ISTHMIA

—

VOLUME II

TOPOGRAPHY AND ARCHITECTURE

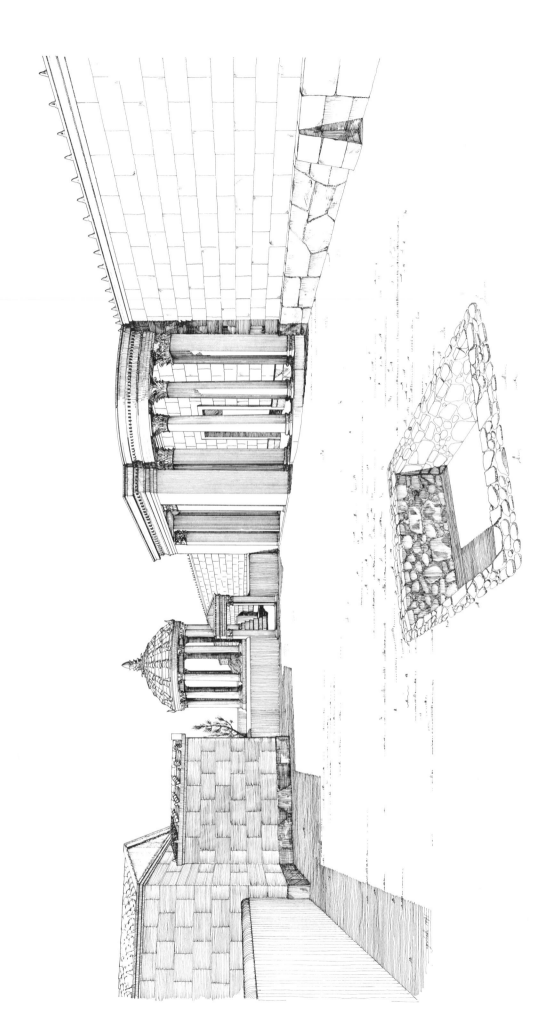

Palaimonion, from East, Restored by A. G. Grulich

ISTHMIA

EXCAVATIONS BY THE UNIVERSITY OF CHICAGO

UNDER THE AUSPICES OF

THE AMERICAN SCHOOL OF CLASSICAL STUDIES AT ATHENS

VOLUME II

TOPOGRAPHY
AND ARCHITECTURE

BY

OSCAR BRONEER

AMERICAN SCHOOL OF CLASSICAL STUDIES AT ATHENS
PRINCETON, NEW JERSEY
1973

PUBLISHED WITH THE AID OF A GRANT FROM THE MERRILL TRUST

PRINTED IN GERMANY *at* J.J.AUGUSTIN, GLÜCKSTADT

PREFACE

The Isthmian Sanctuary of Poseidon was excavated from 1952 to 1960 by the University of Chicago in cooperation with the American School of Classical Studies at Athens. During those years the excavation of the two major precincts, those of Poseidon and Palaimon, was completed, except for some supplementary digging carried on subsequently in connection with preparation of the final publication. Other areas, more or less directly connected with the cult of Poseidon and the Isthmian Games, were also fully or partly excavated. Chief among these is the Theater, which is both functionally and topographically a part of the Sanctuary. Elizabeth R. Gebhard, who supervised the excavation in the Theater, has published the results of her studies as a separate volume issued by the Chicago University Press. Other areas wholly or partly cleared are the Later Stadium, the Sacred Glen, and the West Foundation, which may have been part of the Hippodrome. The publication of the work in these areas is included in the present volume.

On the Rachi, southwest of the temenos of Poseidon, Chrysoula Kardara had charge of excavation in a commercial complex devoted to textile industry. She has presented her conclusions in a preliminary article that appeared in *A.J.A.*, LXV, 1961, pp. 261–266. A final study of this area will appear in a later volume of the Isthmia series.

While work was in progress in and near the Sanctuary, three lines of fortifications across the Isthmus were investigated. The earliest of these, the Cyclopean Wall, I have published in two articles in *Hesperia*: XXV, 1966, pp. 346–362, and XXXVII, 1968, pp. 25–35. James R. Wiseman excavated along the line of a Hellenistic fortification which he published in considerable detail in *Hesperia*, XXXII, 1963, pp. 248–275. Professor Demetrios Pallas began excavation at the South Gate of the Early Christian Fortress, within which stands the Church of St. John the Prodromos. The University of California at Los Angeles took over the excavations at Isthmia in 1967 under the direction of Paul A. Clement. During the first season some supplementary work was carried on in the areas of the earlier campaigns, chiefly in the Theater and in the northwest corner of the temenos of Poseidon. The current series of volumes will comprise only the results of the excavations conducted by the University of Chicago.

Volumes I and II of the Isthmia publications were originally planned as a single volume. As study progressed it became evident that the material from the two Temples of Poseidon alone was sufficient to fill a single volume.

After the devastation of the Sanctuary in the early Christian era, when buildings were pulled down to provide material for the fortress and trans-Isthmian fortification, little remained standing to mark the site of the Isthmian Games. Because of the thoroughgoing destruction, it has been necessary to engage in minute description of architectural details which could otherwise have been adequately presented merely by photographs and drawings. In spite of their fragmentary state, however, several of the monuments, notably the Stadia, the Cult Caves, the Palaimonion, and what I believe to be the Hippodrome, contain features of special interest to archaeologists and to students of Ancient Athletics and Religion.

In the preparation of this volume I have received assistance from many sources. The architects at work through the years are many: chief among them are the late George V. Peschke (Plans II with later additions by others, IX, X; Plates 53, b, 59, a and 66); the late Piet de Jong (Plates 68, a, 72 revised by

W. B. D., Jr., 73—75, 89, 90); William B. Dinsmoor, Jr. (Plans I, III revised by Gene Grulich, IV, VI; Plates 52, a, 60, 61, 65, revision of 72, 78, 79, 80); Gene Grulich (Frontispiece, revision of Plan III, Plans V, VII, VIII; Plates 52, c, 53, a, revision of 54, a, 64, 67, 68, a, 69, 71, 84, 88, a, 91—95, 96, a, 97, 98); and Joseph W. Shaw (Plates 54, a, c, d, 56—58, 70, 76, 78, 79). Others who have worked on plans and drawings are Helen Besi, John L. Czarnowaki, John G. Garner, Jr., Margie Grulich, David Peck, Diane G. Peck, Oliver M. Unwin, Jr., and Charles K. Williams, II. The colored reproductions of the wall paintings for color Plates A and B and the drawings in Plate 62 from the Fountain in the Later Stadium were made by Mary Koutroubaki Shaw.

Excavators in charge of trenches were Katherine Abramovitch, Olga Alexandri, Robert Charles, Elizabeth Courtney, Evangeliki P. Deïlaki, William P. Donovan, Elizabeth R. Gebhard, Paul G. Gebhart, John G. Hawthorne, Dorothy K. Hill, Chrysoula Kardara, Ann Konrad Knudsen, David G. Mitten, John Overbeck, Demetrios Pallas, Joan Ferguson Peck, Margaret Phillips, Laura Fahy Robertson, Françoise Rosen, Miriam Ross, Ione M. Shear, Esther A. Smith, Connie Mitchell Stroud, Gustavus F. Swift, Jr., Matthew Wiencke, James R. Wiseman, and the late Eunice Work. Other assistants, engaged in work on the inventories and manuscript, are Julie Boegehold, Margot Camp, Dian Duryea, Helen von Raits Geagan, Charlotte Brodkey Moore, Sally Cook Nesson, Gatewood Folger Overbeck, Joan Ferguson Peck, Margaret Phillips, Lucy deG. Owen, Laura Fahy Robertson, Judy Sheldon, Esther A. Smith, Connie Mitchell Stroud, Randy Warner and the late Eunice Work. In the final stages of the work Judith Kellogg and Geraldine Gilligan rendered invaluable service to the author. In the tedious work of proofreading and making of the index I was assisted by Anna Manzoni.

It is a pleasure also to acknowledge my indebtedness to Lucy Shoe Meritt, former Editor of Publications of the American School of Classical Studies, who prepared the manuscript for the printer, and to her successor, Marian H. McAllister, for eliminating errors in the typewritten text and in the proofs.

The financial support for preparation of Volume II came from sources acknowledged in the preface to *Isthmia* I. To these and to the University of Chicago, The American School of Classical Studies, and to the Archaeological Service of the Greek government I am greatly indebted for their cooperation and support of my work during the years of excavation and study of the Sanctuary of Poseidon and the site of the Isthmian Games.

ANCIENT CORINTH, GREECE   OSCAR BRONEER

CONTENTS

CONTENTS

CONTENTS

ILLUSTRATIONS

PLATES

PLANS

ABBREVIATIONS

A.J.A.= American Journal of Archaeology.

B.C.H. = Bulletin de correspondance hellénique.

B.S.A. = Annual of the British School at Athens.

Cl. Phil. = Classical Philology.

Corinth, I = Harold North Fowler and others, *Introduction, Topography, Architecture,* Cambridge, Mass., 1932.

I, iii = Robert L. Scranton, *Monuments in the Lower Agora and North of the Archaic Temple,* Princeton, 1951.

I, iv = Oscar Broneer, *The South Stoa and its Roman Successors,* Princeton, 1954.

II = Richard Stillwell, *The Theatre,* Princeton, 1952.

III, i = Carl W. Blegen, Richard Stillwell and others, *Acrocorinth, Excavations in 1926,* Cambridge, Mass., 1930.

III, ii = Rhys Carpenter and Antoine Bon, *The Defenses of Acrocorinth and the Lower Town,* Cambridge, Mass., 1936.

VI = Katherine M. Edwards, *The Coins, 1896–1929,* Cambridge, Mass., 1933.

VIII, iii = John H. Kent, *The Inscriptions, 1926–1950,* Princeton, 1966.

XII = Gladys R. Davidson, *The Minor Objects,* Princeton, 1952.

XIV = Carl A. Roebuck, *The Asklepieion and Lerna,* Princeton, 1951.

Δελτ. = Ἀρχαιολογικὸν Δελτίον.

Dinsmoor, *AAG* = William B. Dinsmoor, *The Architecture of Ancient Greece³,* London and New York, 1950.

Dittenberger, *Syll.³* = Wilhelm Dittenberger, *Sylloge Inscriptionum Graecarum³,* Leipzig, 1915–1924.

Gardiner, *Athletics* = E. Norman Gardiner, *Athletics of the Ancient World,* Oxford, 1930.

Olympia = E. Norman Gardiner, *Olympia, Its History and Remains,* Oxford, 1925.

Gebhard, *Theater at Isthmia* = Elizabeth R. Gebhard, *The Theater at Isthmia,* Chicago, 1973.

Harris, *Greek Athletes* = H. A. Harris, *Greek Athletes and Athletics,* Bloomington, 1966.

I.G. = Inscriptiones Graecae.

Isthmia, I = Oscar Broneer, *Temple of Poseidon,* Princeton, 1971.

Jannoray, *Le Gymnase* = Jean Jannoray, *Fouilles de Delphes,* II, *Le Gymnase,* Paris, 1953.

Jüthner-Brein, *Athlet. Leibesüb.* = Julius Jüthner, *Die athletischen Leibesübungen der Griechen.* I, *Geschichte der Leibesübungen,* ed. by Friedrich Brein (Österreichische Akademie der Wissenschaften, Philosophisch-Historische Klasse, *Sitzungsberichte,* 249. Band 1. Abhandlung), Vienna, 1965.

Kock, *Com. Att. Frag.* = Theodorus Kock, *Comicorum Atticorum Fragmenta,* Leipzig, 1880–1888.

Kunze, *Neue Deutsche Ausgrabungen* = Emil Kunze, *Neue Deutsche Ausgrabungen im Mittelmeergebiet und im vorderen Orient,* Berlin, 1959.

Moretti, *Iscr. Agon. Gr.* = Luigi Moretti, *Iscrizione Agonistiche Greche, Studi Pubblicati dall'Istituto Italiano per la Storia Antica,* XII, Rome, 1953.

Nilsson, *Geschichte Gr. Rel.* = Martin P. Nilsson, *Geschichte der griechischen Religion*

I, *Die Religion Griechenlands bis auf die griechische Weltherrschaft²* (= *Handbuch der Altertumswissenschaft,* 2,1), Munich, 1955.

II, *Die hellenistische und römische Zeit²* (= *Handbuch der Altertumswissenschaft,* 2,2), Munich, 1961.

Op. Sel. = Martin P. Nilsson, *Opuscula Selecta linguis anglica, francogallica, germanica conscripta* (Skrifter utgivna av Svenska Institutet i Athen, 8⁰, II), Lund, 1951–1960.

Num. Chron. = Numismatic Chronicle.

R.E. = Paulys Real-Encyclopädie der classischen Altertumswissenschaft, Neue Bearbeitung, Stuttgart, 1894– .

Will, *Korinthiaka* = Édouard Will, *Korinthiaka,* Paris, 1955.

INTRODUCTION

THE SITE

The area which the ancients chose as the site of the Isthmian Sanctuary is a gently sloping ground, bordered on the north by the deep Northwest Gully and on the south by a prominent ridge, the Rachi,[1] which reaches a height of somewhat over one hundred meters above the sea (Plan I, Pls. 1, 2, b). The direction of the gully and of the ridge is from southwest to northeast, and several small rivulets starting below the ridge have cut the lower slopes into broad strips (Pl. 51). Before the construction of any buildings the terrain was probably heavily wooded. All around the Sanctuary to the north and south there are now groves of pine trees (Pls. 2, 51) covering the hillsides, and the only parts which are not wooded are those that have been cleared and turned into agricultural land. The prominence of the pine is reflected in the mythology, for it was here that Theseus met Sinis the Pine-Bender,[2] who seized his victims and tied their limbs to trees which he had bent down and then let fly apart.[3] The same factor may have determined the choice of the pine for the victor's crown in the early period.[4] In Pausanias' day a row of pine trees, which probably had been planted, lined the avenue between the Later Stadium and the temenos of Poseidon.

Because the terrain would have been more wooded in antiquity, it was probably less scored with stream beds than is now the case, and the actual site of the Temple was more nearly level, sloping gently toward the ravine in the north. Upon this terrain the builders of the first Temple imposed a rigid east-west orientation. As the Sanctuary grew in extent, this orientation, determined by religious usage rather than by the lay of the land, came to involve considerable landscaping. The deep gully in the northwest corner and the gradually sloping ground toward the east had to be raised to the level of the area where the Temple stood; and in the southwest corner of the temenos, where the ground level was higher than the stylobate of the Temple, the original surface was eventually lowered. This incongruity of the orientation of the Temple with the natural lay of the land accounts for certain features of the early temenos which cannot be explained on purely structural grounds. Thus the orientation of the pre-Roman temenos wall and of some of the early buildings seems to conform to the configuration of the land rather than the architectural layout determined by the Temple; and yet the Archaic Temple is the earliest building of which we have any knowledge.

---

[1] The inhabitants of the village of Kyras Vrysi seem to be unaware of the existence of any name other than Rachi, i.e. Ridge. In the early excavation reports (*Hesperia*, XXII, 1953, p. 194) the name is erroneously spelled Rache. The name Pipinia, which appears on some maps (Army Map Service M 708), is applied to another height south of the Later Stadium.

[2] Pausanias, II, 1, 4.

[3] In the earliest version of the myth there may have been no reference to this form of execution; rather, Sinis challenged his victims to a contest of strength which consisted of bending a large tree to the ground. Those who failed in the contest were dispatched by the monster. This story is reminiscent of the founding myth of the Olympic games, in which the losers in the chariot race were slain by Oinomaos. See E. M. W. Tillyard, *J.H.S.*, XXXIII, 1913, pp. 296–312; and Joh. Schmidt, *R.E.*, *s.v.* II Reihe, V Sinis.

[4] On the Isthmian crowns see O. Broneer, *A.J.A.*, LXVI, 1962, pp. 259–263. At the present time the pine trees of the Isthmia region constitute an important source of income to the land owners, who collect the resin to sell for use in the resinated wine and for the production of turpentine.

In addition to the gully which cuts across the northwest corner of the temenos (Pl. 51), there was a less prominent stream bed farther east in the area occupied by the Theater. This ran more nearly south to north, almost to the axis of the cavea. Through the construction of the Theater, the ground level was altered to such an extent that the original stream bed has virtually disappeared. East of the temenos of Poseidon the area is now limited by the Early Christian fortress commonly known as the Fortress of Justinian. Numerous surface finds and trenches dug here by British archaeologists in the 1930's, and more recently by American excavators,[5] have made it clear that this whole lower plateau between the Theater and the Later Stadium was occupied by buildings, at least in late Roman times.

The natural hollow chosen as the site of the Later Stadium was another stream bed oriented like the Rachi from southwest to northeast (Pl. 51). Its water emptied into the large ravine north of the Sanctuary, which is a continuation of the tortuous Northwest Gully referred to above. The latter begins at the west end of the village of Kyras Vrysi and extends almost straight north for a distance of six hundred meters, then turns eastward and terminates in the small alluvial plain at the east end of the Corinth Canal. The Rachi itself (Pl. 2, b) seems not to have been occupied before the fifth century B.C.,[6] and the commercial buildings that have been excavated near its northeast end are of still later date. Farther west the whole top of the ridge has been cut away by extensive stone quarrying carried on both in ancient and in modern times, so that its original shape and height can no longer be determined.

West of the Sanctuary the terrain now occupied by the village of Kyras Vrysi[7] rises gradually toward the west and then falls abruptly toward the Northwest Gully, the largest of the stream beds in the vicinity. At its upper end, near the western edge of the modern village, there is a spring which gave its name to the modern community (Pl. 51, lower left corner). At present the flow is limited, because the area to the west has been tapped with numerous wells from which water is pumped to irrigate the fields and to supply water to the village. In ancient times the flow of water would have been more copious. On the right bank of this stream bed, to the north of the spring, an elaborate system of water works from classical Greek times was observed and described by the two members of the British School who made a preliminary study of Isthmia in 1931–32.[8] Some channels and reservoirs, which now lie at a level some ten meters above the present bottom of the gully, show the amount of erosion that has taken place since the fifth century B.C. There are indications also of buildings constructed on the farther slope, west of the Northwest Gully. The capital of a Doric column, probably from the early part of the fifth century, was plowed up in the field in this area, but this may have been brought there from some other part of the Isthmian Sanctuary and built into a structure of later date.

To the east and south of the Northwest Gully, some four hundred meters southwest of the Temple of Poseidon, was the area known as the Sacred Glen, Ἱερὰ Νάπη[9] (Plan I), which contained several shrines

---

[5] R. J. H. Jenkins and H. Megaw, B.S.A., XXXII, 1931–32, p. 68; and O. Broneer, Hesperia, XXXI, 1962, p. 18, no. 2, pl. 9, a. The recent excavations carried on by the University of California at Los Angeles have produced new evidence for the date of the Fortress. The work in the Fortress has not been completed, but on the evidence already produced the director of these excavations, Paul A. Clement, would now date both the Fortress and the trans-Isthmian wall in the fourth century after Christ. See Paul Clement, Δελτ., XXIII, 1968, Χρονικά, pp. 139–140; Georges Daux, B.C.H., XCII, 1968, pp. 773–782; cf. P. M. Fraser, J.H.S., LXXXIX, 1969, Archaeological Reports for 1968–69, pp. 8–9; and Miriam Ervin (Caskey), A.J.A., LXXIII, 1969, p. 345.

[6] Chrysoula Kardara, A.J.A., LXV, 1961, pp. 261–266. A complete study of the Rachi is being prepared by the same author for the series of Isthmia publications.

[7] The name of the village Κύρας Βρύση is sometimes written Κύρας ἡ Βρύση or Κύρα Βρύση. The word order, with the genitive preceding the noun, may be derived from Albanian, which has the form Kriezonis. It is possible, however, that the name originated as a corruption of Κρύα Βρύση. Villages with such a name occur elsewhere in Greece. There is one other village of the same name in the nomos of Corinthia, near Zevgolatio west of Ancient Corinth; another is in Thessaly not far from Karditsa.

[8] See above, note 5.

[9] The name, which is not mentioned by Pausanias, occurs in an inscription, once set up in the Isthmian Sanctuary and now in the Museo Lapidario at Verona; I.G., IV, 203, line 15; and Hesperia, VIII, 1939, pp. 181–190; Louis Robert, Hellenica, I, 1940, pp. 44–53. The general location of this adjunct to the Isthmian Sanctuary can be determined from two

of deities whose cults were attached to that of Poseidon. Probably this formed the westernmost limit of the Isthmian Sanctuary in the broad sense.[10] It measures about four hundred meters from northwest to southeast and seven hundred meters on the long axis, northeast to southwest. Farther to the southwest, about two kilometers (1.3 miles) from the Temple of Poseidon, an isolated monument, the West Foundation, was constructed in the fourth century B.C.; this too may have been related to, though physically unconnected with, the Isthmian Sanctuary.[11] Somewhere between the Sacred Glen and this foundation, and probably in front of the monument, we must look for the Hippodrome.

In Roman times building activities extended the area still farther, especially toward the north and east. The Sanctuary in the larger sense comprised the whole terrain later occupied by the Early Christian fortress as far as the Northeast Gate. This is shown by numerous foundations protruding above the ground, all of which seem to be of Roman date. Farther south, a little northeast of the Later Stadium, the ruins of a large building are visible above the ground. To judge by its construction it seems to be a Roman bath or gymnasium. As yet no excavation has been done in this area. Remains of other buildings are found still farther east. North of the Temple of Poseidon, at a distance of one hundred and thirty meters, are ruins of another large building. Here test trenches dug in 1954 and 1970 exposed parts of some rooms with hypocaust, showing that this was a Roman bath[12] (Plan I, Pl. 51).

The site was well chosen for a sanctuary, with a superb view in all directions. From the façade of the Temple one looks straight out toward the Saronic Gulf (Pl. 3, a). On the left appear the wooded slopes of the Perachora peninsula and the irregular skyline of the Gerania Mountain (Pl. 2, a). Toward the right the Rachi and the north edge of the high plateau south of the Later Stadium limit the distant view. Almost directly in the west rises the prominent rock of Acrocorinth, clearly visible from the Temple site (Pl. 3, b). The myth relating to the rivalry between Helios and Poseidon,[13] to which the ancients ascribed the choice of site of the Isthmian Games, could have originated from the physical properties of the land. The isolated mountain in the west, as seen from the site of the Temple of Poseidon, appears to challenge the Lord of the blue waters of the Saronic Gulf.

THE BUILDING COMPLEX

It is interesting to speculate about the reason for the original choice of this particular spot on the Isthmus as a Sanctuary of Poseidon and site of the Isthmian Games. The natural features described above seem sufficiently favorable for such a purpose, but the same could certainly be said about other sites in the Corinthia. There is a practical reason, however: the Sanctuary was located at the narrowest point of the Isthmus, near the road which led from Athens and the north of Greece into the Peloponnesos (below, pp. 18, 122). Such a road must have existed from very early times, as the story of Theseus' route from Troizen to Athens would indicate. By the time that the Sanctuary had assumed Panhellenic importance, this road was in common use.

---

dedications to Demeter, whose shrine is mentioned in the inscription as being in the Hiera Nape; O. Broneer, *Hesperia*, XXVIII, 1959, p. 323, no. 3, p. 326, no. 1; XXXI, 1962, pp. 14–16; *Biblical Archaeologist Reader*, II, 1964, p. 409; and John L. Caskey, *Hesperia*, XXIX, 1960, pp. 168–172. See also below, pp. 113–116.

[10] In the present publication the term "Sanctuary" is used to denote the whole area connected with the cults and games at Isthmia. For the precinct proper surrounding the Temple, the word "temenos" is used. The separate precinct of Palaimon appears as Palaimonion, as distinct from the cult building, which is referred to as the Temple of Palaimon. For the sacred area within which this Temple is located, the term "peribolos" is used.

[11] Its location is shown in the inset, Plan I, and a description of the monument follows in a later chapter, pp. 117–122.

[12] *Hesperia*, XXIV, 1955, pp. 123–124. In 1970 further digging was done in this area, and a sizable section of the building was exposed close to the trans-Isthmian wall.

[13] Pausanias, II, 1, 6: "The Corinthians say that Poseidon entered into dispute with Helios concerning the land and that Briareos became arbitrator; he assigned the Isthmus and the adjoining area to Poseidon and gave to Helios the height (Acrocorinth) above the city."

Whatever led the Corinthians to establish the Sanctuary here, the construction of the first Temple and the beginning of the games may have coincided in time. The traditional date of the founding, or reorganization, of the Isthmian Games is 582 (or 580) B.C.,[14] but the first Temple of Poseidon is a full century earlier. The cult must have gained importance rapidly, to judge from the size of the Archaic Temple and the rich votive offerings found among its ruins. The seventh and sixth centuries cover the reign of the Corinthian tyrants, whose exact date is still a matter of dispute among historians. By the earliest reckoning, Kypselos seized power in the city during the year 657 B.C.; those who, with Beloch, follow the later reckoning would bring this event down to *ca.* 610 B.C.[15] Either of these two dates seems too late for the construction of the Archaic Temple, which was probably built in the time of the Bacchiads, early in the seventh century.[16] The next building of which we have any knowledge is the Archaic Stadium, the traces of which can be recognized among the ruins of its successor.

The fire that destroyed the Archaic Temple coincides in time approximately with the Persian invasion of Greece, although the two events are apparently unrelated. The destruction of the Temple seems not to have hampered building activities in the Sanctuary but rather to have hastened them. A new and much larger temple was built before the middle of the fifth century, and sometime before the end of that century the Earlier Stadium had replaced its primitive, archaic predecessor. At about the turn of the century the first construction of the Theater took place, but a permanent stone theater was not built till near the end of the fourth century. About the middle of that century the two Cult Caves ceased to be used, and somewhat later the Earlier Stadium was abandoned and a new stadium with perfected plan was built outside the temenos. There were other building activities at some distance from the Temple, in the Sacred Glen toward the west and on the Rachi to the south. As early as the fifth century B.C. the Isthmian Sanctuary had acquired importance as a center of culture and athletics, and on several occasions it became a meeting place of the Hellenic world. Then in 146 B.C. the destruction of Corinth brought a sudden end to activities at Isthmia, and for the next two hundred years there is little to show what took place at the original site of the games. Did these continue to be held at Isthmia or were they transferred to Sikyon? The evidence is ambiguous, but the latter alternative seems probable. The destruction of the Long Altar and the existence of a wagon road directly in front of the Temple point up the ruinous condition of the Sanctuary.[17] Perhaps at that time the monuments along the north side of the Temple were removed, and the Theater probably fell into disuse. Between the destruction of Corinth and the middle of the first century after Christ we find few certain traces of building activities in the Sanctuary of Poseidon.

The earliest signs of reoccupation occur in the area previously occupied by the Earlier Stadium. Here a new precinct came into existence, dedicated to the founding hero, Melikertes-Palaimon. Doubtless his worship at Isthmia began earlier, but if this was the case, there are no material remains to indicate its existence. He may well have had an altar in the Earlier Stadium, since his later cult place was built there. At first it seems to have centered about one or more sacrificial pits; the circular temple with its underground passage was built later. About the middle of the first century a precinct wall was built around the Temple of Poseidon and a new altar was constructed. The first Roman reconstruction of the Theater, which may have been made for Nero's visit in the year A.D. 66 or 67, should be considered as part of the same program of rebuilding the dilapidated structures of the Sanctuary. About a century

---

[14] This, according to Solinus, VII, 14, took place in the 49th Olympiad, either in the second or the fourth year. See below, p. 65, note 76, and K. Schneider, *R.E.*, *s.v.* Isthmia, col. 248. It is a matter of interest that the earliest pottery found in graves of the large cemetery west of the village of Kyras Vrysi is dated in the second or third decade of the sixth century B.C., i.e. about the time of the traditional date of the reorganization and internationalization of the Isthmian Games; Paul A. Clement, Δελτ., XXIV, 1969, Χρονικά, p. 119.

[15] For a full discussion of this problem see E. Will, *Korinthiaka*, pp. 363–440, who arrived (not without hesitation) at a date *ca.* 620–550 B.C. for the reign of the Kypselid dynasty. Cf. also Carl A. Roebuck, *Hesperia*, XLI, 1972, p. 127.

[16] *Isthmia*, I, pp. 53–55.

[17] *Ibid.*, pp. 100–103; and see below, p. 21.

later a wealthy high priest of Poseidon, Publius Licinius Priscus Iuventianus, endowed the Sanctuary with many new buildings. His priesthood seems to coincide with the last great period of building activity in the Sanctuary, when imposing stoas were projected and partly constructed on all four sides of the temenos of Poseidon, the Temple of Palaimon was built, and a reconstructed and enlarged Theater was planned but never completed.

After this spurt of construction in the second century after Christ no important buildings were erected within the temenos or in the immediate vicinity. From the excavations in these areas there is little to show for the existence of the cult in the third and fourth centuries after Christ. Ceramic evidence shows that the site had been abandoned as a Sanctuary by the end of the fourth century, and debris covered the floors of the ancient buildings. The final event in the history of the Sanctuary is the total demolition of the classical building complex and the construction of the trans-Isthmian wall with its massive Fortress.[18] If, as now seems likely, these were built in Early Christian times, they would have been repaired and strengthened during the reign of the Emperor Justinian. Subsequent to this event no buildings of any note were constructed on the site of the Sanctuary, and when the excavations began in 1952, the area was a plowed field with here and there some scattered building blocks projecting above the surface. The very location of the Temple of Poseidon had become an archaeological problem.

EXPLORATIONS OF THE SITE

The Isthmian Sanctuary has been studied sporadically for some ninety years, and some of the earlier travelers described the site and made observations of the visible ruins.[19] The first excavation was undertaken by Paul Monceaux[20] in 1883. He limited his investigation to the Fortress, which he identified with the sacred precinct enclosing the temples of Poseidon and Palaimon. This erroneous information was repeated by several later scholars, even after it had been pointed out by Fimmen[21] that the wall must be dated in Christian times. Monceaux observed the many fragments of Doric column drums among the debris of the wall, and in studying these fragments he made another unfortunate error, which was likewise repeated by his successors. He calculated that the columns had only sixteen flutes. On this basis the archaeologists dated the Temple in early archaic times. A number of Ionic column drums, now scattered about at the Northeast Gate, Monceaux took to be from the Temple of Palaimon, and he located both temples in the area now occupied by the Church of St. John. Thus the precinct wall of classical Greek times was supposed to have been constructed with material from the two temples, which were still standing in the time of Pausanias! Frazer, to be sure, assumed that the drums, which he said "had been sawn from top to bottom,"[22] were employed in repairing the enclosing wall of the Sanctuary. In 1925 Harold North Fowler and Charles Alexander Robinson, Jr. made a study of the ancient sites in the Corinthia and published their findings in an extensive chapter in *Corinth*, I. Fowler, who based his study chiefly on Monceaux's and Frazer's observations, made no reference to Fimmen's article in Pauly-Wissowa, which had appeared twelve years earlier.

In 1932 R. J. H. Jenkins and A. H. S. Megaw of the British School dug numerous trenches at various points in the Isthmian region and published their conclusions in the *British School Annual*[23] and the *Journal of Hellenic Studies*.[24] The two English scholars corrected several of the errors that had been repeated in earlier publications. They showed that the Doric columns of the Temple had twenty, not six-

---

[18] For the date of these events see above, note 5.
[19] These sources are listed and discussed by Harold N. Fowler, *Corinth*, I, pp. 49–71.
[20] *Gazette Archéologique*, IX, 1884, pp. 273–285, 354–363; X, 1885, pp. 205–214.
[21] *R.E.*, IX, 2, Cols. 2261–2262.
[22] *Pausanias' Description of Greece*, III, p. 11. The columns were not sawn but split by crude hacking.
[23] *B.S.A.*, XXXII, 1931–32, pp. 68–89.
[24] *J.H.S.*, LII, 1932, p. 244.

teen, flutes and thus could be dated much later than Monceaux had supposed. In his study of the Isthmian Wall and the Fortress, Megaw arrived at the same conclusion as Fimmen, i.e. that the wall belonged to the time of Justinian. In an attempt to establish the location of the Temple of Poseidon they dug several trenches within the Fortress itself and to the west of it. Having failed to discover recognizable traces of buildings in that area, they investigated the banks of the deep gorge to the north and west of the modern village, and there they found ample evidence for building activities in Greek classical times. Having cleared and studied an impressive system of water channels and reservoirs of that period, they concluded that the Temple had been located in that vicinity, and they assumed that earthquakes and erosions had obliterated all traces of its existence.

The site of the Temple was revealed in 1952 during the first exploratory campaign by the University of Chicago expedition.[25] The location of the Temple had been correctly conjectured by Fimmen and Knackfuss in 1913, but the small trenches dug by the two English excavators in this area did not expose any recognizable traces of the building. The discovery of the Temple foundation now provided the key to the topography. Over the next ten years excavations were carried on which resulted in the complete clearing of the temenos of Poseidon, the adjoining precinct of Palaimon, and the Theater.[26] Other buildings not directly connected with the temenos were excavated on the Rachi to the south and in the Sacred Glen in the western part of the village. The investigations have also included a study of the Isthmian fortification walls,[27] the West Foundation, and the Later Stadium. These monuments will be described in subsequent pages of this volume and in the other volumes of the series.

PREHISTORIC REMAINS

Not much has been found in the vicinity of the Temple to indicate very high antiquity of the cult. A few small fragments of Neolithic pottery came from the fill beneath the skene of the Theater, and these might have been carried down by water in the rivulet mentioned above. A deposit of Early Helladic vases came to light in the gully to the northwest of the Temple,[28] and scattered fragments of Early Helladic ware have been found throughout the area. The Middle Helladic period is more sparingly represented by a handful of matt-painted sherds.[29] The same is true of the Late Helladic period. Mycenaean potsherds have been found in many parts of the excavations,[30] but they are thinly scattered and very small. They are enough to show that the site of the future Sanctuary was not wholly unoccupied in the fourteenth and thirteenth centuries B.C., but it would be rash to conclude from these insignificant finds that the cult of Poseidon had any such distant ancestry. Not before the end of the Mycenaean period did the Isthmus come into prominence, and then only as a point of communication and line of defense.[31]

---

[25] *Hesperia*, XXII, 1953, pp. 182–195.

[26] Since the first campaign in 1952 the following excavation reports and preliminary articles have been published: *Hesperia*, XXIV, 1955, pp. 110–141; XXVII, 1958, pp. 1–37; XXVIII, 1959, pp. 298–343; XXXI, 1962, pp. 1–25; *Archaeology*, VIII, 1955, pp. 56–62; IX, 1956, pp. 134–137, 268–272; XIII, 1960, pp. 105–109; *Antiquity*, XXXII, 1958, pp. 80–88; *Klio*, XXXIX, 1961, pp. 249–270; *Atti del Settimo Congresso Internazionale di Archeologia Classica*, I, 1961, pp. 243–249; Χαριστήριον εἰς ᾿Αναστάσιον Κ. ᾿Ορλάνδον, III, 1964, pp. 61–85. The Theater is published by Elizabeth R. Gebhard, *The Theater at Isthmia*, Chicago, 1973.

[27] James R. Wiseman, *Hesperia*, XXXII, 1963, pp. 248–275.

[28] Esther A. Smith, *Hesperia*, XXIV, 1955, pp. 142–146.

[29] *Ibid.*, p. 143.

[30] *Ibid.*, especially pl. 57, a; O. Broneer, *Hesperia*, XXVII, 1958, pp. 27–28.

[31] On the fortification of the Isthmus at the end of the Mycenaean period, see O. Broneer, *Atti del Settimo Congresso Internazionale di Archeologia Classica*, I, pp. 243–249; *Antiquity*, XXXII, 1958, pp. 80–83; *Hesperia*, XXXV, 1966, pp. 346–362; XXXVII, 1968, pp. 25–35; Niki C. Scoufopoulos, *Mycenaean Citadels*, Göteborg, 1971, pp. 57–58. Chrysoula Kardara (*Athens Annals of Archaeology*, IV, 1971, pp. 85–89) reverts to our original supposition that the Cyclopean Wall was intended not as a fortification, but as retaining wall for a road. This explanation, I believe, has to be discarded for three reasons: a) in the lower village of Isthmia the wall has two faces built with large blocks in a stretch traceable for a

The Cyclopean Wall (Plans I, II), built at the end of L. H. III B, apparently crossed the west end of the temenos of Poseidon,[32] thus leaving the site of the Temple and most of the Sanctuary unprotected on the north side. This is a clear indication that the cult of the Isthmian Poseidon was unknown at the turn from the thirteenth to the twelfth century B.C.

The paucity of prehistoric antiquities is somewhat surprising in view of the role that the Isthmia played in mythology. It was Corinth and the Corinthia, however, not the terrain about the Sanctuary at the narrow point of the Isthmus, that became thickly settled in prehistoric times. Pottery from the Geometric period is slightly more abundant, especially late Geometric sherds. These and two bronze figurines indicate that the site was occupied by that time, possibly even as a sanctuary. A significant concentration of pottery, however, does not occur before the Protocorinthian period. Judging solely by the antiquities found on the site, one would conclude that the cult of Poseidon became firmly established on the Isthmus near the end of the eighth century B.C.

---

distance of 25 m. on level ground (*Hesperia*, XXXV, 1966, p. 350, fig. 2, 5), where no such retaining walls would have been required; b) a little farther west (*ibid.*, fig. 2, 4) there is a shorter stretch, only 8.40 m., which extends up the slope of a hill too steep for wheel traffic; and c) the addition of small towers, always on the north side, would hardly have been necessary in a retaining wall for a road.

[32] When the Temple precinct was landscaped after the construction of the Classical Temple, the Cyclopean Wall was broken up and the material was then, so it appears, thrown into the Large Circular Pit. See below, p. 23, note 21, and *Hesperia*, XXXVII, 1968, p. 29.

THE PRE-ROMAN SANCTUARY

TEMENOS OF POSEIDON

NORTH SIDE

TERRACE WALLS IN NORTHWEST CORNER

There is little preserved from which to reconstruct the temenos wall of the Greek period. The ground level was considerably lower in the northwest corner than in the rest of the area; and this became from earliest times a convenient dumping place for unwanted debris. A series of retaining walls have been uncovered there on the slope of the gully, the earliest of which (NG¹) goes back to archaic times. This has been exposed for a length of *ca.* 8 m. (Plans II–IV, Pl. 4, a). It is constructed of large, roughly hewn stones and has a comparatively smooth face on the northwest side. The exposed section is standing in one place to a height of two meters. Most of the stones are arranged as irregular headers, with only the ends showing on the face of the wall. One block at the exposed top measures 1.12 × 0.72 × 0.60 m., and there are others which appear to be larger. This wall probably marks the northern limit of the Sanctuary in the earliest period of its existence. It has a superficial resemblance to Cyclopean masonry, but the few pottery sherds found in the fill close to the wall are archaic Greek.

South of wall NG¹ and at a higher level, another rough wall (NG²) has been exposed. Some of the stones in it have the characteristic rope marks of the building blocks from the Archaic Temple; consequently the wall was put up after the destruction to retain the rubble that was dumped down the gully. Of still later date is a third retaining wall, NG³, higher up the slope. This is constructed with large stones set vertically at intervals and with smaller stones filling the interstices. One large block, seen at the left end of the wall in Plate 4, b, has been identified as a floor slab from the Classical Temple of Poseidon.[1] This must have been placed in the wall after the fire of 390 B.C.; consequently the retaining wall was built in the fourth century B.C. The construction is rather similar to the early retaining wall in the West Foundation, which can be dated by pottery to the fourth century B.C. (below, p. 119). These retaining walls, NG² and NG³, are loosely constructed without foundation (Pl. 4, b); they were put up as temporary supports for the fill thrown over the edge of the gully from time to time. The lower of the two has collapsed since the photograph was made.

Some seven meters to the south of wall NG¹ and at a very much higher level (Plan II), there is preserved an early roadbed (Plan IV, A, see below, p. 18), oriented roughly like that wall, its surface being *ca.* 1.75 m. below the level of the precinct in the last Roman period. Its early date is shown by the fact that it was found buried under rubble from the burned Archaic Temple (Pl. 4, c). This fill, which extended down to the roadbed, indicates that the road was in use until the destruction of the Temple, *ca.* 480–470 B.C.

The rubble dumped in the gully above the debris from the Archaic Temple and farther north contained large quantities of calcined marble roof tiles from the fire which damaged the fifth-century Temple in the year 390 B.C., after which the third of the three retaining walls, NG³, was built. This, however,

---

[1] *Isthmia*, I, pp. 70, 114–115, no. BB 115.

did not put an end to the northward extension of the Sanctuary; for much of the fill north of these walls contained pottery of Hellenistic and later times. Some of it seems to have been thrown in during the first Roman reconstruction, probably during the reign of Claudius or perhaps somewhat later.[2]

North Wall and North Propylon

The final alteration in this area was made when the heavy foundation for the unfinished North Stoa was laid (below, pp. 81–82). To the north of this foundation, about halfway between the east and west ends of the temenos, a complex of walls has been exposed which clearly antedates the Roman reconstructions. The easternmost of these is the north temenos wall NP[1], oriented northeast to southwest (Pls. 4, d, 52, a). Of the wall itself only two stones, a and b (Pl. 52, a), are preserved in place, but their orientation indicates that they belong to a single structure. On the assumption that the intervening blocks have all been removed we may thus reconstruct a wall, measuring 0.60 m. in thickness and traceable for a length of 9.50 m. Block a at the northeast end owes its preservation to the fact that it is embedded in a Roman foundation running northward from the east end of the existing foundation for the projected North Stoa. Trial pits dug farther to the northeast failed to reveal other traces of the earlier wall. Block b at the southwest end measures 1.39 m. in length. Its southeast face has been trimmed back at the top, leaving a raised panel, 0.04 m. thick; the southwest end is similarly rusticated. The northwest face has anathyrosis at the end, and here a somewhat thinner wall, NP[2], extends at right angles toward the northwest. The total length of this wall, including the thickness of the long wall NP[1], was 3.67 m., but one block at the northwest end is now missing. At this point a foundation, NP[3], extending at right angles toward the southwest, continues for a length of 5.30 m. It does not seem to have gone farther in that direction. At its southwest end, at c, the top surface has been roughened over a width of 0.55 m., and here a wall, NP[4], all the stones of which are now missing, must have extended perpendicularly toward the southeast. Two square areas, d and e, on the top of wall NP[3] are roughened in the same way as c, probably indicating that some masonry rested on these spots. Along the northwest edge of NP[3] there is a well-marked setting line for the next course, which was set back 0.07 m. from the edge. A row of irregular stones, f-f, set against the northwest face of the foundation seems to belong to the same construction but did not support any part of the superstructure. One of the blocks, which must be re-used, has a double setting line. A broad foundation or sill, NP[5], of much heavier construction runs parallel to NP[3], 3.51 m. farther to the southeast. This foundation, consisting of four large blocks, is separated from the southwest end of the long wall NP[1] by 0.86 m. A setting line 0.125 m. from the southeast edge indicates that the second course was not in line with wall NP[1] but was set back 0.15 m. from its southeast face. The length of the heavy foundation NP[5] is only 2.02 m., and its width varies between 1.08 m. and 1.52 m. What is preserved is probably the total length, since there is no anathyrosis at either end. Here too are two roughened areas, g and h, 1.02 m. wide, marked off by setting lines.

The foundation described above, anomalous as it appears at first sight, must belong to a rectangular structure jutting out from the northwest face of a long wall. In all probability this was a propylon, henceforth to be called the North Propylon (Plans III, IV, Pl. 52, a). Although no part is preserved above the foundations, the plan would be suitable to a building having a porch with two columns between antae on the outside and triple doorways opening on the temenos.[3] There are, however, no pivot holes for the doors. The orientation, so very different from that of the Temple, can be explained by the fact that

---

[2] So far as it is possible to fix the date, this seems to be the earliest large scale reconstruction of the Sanctuary after the destruction of Corinth in 146 B.C. The first Roman reconstruction in the Theater may have been undertaken in expectation of Nero's visit in A.D. 66 or 67; Gebhard, *Theater at Isthmia*, pp. 84–87. The early Roman temenos wall and the second Altar of Poseidon appear to have been built about the same time.

[3] This is the simplest form of propylon found in many sanctuaries. Cf. Gorham P. Stevens, *Hesperia*, V, 1936, p. 478, fig. 31. It contains the basic elements found in all the more monumental gateways. See paper presented by James R. Carpenter on "The Origin of the Propylon in Greek Architecture," *A.J.A.*, LXXIII, 1969, p. 233. The complete text of this important study has not yet been published.

the wall follows approximately the line of the archaic road. The Propylon may have formed a subsidiary approach into the temenos of Poseidon; the main entrance was, as in Roman times, from the east (below, pp. 15–16). The stretch of road laid bare west of the North Propylon had been concealed under debris from the Archaic Temple at a time much earlier than the construction of the Propylon, but there are indications that a road ran at a higher level approximately along the same line at a later period.

West of the North Propylon there are remains of several walls or foundations of walls of a very irregular nature. They are earlier than the north temenos wall of Roman times, and one actually extends under the foundation for that wall. They do not follow the orientation either of the North Propylon or of the later temenos. Going from east to west we find first a very rough wall, NP⁶, extending northward for nearly three meters from the rear face of the later temenos wall. It contains only one large building block and several smaller stones which are not in a straight line with the large block. The longest of the four walls, NP⁷, consists of four large blocks with a total length of ca. 4.50 m., extending northwestward from the south end of wall NP⁶. The four blocks, which are not in a straight line, rest on earth without a proper foundation. One of the blocks has a deep wheel rut at one end, but it does not seem to have been made in its present position. A third wall of two large blocks, NP⁸, which runs nearly parallel to NP⁷ at a distance of ca. 1.50 m., is exposed for a little over two meters. Its southeast end lies hidden beneath the north temenos wall. The blocks have wheel ruts, or what appear to be such, but since they do not run parallel to each other they must have been made before the blocks were laid in their present position. Like the other walls in this area, NP⁸ lacks foundation. Across the northwest end of wall NP⁸ are two stones of a fourth wall, NP⁹, extending from northeast to southwest and constructed very much like the others without foundations or proper fittings of the joints. The fill on which these blocks rest seems to be chiefly debris from the Archaic Temple, and it is likely that they, like two of the walls in the northwest corner of the temenos, NG² and NG³, are temporary retaining walls, roughly constructed to contain the earth thrown over the edge from time to time.

MONUMENT BASES

In the space between the Temple and the later Roman temenos wall the ancient ground level, except in the northwest sector, would have been only slightly above bedrock, and in many places the rock surface was exposed. Over most of this area there are indications of roads, whose period of use cannot readily be determined (below, pp. 20–22). Some foundations for monuments remain in situ, most of which have a different orientation from that of the Temple and are probably earlier than the first Roman reconstruction (Plans II, III). Beginning at the east end of the north side, we find a foundation of a small monument, M¹ (Pl. 5, a), the exact shape of which is uncertain. Its orientation deviates from the east-to-west direction of the Roman temenos wall. What remains of the foundation measures 2.85 × 2.05 m. Stones are preserved only along the south flank and the east end, where the level of the rock is low. The southeast corner has been worn off by wheel traffic on a road that passed from east to west during Roman times. The base would have been sufficiently large for an equestrian statue, but since nothing is preserved above the lowest course of stones, it is uncertain what kind of monument it supported.

Some seven meters farther west and three meters south of the late Roman temenos wall there is a second base, M³, oriented almost due east to west. It measures 2.65 m. in length and 0.87 m. in width and consists of a single row of three thin slabs, only some ten centimeters thick. It is not clear whether this was the original thickness, because the area seems to have been leveled off in later times, and the full thickness may have been greater. The slabs were first thought to have served as cover of a grave, but there is no depression in the rock underneath the stones. A little to the east of this base three small stones, M², lie in what may be their original position, but they have been so mutilated that no conclusion can be drawn regarding their original condition. They are indicated on the actual state plan, Plan II, but are not shown on the restored plan, Plan III. Nearly nineteen meters farther west there is a square base, M⁴ (Pl. 5, b, left), measuring 1.50 × 1.50 m. in area and consisting of two rectangular blocks, the top of which is nearly even with the ground level of Roman times.

Less than one meter to the west of this small foundation stood the largest of the pre-Roman monuments north of the Temple, M⁵ (Pl. 5, b, c). The orientation of M⁵ is very nearly the same as that of the smaller base, M⁴. What remains of M⁵ is a large T-shaped foundation, measuring 9.00 m. from east to west along the north edge and 6.30 m. from north to south. At the northeast corner two blocks, measuring 0.90 × 1.27 m. in area, form a projecting wing. In the middle along the east edge the tops of the stones project roughly over an area slightly less than 2.00 m. long and 0.50 m. wide. At the north end of this projection there is a roughly circular hole, ca. 0.10 m. in diameter, extending through the thickness of the block. At the northwest corner there is a much larger wing consisting of eight blocks, the combined area of which measures 2.75 m. from east to west and slightly less than 2.00 m. from north to south. Here, as at the east edge of the foundation, the final dressing at the top stops short of the end of the blocks, leaving a rough border along the west edge of the wing. Thus the monument supported by the existing foundation was set back somewhat from the east and west edges of the foundation. The middle part of the monument between the two wings and extending southward has a length of somewhat over five meters from east to west. The edges are very irregular both here and at the two wings so that the measurements given are only approximate. The main part of the base, not counting the wings, consists of five rows with ten large blocks in each row. They are all oriented from east to west like the monument, whose orientation deviates considerably from the cardinal points of the compass. The whole southern part of M⁵ has been deeply worn away since the monument was removed, and wagon ruts are clearly visible running from east to west. The material is a soft, rough poros which weathers and disintegrates very easily. Since no stones remain above the first course of the foundation, there is nothing to indicate what purpose the monument served. Its pre-Roman date is indicated both by the orientation and by its relationship to an early water channel to be described below (pp. 24–25). It is clear that this channel existed before the foundation was laid and was interrupted by the monument. A detour was then made along the north edge of the foundation (Plan III, Pl. 5, c). If we are correct in our identification of the North Propylon, it is conceivable that foundation M⁵ supported an inner entranceway of some kind. It does not connect with any wall now visible, so that if a gateway stood here it would have been purely ornamental. The foundation is large enough for a treasury or even a small temple, but the two wings of unequal size would seem to preclude any such use.[4]

West of M⁵ and separated from its northwest wing by a distance of 1.12 m. is the foundation of a rectangular monument, M⁶ (Pls. 5, c, d, 6, a), measuring 2.10 m. from north to south and 1.44 m. from east to west. Two courses of stones are preserved, and the top course has deep grooves from wheel ruts (Pl. 6, a) extending diagonally from east to west. Like M⁵ it is later than the early water channel which it interrupts, and the channel's detour seems to have taken cognizance of the existence of the monument. In other words, the water channel through its detour functioned for some time after M⁵ and M⁶ had been constructed.

The next monument, M⁷ (Pl. 6, a), which is oriented like the preceding two, is situated two meters west of M⁶. It measures ca. 3.00 m. from north to south and 1.39 m. from east to west and consists of five large blocks laid at right angles to the line of the base. As in the case of the other foundations, its top surface has been deeply scored by the wheel ruts of the east-west road. Two of the deeper ruts are ca. 1.35 m. apart, which would indicate the approximate distance between wheels of the carts. At the north end of the foundation there are traces of another road coming from the northeast. It had obviously been in use over a long period because at one point the stone has been worn down to a depth of 0.13 m. This may be the same road (B), which has left visible traces a little farther to the north on the side of the detour of the early water channel at the northwest corner of M⁵ (Pl. 5, c, d). This road is

[4] The monument might have been shaped somewhat like the large altar in the Corinthian Agora, which faced the east; *Corinth*, I, iii, pp. 139–141, figs. 67, 68.

earlier than the east-west road and at a lower level, some half a meter below the surface of the temenos of Roman times. This proves clearly that both the road and the three monuments, M⁵–M⁷, are to be dated before the Roman era.

At a distance of only 0.70 m. west of M⁷ there was a small monument, M⁸ (Pl. 6, a, top), the foundation of which measures 0.98 m. from east to west and 0.94 m. from north to south. This too has been deeply worn by wheel traffic, but at a later period the wheel ruts were filled up with road metal of such hard consistency that it is difficult to distinguish it from the poros stone underneath. The two monuments M⁷ and M⁸ are later than the final destruction of the early water channel, which they cut off. Sections of the channel are preserved at the east edge of M⁷ and between M⁷ and M⁸. Since the detour of the channel was laid after M⁵ and M⁶ had been constructed, these two bases are obviously earlier than M⁷ and M⁸. It is, of course, impossible to determine what monuments the two bases supported, except that the larger of the two would be of suitable size and shape for an equestrian statue and the dimensions of the smaller, M⁸, would fit a statue base for a standing figure.

One other monument on the north side that may belong to pre-Roman times is a small base, M⁹, 41 m. west of M⁸ and *ca.* 12 m. northwest of the northwest corner of the Temple (Plans II, III). It measures 1.20 m. from north to south and 1.26 m. from east to west and consists of two blocks. The top has been roughly cut down. This may have been done when the early Roman temenos wall was constructed; the junction of the north and west arms of that wall comes exactly at M⁹. The only reason for dating this base before the Roman era is its orientation, which deviates from that of the Temple and follows approximately the orientation of the monuments described above. It corresponds roughly to the direction of the archaic road discovered beneath the fill from the Archaic Temple and to the line of its successor at a higher level.

WEST END

West of the Temple of Poseidon the terrain originally sloped down toward the north and east. During the last Roman reconstruction the ground level in the southwest corner was lowered by about 2.50 m.; and the northwest corner, where the ground sloped steeply toward the north gully, was raised artificially by further addition of earth fill. At the points where three early water channels, WChs I–III (below, pp. 24–26) traversed the area north of the West Waterworks the ground level remained almost unchanged; this is shown by the fact that these channels, originally designed to be without cover, lie only a little below the level of the Late Roman period. Here the surface of the temenos was raised slightly when the West Stoa was constructed; and these channels, then no longer in use, became concealed beneath the Stoa floor and the level of the temenos east of the Stoa. In view of the changes that took place when the Stoa was built, there is little to show the condition of the area before the Roman era. The West Waterworks, which will be described in a later chapter, indicate that the space was occupied to a certain extent by buildings of a sacred character, probably related to the cults of the Sanctuary. The irregular shape of the West Waterworks was probably determined by the existence of other buildings in the vicinity. The Large Circular Pit contained immense quantities of unhewn stones which had served some purpose in that part of the Sanctuary. Many of them are very large and too rough to have been used in the walls of a building. The most likely explanation is that they came from the Cyclopean Wall, which crossed diagonally the southwest corner of what later became the sacred precinct. Where it traversed the southwest end of the temenos, this wall would have been removed some time after the destruction of the Archaic Temple, probably in connection with the construction of the fifth-century Temple.⁵ The exact line of the wall can no longer be determined, and its extension toward the north has not been discovered, if it was ever constructed beyond the Sanctuary.⁶

⁵ See above, p. 7, and note 32.

⁶ There are good reasons for supposing that the Cyclopean Wall was never completed; O. Broneer, *Hesperia*, XXXVII, 1968, pp. 33–35.

SOUTH SIDE

On the south side, as at the west end, the temenos has undergone radical alterations, and the original condition can no longer be reconstructed. From the southwest corner of the temenos and almost as far east as the east end of the Temple, the original ground level was lowered when the South Stoa was constructed. At the east end of this area, however, the ground slopes down toward the Earlier Stadium. The formal approach to the racecourse begins near the southeast corner of the Temple, leaving a space only 5.50 m. wide between an ornamental gateway at the entrance to the Stadium ramp and the Temple foundation (Plans III, IV). This became a vital junction in the layout of the temenos, since the processions formed at the Long Altar had to pass through this point to reach the Stadium. On the rising ground west of the ramp, there is a "polygonal" wall marking the eastern limit of the upper terrace (Plans II–IV, Pl. 6, b). This wall, which is earlier than the first Roman reconstruction, is made partly of re-used blocks, smoothly dressed and fitted with tight joints. It makes several angles, hence the designation "polygonal". There is a long narrow retaining wall running nearly parallel to the Temple for a distance of 32.12 m., beginning at a point opposite the west cella wall and extending eastward to about 8.00 m. west of the southeast corner of the Temple.[7] It is 0.29 m. high and *ca.* 0.38 m. wide at the top and has a smooth face on the north side toward the Temple, but is left rough on the south (Pl. 6, c). The top shows signs of wear, and it seems to have served as the lower of two steps. It would have formed a curb and the approach to an area on the south at a somewhat higher level than the euthynteria of the Classical Temple. The first preserved block at the west end has anathyrosis, showing that there was at least one more block; but two meters west of this point the natural rock rises considerably above the level of the curb, which cannot have extended farther west.

At the east end (Plans III, IV) the curb forms an obtuse angle with the "polygonal" wall, which makes two more obtuse angles and extends southward as far as the reservoir that supplied water for the Earlier Stadium (below, pp. 27, 48). The first, i.e. northern, stretch of the "polygonal" wall is 6.85 m. long and 0.62 m. wide. It has a setting line 0.30 m. from the east edge, which is considerably worn and crumbly, whereas the west half is well preserved. The setting line indicates a second course of stones, set back to become the upper of two steps, which formed the ascent from the lower area in front of the Temple of Poseidon to the upper terrace enclosed by the wall. The second stretch is 5.40 m. in length, but what is preserved here is one course lower than the section farther north. Here too are traces of a setting line (Plan VII), only 0.10 m. from the east edge; and at one point there is a second setting line at right angles to it marking the end of a block in the second course. The existing foundation is *ca.* 0.66 m. broad, but the wall that rested on it was a great deal lighter. From this second angle in the "polygonal" wall the next stretch extended 17.90 m. to the edge of the Stadium reservoir. Two small blocks, possibly in their original position, remain from the second course. The foundation is preserved for a length of 6.92 m.; beyond that point only the footing trench cut in rock shows the line of the wall, which seems to have made one more slight bend. At the south end the trench, for a distance of two meters, is filled with rubble masonry; this was probably put in later than the well-built sections described above. The footing trench extends to the northeast edge of the reservoir, but there is no indication that it went across to the other side; consequently we must assume that it stopped here. Where the wall reached the reservoir there was a parapet, probably forming a sluice for regulating the flow of water into the Stadium (below, pp. 27, 48, Pl. 13, b). The fact that the wall terminated exactly at this point is an indication of early date, since the reservoir must be dated as early as the fifth century B.C.

---

[7] *Isthmia*, I, p. 4, pl. II.

EAST END

At the southeast corner of the Temple of Poseidon a rectangular base, M[13] (Plans III, IV), stands close to the foundation. It measures *ca.* 2.00 m. in length from north to south and is preserved to a width of 0.97 m. Where it stands the rock has been dressed down, and the south end of the base has a cutting indicating that another monument abutted against it. The base, which is made out of a single block, is now preserved to a height of 0.25 m. but was originally higher. It was once, probably in Roman times, converted into a rectangular basin, and remains of lime on the uneven bottom show that it had served as a trough for slaking lime. In its original form it probably supported a monument of some kind. Its date is uncertain.

SACRIFICIAL AREA

In the area between the Long Altar[8] and the eastern limit of the temenos, the southeast corner was in Greek times occupied by the Earlier Stadium, and there was probably a temenos wall or some simple enclosure limiting the sacred area toward the east. One monument of pre-Roman date is the East Gateway, to be described below. Its location, some forty meters distant from the Temple façade, marks the eastern limit of an open area that included the Long Altar and was, like its Early Roman counterpart (below, p. 72), designed to serve the ritual and sacrificial requirements of the cult. The ground level in this area, which originally sloped down toward the east, was later raised to the approximate height of the later Roman precinct level. In archaic times, before the level was raised, this sloping ground, at least as far east as the foundation for the rear wall of the East Stoa, was part of the Temple precinct. This is shown by an extensive sacrificial area strewn with bones, ash, and sea pebbles.[9] It does not seem, at that early period, to have been enclosed with a wall; at least no trace of such an enclosure has appeared in the excavation. The ground level was raised in two stages. From the Long Altar, where the ground begins to slope down as far east as the west side of the Roman Altar, the fill consisted chiefly of debris from the Archaic Temple (Pl. 6, d), and this would have been thrown in at the time of construction of the fifth century Temple. In the area farther east later occupied by the East Stoa the accumulation of earth was deeper. The bottom layer contained tiles and stones from the Archaic Temple, and underneath on the hard-packed floor lay strewn the pebbles and ash from the sacrifices of archaic times. The upper part of the fill consisted chiefly of debris from the destruction of 390 B.C. (Pls. 7, a, 52, b). There was, of course, no definite line of demarcation between the two layers, but over most of this area the later fill overlay the archaic debris. The consistency of this fill gives the impression that the area had not been formally landscaped until after the fire of 390 B.C.

EAST GATEWAY

About 40 m. east of the Temple of Poseidon and a little to the south of the Temple axis, there is a heavy foundation constructed with large, squared blocks (M[17], Plans III, V). The courses preserved at the top are made of a very soft shell limestone which has disintegrated to such an extent as to obliterate the joints completely (Pl. 7, b). All that could be seen before excavation was a low mound strewn with oyster shells from the decomposed stones. The lower courses, however, are made of a brittle limestone which tends to crumble and become sand. Originally, the foundation appears to have been T-shaped, but the north wing cannot now be seen, being partly destroyed and completely covered over by the construction of a late Roman cistern (below, p. 96). The central part of the foundation, exclusive of the wings, measures 4.80 m. from east to west, and 4.65 m. from north to south. The east face has been laid bare down to the lowest course (Plan V, Section B–B, Pl. 7, c), and here the total height, from the bottom to the highest preserved part of the foundation, is 3.30 m. The western half of the foundation

---

[8] *Isthmia*, I, pp. 98–101.
[9] *Ibid.*, pp. 55–56.

was more than twice as broad. Here a wing, 2.00 m. wide, extends 2.65 m. toward the south, and presumably there was a similar wing on the north in the area of the cistern. The west face of the foundation has been partly exposed in a small pit between it and the rear wall of the East Stoa, which here forms one of its regular buttresses in the rear (the south face of the buttress is shown in Plan V, Section A–A). If the two wings were symmetrical in size and disposition, the full width, north to south, on the west face of the foundation would have been close to 10.00 m. (4.65 m. + (2 × 2.65 m.) = 9.95 m.).

The stones are laid in a consistent system of headers and stretchers, but the dimensions of the blocks vary a great deal. Thus, on the east face there are four stretchers in alternating courses, occupying the combined width of seven headers (Plan V, Section B–B, Pl. 7, c). The individual blocks measure 1.10–1.30 m. in length, *ca.* 0.60 m. in width, and *ca.* 1.41 m. in height. The lowest course, which rests on stereo, was laid in a trench 0.30 m. deep. In spite of the slight irregularity in the dimensions of the blocks, it is likely that they were intended in their rough form to measure $4 \times 2 \times 1\frac{1}{3}$ ancient feet of the Hellenistic foot length of 0.302 m.[10]

Both in material and construction this foundation differs radically from any of the other foundations in the Sanctuary. It resembles more closely the construction of the West Foundation (below, p. 117). Although no blocks from the original superstructure have been identified, the shape of the foundation suggests a gateway, and its location would indicate that this was the principal entrance into the pre-Roman temenos of Poseidon. The central part of the foundation would have supported an ornamental gateway, probably with two columns on the east façade, perhaps with flanking walls forming antae. There were probably two columns *in antis* facing the Temple, with the doorway somewhere between the two façades. The two wings would hardly have consisted of solid masonry, for which there would be no structural reason. They may have contained niches for two statues facing the temenos, or, more likely, there was a covered passage on either side of the main gateway. In Plate 52, c four plans are presented for possible restoration of the East Gateway in the pre-Roman period.

Before the first Roman reconstruction there were, so far as our excavations show, no walls abutting against the wings on the north and south sides. The temenos enclosure may have consisted merely of a wooden fence or perhaps only horos stones, leaving the Gateway as an isolated structure, ornamental and formal rather than practical. The roof would have formed gables on four sides. Numerous fragments of small Doric columns were found in the vicinity, and some of these would be of suitable size for a structure of this kind.[11] In the absence of definitely attributable members, no convincing architectural restoration can be made of the East Gateway. (On the Roman reconstruction of the building, see below, p. 74.)

For the date of the East Gateway, the fire damage to the Poseidon Temple in 390 B.C. provides a terminus *post quem*, since the foundation extended through the debris and could not have been laid before the area had been landscaped after the fire. There are traces of the footing trench in the loose earth fill east of the foundation; these are indicated in Plan V, Section A–A, right. On the other hand, the regular construction with headers and stretchers in alternate courses is more characteristic of classical Greek masonry than of Roman work. The East Gateway was probably built in the course of the fourth century B.C. as part of the reconstruction work undertaken to condition the Sanctuary at the time of Alexander, when the temenos needed enlargement to provide space for processions and ritual functions east of the Temple of Poseidon.

EARLY REMAINS NORTH OF THE EAST GATEWAY

In the north half of the area, some 18 m. north of the East Gateway, there is a solidly built terrace wall preserved to a length of 8.70 m., which probably goes back to pre-Roman times (Plans II–IV). It is

[10] For the foot length in use in the Corinthia in the fourth century B.C. and later, see below, pp. 63–64, and *ibid.*, Appendix I, pp. 174–181.

[11] *Ibid.*, p. 118, nos. C 34–68.

oriented northwest to southeast. The northeast face is smooth and the other face is uneven. This shows that it was built as a retaining wall, indicating that the ground level southwest of the wall was considerably higher than on the northeast side. Furthermore, not only the wall but the individual blocks slope perceptibly down toward the southeast, which would not be the case had the wall been intended as foundation for a building. The southeast part of the wall, for a length of 3.10 m., is built of rather large squared blocks (Pl. 7, d, middle), some of which are re-used. They were laid without the use of mortar, the interstices being filled with earth and stone chips. The largest is 1.23 m. long. Both the northeast face and the top of the block are very smoothly finished, and the rear face seems to have anathyrosis. In the top are preserved four scratch lines forming a rough asterisk, and near the southeast end is what appears to be a shifting notch. It is obvious that the block had been prepared for some other use before being placed in its present position. At the northwest end of the southeast section of the wall an unfluted column drum is built into the masonry. It is preserved to a height of 0.74 m. and had a diameter in excess of 0.44 m. The lower part of the drum, to a height of 0.30 m., had a greater diameter than the upper end and its surface is now rather rough. The upper part retains traces of a very hard, smooth stucco, ca. 6 mm. thick. The rest of the wall, northwest of the column drum, is made in a somewhat different technique (Pl. 7, d). The wall is here preserved to a maximum height of 0.60 m. The first course consists of rather large blocks, comparable in size to those in the southeast stretch just described. Above these larger stones is a second course of much smaller stones of irregular shape laid in lime mortar and with the joints smoothly filled on the northeast face. At the northwest end the wall has been cut through by the heavy foundation for the colonnade of the East Stoa. West of this foundation a stretch of the wall is preserved to a length of 1.20 m., but the footing trench extends 0.90 m. beyond the end of the wall and then stops dead. Here the ground level at the time when the wall was built seems to have been even with the top of the wall; consequently there was no need for the terrace wall to continue farther northwest. At the southeast end the wall is interrupted by the foundation for the rear wall of the East Stoa, and no trace of the terrace wall or of its footing trench has been found east of this foundation. The orientation of the wall, somewhat similar to but not identical with that of the Earlier Stadium and the North Propylon, seems to indicate that the wall existed before the construction of the early Roman temenos walls, which follow the orientation of the Temple of Poseidon. It served as a supporting wall for the higher terrace to the southwest, and probably marks the limit of the temenos toward the northeast in the pre-Roman period. If this is correct, the Northeast Altar Terrace and the Northeast Cave, to be described below, were at that time outside the temenos of Poseidon. The area has been too much disturbed by later building activities to show the line of the temenos enclosure between the East Gateway and the terrace wall.

At a distance of ca. 4.50 m. northeast of the terrace wall there is a very rough foundation of large stones (Plan II, Pl. 7, d), two of which have grooves in the top as they now lie; these were probably from the Archaic Temple. The foundation has a thickness of over 1.50 m. That it belongs to a comparatively early period is shown by the fact that the rear foundation of the East Stoa cuts through some of the blocks diagonally. What is preserved appears to be a very rough subfoundation, which may have extended northwestward to the west side of the rear East Stoa foundation. Some unshaped blocks appearing at the edge of the Stoa foundation trench seem to indicate that the rough foundation extended farther in that direction. It may be part of a lower retaining wall built to prevent the earth of the upper area to the southwest from washing down toward the Northeast Altar Terrace.

In the far northeast corner of the temenos few clear remains of pre-Roman buildings have appeared, but near the north end of the East Stoa there is preserved a threshold which, to judge by its orientation, may belong to the Greek period (Pl. 6, e; for its location see Plan II). It consists of two blocks with a total length of 1.675 m. and a width of 0.55 m. The door opening, as indicated by pivot holes and cuttings for door jambs, would have been about 1.29 m. wide. A square cutting for a door stop to the right of center shows that there were two leaves to the door. On the threshold are remains of stucco, consisting of natural cement and fine gravel. The north end abuts against an east-west wall made with uncut stones laid in earth mortar. The threshold, together with the adjoining wall, is all that remains of some small building, probably connected with the Sanctuary in pre-Roman times.

PRE-ROMAN ROADS

Several ancient roads run through parts of the Sanctuary, and some of these have been mentioned above. As links of communication they provide a useful index to conditions of the Sanctuary at different periods. Some of these roads give evidence of long and frequent use, which means that the Sanctuary lay close to an important thoroughfare. There are good reasons for believing that this was the case even before the earliest traceable period of the Sanctuary.[12] A glance at a map of Greece will show that a road coming from Athens, following the shoreline of the Saronic Gulf and continuing westward in the direction of Ancient Corinth, would have passed through, or very close to, the Sanctuary of Poseidon (Plan I, Pl. 51). Probably it forked somewhere near the east end of the Corinth canal,[13] one branch continuing along the shore toward Kenchreai, Epidauros, and Troizen, and the other leading westward through the town of Kromna[14] toward Corinth and Sikyon. The former of these is the road that Theseus took from Troizen to Athens when he cleared the route of the monsters that made travel precarious. It was at Isthmia, near the juncture of the two roads, that he encountered and dispatched Sinis the Pine-Bender.

Archaic Road

The earliest road within the area of the later temenos runs along the bank of the gully northwest of the Temple of Poseidon (Plan IV, Road A). Three stretches of the road have been exposed. The eastern-most and longest section (Pl. 8), *ca.* 30 m., begins 17 m. west of the North Propylon, at the point where the road has been cut off by the foundation for the late Roman temenos wall. Originally the road, skirting the north edge of the Temple precinct, must have continued eastward in the direction of the Theater. There are indications of a road along the same line north of the North Propylon, and this seems to have been in use also at a later period. At the eastern end of the long stretch, close to the Roman temenos wall, the roadbed is *ca.* 1.63 m. below the temenos level of Roman times; farther west it descends to a somewhat lower level, then rises again gently toward the west. Along the south edge, where the living rock was exposed at the level of the road, wheel ruts are visible, but in the northern part the road metal consists of smooth hard-packed earth.

Road (A), which runs at an angle of 20⁰ to the long axis of the Temple, had obviously been in use over a long period. Its first use probably goes back to the time of construction of the Archaic Temple and perhaps earlier. When the Temple was destroyed by fire *ca.* 475 B.C., the debris from the fire was dumped on the roadbed, where it reached a depth of well over one meter. It was here that most of the building blocks from the Archaic Temple were found, and among them the pieces of the shattered marble

---

[12] *Hesperia*, XXXVII, 1968, p. 26, and note 3.

[13] Two cart roads still in existence probably follow very nearly the lines of the ancient roads. The main highway which now leads from Athens to the Peloponnesos forks close to New Corinth. The direction of this road in the Corinthia is determined by two factors which came into existence in the last century, the Corinth Canal and the new city of Corinth. In ancient times the route from the Isthmian Sanctuary to Corinth led almost due west and entered the city from the east through the "Kenchrean Gate." A. W. Parsons, *Corinth*, III, ii, pp. 94–99, postulated a more northerly route coming in by way of the "Isthmian Gate" through the East Long Wall, then through some gate in the north wall of the city. Cf. Henry S. Robinson, *The Urban Development of Ancient Corinth*, Athens, 1965, map on p. 5.

[14] This town, probably no more than a farming community, is mentioned in a passage of Kallimachos; its location became known in 1960 through our excavations along the Hellenistic wall across the Isthmus; cf. James R. Wiseman, *Hesperia*, XXXII, 1963, pp. 271–272, who gives references to the ancient sources. The road from the Isthmus to Ancient Corinth would have joined the road from Kenchreai somewhere between Kromna and the modern village of Hexamilia.

perirrhanterion.[15] At one time the road ran at a higher level; this is shown by wheel ruts in the rocks along the south edge at a height of 0.75–0.90 m. above the road level preserved farther north. The surface of the hillside would have kept changing as the earth washed down the slope, and the road moved gradually to lower levels during the long period of the Archaic Temple's existence. This is the opposite of what happens in more level areas, where the ground rises so that the earliest roadbeds are at the lowest level.

At the west end of the long easternmost stretch of the archaic road a small part of the Roman road for a length of 8.50 m. has been left as found. The Roman roadbed, which overlies the archaic fill from the Temple, is at a level ca. 1.09 m. above that of the archaic road. A second stretch of the early road, 11.50 m. long, has been exposed farther west, and here the archaic road level was only ca. 0.50 m. below that of the Roman road. At this point both the archaic road and its later successor made a slight S-turn to avoid running too close to the steep slope of the gully (Pl. 9, a, right). The roadbed in this stretch was found encumbered with building blocks, mostly from the stylobate of the Archaic Temple (Pl. 9, b, lower left). They lay flat on the road metal with no intervening fill. This shows that the road was in use until fire destroyed the Temple.

Where the foundations of the West Stoa cut across the ancient road (Pl. 9, b, center), some of the surface of the Roman temenos has been left above the archaic road, extending as far west as the rear wall of the Stoa, a distance of 9.50 m. Here the archaic road was only about 0.30 m. below the level of the Roman temenos. West of the rear wall of the West Stoa, an area measuring 23 m. in length from east to west has been excavated (Pl. 9, b, center), and here many successive layers of road metal have been exposed, extending in time through several centuries from archaic to late Roman.[16] Over much of this area the surface of the rock formed the roadbed; consequently there is little difference in level between the early and the later roads. Some fifty meters west of the excavated area there is a rough retaining wall of uncut stones (Pl. 9, d), now concealed beneath an olive grove. Its orientation is about the same as that of the archaic road, and in construction it resembles the early retaining wall NG[1], which we have found reasons to date to the early years of the Sanctuary. It is likely that this row of stones formed a retaining wall for the archaic road on the gentle slope at the head of the gully.

The earliest terrace wall, NG[1], in the northwest corner of the temenos and the archaic road, which is oriented somewhat similarly, indicate the line of the temenos boundary toward the north in pre-Roman times. This would have resulted in a precinct of very irregular shape, such as existed at other early sanctuaries, e.g. the archaic Sanctuary of Aphaia on Aigina.[17] The earliest plan to establish a rectangular temenos with the same orientation as the Temple was not made before the reorganization and repairs of the Sanctuary in the first century of our era.

CLASSICAL ROAD

One road of comparatively early date has been partly exposed north of monument M[5] (Plan IV, Road B, Pl. 5, d, lower right); this too shows use over a long period and at different levels. The road metal consists of stones and gravel packed together with earth into a very hard solid mass. This road

[15] *Isthmia*, I, pp. 6, 11–12, pl. 7.

[16] The westernmost sector (shown on Plan II) in which these roads appeared was excavated in 1967 by the expedition from the University of California at Los Angeles; Paul Clement, Δελτ., XXIII, 1968, Χρονικά, p. 139.

[17] See E. Fiechter, *Aigina, Das Heiligtum der Aphaia*, Plan 5, opp. p. 154; and cf. the temenos of Hephaistos and Athena in Athens, Homer A. Thompson, *The Athenian Agora*, 1962, pp. 28, 38–39, figs. 6, 8, 9; with R. E. Wycherley, *Athenian Agora*, XIV, *The Agora of Athens*, 1972, pp. 143, 149. The tendency toward the development of a rectangular precinct with the Temple in the middle is best exemplified in the Aphaia Sanctuary. Cf. the two plans, an early mid-sixth century one of irregular shape and the later, nearly rectangular plan from the early fifth century, reproduced in Vincent Scully, *The Earth, the Temple, and the Gods*, figs. 299–300. In the precinct of Apollo at Didyma, part of the curving archaic temenos wall surrounding the temple was retained after the construction of the later building; Th. Wiegand and H. Knackfuss, *Didyma*, I, 3, pl. 79, reproduced in H. Berve, G. Gruben, M. Hirmer, *Greek Temples, Theaters and Shrines*, p. 463, fig. 129.

seems to have had approximately the same orientation as the archaic road, but its level is 0.767 m. higher and only *ca.* 0.87 m. below the temenos level of Roman times. There are at least two distinct levels, one *ca.* 0.18 m. below the later road level, but it is likely that the road in the two periods had the same direction. This road was in use after the construction of monument M⁵, the northwest corner of which has been worn away by the wheel traffic. The fill above the road contained numerous fragments from the Classical Temple damaged by fire in 390 B.C. and also a small amount of pottery of late Hellenistic times, including some sherds of Megarian bowls. Thus the road, which existed while monument M⁵ was standing, continued to be used for a long time, probably till the destruction of Corinth in 146 B.C. It seems to be the successor of the archaic road (A), raised to this higher level when the area north of the Temple was landscaped after the fire that destroyed the Archaic Temple. Since Road (A) was blocked by debris at the time of the construction of the Classical Temple, we may assume that the later Road (B) came into use in the fifth century. The line of this road is indicated by the earliest of the water channels, WCh I (p. 24), which is probably of the same date. Such conduits frequently follow close to the roadbeds, where no building foundations interfered with the making of the channels.

EARLIER HELLENISTIC ROAD

Another road of pre-Roman times existed in the area later covered by the Sanctuary of Palaimon (Plan IV, Road C). It runs approximately northeast to southwest, a little to the south of the foundation for the Temple of Palaimon. When it was first exposed in the excavations, the wheel ruts, *ca.* 1.40 m. apart,[18] were clearly visible (Pl. 9, c, lower center). The road rose gradually from east to west. Where it crossed the later starting line of the Earlier Stadium the road surface was only a few centimeters above the level of the stone sill; but at the corner of the Temple, where the road passes over the water channel of the Stadium, it was *ca.* 0.30 m. above this channel. The road metal is comparatively hard, formed out of gravel and earth and easily distinguishable from the whitish surfacing of the Stadium. Since the road passes over both the later starting line and the water channel on the southwest side of the Earlier Stadium, it must have come into use after this Stadium had been abandoned and the Later Stadium constructed farther to the southeast (below, pp. 52, 65–66). On the other hand, some of the early temenos walls of the Palaimonion overlie the road; consequently it cannot have been open to traffic after the first construction of the Palaimonion. When the Temple of Palaimon was built at a still later date, the ground level east of the Temple façade had risen to a height of nearly half a meter above the surface of the Earlier Stadium and above the level of the road. The deep accumulation of earth over the roadbed indicates that the area had been left unoccupied for a long time between the abandonment of the road and the construction of the Temple. Thus if the Later Stadium was constructed, as is probable, in the second half of the fourth century B.C., the road would have been in use from that time to the middle of the second century B.C. Its direction, which differs from that of the road of classical times north of the Temple, indicates that Road (C), coming from the east, forked somewhere east of the Sanctuary, both branches leading westward, one (Road D) north, the other (Road C) south of the Temple of Poseidon. There is no evidence to show whether the two branches were in use simultaneously or came into existence at different times. The northern branch seems to have been used for a longer period than the southern, and it is possible that the two roads converged west of the temenos and continued as a single route toward Corinth.

LATER HELLENISTIC ROADS

Three roads have left distinct marks on the foundation for the Long Altar. At the very north end the topmost course of stones has been worn away by a road coming from the southeast and rounding the

---

[18] The width of ancient carts, as measured by the wheel ruts, was *ca.* 1.35–1.50 m. The earlier roads in the Corinth Agora are *ca.* 1.45–1.50 m. wide; the Late Roman and Byzantine roads at the Northeast Gate in the Fortress at Isthmia are somewhat narrower, *ca.* 1.40 m.

corner before continuing in a westward direction (Plans II, IV, Road F, Pl. 10, a, foreground); this seems to indicate that the Altar was standing when the road was in use. The top of the exposed foundation, however, has also been worn smooth, seemingly by road traffic, and this must be later than the destruction of the Altar. At a distance of three meters south of the north end of the Altar there are two deep wheel ruts crossing the foundation at an angle (Plans II–IV, Road E, Pl. 10, a). Each rut is *ca.* 0.60 m. wide and 0.16 m. deep, showing that this second road had been in use for a long time. East of the Altar the area has been raised in later times, but the line of the road can be seen on both sides of the foundation for the façade of the East Stoa. All the Roman foundations which cross the roadbed in this area still stand considerably higher than the roadbeds; consequently the Roads (E) and (F) were abandoned and covered over before the Roman foundations were laid down.

The third road, (D) (Pl. 10, b), which crossed the Altar foundation 16.00 m. south of the north end, has ruts even more pronounced than are those of Road (E). They are *ca.* 0.75 m. wide and nearly 0.20 m. deep, made by carts with a wheel base *ca.* 1.40 m. wide. The road comes from the southeast and continues northwestward, skirting the northeast corner of the Temple, then turning westward at the point where the three roads (D), (E), and (F) come together (Plan IV). From this juncture the road can be traced toward the southeast for a distance of about 100 m.

Like the second of the two roads at the north end of the Altar, Road (D), near the middle of the foundation, is intercepted by the Roman foundations, including that of the early Roman temenos wall. This fact is crucial for the chronology of the Sanctuary. Road (D) must be dated after the destruction of the Altar but before the construction of the first Roman temenos wall, and the same is true of Road (E) farther north. These two roads, which saw heavy use over a long period of time, can hardly have been in operation while the Temple with its related structures was open as the principal cult place in the Sanctuary. The demolition of the Altar would have taken place after the sack of Corinth in 146 B.C., and the two roads would have come into use while the temenos lay virtually abandoned after that event. Furthermore, these roads, (D) and (E), ceased to be used before the construction of the early Roman temenos walls, which we have reasons to date about the middle of the first century after Christ. Thus the two roads carried traffic across the Sanctuary over a period of some 200 years, from the destruction of Corinth under Mummius to the reign of Claudius. The first of the three roads, (F), at the north end of the Altar foundation might have existed while the Altar was still standing and perhaps continued in use for a short time after the demolition had begun. It was doubtless the predecessor of the two later roads, (D) and (E), which crossed the foundation farther south. Thus Road (F) may be dated somewhat earlier, but the two later roads, (D) and (E), cannot be earlier than the late Hellenistic period. It is not clear whether these two roads were in use simultaneously or successively, but the fact that they seem to come from the same general direction would favor the second alternative. If, as seems likely, the Altar was demolished gradually, beginning at the north end (below, p. 69), the southernmost of the three roads, (D), would have been the last to come into use.

Some ten meters west of the north end of the Altar, where the three roads come together (Plan IV), there is a rough pavement of poros blocks, which show wear in the top from the use of carts. The single road west of the juncture did not run close to the Temple, but turned slightly northward into the area north of the earlier Roman temenos wall. Between this wall and the later Roman temenos wall the ancient ground level is deeply scored by wheel ruts of different periods. Some of them, having a straight east-west direction, are probably of later date, but the three roads (D), (E) and (F) that crossed the Altar foundation and then united into one seem to have cut across the area from east-southeast toward west-northwest. The deep wheel ruts observed on the foundations for monuments M^6, M^7, and M^8 (above, pp. 12–13) probably belong chiefly to this period of interrupted use of the Sanctuary. The ground level here, however, in the Roman period was approximately the same as in late Hellenistic times. Farther west the road turned slightly southward again and then continued in a direction somewhat south of west. The roadbed, which was cut through by the foundation trench for the earlier Roman west temenos wall, is here *ca.* 0.25 m. below the ground level of the late Roman period. The principal line of the road has been exposed about eight meters north of the West Gate that formed the exit of the later Roman road (H) through the West Stoa. The pavement of the earlier road is a hard macadam, made of gravel, clay, and small stones, and the two foundations for the West Stoa cut across it.

East of the Long Altar there are traces of another road, (G), north of (F), also of pre-Roman times; this is shown by the fact that the foundations of the early Roman temenos wall and of the East Stoa overlie the roadbed. All four roads, (D)–(G), coming from the southeast and uniting into a single route north of the northeast corner of the Poseidon Temple, are probably branches of the same thoroughfare. During the period of inactivity in the Sanctuary these cart roads, which in many places cannot be traced with certainty, changed their lines of direction gradually before they reached the northeast corner of the Temple, where they formed a single roadbed. East of the Altar the road metal, with more or less distinct traces of use, extends over a large area, and the wheel ruts run together so as to make it difficult to separate them into distinct routes. On Plan IV they are marked as individual roads, but it is only in a few places, e.g. where they cross the Altar foundation, that the individual wheel tracks appear.

PRE-ROMAN WATERWORKS

The need for an adequate water supply in the Isthmian Sanctuary seems to have created a perpetual problem both in Greek and Roman times. A large number of water channels crisscross the excavations, and in the majority of cases the direction is from west to east. Since none of these channels have been traced beyond the west edge of the excavated area, it is not clear whether they all tapped the same source. At the west edge of the modern village there is a spring which reputedly gave the name Kyras Vrysi to the village, and this may have been the original source of the whole network of channels. In ancient times, before the underground water was tapped with deep wells west of the fountain, the source was far more copious than it is at the present time. This can be seen by the deep erosion in the gully, which begins near the spring and continues southeastward to the sea; at present the flow of water is a mere trickle. In addition to the channels which brought water from afar, rainwater was collected from the roofs of the buildings and stored in reservoirs.

LARGE CIRCULAR PIT

The quest for water may explain the reason for a surprisingly large pit or well discovered in the vicinity of the Sanctuary. One of the early campaigns revealed a circular depression (Pl. 10, c), located some 43 meters almost due south of the southwest corner of the Temple of Poseidon (Plans II–IV). The mouth of the shaft, with a diameter of almost five meters, is cut in solid rock extending to a depth of 0.50–1.25 m. The rest of the shaft is cut through marl or hard clay, which in certain places tends to crumble and cave in (Pl. 11, a). It was at first thought that this large circular cutting was a wading pool, similar to those found in other sanctuaries connected with games,[19] but it took three seasons of digging to reach the bottom, at a depth of 19.75 m. The shaft is very nearly a perfect circle at the top, but near the bottom it becomes slightly elliptical.[20] The marks of the well-diggers' tools were clearly visible on the walls of the shaft at the time of our excavations. At the rim there is a shallow cutting in the rock,

[19] On the pool in the gymnasium at Eretria, R. B. Richardson, *A.J.A.*, XI, 1896, pp. 153–156, fig. 1. At Delphi the circular pool measures 9.70 m. in diameter and 1.30 m. in depth; Jannoray, *Le Gymnase*, p. 61, pls. I, II, XXV. At Olympia the circular structure (diam. 7.80–8.04 m.) north of the Workshop of Pheidias, originally regarded as a heroon (*Olympia*, Text II, pp. 105–107, 165–167, and Plates, vol. I, pls. LXXI, LXXII; Gardiner, *Olympia*, pp. 204–205) was later identified as "sweat bath" (Emil Kunze, *Olympiabericht*, IV, 1944, pp. 39–40, pl. 11; *Neue Deutsche Ausgrabungen*, pp. 275–276).

[20] The shaft measures *ca.* 5.00 m. in diameter at the top; farther down it is not a perfect circle, but the deviation is slight.

0.87 m. wide (Plans III, IV, Pl. 10, d), which must have been made as bedding for a surrounding parapet. Where there were natural depressions in the rock, small stones were set in to produce a level surface.

The shaft does not terminate evenly at the bottom. There is a trench, *ca.* 1.00 m. wide and 0.45 m. deep, around the edge with two bridging dikes directly across from each other. This would seem to indicate that the well was left in an unfinished state, and it is conceivable that the inflow of water prevented the well-diggers from finishing the bottom smoothly. The reason for the trench around the edge is obvious. It would have been cut by the master well-digger, whose task it was to make the shaft circular and the edges as nearly vertical as possible. After the trench had been dug to a convenient depth, the removal of the middle part required no careful measuring. The two dikes were probably left in order to facilitate the removal of the water. The workmen detailed to bail out the water would be engaged in one half of the trench while digging continued on the other side. In our excavation of the pit we followed much the same system and found this a convenient and time-saving device. Although the water in spring-time may rise to a height of nearly four meters above the bottom, at the end of the summer when the ground water is at a low level, we were able to continue operations even without installing a mechanical pump. One gang of workmen bailing with the use of a simple hand-operated windlass was able to keep the water level down so as to permit excavation of the shaft (Pl. 11, a). Thus if the immense pit was dug to provide the Sanctuary with water, it may have served its purpose reasonably well for the time of the year, April to May, when the Isthmian Games were celebrated, but it was not a dependable source at all seasons. The deep stratum of marl that extends down below the bottom of the well is virtually impervious to water, and the well-diggers never encountered a gravelly, water-bearing stratum. The present inflow is rather surface water seeping through the cracks in the rock at the top, but this flow is seasonal and too meager to provide a steady water supply.

The failure of the pit to meet the need for water the year around was probably the reason why it was abandoned at an early period. The fill of the shaft contained enormous quantities of large stones[21] and earth, and mixed with these were many dedications of bronze and terracotta, fragments of poros sculpture, a few pieces of archaic inscriptions, one nearly complete terracotta perirrhanterion and fragments of many others, and enormous quantities of pottery (see Appendix I, showing the contents of the Large Circular Pit, pp. 135–136). Except for the top part, which contained some mixed fill, the shaft appears to have been filled up at one time not much later than the middle of the fifth century B.C. Near the bottom were found two Attic lekythoi from the period of the Emporion Painter and the Haimon Painter, which have been dated to about 480–470 B.C.[22] Several Attic lamps datable to the first quarter of the fifth century also came from the lower levels.

The great well does not seem to have been abandoned until after some period of use. Among the numerous undressed stones found in the shaft, there is one block of a curbing (Pl. 53, a). It measures 0.973 m. in length on the inside, 0.748 m. in height, and 0.28 m. in thickness. It is fairly smoothly finished on all sides and has anathyrosis at the ends. The edge is smooth and well preserved; the top is somewhat weathered and worn. There are traces of clamp cuttings at the ends, probably for double-T clamps, but they are not well preserved. The curvature fits a circle of about the same diameter as that of the well-shaft. The weathered top of the curb stone shows that the well had been in use for some time, but there are no rope marks. To make up for the meager inflow, the immense shaft would have

---

[21] The immense quantities of uncut stones, now used as foundations for the walls enclosing the neighboring school playground (Pls. 3, b, upper left, 9, b), are too numerous and homogeneous to be a haphazard collection of field stones. They were probably thrown into the Pit when part of the Cyclopean Wall that crossed the southwest corner of the temenos was demolished. The most likely time for that operation is after the construction of the Classical Temple when the precinct was being landscaped (above pp. 6–7, notes 31, 32).

[22] IP 2441 and 2351; *Hesperia*, XXXI, 1962, pp. 22–23, nos. 1 and 2. For the shape cf. Emilie Haspels, *Attic Black-Figured Lekythoi*, pp. 166–167, pl. 48, 4 a, b, by the Emporion Painter, whose works she dates about 470 B.C.

served as a sizeable reservoir;[23] this seems the most logical explanation for the large diameter. Possibly the well was abandoned and filled up at the time when the early water channel, WCh I (below, p. 25), was made to bring water from the natural spring to the Sanctuary.

The possibility cannot be excluded that the shaft was dug to serve some purpose more directly connected with the cult of Poseidon. There are other sanctuaries of the same god in which comparable pits have been discovered.[24] If, however, the pit at Isthmia had been dug to serve some such purpose, it is difficult to explain why it was abandoned at such an early date. The first Temple of Poseidon was destroyed by fire about the time of the Persian Wars, in other words, somewhat earlier than the filling up of the Large Circular Pit. Although the pottery from the debris of the Temple points to nearly the same period as that from the Pit, it is likely that the shaft was filled up after the Classical Temple had been constructed. In the debris thrown away into the North Gully and east of the Temple after the fire there is a large admixture of ash, and most of the stones and many tiles show the effect of the fire. The debris thrown into the well-shaft, on the other hand, did not contain ashes and charred objects to any appreciable extent. After it had been decided that the pit was no longer needed, it became such a convenient place for the disposal of rubbish that some of the debris from the burned Temple would certainly have found its way into the shaft, had this been available for dumping at that time. The building blocks from the Archaic Temple with their telltale rope marks and the heavy roof tiles of the building formed a conspicuous portion of the fill in the North Gully, and the scarcity of such material among the contents of the Pit would indicate either that this was still open and used for water when the debris from the Archaic Temple was discarded or that the shaft had been filled up before the destruction of the Temple. Some of the pottery from the shaft is later than 470 B.C. (Appendix I, pp. 135–136), and it is likely that the Pit was filled up when the area of the temenos was landscaped some time after the construction of the Classical Temple.

WATER CHANNELS

The earliest of the conduits that brought water to the Sanctuary from the west is an open channel, WCh I, dug in the earth and lined with a hard, watertight cement both on the bottom and on the sides (Plans III, IV, WCh I, Pl. 11, b). Wherever it is cut in poros blocks it has been mended or re-routed at a later period. It is almost rectangular in section but is slightly wider at the top than at the bottom. This channel has not been laid bare in its entire length, but small cross trenches dug at short intervals have enabled us to trace its course for a total distance of 115 m., from its preserved west end, twenty meters west of the West Stoa, to the point where it is broken up east of monument base M⁵. Like the other east-west conduits, it had its source somewhere west of the Sanctuary, probably at the fountain mentioned above, some five hundred meters west of the Sanctuary. Through most of its exposed length west of the temenos it was found covered, partly with marble roof tiles from the fifth-century Temple. These, having been made available after the fire of 390 B.C., show the comparatively early date of WCh I. The cover is certainly a later addition; originally the channel was intended to be left open. A little to the west of the West Stoa there is a well-preserved section of the channel without cover; within the Stoa

---

[23] The water at the end of the rainy season reached a depth of *ca.* five meters. There would have been 98.175 cu. m., or 25,936 gallons at that time of the year.

[24] A conspicuous example is the Sanctuary of Poseidon at Molykrion; A. K. Orlandos, Δελτ., IX, 1924–25, Παράρτημα, pp. 55–64. In Athens, where Poseidon was identified with Erechtheus, he had his θάλασσα in the Erechtheion; N. Kontoleon, Τὸ Ἐρέχθειον, pp. 34–37; and cf. D. I. Pallas, Ἡ Θάλασσα τῶν Ἐκκλησιῶν, pp. 148–156; Gorham P. Stevens *et al., The Erechtheum*, pp. 168–171, 312–313, 490–491. There was a place near Mantineia in which waves of the sea appeared within the sanctuary of Poseidon (Pausanias VIII, 10, 2–3); and Pausanias (I, 26, 5 and VIII, 10, 4) mentions another sanctuary in Asia Minor in which similar phenomena were observed. If the circular pit at Isthmia was indeed intended as a Thalassa, it is conceivable that it had something to do with the origin of the myth about the secret burial place of Neleus, who was the son of Poseidon (Pausanias II, 2, 2). Further speculation along this line would lead too far from factual reality.

itself only the bottom of the channel remains. Close to the Stoa stylobate, however, the channel is well preserved, and here a second channel, WCh II, branches off toward the southeast (Pl. 11, b). That WCh II is later than WCh I is shown by the fact that its bottom is lower than that of the earlier channel, which runs north of east in the area north of the Temple of Poseidon. It is likely that WCh I continued to carry water toward the northeast after WCh II had been made. The two differ markedly in workmanship, as will be shown below. One well-preserved section of WCh I has been exposed just east of the stylobate for the West Stoa (Pl. 11, b, lower left). Here it measures 0.14 m. in width at the bottom, 0.145 m. at the top, and 0.07 m. in depth. It is carefully made with a hard cement and sharp corners at the top. There is no cover and no rabbet for one, as there would have been had cover slabs been intended from the beginning.

From the point of juncture of channels WCh I and II the former turns slightly northward and continues in an almost straight line toward the northeast. At the northwest corner of the foundation for the Classical Temple the channel makes a bend turning slightly southward. It is clear that WCh I is later than the Classical Temple, though perhaps not much later. At the bend, where a length of 2.50 m. has been exposed, it measures 0.146 m. in width at the bottom and almost the same at the top. The depth here is 0.05 m. at the south edge and 0.06 m. at the north edge. The construction and dimensions of the channel remain approximately the same throughout. At the very corner of the Temple foundation there are some terracotta bricks covering WCh I (Pl. 11, c, right), but these seem to be of much later date than the channel itself. In some places where the channel has been exposed it is roofed with terracotta cover tiles of the Lakonian type; at other points there are no indications of cover at all.

There are traces of the channel on both sides of the foundation for monument M[7] (above, p. 12). At the east edge of this base the nature of the channel changes. Here it turns northward and continues in a curved line north of the foundations for monuments M[6] and M[5]. This section, however, which will be described below, is not an original part of WCh I but a detour made to avoid the two foundations. Between the east edge of M[6] and the west edge of M[5] a small section of the original channel is preserved, here covered with Lakonian cover tiles (Pl. 5, c, center). The last extant portion of the original channel (Pl. 5, b, lower right) is found a little to the east of the foundation for M[5]. Here a small section, 0.80 m. long, remains *in situ*, but only the bottom and south wall of the channel are preserved. Further digging beyond this point showed that the channel was interrupted and broken up when the north temenos wall was constructed in Roman times, and nothing more is preserved of WCh I or of its detour. From the direction of the channel at this point one would conclude that it was intended to bring water to the area of the Theater, but no water channel of this type or of this early date has been found in the Theater excavation.

Returning now to the beginning of the detour east of M[7] we find that the channel has here been cut out of poros blocks, varying in length but measuring *ca.* 0.33 m. in width at the top (Pl. 11, d). The channel also has different dimensions here. It measures only 0.112 m. in width at the bottom and 0.125 m. at the top, and the depth has been increased to *ca.* 0.16 m. Over the west end of this detour four cover slabs of poros with a total length of 2.70 m. are still in place, and it is obvious that the whole detour was intended to be similarly covered. The channel skirts the northwest corner of foundation M[5], then turns a little toward the south, and continues eastward very close to the monument foundation. It is here cut in large poros blocks, which seem to be part of the foundation of M[5], and the cover slabs are partly preserved. Both the channel itself and the blocks in which it was cut have been worn down by cart wheels on a road (Plan IV, Road B) that ran close to the north edge of monument M[5] (Pl. 11, d). The detour of the channel has been exposed at the northwest and northeast corners of M[5], and in both places are remains of poros cover slabs. At the northeast corner it makes a slight southward bend and continues east of M[5] for a distance of one meter. A little beyond this point the detour would have joined the original channel, but the actual junction is not preserved. There is now a gap of 0.17 m. between the east end of the detour and the west end of the small section of original channel described above (Pl. 5, b). The whole area here was much disturbed in Roman times when the foundation for the east end of the projected North Stoa was laid and later when the north temenos wall was built.

Summarizing the above description we observe that WCh I is earlier than WCh II but later than the foundation for the fifth-century Temple. It is earlier than the foundations for M^6, M^7, and M^8, by which the original channel was interrupted. On the other hand, when M^5 and M^6 were built WCh I was still in use, since it proved necessary to construct the detour to the north of these foundations. After the later monument bases, M^7 and M^8, had been built, WCh I with its detour can no longer have carried water.

Where WCh II branches off from WCh I just west of the foundation for the façade of the West Stoa (Pl. 11, b) the later channel, WCh II, is at a level *ca.* 0.06 m. below that of WCh I. This, as is pointed out above, need not imply that the original course of WCh I ceased to be used after WCh II was made. The outflow at the junction could have been blocked so as to turn the water into either of the two channels. WCh II, which must have been in use over a long period, was made with walls and bottom of cement, but it is much less regular than WCh I, and the walls flare out toward the top. At the junction WCh II measures 0.10 m. in width at the bottom and 0.15 m. at the top, and *ca.* 0.055 m. in depth. The sides are rounded and uneven, clearly not intended to receive cover slabs. A little to the east of the junction WCh II turns toward the southeast. Here it is in rather poor condition and its sides have been mended with roof tiles from the Classical Temple. At a distance of nine meters from the junction of the two channels another branch, WCh III (Pl. 12, a, upper right), takes off almost at right angles toward the southwest, continuing for a distance of 7.60 m. to a circular manhole of the West Waterworks (Pl. 12, b, lower right). This short channel is larger than either I or II and very uneven, both in width and in depth. At one point near the manhole it is only 0.11 m. wide at the bottom; farther north it widens to 0.18 m., and the depth is *ca.* 0.12 m. This was intended to bring water from WCh II to the West Waterworks (below, pp. 27–29) with its long reservoir. The short branch WCh III is at a slightly lower level than WCh II.

Beyond the point where WCh III branches off from WCh II the latter continued toward the southeast, and after some gentle curves it emptied its water into the reservoir of the Earlier Stadium. Just beyond the junction of WCh II and WCh III, the former makes a detour toward the north for a distance of seven meters. At its west end the detour makes a slight bend toward the north, and at the other end, where it rejoins WCh II, it makes a sharp southward curve. At this point, however, a late foundation built across the original channel and the detour has caused the destruction of both. The detour was made almost entirely out of cover tiles from the fifth-century Temple (Pl. 12, a, c). At the bottom these tiles are laid upside down, their hollow underside forming the channel, and similar tiles were placed right side up as cover. Most of them are well preserved, but there are slight traces of fire on some of the fragments. We may thus date the detour as well as the repairs to WCh II after the fire of 390 B.C.[25] Although most of the roof tiles were then calcined from the heat and broken into small fragments, there may have been parts of the Temple in which they escaped the direct effect of the fire and thus could be used for the construction of the detour to WCh II as well as for covers in parts of WCh I. It is unlikely that so many marble roof tiles would have been available at any time for such a use except after the fire in the Temple. The purpose of the detour is not now apparent, but after it had been made the detoured section of the original channel cannot have been used, although it is still nearly undamaged. The edge of the first cover tile at the bottom of the detour projects *ca.* 0.05 m. above the bottom of the original channel so as to prevent the water from flowing through the straight channel at this point (Pl. 12, c, right center).

Beyond the point where the detour rejoined the original channel, the latter is comparatively well preserved for a distance of 24.00 m. up to the point where it is interrupted by the early Roman south temenos wall. This stretch is covered with a patchwork of marble and terracotta cover tiles and stone

[25] *Isthmia*, I, pp. 90, 92.

slabs (Pl. 12, d); but part of the channel was found without cover, although it is here so far below the surface that it could not have been intended as an open conduit. The poros blocks in the south temenos wall of the first century after Christ rest directly on the edges of the channel. Some stones packed into the channel at the point of crossing and long stretches where the cover slabs are missing indicate that the water could not have flowed through the channel after the wall had been constructed. It is unlikely, in fact, that WCh II was used at all during the Roman period. Beyond the point where the channel passed under the temenos wall it continued for a distance of 22.00 m. until it emptied into the Earlier Stadium reservoir (Pl. 13, a). Here the channel, as far as it has been exposed, was left partly open and partly covered with poros slabs and large pieces of marble pantiles from the fifth-century Temple. For the last seven meters before it issues into the reservoir the channel is poorly preserved. The ground level here was lowered in late Roman times when the South Stoa was built, and this operation caused the destruction of the water channel.

STADIUM RESERVOIR

The Stadium reservoir was originally underground, but when the South Stoa was constructed the roof at the northwest end was cut away for a stretch of seven meters; the rest is still below ground. The reservoir has a length of 17.00 m., and it varies in width at the bottom between 0.45 m. and 0.75 m. At the lower, southeast end it measures 1.20 m. in height, but at the now unroofed upper end (Pl. 13, a) it would have been less high. The floor slopes down toward the southeast, the difference in level between the two ends amounting to 0.845 m. The sides of the reservoir are very uneven. Where the diggers encountered hard rocks imbedded in the soft marl, they did not cut them away but left them projecting into the channel and covered them over with stucco (Pl. 13, a). Where the reservoir is now open to the sky at the northwest end there was a descent, as shown by the existence of steps in the sides. The walls, roof, and floor are covered with a heavy, watertight stucco of very hard consistency and containing gravel. At the southeast end (Pl. 13, b) there was a stone screen across the reservoir, probably with a sluice for regulating the flow of water into the Stadium area (Plan VIII). At the southwest edge the poros slab which closed the reservoir is preserved to a height of 0.95 m., and the line of the slab is visible at the bottom. There were two poros piers, one on either side of the reservoir, which held the thin slab in place. Only the pier on the southwest side is preserved; of the corresponding pier on the other side only the cutting in rock remains. Close to the screen on the northwest side steps were made in the sides of the reservoir, showing that there was a second descent at this point. When the Temple of Palaimon was constructed in Roman times, the barrier across the reservoir was cut away and the sides were patched with a heavy lime mortar of characteristic Roman type, like that used to cover the walls and floor of the crypt underneath the floor of the Temple. At that time the reservoir became part of this covered passage, in which the oath ceremonies took place (below, p. 111).

Originally, however, the reservoir was designed to provide the Stadium with water, as the two channels at the curved end of the racecourse and the large basins at the ends of the starting line indicate. At the farthest preserved point the floor of the reservoir is 0.105 m. below the upper of the two channels, but 0.07 m. above the bottom of the lower channel. The connection of the two channels with the reservoir was destroyed when the foundation for the Temple of Palaimon was laid. It is not clear why there were two parallel channels instead of one. It may be that the upper one is the earlier and that the lower channel was made to permit the water to flow into the Stadium when the level in the reservoir was low. (For a description of the channels in the Stadium see below, p. 48.)

WEST WATERWORKS

We return now to the point where the detour takes off from WCh II, a little to the east of the stylobate of the West Stoa. At the northwest end of this detour the short channel, WCh III, described above, brought water from the common source of channels WCh I–III and emptied it into a circular manhole (Pl. 12, b, lower right), which measures 1.04 m. in diameter at its widest point and reaches a depth of 2.20 m. below the floor of the channel. On either side of the manhole are steps (Pl. 53, b, Section E–F), and on the south there is an opening into a reservoir, which extends southward for a total length of 43.50 m. (Plans II–IV). The floor of the reservoir is 0.135 m. above the floor of the manhole. Near the opening the reservoir measures 0.70 m. in width at the bottom, and its total height would have been *ca.* 2.20 m. The walls converged toward the top, but nowhere in this part is the top preserved. The roof was cut away when the ground level was lowered before the West and South Stoas were constructed, and by that time the West Waterworks had fallen into disuse and were filled with earth. From the first manhole the reservoir extends almost due south to a second manhole, a distance of 18.20 m. There, close to the foundation for the façade of the South Stoa, the reservoir turns slightly westward into the public school lot, where it terminates in an oval manhole. This last section, between the second and the third manholes, is still underground. Here the reservoir measures 0.85 m. in width at the bottom (but narrows toward the top) and *ca.* 1.80 m. in height. If we calculate a mean width of 0.65 m. and a mean height of 2.00 m., the total capacity of the reservoir would have amounted to *ca.* 56.55 cu. m. (14,939 gallons).

There were no proper draw basins, and the water would have been accessible only through the manholes. On the west side of the first manhole, where the reservoir begins, a terracotta pipe extends for a distance of three meters toward the northwest and there empties into a rectangular tank measuring 0.91 m. in length, 0.557 m. in width at the top, and 1.27 m. in depth. The pipe takes off at the height of 1.93 m. above the bottom of the manhole and issues 0.66 m. above the bottom of the tank (Pl. 53, b, Sections A–B and E–F). Thus before any of the water could flow into the tank, it had to rise almost to the top of the reservoir. A parapet, 0.17 m. thick, separates the tank from a small room of irregular shape approached by two stairways (Pls. 12, b, 53, b). The parapet is not preserved to its original height; this is shown by two dowels in the top, set in lead, probably for fastening a moulded coping. The room to the north of the tank has a maximum length of 4.08 m. from east to west and a maximum width of 3.30 m. from north to south. A stairway, four steps of which now remain, forms the descent in the northwest corner of the room, and a second stairway with only three steps preserved is situated in the northeast corner. On the west side of the room is a bench, 1.85 m. long, 0.32 m. high, and 0.40 m. broad. The walls and floor of the room, the steps of the two stairs, the bench, and the rectangular tank are all covered with a hard, watertight stucco, similar to that used in the reservoir. The irregular shape of the room, with its two stairways, may have been caused by the existence of some buildings at a higher level, which were removed when the ground level was lowered prior to the construction of the West Stoa, but there are no traces of foundations for such structures. It cannot now be determined whether the room with its appurtenances was roofed over; more likely it was left open to the sky.

There are several features in this complex which cannot be explained on purely utilitarian grounds. The long reservoir, with its three manholes, was probably no more than a cistern for storing water, which reached the Sanctuary in a meager flow and had to be collected in large quantities and kept cool for use at the Isthmian festival. But the irregularly shaped room with its double approach, its bench and tank cannot have been designed as a public fountain. The tank might be thought of as a draw basin, but this cannot have been its real purpose, inasmuch as it received no water until the water level had risen nearly two meters in the manhole, i.e. almost to the top of the reservoir. A draw basin receiving its water at this high level would soon have run dry if it had been in frequent use. Once the tank had been filled with water, however, a considerable quantity would have remained below the inlet, even when the water level in the reservoir was too low to flow into the tank. From these peculiar features we may judge that only small quantities of water were required, and that precautions were taken so that the tank would always contain some water after the flow through the pipe had ceased. Such sparing use of water, designed not to give out when the inlet was cut off, could hardly be designed for secular use but is likely to have played a role in a religious rite, possibly some kind of baptismal act such as is known from other sanctuaries.[26] This conclusion is further confirmed by the discovery of a peculiar vase, which seems to have been employed as a cult vessel (Pl. 14, c). It was found together with a great deal of coarse pottery in the fill of the first manhole. The vase (IP 363), which has a height of 0.316 m. and greatest diameter of 0.296 m., is made of pale buff clay, rather powdery on the surface. The rim is profiled, and its lower edge is scalloped. On the shoulder are parallel grooves and wavy lines impressed in the clay while it was still soft. On each side of the two handles is a circular disk, decorated with concentric circles. Over each handle a moulded snake is represented as crawling up to the rim and looking into the interior, perhaps intending to drink of its contents. On their heads are crest-like projections, and their eyes and the scales on their skin are indicated by small depressions made in the wet clay. The rim, the handles, and the snakes are covered with a thin, light brown wash; the rest of the vase is unglazed. The peculiar shape of the krater and its plastic decoration indicate ritual use and, specifically, in connection with some chthonic cult.[27] No other cult objects were discovered to throw light on the identity of the deity to whom this baptismal cult place was dedicated.

What has been said above regarding the ritual use of water from the tank does not apply to the water in the reservoir. This supply, which could be reached through the three manholes south of the shrine, was sufficiently large to be of common use during the festivals. A comparatively early date is indicated by the fact that marble tiles, discarded after the fire in the Temple of Poseidon in 390 B.C., were used to patch the conduit (west part of WCh II) that brought water both to the West Waterworks and to the Earlier Stadium. This is based on the likely assumption that Water Channels II and III are of approximately the same date. The reservoir and the adjoining cult room seem to have continued in use until late Hellenistic times. Pottery pointing to such dates[28] was found in the fill of the cult room and in the second manhole close to the front foundation of the South Stoa. The pottery from the manhole includes fragments of Megarian bowls and late Hellenistic lamps, but no Roman pottery. The West Waterworks probably continued in use until the destruction of Corinth in 146 B.C. and did not reopen after that. This is one of the several features indicative of interruption in the functions of the Sanctuary at that time. The pottery from the manholes may have been thrown in during the reconditioning of the Sanctuary after the return of the Isthmian Games to Corinthian management in the early first century after Christ.

NORTHWEST RESERVOIR

Another reservoir of much greater capacity has been excavated about one hundred meters northwest of the Temple of Poseidon, in the garden of Takis Gerzelis (Plan I). Four manholes were made when

[26] Some kind of baptism or purification by sprinkling of water played a part in the Eleusinian rites of initiation; K. Kourouniotes, Ἐλευσίς, Ὁδηγὸς τῶν Ἀνασκαφῶν καὶ τοῦ Μουσείου, p. 19 (English Edition, p. 29); cf. G. E. Mylonas, *Eleusis and the Eleusinian Mysteries*, p. 236, note 61, fig. 70. The West Waterworks may be compared to the Lustral Room in the Temple of Asklepios at Corinth; Carl Roebuck, *Corinth*, XIV, pp. 46–51, 158. For the occurrence of ritual baths in pagan cults and their relation to the Christian baptism see D. I. Pallas, Ἡ Θάλασσα τῶν Ἐκκλησιῶν, pp. 48–49, 150–156.

[27] On the occurrence of the snake in cults of the dead and of the chthonic gods see Martin P. Nilsson, *Geschichte Gr. Rel.*, I³, pp. 198, 404–411, 441, 796, and *Minoan-Mycenaean Religion*, pp. 320–329; A. B. Cook, *Zeus*, II, 2, pp. 1059–1068. Fragments of another snake vase of later date came to light in 1970 in an area east of the Palaimonion, where cult lamps and other objects were found that point to ritual use.

[28] The snake vase (IP 363) may be early Roman. The decoration—impressed wavy lines, scalloped edge of the rim—are paralleled on some bowls with high foot recently discovered in the Sanctuary of Demeter on the north slope of Acrocorinth. These are of red clay, very different from that of the snake vase. The bowls have been dated in early Roman times. I owe the reference to these bowls to Sharon Herbert; Nancy Bookides, *Hesperia*, XXXVIII, 1969, p. 303, pl. 79, e. The disks on the handles of the snake vase are reminiscent of the disks on volute kraters of earlier date; actually they are more likely to have been borrowed from the handle attachments of bronze vessels, imitated in terracotta perirrhanteria and mortars of Classical Greek and Hellenistic times; cf. *Hesperia*, XXXI, 1962, pl. 10, a and d. The buff, mealy fabric is similar to that of much coarse pottery of Corinth. The snake krater seems to be a cult vessel of peculiar shape with no close parallels.

the reservoir was constructed; later, having been lined with stucco, they would have served as wells through which the water was drawn.

The description properly begins with a broad stairway (Pls. 13, c–e, 54, a, c, d) leading down to a large clearing basin. The stairway descends from southeast to northwest, and the whole reservoir is oriented in this way (Plan I, Pl. 54, a), very nearly like the Earlier Stadium. Only the top of the stairway near the surface had been damaged and has since been repaired; the rest was found in good state of preservation. The whole stair-shaft has been cut in the virgin soil, and the surface covered with stucco. Twenty steps are preserved, and there may have been a few more at the top (Pl. 54, c). The risers measure *ca.* 0.25 m. and the treads 0.30 m., but there are slight variations. The edges are carefully beveled to prevent chipping and wear. The width of the stairway is 1.52 m. at the top step and 1.60 m. at the bottom; and it narrows gradually toward the arched ceiling to a width of *ca.* 1.10 m. The total height from the steps to the top of the vault is *ca.* 1.75 m. at the top of the shaft and 2.00 m. at the bottom.

The stairway descends into a clearing basin, measuring 3.23 × 3.00 m. in area. The floor slopes very gradually toward the east corner where there is a depression, 0.27 m. in diameter and 0.085 m. deep, made to facilitate the cleaning of the basin (Pls. 13, d, 54, d, left). The walls rise to a height of *ca.* 1.65 m., and the ceiling is hipped, with a maximum height of 2.07 m. above the floor. In the south corner of the basin is the opening into the reservoir (Pls. 13, e, 54, a, c, d). When the water in the basin had risen to a height of 0.30 m., it would flow over the lip into the reservoir, the floor of which is 1.38 m. below that of the clearing basin. The walls, ceiling, and floor of the basin as well as the steps and shaft of the stairway are all covered with watertight cement, for the most part well preserved. There is no inlet except through the stairway; consequently the water, whatever its source, must have cascaded down over the steps into the basin.

At a distance of 34.50 m. to the southeast of the stairhead there is preserved part of an open water channel (Pl. 54, a) that probably brought water to the Northwest Reservoir. Only a short section, 1.50 m. long, has been exposed on the north side of a house formerly owned by Stavros Spanos and recently purchased by the University of California and now used as the excavation architect's office. The channel extends southeastward under the Spanos house, but on the south side of the house where the ground level is lower no trace of it has been found. It is made like WCh I and measures 0.133 m. in width and 0.12 m. in depth. Another short section of the channel, 1.65 m. long, appears nine meters farther northwest, showing that the channel ran almost straight for a distance of at least 12.00 m. If extended with a slight bend toward the northwest, it would reach the reservoir at the top of the stairway. The channel, cut in rock where it is now visible, was probably, to judge by its resemblance to WCh I, intended to be without cover. Since its direction points toward the Temple of Poseidon, it is likely that the rain water from that building was somehow collected and brought through this conduit to the reservoir. Coming from such a source and brought in an open channel, the water would have had to be cleared before being used, and this explains the need of such a large and elaborate clearing basin.

The builders or cleaners of the settling basin immortalized themselves with certain designs smeared with wet plaster on the walls and ceiling (Pl. 54, b). There are several impressions from hands, and one circle divided by four lines into eight sectors. Another design seems to be an outline of an amphora. These are mere doodlings by idle hands.

The first branch of the reservoir extends southwestward for a distance of 23.44 m. from the opening in the side of the clearing basin. At the bottom it is 0.94 m. wide and narrows toward the top to only 0.53 m. The vaulted roof rises to a height of 2.35 m. above the floor. At a distance of 12.28 m. from the draw basin there is an oval manhole with steps inside, 14 on one side and 13 on the other (Pl. 54, d, Section B–B). The manhole measures 1.05 × 0.62 m. in section, and directly below it is an oval depression, 0.38 m. deep, in the floor of the reservoir. A second, longer branch of the reservoir begins at a distance of 18.82 m. from the clearing basin and extends 41.43 m. toward the southeast, at right angles to the shorter branch and parallel to the line of the stairway. A little beyond the juncture the second branch measures 0.84 m. in width at the bottom and 2.42 m. in height. There are three manholes in this branch, the last of which is at the very end of the reservoir, here 2.42 m. high and 0.76 m. wide at the bottom. The oval manhole at the end measures 0.97 × 0.55 m. in section; at the bottom is an oval depression 0.50 m. below the floor of the reservoir. On both sides of the manhole are steps, measuring *ca.* 0.22 m. in width and 0.12 m. in depth, 16 on one side and 17 on the other. In addition to the steps there are two triangular niches, probably intended to hold lamps. This manhole is oriented with the long axis in line with the reservoir. The second manhole from the end is oriented at right angles to the reservoir, and here the steps begin at the two corners made by the reservoir and the manhole. There are 17 steps on one side and 18 on the other. There is one cutting for a lamp, halfway up the shaft; in other respects it is similar to the manhole at the end. The third manhole from the end is on the side of the channel and oriented at right angles to it. Before the excavations began, this had been discovered by the owners of the lot, who cleared the shaft to the bottom and then continued digging to a much greater depth until they reached water. It was this operation that led to the discovery of the Northwest Reservoir. The walls, bottom, and roof of the reservoir as well as the manhole shafts are covered with a heavy and very hard, watertight stucco, *ca.* two to four centimeters thick. Most of the stucco is well preserved, but in places it has fallen down. It was applied directly on the hard clay in which the reservoir was dug. The combined length of the two branches is a little short of 65 m., and the total capacity would amount to some 110 cu. m., nearly 30,000 gallons.

This is the largest and most elaborate of the pre-Roman waterworks excavated in the vicinity of the Sanctuary. There is no evidence for the date of its construction; on the analogy of similar reservoirs at Perachora and Corinth, it is probably to be dated in the fourth century B.C.[29] It seems to have continued in use till the destruction of Corinth in 146 B.C., but the manholes were open as late as the first century after Christ; this is shown by a small number of Roman sherds from the fill. The bulk of the pottery is Hellenistic and earlier.

NORTHEAST ALTAR TERRACE

This monument is located at the northeast corner of the temenos of Poseidon, near the entrance to the Northeast Cave (Plans II–IV). It is oriented southeast to northwest and consists of three walls, forming a Γ, with the open end to the northwest (Pl. 55, a). The northeast wall, which is standing to a height of 1.78 m., is 0.43 m. thick and has a length of 6.23 m. Its full original length is preserved, but the northwest end, which abutted against an irregular bank of earth, is not finished in a straight vertical line. The wall is made in three courses of unequal height (Pl. 14, a). The outer surface is rather roughly finished, and there are drafted bands in places both below and above the horizontal joints, but not along the vertical joints (Pl. 55, b). Some of the latter are slightly beveled, in each case on the right side of the joint as one faces the wall. The top course is set back 0.03–0.05 m. from the face of the two lower courses, and the offset turns the corner and continues on the southeast face (Pl. 14, b). This would indicate that only the highest preserved course belongs to the superstructure and the rest would be founda-

---

[29] At Corinth a system of tunnels and reservoirs, larger and more elaborate than those at Isthmia, have been discovered in the vicinity of the Anaploga. They have not all been fully explored. H. S. Robinson, *Hesperia*, XXXVIII, 1969, pp. 1–8, states that "there is no reason to suppose that the system antedates the fourth century B.C.," but he is dealing here with a small part of the system between manholes 3 and 10. Part of the system went out of use in the fourth century B.C., part continued till the sack of Corinth by Mummius. At Perachora several cisterns, not all of the same period, have been found. The most elaborate one, which shows some resemblance to ours, Humfry Payne (*Perachora*, I, pp. 11–13, fig. 5) thought to be "probably at least as early as the fifth century B.C.," but he admitted that he had "not yet got evidence for its date." It resembles, though much deeper, the Fountain of Upper Peirene on Acrocorinth, the architecture of which Richard Stillwell has dated in the early part of the fourth century B.C. (*Corinth*, III, i, p. 45). This seems to offer the best evidence for the date of construction of these elaborate waterworks in the Corinthia.

tion, although the northeast face of all three courses was intended to be visible when the wall was built. On the middle course near the east corner is an inscription, ONVMANTIO႘[30] (Pls. 14, e, 55, b), in letters measuring 0.10–0.13 m. in height.

On the inside only the top course of the wall has been finished in a nearly straight line; the stones in the other courses, which would have been hidden, project unevenly. Although the building seems designed for a ground level at the bottom of the highest course now preserved, the fill inside the structure indicates that the floor was raised at least to the top of that course. In the top of the wall are pry holes, showing that there was at least one more course of stones. The southeast wall (Pl. 14, b) measures 5.45 m. in length, but here only three blocks of the top course are preserved at the east corner; the rest were removed when the foundation for the rear wall of the East Stoa was laid. Of the southwest wall (Pl. 14, b, upper left), which is only 3.48 m. long, a little more than half as long as the corresponding northeast wall, two of the high blocks are preserved at the northwest end. They rest partly on stereo, and the wall abuts against the rock, which has been cut down in a rough vertical line at that point. The wall never seems to have extended farther toward the northwest.

The ground level in this part of the Sanctuary appears to have been higher in Greek times than in the first Roman period, when a cart road ran across the foundation from east to west. In the second century after Christ the level was raised. The foundation for the rear wall of the East Stoa then cut through the Altar Terrace diagonally and caused much destruction, particularly at the south corner. Below the upper, contaminated strata, the fill close to the foundation on the inside was consistently pre-Roman, and the same is true of the earth packed against the face of the high northeast wall. But the pottery culled from those places, so far as it can be dated, belongs chiefly to the fifth century B.C. and earlier, and this seems too early to serve as a useful criterion for dating the Terrace. The stratification shows that the outside fill was put in after the wall had been built, since there is no sign of a footing trench. A better indication of date is furnished by the inscription (Pls. 14, e, 55, b), the letter forms of which seem to fit the second half of the fourth century B.C. The upsilon has the V-form, and the upright strokes of the mu converge toward the top. The vertical strokes of the nu, however, are parallel or nearly so. The inscription need not of course be as early as the Terrace, but in any case it must have been made before the space northeast of the wall had been filled in.

Whatever structure the Terrace supported, it probably did not survive the destruction in the second century B.C. A terracotta pipe, which ran diagonally across the foundation (Pls. 14, a, 55, a) may have brought water to the large Roman cistern farther east. Furthermore, the northeast and southeast walls have been deeply scored at the east corner by wheel traffic of different periods (Plan IV, Road H).

A construction of this kind, with two flanking walls of unequal length joined by a crosswall at one end, can hardly have been part of a roofed building. It probably served as retaining wall for a terrace that may have supported an altar. It is not likely to have been functionally connected with the Northeast Cave, since the Terrace seems to have been entered from the west or northwest at a level more than two meters above the entrance court in front of the two cave chambers (below, pp. 33–37), and there are no visible means of communication between the two levels. One object, found in the east corner of the Terrace, may point to sacral use of the area. This is a small terracotta thymiaterion (IP 1334, Pl. 14, d), which was discovered in perfect condition about a half meter below the modern ground level. It is large enough to have been used for incense, but it is not blackened on the inside, and what was found is probably only the foot supporting the thymiaterion proper.[31] It may have been intended as a votive gift and

---

[30] *Hesperia*, XXXI, 1962, p. 4. The inscription will be published by Michael Jameson together with the other epigraphical material of pre-Roman times from Isthmia.

[31] Thymiateria are listed by Greek authors (Herodotos, IV, 162; Thucydides, VI, 46, 3) and in inscriptions among the objects dedicated to various deities; W. H. D. Rouse, *Greek Votive Offerings*, pp. 395, 398, 400, 402; C. G. Yavis, *Greek Altars*, pp. 9, 10. On Delos were found many censors of comparable shapes (W. Deonna, *Délos*, XVIII, *Le Mobilier Délien*, pp. 377–379, pl. CV); and one came from a Hellenistic (*ca.* 250 B.C.) deposit at Corinth (Gladys R. Davidson,

never used for incense. The context in which it was found was so late, however, that its relation to the Altar Terrace should not be unduly stressed.

Nothing else was discovered that would throw further light on the purpose of the Terrace or the identity of the divinity worshiped in this area. Pausanias mentions an altar of the Cyclops,[32] but he gives no clue to its location, and the Terrace seems too late to be identified with it. One would expect to find early pottery in the area occupied by such a structure. Other deities received worship on the Isthmus,[33] but in the absence of evidence it must remain unknown what god or hero had his cult place on the Altar Terrace.

CULT CAVES

NORTHEAST CAVE

The temenos of Poseidon occupies a nearly level plateau, in the northern half of which a comparatively thin cap of limestone rock rests on a layer of hard clay or marl. This thin crust of rock breaks off in an irregular line along the north edge, and at the east end of the temenos the rocky ledge extends diagonally from southwest to northeast, the two lines coming together at the northeast corner. Here the rock forms the roof of a cave, which appears to have been a natural formation made by erosion, leaving the hard rock projecting (Pl. 15, a). This natural cave has been enlarged and divided into two chambers, each with its own entrance from the south. In front of the cave a large area was artificially leveled off, and this was probably separated into two parts, each forming an entrance court from which a stairway led down into one of the cave chambers. The courts were largely destroyed in Roman times, when a large cistern was built in the southeast corner (Pl. 55, a).

The court in front of the west entrance is the better preserved. It has a length of eight meters from north to south and a width of *ca.* six meters, but originally it was probably somewhat larger. Toward the north and northwest the ancient ground level was at a height nearly three meters above the floor of the court. The Northeast Altar Terrace, constructed probably as early as the second half of the fourth century B.C., may have cut away the southwest corner of the court. The inscription and sherds from the earth fill packed against the terrace wall indicate the approximate date of the wall itself, which must be later than the entrance court. The original features of the court, obliterated through these changes, may have comprised a kitchen and other paraphernalia connected with the use of the caves, but none of this is now preserved. To the south of the west entrance there is a small, irregular niche in the rock, which seems to have been made artificially, and at the northeast edge there is a low embankment of rough stones and clay dividing the west court from the east (Pl. 55, a). The floor of the court, which is not entirely even, consists of tamped clay. The fill close to the wall of the Altar Terrace in the northwest

---

Corinth, XII, p. 131, pl. 66, no. 893). The Delos and Corinth examples are made in "two stories." The lower and much taller part resembles the one from Isthmia, which must have served as a standard for a separate section that would have held the incense. This explains the absence of any trace of burning.

[32] Pausanias (II, 2, 1). The inscription in Verona, *I.G.*, IV, 203, contains a reference to Altars of the Ancestral Gods, which Frazer thought might include the Altar of the Cyclops. The Cyclops were but rarely recipients of cult observances; Ulrich von Wilamowitz-Moellendorff, *Der Glaube der Hellenen*, I, p. 277. As the superhuman artificers, who fashioned the thunderbolt of Zeus and the trident of Poseidon, they may have been honored by the early metal workers of Corinth. The chief Cyclops, Polyphemos, could have had claim to worship at Isthmia as son of Poseidon, but he was at home in Sicily and seems to have been unrelated to the tradition of Cyclopic craftsmanship. In Attic mythology Cyclops was the father of Zeuxippos, who had Sikyonian and Corinthian connections; O. Broneer, *Hesperia*, XI, 1942, pp. 136–139; Will, *Korinthiaka*, pp. 136–137.

[33] On deities known to have been worshiped at Isthmia, see Pausanias, *loc. cit.*, and *I.G.*, IV, 203, which begins with a dedication to the Ancestral Gods; Will, *Korinthiaka*, pp. 176–212; and O. Broneer, *Klio*, XXXIX, 1961, p. 251.

corner of the court contained pottery sherds from the fourth century B.C. and earlier. At the very bottom of the fill in this area, directly on the floor of the court, were found three gold Darics which probably date from the fifth century B.C.[34]

Of the court in front of the eastern chamber very little now remains, its south end having been cut away when the large Roman cistern was constructed. In the northeastern part two parallel walls, apparently of late date, stand to a height of 1.50 m. above the level of the court. They are built with stones of irregular shape laid in earth mortar.

The west chamber (Pl. 56, b) was reached from the court by means of a stairway, with seven steps preserved, all cut in the native clay. This leads down to a passage 3.85 m. long, at the inner end of which there is a niche, 0.55 m. wide and 0.75 m. deep (Pls. 15, b, upper right, 56, a, right). On the left side of the niche the clay has been cut away to form a roughly shaped "throne." The niche is undoubtedly original, but the rough pick marks in the upper part of the walls indicate that it has been reshaped to some extent in later times. These tool marks extend all around the "throne" and may indicate that this is a later formation. In the first period the width of the niche, 0.55 m., was the same as now, and it seems to have extended to the same depth, ca. 0.75 m. The niche with its "throne" was at first thought to be the place of a presiding magistrate, but for such a purpose the seat seems too rough and small. It is more likely that the niche was made as the opening into a side chamber, like those found in the Theater Cave (below, pp. 39, 40), and that for some reason the work was never completed. The rough pick marks were probably made in Roman times when the niche was slightly enlarged.

The passage has a width of 1.22 m. at the foot of the stairs and 1.42 m. at the inner end. On the left side were two couches cut in the native clay and arranged alongside the passage, and a single couch at right angles to the others (Pls. 15, b, 56, c, 3). The two nearest the stairway have been partly covered over by a Roman retaining wall and a late pier, so that only the outer edge is now visible (Pl. 15, c). The exposed couches are ca. 0.80 m. wide and 1.65 m. long, including the headrest, but their dimensions vary a great deal. The top of each couch is sunk below the surrounding rim, probably to hold a mattress or rug in place. The headrest in each case is on the right as one faces the couch so that the occupant, reclining on his left elbow, would have the right hand free. On the right side of the corridor there were two couches, one of which has been largely obliterated by the cutting of a passage into the adjoining cave chamber. The second couch, however, is well preserved. It has a hole through the outer edge (Pl. 15, d, lower edge), presumably to permit water dripping down from the roof and collecting in the hollow to run off. At the northwest end of the corridor there was a depression in the floor (Pl. 56, a), measuring 0.80 × 0.50 m. in area and 0.12 m. in depth. It contained a few sherds, all classical Greek and probably not later than the fifth century B.C.

On the right side as one descends the west stairway there was at one time a passageway between the two chambers (Pl. 15, d). The floor is ca. 0.10 m. higher than the floor of the main passage in the west chamber. The connecting passage did not run straight but made a dog-leg curve toward the entrance in the east chamber. It had a width of 1.25 m. at the east end and 0.90 m. at the west end. It is not possible now to determine whether this connecting passage was part of the original arrangement of the cave; it seems more likely to have been made at a later period to provide communication between the two chambers. If it had been part of the original plan it would be difficult to explain the need for two stairways. However that may be, the connecting passageway appears to have been abandoned while the cave chambers were still in use, and two shallow pits were dug and their sides partly built up on the floor of the passage (Pl. 56, b). They measure respectively 0.53 × 0.33 m. and 0.50 × 0.32 m. in area and only ca. 0.14 m. in depth.

---

[34] *Hesperia*, XXXI, 1962, p. 21, pl. 2, b. The weight of the three coins is 8.33, 8.32, 8.31 grams. Although the Darics do not permit dating within close limits, the type showing the running king with bow and spear was in circulation between 486 and 331 B.C. I am indebted to Margaret Thompson and Ross Holloway for comments on these coins; see also E. S. G. Robinson, *Num. Chron.*, XVIII, 1958, pp. 187–193.

When the pits were first discovered they were neatly covered over with two large pieces of Corinthian roof tiles (Pl. 15, d). Along the east and north edges were some irregular stones fitting closely to the edges of the tiles; they seem to have been placed there when the pits were made. The northern pit contained some animal bones and a few small, nondescript sherds; the other was completely empty. The fact that the two pits had been so carefully covered would seem to indicate that they had served as receptacles for some objects, which have completely disintegrated. One might imagine the deposit of some sacrificial food that left little or no trace in the earth.

The east cave chamber is reached by a stairway cut in clay with five steps preserved. From the bottom of the stair a passage, less regular in shape than that in the adjoining chamber, extends inward for a distance of 4.85 m. Beginning at the foot of the stairs there was a couch on the left, now largely restored, which was not arranged parallel to the passage. In the next space there is now no couch preserved but there may have been one that has been removed, and beyond this point there is a well-preserved couch on the left side of the passage. In the middle of this couch is a cavity, 0.50 m. in diameter and 0.23 m. deep, which was probably made at a late period, perhaps after the cave was no longer used in its original capacity. In the floor of the corridor directly in front of the couch was another, smaller circular cutting, 0.13 m. in diameter and 0.12 m. deep. When this was discovered it was filled with carbonized wood. At the inner end of the corridor and at right angles to it there was a third couch, and on the right side two more couches. The passage, which in the middle had a width of 1.57 m., is narrowed to 0.84 m. at the inner end. Here a small bench, as high as the couches, has been left on each side, probably to serve as table support in front of the adjoining couches. To the right of the entrance is the opening into an irregular arm of the cave of natural formation, on the north side of which a sixth couch has been shaped. Beyond the couch, on the same side, the level area continues, but this does not seem to have been made into a couch. Thus the total number of couches in the two chambers seems to have been eleven. On the floor of the side chamber and in the passage itself were found a small number of sherds, which date chiefly from the fifth century B.C., but a few may be somewhat later. These would derive from the original use of the cave.

If we are correct in thinking that the passage uniting the two chambers is later than the original construction, one couch in the east chamber would have been removed when this passage was cut. Thus in the original arrangement (Pl. 56, c, Couches 2', 3' and 5', 6'), there were probably two couches placed end to end on each side of the main passage, and a fifth couch, 4', at the end of the passage turned at right angles to the others. Since the cult use of the cave (below, pp. 45–46) seems to have required six couches, the sixth one, 6', was cut out of the left side of the eastern branch. Then, when the connecting passage was made, the number was reduced to five, and to restore the cave to its original capacity a sixth couch, 1', was made on the left side at the foot of the stair. This might explain the peculiar angle of the couch in its relationship to the central passage, which is oriented like the stairway.

In Roman times a retaining wall built with stones laid in hard mortar was erected on the south side of the west chamber. The wall is L-shaped (Pl. 15, c), its long arm measuring 3.30 m. and the short arm 0.87 m. in length. The wall extends almost down to the first couch on the left side (Pl. 15, c, lower left) and rests partly on the stairway. It reaches to the roof of the cave and was clearly constructed in support of it. In the approximate middle of the wall, 1.30 m. above the floor of the corridor, there was originally an opening (Pls. 15, c, upper left, 56, a), the lower part of which is 0.63 m. wide and 0.70 m. high. Above this window or niche there seems to have been a larger one, 1.45 m. wide, which extended all the way to the top. Both openings, which formed a single T-shaped aperture, are filled with rough masonry of a later period. They can hardly have been intended to admit light into the chamber, for the fill outside seemed to be undisturbed debris from the fire of 390 B.C. in the Temple, and in any case the rock comes up so high that it would have shut out most of the light.

The shorter arm of the retaining wall (Pl. 15, c, right), which forms an attached pier, extends across the corridor, and does not rest on the floor but on rubble fill, 0.80 m. deep. It is obvious that when the retaining walls were constructed, the fill had risen to that height, covering the couches and concealing the original arrangement of the cave. This arm of the retaining wall has a slit window like an archer-slot in a fortification wall but with the narrow opening toward the outside. This may have been made to provide light in the inner, left corner of the chamber. It is conceivable, however, that the chamber had been used as refuge during some local disturbance and that the slit window was intended to provide a view to the outside, and perhaps as a vantage point from which arrows could be shot at intruders. The opening is at the proper height for such a purpose, *ca.* 1.00 m. above the floor level that existed when the retaining walls were built.

On the right side of the stair into the west chamber there is a pier of heavy masonry (Pls. 15, a, 16, a), measuring 1.22 × 0.63 m. in section, and extending from the level of the couches up to the roof of the cave. The pier rests on earth and is built of large poros blocks without the use of mortar. Hence it was probably not put in at the same time as the L-shaped retaining wall, which is constructed mostly with small stones laid in lime mortar. At a later period the entrance to the west chamber was completely blocked up, and the cave was entered only from the east. At some time subsequent to the original use of the cave, the partition dividing the cave into two chambers was removed.

From the objects found in the Northeast Cave and the features of the two chambers we can follow to a certain extent the changes made through several centuries of use. In the natural, shallow cavern formed by erosion the two chambers with their dining couches and serving tables were scooped out beneath the overhanging ledge of rock, and the stairs from the higher area to the south were carved in hard clay. At the same time the area in front of the cave was shaped into two separate entrance courts. The inception of this work is doubtless to be sought in the sphere of religious cult practices. In the fourth century B.C. a small area to the west of the court was walled off and turned into the Northeast Altar Terrace. Whatever was the nature of that structure, the great difference in level indicates that the Altar Terrace and the Northeast Cave were functionally unconnected. Not much later the cave appears to have been abandoned, and the area of the courts filled to a height of some two meters. Some of the debris thrown into the courts rolled down the stairs into the cave. This happened after the Temple of Poseidon had been damaged in the fire of 390 B.C., as is shown by fragments of the marble sima, column fragments, etc., found in the lower stratum of the two chambers. A large bronze knocker, discovered a little south of the west entrance (Pl. 16, a), is probably from the Temple doors.[35] This and the three gold Darics from the same place presumably came into the court area with debris after the fire in 390 B.C.

The east chamber seems to have undergone several changes, one or perhaps two of them dating back to the time when the cave was in use as a dining room (below, pp. 42–46). These will account for certain irregularities not found in the west chamber or in the Theater Cave. In the first period there were probably two couches in a straight line to the left of the passage (Pl. 56, c, 2', 3'), and the first couch, 1', left of the stair did not then exist. When it was later decided to cut an opening between the two chambers, what was then the first couch on the left (Pl. 56, c, 2') had to be sacrificed, and to take its place a new couch was carved out of the clay bank at the foot of the stairway (Pl. 56, c, 1'). It is possible, however, that couch 1' belongs to the original arrangement, in which there would then have been no couch in the east branch. Then after couch 2' had been sacrificed to form an opening between the two chambers, couch 6' was added in the east arm of the cave. This is the arrangement indicated in Plate 56, c. The two cavities to the right of the west stairway were made in the floor of this passage before the cave was discarded as a dining room in the fifth or early fourth century B.C. This explains the use of large Corinthian tiles as covers, though it is not clear what purpose these shallow depressions had served.

The next change took place during the reconstruction of the Sanctuary in the first century after Christ. The cave was then rediscovered and most of the fill which had accumulated was probably removed. This

---

[35] The architectural pieces and the door knocker from the Temple have been published in *Isthmia*, I, p. 170, no. M 71, pl. 38, c, d.

accounts for the almost total absence of pottery and other objects associated with the early use of the chamber. The reopening may have been occasioned by the construction of the large vaulted cistern, which must have entailed extensive excavation of the surrounding area. Only the east entrance to the cave chambers seems to have been opened up, and to make the west chamber accessible, a passage was cut in the rear of the cave through the partition between the two chambers. The original passage at the foot of the west stairway may have been blocked by debris. Later on the whole partition was removed. This would have weakened the roof, from which even now large chunks of rock continuously break loose and fall down. To prevent further damage the L-shaped wall along the south edge of the west chamber was built. By that time accumulation of debris had reached a height of *ca.* 0.80 m. above the floor of the passages. Since this loose fill was left undisturbed and the wall built on top of it, the cave cannot have served its original function. Nevertheless it continued in use, probably for storage, and the precarious condition of the roof necessitated construction of the large pier north of the west stairway. Still later a rubble wall was constructed from this pier toward the south (Pl. 16, b, upper right), probably to prevent earth from washing down into the chamber where the west stairway had been. When the East Stoa was built in the second century after Christ, the ground level in front of the cave was raised, but the east entrance continued to be used; and here, at a high level, two parallel walls were later constructed east of the entrance. These are poorly built of rough stones laid in earth mortar and resting on earth fill; they were probably intended to prevent earth from completely filling the cave. That this continued to be accessible until a very late period is shown by further shoring of the roof. Pieces of columns and other architectural members were inserted underneath the stone cap behind the great stone pier (Pl. 16, c, center). By that time the two chambers must have been largely filled up, since this shoring rested on earth fill some two meters above the floor. Eventually the east opening too became closed up with debris, and at the time of our excavation the whole cave with its entrance courts was completely buried below the surface of a plowed field.

THEATER CAVE

At the upper edge of the cavea, a little to the east of the axis of the Theater, there is a second cave, also divided into two chambers, each with its entrance court (Pl. 57). Here too the overhanging ledge of rock probably suggested the enlargement and utilization of the space underneath.

The entrance court of the western chamber has been considerably modified since the first use of the cave. In the latest reconstruction of the Theater, two heavy piers for support of the outer wall were built inside the court (Pl. 16, d). The area of the court is irregular, measuring 3.10 m. from north to south and 6.72 m. from east to west. It was entered from the north by a ramp, 0.94 m. wide, directly opposite the door into the chamber. To the right of the entrance below the floor of the court there was a pit, originally measuring 2.30 m. from east to west and 1.80 m. from north to south and nearly 1.50 m. in depth. This had been dug in the hard clay, and the lumps of clay thrown back into the hole. Mixed with them were a very few nondescript potsherds and pieces of coal. A large wooden post, with a diameter of 0.16 m., had stood upright in the middle of the pit. The wood had decayed, leaving a vertical hole through the fill. From the north side a slanting passage or chute, only 0.55 m. wide and 1.50 m. long, leads down into the pit (Pl. 58, a). When this was discovered it contained several large marble slabs, one terracotta cover tile, two large pitchers of coarse ware, and a small pitcher with trefoil mouth (Pl. 17, a). The passage extends to the north of the court, where there is a narrow opening from above. On the west side there was a similar but smaller chute, 0.40 m. wide, which was found blocked with boulders and earth fill (Pl. 17, d, lower left). It is difficult to understand what purpose these chute-like passages were intended to serve; possibly they were made to facilitate cleaning.

In the northwest corner of the court there is a large poros block, 0.76 × 0.65 m. in area and 0.52 m. high above the floor (Pl. 17, b, c). In the top is a large depression, now covered with cement, which has formed a series of circular ridges; these seem to have resulted from the impression of some kind of wicker basket or tray pressed down into the cavity while the cement was wet (Pl. 17, b). Opening into the clay bank from the west edge of this table there is an oven-like niche (Pl. 17, c) which had a domed top formed by a terracotta pithos lying on its side and with the lower part chipped away (Pl. 17, d). The pithos measures on the inside 0.54 m. in diameter at the mouth and 0.53 m. in depth. The floor below the pithos and the top of the stone in front of it were found covered with a hard stucco. Originally there was a semicircular cavity in the north wall of the court opposite the table (Pl. 17, d); this had at some later time been filled with stone and clay mortar. The pithos seems to have been used chiefly as a covered extension of the top of the table. Although it looks like an oven, the total absence of ash and blackening on the inside shows that it was not used for fire. South of the pithos, along the west wall of the court, there was a ledge which had perhaps been used as a couch. A second couch seems to have existed to the east of it, on the right side of the door into the chamber, and there may have been a third one on the left side. The piers of the Theater construction now largely cover the space that may have been occupied by these couches.

In the corner to the left of the ramp that leads into the court, there is a circular cavity shaped like a pithos and carved out of the natural clay and covered with hard stucco (Pls. 57, a, 58, a). It has a maximum diameter of 0.70 m. and a depth of 0.61 m. below the floor of the cave; but in the corner the edge is at a considerably higher level. The "pithos" was found filled to the top with seventeen pottery vessels of common household ware (Pl. 17, e). They were all stacked upside down, the smaller at the bottom, the larger near the top, as if they had been washed and left to run dry. These vessels, some of which are blackened from use over the fire, reveal the date of the original use of the caves and throw further light on the purpose that they served (below, pp. 42–46).

In the northeast corner the clay bank juts out into the court for a distance of 1.43 m. and then cuts back toward the east *ca.* 2.00 m. In the corner formed by this mass of natural clay and the east wall of the court, there is a shelf, 0.82 m. wide and 0.55 m. deep, its top at a height of 0.46 m. above the floor of the court. At the rear edge of this area there were originally three circular depressions used as burners for a kitchen stove (Pls. 18, a, 57, a). Only one is now well enough preserved to be measured; it is 0.183 m. wide at the top and 0.19 m. deep. The burners were constructed partly with bricks and clay mortar and partly gouged out of the clay bank. When first discovered they showed considerable signs of burning, and in front of them on the shelf were found quantities of ash. Close to the stove on the south side, the kitchen area opens into a large room which may have been roughly circular, *ca.* 1.80 m. in diameter; this was used as a pantry, containing facilities for washing dishes. On the north side there is a slight depression in the floor, 0.16 m. in diameter and 0.07 m. deep, which served as the sink (Pl. 18, b). This is indicated by a covered drain, extending from the sink diagonally across the court below the floor and emptying its contents into the disposal pit (Pls. 18, b, 57, a, b). The channel, which is cut in the hard clay and covered with terracotta cover tiles of the Corinthian type, has a perceptible slope toward the disposal pit. These culinary arrangements, repeated also in the east entrance court, leave no doubt that meals were prepared in the entrance courts.

The chamber is entered from the court through a narrow doorway, 0.70 m. wide, with a profiled door trim cut in clay on the outside (Pl. 16, d). The door jambs, preserved only at the bottom, are 1.22 m. broad; and the descent from the court is over two low, broad steps. There is no indication that a door had existed, and the entrance would either have been left open or closed by a curtain of cloth or matting. The chamber measures 4.45 m. in length and 3.10 m. in width. The ceiling has been carved as a vault (Pl. 18, c) with a maximum height of 2.36 m. in the middle. There were five couches along three of the walls (Pl. 57, b), but they have all been cut away, leaving only the rough surface to indicate their number and size (trace of a headrest is shown by arrow, Pl. 18, c). From these traces we learn that the couches were somewhat larger than those in the Northeast Cave. They measured *ca.* 1.90 m. in length and 0.97 m. in width, and rose to a height of *ca.* 0.30 m. above the floor of the chamber. The walls above the couches were stuccoed up to a height of 0.65 m. above the level of the couches (Pl. 19, a, lower left). Higher up, the wall has been roughly cut back, indicating that there was a raised band or cornice above the stuccoed dado; but the upper part of the walls and the vault appear to have been unstuccoed.

On each side of the doorway on the inside there is a plain vertical trim, 0.14 m. wide. On the north wall a raised horizontal band extends 0.93 m. westward from the door trim, and above it is a niche, 0.66 m. wide, 0.35 m. deep, and *ca.* 0.44 m. high, cut out of the native clay (Pls. 19, a, b, 58, b). The top of the niche is arched. The floor, which is 0.93 m. above the floor of the cave, retains part of a heavy coat of stucco, but the walls are unstuccoed. On the wall below the niche an area, 0.95 m. wide and 0.81 m. high, has been trimmed back, and within this recessed space a circular cutting with an arched trim around the edge (Pl. 19, a, b) extends 0.30 m. below the floor of the cave (Pl. 58, b). The niche with the circular cavity in the wall gives the effect of an altar, and it is probable that it served some religious purpose in connection with the use of the cave. A terracotta amphora would have fitted into the cutting below the niche.

In the northwest corner just beyond the niche a door opening, 0.68 m. wide, gave access into a side chamber (Pls. 19, a, 57, a, b, 58, b). On the left of the entrance into this room a projecting door trim sets off the door from the first couch on the right side of the main room. The side chamber now measures three meters from north to south, 2.20 m. from east to west and 2.50 m. in height, but was originally smaller. It seems to have been enlarged in Roman times, and at that time a separate stairway (Pl. 58, b) was made leading up into the cavea of the Theater. Also at some late period a hole was cut through the roof in the northwest corner providing access from the top. When the cave was excavated the side chamber was found filled with earth and broken roof tiles, many with stamps of Roman times.[36] The contents of the main chamber were all of late date. At the southwest corner a coin of George I (1882) was found only a few centimeters above the floor.

East of the west entrance court is a second court giving access to the east chamber of the Theater Cave (Pl. 57, a, b). It was separated from the kitchen area of the west court by a clay mass *ca.* 2.50 m. thick. The court proper measures 5.35 m. in length from east to west and 3.00 m. in width. At the west edge there is a small disposal pit (Pls. 18, d, lower right, 57, b), measuring 1.07 m. in length, *ca.* 0.84 m. in width, and 0.92 m. in depth. This is cut partly out of the west wall of the court and partly below the floor. Close to it, a little to the southeast, is the kitchen stove, 1.60 m. long and 0.90 m. wide, raised *ca.* 0.50 m. above the floor of the court (Pl. 18, d, center). At its west end are two circular depressions, which had served as burners, and there may have been a third in the southeast corner. Over the whole kitchen and in the court directly below it, as well as in the pit, was found a deposit of ash and kitchen debris. There is no doubt that meals served in the cave chamber were prepared in this place. The east end of the kitchen stove area is occupied by a large stone trough (Pl. 18, d, left), 0.84 × 0.57 m. in area and 0.45 m. in height. Its top is 0.85 m. above the floor of the court. The rectangular depression measures 0.50 × 0.37 m. in area and is only 0.06 m. deep. The broad slanting rim of the shallow basin is covered with a hard cement, but the bottom is left unstuccoed. This stone, which lies right at the entrance into the cave, seems to have been a table corresponding to the covered table in the northwest corner of the west court. It is too shallow for a dishwater basin, and the fact that only the rim, not the bottom, is stuccoed precludes such a use. In the area south of the kitchen several small post holes of varying diameter and depth appeared in the clay bank flanking the entrance into the chamber on the east side. They are smaller than the post hole found in the disposal pit in the court of the west chamber (Pl. 57, a, b).

The space east of the table, to the left of the original entrance into the cave, is now occupied by a large block of rubble masonry from one of the foundation piers of the Theater (Pl. 57, a). The east end

---

[36] These are discussed by Elizabeth Gebhard, *Theater at Isthmia*, pp. 109–110; see also *Hesperia*, XXXI, 1962, p. 10, pl. 5, a.

of the court may have had couches comparable to those assumed to have existed at the west end of the west court. A bench-like projection, 0.43 m. high, existing on all three sides may be the remains of three couches, but the original arrangement is no longer evident.

In Roman times, when the ground level in front of the entrance was higher, seven steps led down to the floor level of the cave (Pls. 57, a, 58, c). The stairway is 0.95 m. wide, and this seems to have been the original width of the entrance way. Only the two bottom steps cut out of native clay existed in the pre-Roman period; the others are built out of stones laid in earth. Some modern steps now lead up from the entrance court to the top of the Roman stair.

The chamber is less regular than the west chamber, and the crumbly nature of the roof has necessitated the construction of piers (Pl. 57, a) to prevent the rock from breaking off. One such pier, made out of large poros blocks laid in lime mortar, was built in Roman times, probably at the time that the stairway was constructed, and a still larger pier had to be added at the time of our excavation. The chamber is an irregular quadrangle, measuring 4.30 m. in length at the entrance and 4.90 m. at the back wall. The width from north to south is 4.42 m. at the west end but only 3.86 m. at the east end. The preserved height, which may be a little more than the original height, is *ca.* 2.20 m. There are six couches cut out of clay, one on the north wall to the west of the entrance, two each along the west and south walls, and one at the east end. They vary somewhat in size but measure approximately 1.60 m. in length and 0.85 m. in width, and they are raised 0.27 m. above the floor of the chamber. The outer edge of the couches is slightly raised, and at one end is a headrest so arranged that the reclining diner could support himself on his left elbow, leaving the right arm free to handle the food. The couches must have been originally provided with mattresses held in place by the raised edge. In the southeast corner there is a rectangular base (Pl. 19, c, lower left), 0.63 × 0.36 m. in area and raised 0.22 m. above the floor. It is cut out of the natural clay, probably intended as support for the trays on which the food was brought in.

The walls of the chamber retain no trace of stucco, and it seems unlikely that there had ever been any. On the couches, however, were found clear traces of a surfacing of hard clay (Pl. 19, c). East of the entrance on the north wall is preserved the lower edge of a cult niche (Pls. 57, b, 58, d), 0.76 m. wide at the bottom, and 1.25 m. above the floor of the chamber. Underneath is a cutting for a wine jar, *ca.* 0.90 m. high and 0.48 m. wide, extending 0.30 m. below the floor. At the bottom it narrows to a blunt point, which would fit the toe of a large amphora. In the northeast corner a door opening, 0.51 m. wide, leads to a small side chamber, only 1.53 m. by 0.77 m. in area. The top of the doorway is not preserved, and the chamber could not be fully excavated because of the perilous condition of the roof. In the southwest corner of the main chamber a manhole shaft (Pls. 57, a, 58, c) has been cut through the bedrock that forms the roof of the cave and continues below the floor. The manhole, which measures 1.05 × 0.63 m. in section, has foot holds on either side. It leads down to a water channel, the bottom of which is 3.30 m. below the floor of the cave. The manhole and the water channel are almost certainly of later date than the chamber with its couches; they were probably cut after the cave had been discarded and was partly filled up. In any case they can have had nothing to do with the original use of the cave.

CHRONOLOGY AND SIGNIFICANCE OF THE CAVES

The close correspondence between the Theater Cave and the Northeast Cave is apparent. In each case there were two chambers whose walls were lined with couches, five in one chamber, six in the other. Each chamber had its own entrance. In these respects the two caves are alike. The cult niche and cutting for a jar and the side chamber found with each compartment of the Theater Cave have no corresponding features in the Northeast Cave, unless the niche in the west chamber, as suggested above, is an abortive attempt to cut out a side chamber. The absence in the Northeast Cave of some of the other features may be accidental, since the Theater Cave is much better preserved. The courts in front of the two chambers of the Northeast Cave, as we have seen, have been modified and curtailed through later building activity in the area. Any provisions for preparing meals that may have existed were probably also removed when the courts were destroyed. Enough is preserved, however, to indicate that the two caves had served the same or similar purposes.

We must now ask whether the caves were in use at the same time or successively. Except for the vases found in the west court of the Theater Cave, no part of the caves' movable furnishings survived the thorough cleanup and re-use in Roman times. But in the west chamber and on the floor of the east branch in the east chamber of the Northeast Cave, we found what seemed to be small uncontaminated deposits below the deep fill of later times. The datable pottery is chiefly of the fifth century and earlier, but some of the pieces appear to be from the fourth century B.C. The limited number of fragments from these two places would tend to show that the cave was in use as early as the fifth century and continued into the fourth. Above these slight accumulations from the period of use, the debris from the fire of 390 B.C. in the Temple of Poseidon formed a deep deposit in the Northeast Cave. The reopening and subsequent use of the cave in the first century after Christ caused contamination of this debris, but the number of architectural fragments found in both chambers is so large that they are likely to have come into the cave during the cleanup after the repairs to the Temple in the fourth century B.C. In the area south of the descent into the west chamber, the debris from the same fire was uncontaminated with later fill. Among the objects from this place is a heavy door knocker of bronze, which probably came from the Temple doors. On the basis of these discoveries we may conclude that the cave ceased to function in its original capacity not long after 390 B.C.

The Theater Cave with its courts yielded very few sherds that could have found their way into the fill on the floor during the period of occupation. With the classical sherds were mixed a few prehistoric fragments, probably washed down from the higher area to the south. The sherds are too few and not sufficiently homogenous to indicate how early the cave came into use. It is clear, however, from the well-preserved vases found in the west court that the Theater Cave was abandoned about the middle of the fourth century B.C. Among the vases in the chute and the pottery pit there are many shapes (Pl. 19, d), but all are household vessels, mostly without decoration, and many of the cooking pots are blackened from use over the fire.[37] There are four mixing bowls of various sizes (Pls. 17, e, 19, d, right), two spouted mortars, five cooking pots with one or two handles, three large pitchers, one casserole with lid, two small jugs with trefoil mouth, and two squat lekythoi. Nearly all are complete, but some had parts of the rim or mouth missing. Those found in the pit had definitely not been discarded as useless but had been carefully stacked upside down and so arranged as to avoid breakage. We may safely assume that they had been left where we found them after the cave had ceased to be used for its original purpose.

Although the evidence of the pottery does not prove conclusively how early the two caves came into use, it would seem on the face of it likely that one succeeded the other. The correspondence in the two-fold division, with separate entrances and with the same number of couches, may be interpreted as an indication that one is earlier and that the later of the two was intended to replace the earlier. And, if there is a difference in date, the Theater Cave is very likely the later. We can only guess at the reason why the Northeast Cave should have been abandoned early in the fourth century B.C. An earthquake might have caused partial collapse, and the constant flaking away of the rock in the roof over the cham-

---

[37] A few of these vases are briefly discussed in the preliminary report, *Hesperia*, XXXI, 1962, pp. 24–25, pls. 2, c, 3, b, d, 12, a–f. Professor Roger Edwards, who has made a thorough study of fourth-century pottery, has concluded that the pottery from the cave deposit is to be dated at about the middle of the fourth century B.C. Consequently the caves must have gone out of use about that time or very soon thereafter. The two small ribbed jugs of "blister ware" seen in Plate 19, d on either side of the spouted mortar are very similar to vases from Athens found in contexts from late fifth century to the second half of the fourth century B.C.; Brian A. Sparkes and Lucy Talcott, *Athenian Agora*, XII, *Black and Plain Pottery*, nos. 1679–1681. The mortar in Plate 19, d belongs to types from Athens dated about the same time; *ibid.*, nos. 1911, 1917. The vases from the cave deposit will be published in final form by D. A. Amyx in a volume devoted to pottery found at Isthmia during the years 1952–1966.

bers, which still continues, may have made them seem unsafe for human occupation. If we are correct in assuming that members of some religious brotherhood had their meals in the caves (see below), the construction of a second cave at the edge of the Theater might have been dictated by ritual require- ments. Similarly, the abandonment of the Theater Cave in the second half of the fourth century prob- ably came as the result of changes in these associations.

Inasmuch as there are no inscriptions or wall paintings or any other representations to throw light on the identity of the human occupants, or of the deity or deities worshiped by them, their identification must remain a matter of conjecture. It is an obvious fact, however, that the interpretation of the caves must be sought in the realm of religious rather than secular usage. The chambers are too small to have served as public dining rooms, and it is unthinkable that they were privately owned establishments. No private houses have been discovered in the vicinity and none would have been permitted in such close proximity to the Sanctuary.

However obvious may be the religious nature of the caves, this fact does not lessen but rather in- creases the difficulties of their interpretation. Religious usage and taboos do not lend themselves to rational explanations. Cult meals entered into the worship of many deities, and religious fraternities and semi-religious associations frequently included such meals in the program of their meetings.[38] Three deities, Dionysos, Poseidon, and Palaimon, may be considered as most likely patrons of the establish- ments. Poseidon was the chief deity of the Isthmus and the divine patron of the Isthmian Games, and his name and emblem—the dolphin and trident—appear on numerous roof tiles from the Theater,[39] all dated to Roman times. The performances in the Theater may well have been, and probably were, held under the patronage of Dionysos, but the real estate was Poseidon's.[40]

Closely associated with Poseidon at Isthmia was the boy-god Melikertes-Palaimon. The two names probably indicate a double origin of the cult, but at Isthmia he was worshiped as Palaimon, the Wrestler.[41] He too, in whose worship mysteries played an important role, might have been the patron of some sacred brotherhood who held their cult meetings in underground places. In his Temple at Isthmia there is a crypt beneath the floor where oaths were administered, presumably to athletes and officials of the Isthmian Games. The Palaimonion, however, is located southeast of the temenos of Poseidon at a considerable distance from the caves. His earlier associations there would have been with the Stadium, and all the material evidence for his cult at Isthmia belongs to a period after the destruction of Corinth and its subsequent restoration by Julius Caesar. Elsewhere in Greece, however, he was associated with Dionysos, and it is conceivable that both Dionysos and Palaimon shared in the religious observances of the occupants in the caves. It is Dionysos who must be given priority in any conjecture concerning the

---

[38] There is an extensive literature on the nature and functions of Greek religious organizations. See Franz Poland, *Geschichte des Griechischen Vereinswesens*, pp. 129–150; Nilsson, *Geschichte der Gr. Rel.*, II², p. 363; *Op. Sel.*, II, pp. 524–541; *The Dionysiac Mysteries of the Hellenistic and Roman Age*, pp. 45–66. A convenient summary of this large subject is presented by Marcus N. Tod in *Sidelights on Greek History*, pp. 71–93; see also W. S. Ferguson and Arthur D. Nock, *Harvard Theological Review*, XXXVII, 1944, pp. 61–174.

[39] See above, p. 39, note 36. A slightly modified copy of the dolphin and trident appears on the cover and title page of this and other volumes of the Isthmia publications.

[40] It would be natural for Poseidon, whose subterranean powers are expressed in his titles Gaieouchos, Seisichthon, Ennosigaios, to have cult place in caves as in water holes. At Tainaros in Lakonia he had a sanctuary like a cave, and there was a festival whose celebrants were called Tainarioi or Tainaristai; Strabo, VIII, 5, 1 (C 363); Pausanias III, 25, 4. Sam Wide, *Lakonische Kulte*, pp. 33–47, lists the pertinent literature. Kruse (*R.E.*, *s.v.* Tainarios) does not believe that the Tainarioi formed a permanent thiasos. The name "Tainaristai" is analogous to "Isthmiastai," the name applied to part- cipants in the Isthmian Games, who gave the title to Aischylos' satyr play, *Theoroi* or *Isthmiastai; Isthmia*, I, p. 57 and note 1.

[41] On the Temple and temenos of Palaimon see below, pp. 99–112; cf. *Hesperia*, XXVIII, 1959, pp. 312–319. Much useful information about the cult is found in Will, *Korinthiaka*, pp. 169–180. Although there was an early cult of the boy-god at Isthmia, all the references to it are of Roman times, and the sanctuary retains no features earlier than the establishment of the Roman colony at Corinth. Will's statement (p. 184) that "il va de soi qu'il (le Palaimonion) était aussi ancien que les mythes qui y étaient attachés," must be reconsidered in the light of recent discoveries. Whatever was the date of the source from which the late writers drew their information concerning the myth, all the available material evidence and the literary sources for the cult are late.

identity of the god worshiped in the caves. Although sacred meals and drink offerings played a role in the worship of other deities, they are, so to speak, a prime requirement in the cult of Dionysos.[42]

Dionysiac associations and their functionaires went by several different names. The evidence for their organization and practices comes from written sources, chiefly inscriptions. The material remains that can be identified as related to these bodies are both meager and difficult to interpret. Some such societies, variously called θίασος, σύνοδος, βακχεῖον, σπεῖρα, operated as organizations of clan or family; others drew their membership from specific crafts or professions. A widely known guild of this kind, the "Artists of Dionysos," οἱ περὶ τὸν Διόνυσον τεχνῖται, functioned in connection with the Isthmian and Nemean Games.[43] It seems to have been active chiefly in the third and second centuries B.C.; in fact the existing inscriptions dealing with organizations of this kind are for the most part Hellenistic and Roman in date. We are much less well informed about the religious or semi-religious societies that existed before the time of Alexander. Since the use of the Isthmian caves would have terminated in the fourth century, it may be questioned whether they can have served as dining chambers for the Artists of Dionysos, but there may well have been other organizations with similar functions at an earlier date.

If we proceed from the likely assumption that it was Dionysos—alone or in association with Palaimon— whose devotees held their ritual meals in the caves, certain features of these dining rooms invite comment. Little need be said about the Northeast Cave, whose furnishings and entrance courts are poorly preserved. For the purpose of interpretation it is the Theater Cave, where the two courts and two chambers present all the essential features in duplicate, that offers the most useful evidence. Although the couches of the west chamber have been crudely hacked away, their size and disposition are quite apparent. The small niche inside the chamber to the right of the entrance would be suitable for cult images, as well as for offerings that might have been placed there in front of the statuettes.[44] The large circular cutting underneath this cult niche is so perfectly shaped for an amphora that it must have been made to hold such a vessel. In both chambers of the Theater Cave we find an entrance into a side chamber, which probably played an important role in the ceremonies enacted in the caves. With no direct light from the outside these small rooms would have been poorly illuminated, and a curtain drawn across the doorway would have secured privacy and shut out all light. Presumably the most sacred and secret parts of the ritual were held in these chambers. They are in a sense paralleled by the crypt in the Temple of Palaimon, in which oaths of the most binding nature were administered in total darkness.[45] Sacred vows and oaths entered into the initiation of members of religious brotherhoods, and these secluded side chambers would have served admirably for the performance of such rites.

In the courts from which the cave chambers were entered we have clear evidence for the preparation of meals. It may not be without significance that the dishes were stacked away in a carefully prepared pit, lined with hard cement. Probably the vases themselves used for the preparation and serving of the meals were considered sacral objects, as Martin P. Nilsson[46] has pointed out in connection with similar

---

[42] Nilsson, *Geschichte der Gr. Rel.*, II², p. 363; *Op. Sel.*, II, p. 536.

[43] The full title of this organization was, with some variations, τὸ κοινὸν τῶν τεχνιτᾶν τῶν ἐξ Ἰσθμοῦ καὶ Νεμέας Dittenberger, *Syll.*, II³, 690. A fragmentary inscription from Corinth refers to this body. The dispute between its members and the rival guild of Dionysiac artists of Athens has been extensively discussed by Franz Poland, *op. cit.*, pp. 136–137; and more recently by Georges Daux in *Delphes au IIe et au Ier siècle*, pp. 356–372. Since the Delphic inscriptions relating to this controversy are all dated in the years 134–112 B.C., when Corinth was all but deserted, the late John H. Kent (*Corinth*, VIII, iii, p. 13) was doubtless right in his suggestion that the Corinth fragment refers to an earlier dispute, prior to 146 B.C. There is, however, no direct evidence for the earlier existence of these guilds.

[44] The niches find their best analogies in rock sanctuaries which are so common in Greece. Similarly the Lares of Roman religion had altars and niches in the walls of private houses. See Nilsson, *Op. Sel.*, III, 278.

[45] *Hesperia*, XXVIII, 1959, pp. 312–319; and see below, pp. 110–112 and note 27.

[46] Martin P. Nilsson, *Eranos*, LIII, 1955, p. 30, where he discusses an inscription from Smyrna, published by J. Keil, *Anzeiger d. österreich. Akad. Wien*, XC, 1953, pp. 16–20, no. 1. The phrase μηδ' ἀθύτοις θυσίαις ἱερῶν ἐπὶ χῖρας ἰά[λειν] according to Nilsson admits of two interpretations. ἄθυτος may mean either "what has not been sacrificed" or "what is not allowed to be sacrificed". "If the former sense is preferred it is forbidden to begin the meal until the dishes have been sacrificed, i.e. devoted to the god, sacralized."

cult meals. We need only bear in mind the care with which kitchen vessels and all tableware have to be handled in Kosher cooking. Perhaps similar stipulations could explain the presence of disposal pits within both entrance courts. Presumably the water in which the pottery had been washed was poured through the covered channel into the large pit of the west court. Are we then to assume that this water too had acquired ritual character?[47] In this connection, the practices in Christian baptism of the Orthodox Church may throw light on the procedure. The baptismal water, which is fundamentally bath water, albeit of a sacral nature, is not poured out just anywhere on the ground or down a drain but into a special pit (βόθρος) from which it sinks into the earth. The disposal pits themselves, so close to the entrance into the chambers, would seem an unsuitable feature in an area devoted to religious use, and this very fact would perhaps indicate that certain regulations demanded that the water be disposed of in this fashion. The cult caves were probably used chiefly or exclusively at the time of the Isthmian Games once every two years, so that the water poured into the pits would have had ample time to seep down and evaporate between festivals. This explanation, if correct, does not account for the presence of the vases and architectural pieces found in the chute of the large pit; presumably these objects were placed there while the caves still functioned as cult rooms and were left, like the dishes in the pottery pit, after the original users of the cave had abandoned it.

The peculiar arrangement in the northwest corner of the west court, with its partly open and partly covered table, was probably made to serve some sacrificial purpose. Fruit and other raw edibles may have been placed there as offerings to the god. In each of the two courts there seem to have been three couches similar to those found within the cave chambers. Perhaps these were used for servants or for initiates awaiting admission to full membership in the brotherhood. Of particular interest are the post holes found both in the west court and at the entrance to the east chamber of the Theater Cave. These may have been used for setting up a wooden framework for a temporary roof (σκιάς) over the outer establishments. Such equipment played a role in other cult places of Dionysos.[48]

An inscription from Italy[49] of the second century after Christ and now in the Metropolitan Museum lists a large number of functionaries in a Dionysiac association. Among them are two guardians of the grotto (ἀντροφύλακες); and other inscriptions, cited by the authors who published the inscription in the Metropolitan Museum, refer to the ἑστίαρχος, κρατηρίαρχος, and ἀρχιμαγαρεύς as titles of such functionaries. Magaron was the name of a Dionysiac grotto[50] in which a πατὴρ σπηλλέον or an ἀρχιμαγαρεύς, presided. These terms probably refer to cave cults of Dionysos, in which eating and drinking entered into the ritual program, and improvised caves were carried on carts in processions in the service of the wine god.[51] An important passage in Athenaios quotes Socrates of Rhodes concerning Mark Antony's visit in Athens in 42 B.C.: "He (Socrates of Rhodes) relates that Antony while in Athens constructed an

---

[47] The question of the disposal of dirty water and refuse is extensively discussed by S. Eitrem, *Opferritus und Voropfer*, pp. 119–132. This has to do chiefly with water used in bathing or washing of hands; little is said about disposal of dishwater after cult meals. For analogous practices in Early Christian Churches cf. D. I. Pallas, Ἡ Θάλασσα τῶν Ἐκκλησιῶν, p. 75.

[48] Martin P. Nilsson, *The Dionysiac Mysteries of the Hellenistic and Roman Age*, p. 61. The references to the use of fresh branches, χλωρὰ ὕλη, may hark back to an earlier tree cult of Dionysos δενδρίτης. The cult name θυλλοφόρος, applied to Dionysos on Kos, denotes the use of κλάδους ἢ φύλλα. Cf. Hesychius, *s.v.* θύλλα.

[49] Published by Achille Vogliano, Franz Cumont, and Christine Alexander in *A.J.A.*, XXXVII, 1933, pp. 215–270.

[50] So Martin P. Nilsson, *The Dionysiac Mysteries of the Hellenistic and Roman Age*, p. 53, note 47, and p. 62; also *Op. Sel.*, II, pp. 524–541, where he comments on the inscription (note 49) in the Metropolitan Museum. The inscription on an altar in Thessalonike, in which the title μαγ[α]ρεύς—or μαγ[ει]ρεύς— (discussed by L. Robert, *Mélanges Bidez*, II, 1934, pp. 795–812) occurs, shows that a cave, σπήλλεον, served as dining room probably for a Dionysiac thiasos. An inscription from Abdera contains a dedication to θεῷ Διονύσῳ καὶ τοῖς συνμύσταις (J. Bousquet, *B.C.H.*, LXII, 1938, pp. 51–54) of a μάγαρον, which, according to Nilsson, has the meaning of Dionysiac cave. Nilsson, *loc. cit.*, rejects the interpretation that the altar in Salonike was a dedication to Mithras or to the Magna Mater. He reverts to the view of Franz Cumont (*A.J.A.*, XXXVII, 1933, p. 259, note 2) that the σπήλλεον was a Dionysiac cave, and the functionaries mentioned in the text are all suitable to the cult of Dionysos.

[51] Athenaios, *Deipn.*, V, 200; Martin P. Nilsson, *Op. Sel.*, II, pp. 535–536; and M. Vollgraff, *B.C.H.*, LI, 1927, pp. 455–456.

improvised pavilion (σχεδία) covered with fresh branches (χλωρᾷ ὕλῃ) *as is (usually) done above the Bacchic Caves;* and after hanging up tambourines and fawnskins and all kinds of other Dionysiac toys in the pavilion, he made himself drunk with his companions."[52] The wooden posts, shown by post holes to have been set up in front of the two cave chambers at Isthmia, may have served as supports for such exhibits.

The number of couches which the caves accommodated is probably significant, in view of the fact that the two caves were similar in that respect. In the Northeast Cave, as we have seen, the disposition of the couches is somewhat irregular, but the number seems to have been the same as in the Theater Cave. The very fact that an isolated couch was carved out of the side in the east branch is an indication that the exact number eleven was important. Similarly the east chamber of the Theater Cave was made irregular in shape in order to make room for six couches along the walls. If we are correct in our conclusion that only one of the two caves was used at one time and that the Theater Cave is the later of the two, this repetition of the number eleven must be of significance. Does it imply that the membership in the association was fixed at exactly eleven? That would seem to be a natural inference, and if it was a guild of performers in the Theater, such a small number would be understandable. But the makers of the caves may have had other reasons for limiting the number of couches to eleven, since that seems to have been a general requirement in dining rooms attached to sanctuaries. Such rooms are usually square or very nearly so. In the Asklepieion at Corinth,[53] which had a row of dining rooms on the east side of the Lerna Square, each room was so designed as to accommodate the length of three couches and the width of one on each side of the square. That would have made twelve couches, but one was omitted to make room for the door, which had to be placed off axis. The eleven couches exactly filled the space, and each couch had a headrest at the right end as one faces the couch. Between the tables and a square hearth in the center there was room enough for the servants to circulate. Other arrangements are of course possible in very large or in smaller chambers, but in the fifth and fourth centuries B.C. eleven couches seem to have become the standard number for the larger dining rooms. This, one would suppose, is the meaning behind Telekleides' enigmatic passage, in which he taunts Perikles for his oversized head, which with all his worries about the affairs of state was big enough to hold eleven couches.[54]

[52] Athenaios, *Deipn.*, IV, p. 148 B.

[53] Carl Roebuck, *Corinth*, XIV, pp. 51–54. Apart from the Asklepieion at Corinth, such dining rooms with eleven couches are found at the Sanctuary of Hera at Perachora (H. Payne, *Perachora*, I, p. 14, who does not mention the number of couches); and in the Sanctuary of Brauronian Artemis (Τὸ Ἔργον, 1961, pp. 22–24, fig. 22), where the late John Papadimitriou uncovered the sacred stoa in which there were nine dining chambers with eleven couches each. An inscription from the sanctuary mentions other dining rooms, two with ten, one with nine, and one with eleven couches. See also J. Papadimitriou, "The Sanctuary of Artemis at Brauron," *Scientific American*, CCVIII, 1963, pp. 110–120. The recently excavated Sanctuary of Demeter and Kore on the slope of Acrocorinth has a whole series of dining rooms, in which the number of couches varied. Ronald S. Stroud, *Hesperia*, XXXVII, 1968, pp. 314–319, estimated that nine banqueters could be accommodated at one time in the Northwest Banquet Hall. A large lustral basin was found in an adjacent room, which also contained couches. There is abundant evidence for the use of water for ritual purification of the diners and perhaps of the utensils as well; Nancy Bookidis, *Hesperia*, XXXVIII, 1969, pp. 297–310, XLI, 1972, pp. 283–317.

[54] Kock, *Com. Att. Frag.*, I, p. 220, Tell. 44. The line from Telekleides is from Plutarch's *Perikles*, III, 4. Τηλεκλείδης... φησιν αὐτὸν (Perikles) ἐν τῇ πόλει "Καρηβαροῦντα, ποτὲ δὲ μόνον ἐκ κεφαλῆς ἑνδεκακλίνου θόρυβον πολὺν ἐξανατέλλειν." The seemingly incongruous epithet ἑνδεκάκλινος may have had the significance of "a very large number." Perhaps the expression goes back to primitive times when counting was done by the fingers of the hand and anything above ten denoted a number too large to be counted. J. M. Edmond, *Fragments of Attic Comedy*, I, pp. 194–195, 44 b, restored the lines from Telekleides and translates them as follows:
μόνος ἐκ κεφαλῆς ἑνδεκακλίνου θόρυβον πολὺν ἐξανατέλλει.
"He alone knows how to give birth to a row from a head that would seat four-and-twenty!"
My suggestion about the origin of eleven as a term to denote a very large number is supported by Karl Menninger's theory about the origin of numbers in *Number Words and Number Symbols* (English Edition, MIT Press, 1969), pp. 46 and especially 83–84: "Anything above that (ten) was 'more'. One and two more than ten was still counted, but anything beyond them was perhaps, as often happens among primitive people, merely considered 'many'." I owe this reference to Menninger's book to the translator, Paul T. Broneer. A different explanation of the figure of speech appears in Joachim Schwarze, *Die Bedeutung des Perikles durch die Attische Komödie*, pp. 98–99; he believes that the figure is borrowed from the myth about the birth of Athena from the head of Zeus.

In buildings specially constructed with a series of dining rooms of equal size and nearly square in form, convenience and proper utilization of space may have been the deciding factors in creating a standard of eleven couches as the optimum. In the case of our caves a single chamber large enough to contain eleven couches, in addition to such apparatus as the religious cults may have demanded, would have become unduly large and would certainly have required interior supports for the roof. The division into two compartments was an obvious solution to this problem. And if the cult niche, the large amphora, and the side chamber played a role in ritual performances held in the caves, the reduplication needs no further explanation. But if all the diners were members of the same organization, why would it have been necessary to have separate entrance courts, each with a kitchen stove, ritual table, disposal pit, and outdoor couches? Such a twofold division of equipment may denote differences in rank among the members. One chamber may have accommodated the hierarchy and the second the rank and file of the organization. In the Theater Cave the western chamber with the smaller number of couches is the better constructed, with its vaulted roof, plastered walls, and larger couches; and the court in front of it is both larger and more elaborately equipped. Whatever was the reason for the reduplication, it is clear that the meals were prepared separately for the two contingents served in the caves.

Many problems concerning the caves are likely to remain unsolved, unless some inscription containing references to them should come out of future excavations. The premise that they had served as dining rooms for some sacred or semi-religious confraternity may be safely admitted, however, for only on that basis can we account for all the peculiar features of these subterranean chambers. Thus they will take their place among the documents relating to the ritual meals of such associations known hitherto only from written sources.

THE STADIA

ARCHAIC STADIUM

In preliminary reports on the Isthmia excavations and in the first volume of the definitive Isthmia publications[55] we have made frequent references to two stadia, an earlier one close to the Temple of Poseidon and a later one located at a different site some 240 meters farther southeast. The available evidence further points to several alternations which in some cases may have involved thoroughgoing rebuilding. Thus in the Earlier Stadium it is possible to distinguish three periods of construction.

Very little remains of the first period. South of the Roman Altar, among the foundations of the East Stoa and at a very much lower level than the Stoa Stylobate there is a prominent stone packing with a length of *ca.* 15.30 m. and a maximum width of 4.00 m. (Plans II, VII). The northeast edge, which is fairly regular, is made with somewhat larger stones and laid with greater care in a straight line. The rest of the stone packing consists of earth and rough field stones thrown in helter skelter (Pl. 20, a). The orientation of the outer face is northwest to southeast. It does not run quite parallel to the stadium retaining walls of later date; the two converge *ca.* 0.90 m. toward the southeast on a stretch of 15 m. Conversely the line of the stone packing converges toward the northwest at about the same rate with the water channels that line the racecourse itself. At a point some fifteen meters farther southeast one of the early trial trenches in the area exposed a similar stone packing, only 1.70 m. long (Plans II, III), with the straight northwest face approximately in line with that of the longer stretch.

Another large stretch of stone packing, close to the modern auto road, has been cleared for a length of 11.50 m. and a maximum width of 3.60 m. (Plan II, Pl. 20, b). The stones are put together in much the same way as in the stretch south of the Roman Altar, and the northeast edge is, if anything, more regular here and made with larger stones. The orientation too is about the same, but the line is here closer to the two parallel retaining walls. Thus at the farthest point of the long stretch south of the

[55] *Isthmia*, I, pp. 10, 174–181; and above, p. 4.

Roman Altar, the northeast edge of the stone packing is at a distance of 9.40 m. from the northeast face of the inner, i.e. southwestern, of the two parallel retaining walls. Close to the modern road the distance between the faces of the same two walls is only 8.15 m. At one point between these two, where the short stretch of the stone packing is preserved, the northeast faces of the same two walls are only about 7.30 m. apart. Since the face of the later wall is straight this variation must be due to a northeast bulge of the northeast edge of the stone packing. The similarity of the two large areas of stone packing and the orientation of their northeast edge is sufficient proof that they belong to a single structure. In the interval between these two areas some trial trenches showed that the ancient ground level has been much disturbed, but there were traces here and there, as shown above, of stone packing of a less regular nature. The total length of the northeast edge, from the northwest end of the stretch south of the Roman Altar to the farthest preserved point at the edge of the modern road, is 67 m., a little more than one-third the length of a stadium. That the stone packing extended farther toward the southeast was shown by many stones of the same kind found and removed in the building lot of Spyridon Venezianos across the road from the area described above.

In the light of the better preserved ruins of the Earlier Stadium in the same area, it now seems all but certain that the stone packing marks the outer, northeastern edge of an embankment in the earliest phase of that building. In order to create a uniform slope for the convenience of the spectators, it was necessary to raise the outer edge above the original ground level, which here sloped away from the racecourse. The slope of the spectatory would have been very gentle, since the comparatively small size and irregular shape of the stones would not have supported a high embankment.

There is little else that can be brought into relation with this early phase of the Stadium. On the southwest side the ground sloped down toward the racecourse so that no artificial embankment had to be provided. At the preserved, northwest end of the Stadium, the Cyclopean Wall would have formed the outer limit of the spectatory on that side (above, p. 7). The two do not run parallel, however; on a distance of 20 m. the face of the Cyclopean Wall converges toward the north with the southwest edge of the racecourse as much as 4.00 m. Furthermore, the most carefully finished face of the wall is toward the racecourse; consequently it could not have been intended as a retaining wall for the embankment, though it was probably left standing and functioned as the boundary of the Stadium area on that side. There is no indication that the embankment was raised above the present top of the wall, and the distance from the wall to the racecourse at the northwest end is only slightly less than the distance from the racecourse to the outer edge of the stone packing on the northeast side.

In the racecourse itself nothing has been found that is early enough to go with the stone packing of the archaic spectatory. Both of the two fairly well preserved starting lines[56] almost certainly belong to later phases, and a third line, second in order of date, of which some uncertain traces are left, is probably also later. Almost no pottery was found that can throw light on the chronology. Our probing in the fill of the stone packing yielded virtually no pottery and no other objects that could be used for dating. One fragment of a large geometric vessel of Attic manufacture (IP 2841) was found in the surfacing of the racecourse, but this seems too early—eighth century B.C.—to have any bearing on the date of the Stadium.

EARLIER STADIUM

Our description of the Earlier Stadium properly begins with the formal entrance way, by which athletes and officials reached the northwest end of the racecourse. The descent from the higher area in front of the Temple of Poseidon was by a ramp, which began *ca.* 5.00 m. south of the southeast corner of the

[56] Although the line at the closed end of the racecourse was the finish line in the single stade race, it served as a starting line for the diaulos, the race in armor, and probably the dolichos. See Harris, *Greek Athletes*, p. 70; Gardiner, *Athletics*, pp. 133–135. In most of the excavated stadia the two lines are approximately alike, but see below, Appendix II, p. 138.

Temple. At that point there are three cuttings in the native rock that seem to have been made for the erection of a temporary ornamental gateway (Plan VII, Pl. 21, a, foreground). They are irregular in shape. The one on the left as you face the Stadium is L-shaped, measuring 0.358 m. from east to west, 0.45 m. from north to south, and 0.33 m. in depth. The middle cutting seems to have been almost square originally, measuring 0.13 × 0.15 m. in area and 0.25 m. in depth. It was later enlarged irregularly toward the north. The cutting on the right measures 0.35 × 0.25 m. in area and *ca.* 0.50 m. in depth. All three are cut in solid rock. Since these three evenly spaced cuttings are found at the very beginning of the ramp, they cannot be accidental depressions or cuttings made at some later time. They could have served suitably as anchorage for three upright posts of a double gateway, set up at the time of the games and decorated with bunting or, more likely, with green boughs and flowers.

From this point two low walls flanked the ramp (Plan VII), which is now interrupted at one point by the foundation for the south temenos wall of the early Roman period. Only the west wall, built of squared blocks of irregular sizes, is now partly preserved; but a cutting for the east wall and two stones which seem to be in their original position show that the ramp was *ca.* 1.90 m. wide at the upper end and presumably about the same at the lower end. The west wall terminated close to the upper of two channels which brought water from the reservoir into the racecourse; and the east wall, which was only 7.75 m. long, did not extend to the edge of the racecourse. The floor of the ramp consists of native rock graded to an even decline and surfaced with tamped earth. Close to the lower end of the ramp are four stones nearly evenly spaced in a row along the water channel at the foot of the spectatory (Plan VII, Pl. 21, b). In the center of each stone is a rectangular socket, measuring *ca.* 0.08 × 0.10 m. in area, and extending through the thickness of the stones. Other stones of the same kind farther southeast may have been removed when the heavy foundation for the façade of the South Stoa was laid. Probably the banners identifying the participating teams were set up in these holes as the atheltes marched down the ramp in formal procession after taking their oaths at the Altar of Poseidon at the beginning of the contests. The holes are too close together to have carried markers for rooting sections in the spectatory. The incline of the ramp was only 1 in 11 or 5° 12′, that of the spectatory somewhat steeper, *ca.* 8° 22′.

The closed end of the Stadium is slightly curved. Typologically it forms an intermediate stage between the straight ends of the stadia at Olympia and Epidauros and the pronounced curve of the later sphendone found in the Later Stadium at Isthmia and elsewhere. Neither at the end nor on the sides were there any proper seats for the spectators, except for special seats of honor to be described below. At the curved end, however, where the rocky ground rose steeply toward the west, there is a series of four very irregular steps (Pl. 21, c), too narrow to have served as seats; they were probably intended primarily as stairs, but may also have accommodated spectators standing up.

At the bottom of the steps two water channels follow the curved end of the Stadium (Plans VII, VIII, Pl. 21, c, d). Where the south ends of the channels connected with the reservoir, they were cut away when the foundation for the Temple of Palaimon was laid, which now covers the south corner of the Stadium (Plans II, VII, VIII). Here would have been another outlet, bringing water from the reservoir to the channel along the southwest side of the racecourse. The two parallel channels are made very much alike and must have been in use simultaneously, even if they were made at different times. They are cut in the soft rock and lined with a heavy cement similar to that used in the Stadium reservoir (above, p. 27) and in Water Channels I–III. Both channels are rather uneven, measuring 0.07–0.115 m. in width and *ca.* 0.125 m. in depth. The two come together at the foot of the ramp to form a single channel (Plan VII, Pl. 21, d) which makes a sharp turn at the north corner of the Stadium, then continues southeastward for a distance of 3.50 m. and there empties into a large basin. The amount of decline of the upper branch from its southernmost preserved end to the junction at the foot of the ramp is 0.12 m., that of the lower branch is 0.15 m.; from there to the edge of the basin there is a further decline of 0.03 m.

The basin (Pl. 21, b) is rectangular with the corners rounded. It measures 1.02 m. in length (northeast to southwest) and 0.73 m. in width at the top. The maximum depth is 0.40 m. At the top is a rim 0.09 m. wide, covered like the inside with hard cement. The beginning of the channel on the other, southeast side of the basin was found broken away, and the piece has now been stuck on with cement. No part of the channel is preserved farther southeast. The corresponding basin at the southwest end of the starting line is in the exact center of the foundation for the Temple of Palaimon (below, p. 110). Unlike its counterpart on the other side, this basin is oval in form (Pl. 22, a), measuring 0.87 × 0.66 m. at the top and 0.31 m. in depth at its deepest point. When the Temple foundation was discovered the basin was not visible, having been filled to the top with stones packed in hard mortar (Pl. 22, b). All traces of the water channel between the basin and the reservoir have disappeared. From the other, southeast side of the basin a channel, cut in blocks of poros and lined with cement, led southeastward along the southwest edge of the racecourse. The first six meters of this branch were cut off by the builders of the Temple of Palaimon. From the southeast corner of the Temple foundation the channel is well preserved for a distance of 7.50 m., as far as the later south temenos wall of the Palaimonion (Pl. 22, c), and another section has been exposed south of the Palaimonion (Plans II, VII). The total length from the basin to the farthest preserved point is *ca.* 21.00 m. On a length of 15.50 m. it has a downward slope of 0.118 m. toward the southeast. If this grade continued uniformly to the other end of the Stadium the decline would have amounted to about 1.46 m. This is nearly twice as steep a gradient as that of the Later Stadium (*ca.* 0.83 m., Plan VI). Besides the two large basins at opposite ends of the starting line, no basins have been found along the channel in the excavated part of the Stadium. In 1959 we dug some pits in the orchard of Michael Papatheodorou on the south side of the modern road in an attempt to find the continuation of the channel on the southwest flank of the racecourse. At the very north edge of the orchard a short section appeared, but beyond that point no part of the Stadium seems to have survived the agricultural operations in the orchards.

The most surprising discovery of the excavation in the Earlier Stadium is a form of starting line, the existence of which was previously known only from literature. It consists of a stone sill with cuttings for upright posts, a triangular pavement with a starter's pit in the axis, and grooves fanning out from the pit (Pl. 59, a). The stones in the pavement are of different sizes, only about 0.15 m. thick. The sill at the base of the triangle is *ca.* 0.24 m. wide and 0.23 m. thick; it extended clear across the racecourse, for a length of 20.42 m. The northeast half (Pl. 22, d), which is perfectly preserved, has nine vertical sockets, measuring *ca.* 0.07 × 0.035 m. at the top and extending through the thickness of the sill. They are spaced with intervals of 1.04–1.055 m., the average distance being 1.049 m. There is a sturdy bronze staple fastened with lead to the edge of the pavement opposite each but one of these sockets. From the staples grooves converge toward the starter's pit (Pl. 23, a), their inner ends forming a circular line, roughly concentric with the circle of the pit at a distance of *ca.* 0.53 m. from its rim. Here, as at their outer ends, a bronze staple set in lead bridges the end of each groove (Pl. 23, b). The pit, which is cut in rock, measures 0.53 m. in diameter and 1.00 m. in depth. It is not at the apex of the triangle; the distance from the rim to the edge of the sill is 1.55 m.

The other, southwest half of the triangle is less well preserved. All the slabs over a length of 4.51 m. were removed when the foundation for the rear wall of the South Stoa was laid, and here the sill is missing for a length of 2.22 m. Only seven of the original nine sockets in the sill together with the far ends of four grooves are now preserved. The southwest end of the sill and the pavement have been laid bare in a tunnel cut through the rubble foundation of the Temple of Palaimon. There were eight grooves and nine sockets in the southwest half, as in the fully preserved northeast half. The two halves were not completely symmetrical, however, as shown in Plate 59, a. All the grooves in the northeast half terminate at a socket in the sill, and one socket, the ninth from the northeast end, has no corresponding groove in the pavement. In the southwest half, the socket close to the acute end of the triangle is likewise without groove, whereas the socket nearest to the middle had such a groove (restored). Thus in each half there is one more socket in the sill than there are grooves in the pavement. The reason for this apparent lack of correspondence of grooves and sockets becomes clear when we consider the operation of the starting device.

The sockets, obviously intended to hold vertical posts of wood, mark the width of the lanes allotted to the several runners. A horizontal piece of wood, only slightly shorter than the width of the lanes, was loosely hinged to one of the posts and manipulated with a string that passed through the groove in the stone pavement and was held in place by the staple at either end. One end of each cord would have been fastened to the horizontal bar, the other end was held by the starter in the pit. As soon as he let go of a string, the bar held by it in a horizontal position would fall of its own weight and hang vertically on the side of the post to which it was hinged. The gate was thus instantaneously opened. Two or four or all sixteen bars, depending on the number of runners in each heat, could be made to fall simultaneously. In the well-preserved northeast half of the sill the bar in each lane was fastened to the post farthest from the middle, i.e. on the northeast side of each lane. The ninth hole from the northeast end, which has no corresponding groove although the sill and pavement are there well preserved, shows that the eighth lane, of the same width as the others, was used. In the other, southwest half the horizontal bars were hinged to the posts on the side nearest to the center, and thus there is no groove leading to the last slot at the southwest end. In other words, the bars in both halves were fastened to posts on the same, i.e. northeast, side of the lanes. The absence of a groove at the ninth slot from the northeast end shows that there was a blind space in the middle, directly in front of the starter's pit.

The total length of the sill, measured from basin to basin, is 20.42 m., and the distance from the northeast basin to the central joint in the pavement, which very nearly bisects the triangle, is 10.10 m., leaving 10.32 m. for the other half. The difference of 0.22 m. may be due to the fact that the basin at the southwest end was smaller—its end is now concealed beneath a wall in the Temple of Palaimon—than the fully exposed basin at the other end. If we assume that 20.42 m. is the correct distance between the two basins, the sill may be divided as follows: $(16 \times 1.049) + 1.10$ (i.e. distance from first socket at northeast end to northeast basin) $+ 1.19$ (i.e. distance between basin and last socket at southwest end) $+ 1.351$ (i.e. blind lane in the center)$=20.425$ m. The width of the blind central lane is calculated by measuring the distance between the edge of the northeast basin and socket 13, which gives 13.99 m. as the width of 13 spaces, 11 of which were normal, used lanes. Hence $13.99 - (11 \times 1.049) + 1.10 = 1.351$ m., the width of the blind lane.

The operation of this elaborate type of starting gate, which has been repeatedly tested and found to function perfectly (Pl. 23, c, d),[57] was discontinued long before the Earlier Stadium was succeeded by the Later Stadium. When the pavement was found it was covered with a layer of hard whitish earth, ca. 0.05 m. thick, with which the race track had been surfaced (Pl. 23, e). A starting line of more conventional form was eventually made 10.93 m. from the line of cuttings in the sill, thus shortening the race track by that much. But that may have been a third starting line in this Stadium. At a distance of only 0.905 m. from the sill at the base of the triangle, the white surfacing of the racecourse is interrupted by a broad (ca. 0.70 m.) stripe of a darker color of earth (Plans II, VII, Pls. 21, c, 22, d). The change in color is very obvious along the southwestern part of the sill, less so in front of the northeastern end. Some foundation or sill seems to have been removed here since the last surfacing of the track. The

---

[57] In the summer each year the members of the Olympic Academy on their way to Olympia make their first stop at Isthmia, where they have the opportunity of testing the operation of the starting gates, unexampled elsewhere and previously known only from literary sources. Since they were first published in a preliminary report (*Hesperia*, XXVII, 1958, pp. 10–15), they have been illustrated by other authors dealing with the ancient stadium; cf. Harris, *Greek Athletes*, pp. 68, 69; Jüthner-Brein, *Athlet. Leibesüb.*, II, part 1, pp. 58–65, 84–85. Both Brein and Harris call them "hysplex." Harris, *loc. cit.*, has misunderstood the mechanism. In his sketches, figs. I and II, he has arranged the sockets with their long axis parallel to the sill and reconstructed a gate on the principle of a railroad semaphore. On paper this looks plausible, but since the sockets, and consequently the posts, are arranged at right angles to the sill, the restoration shown in his figures I and II, pp. 68–69, is incorrect.

width of this stripe is about the same as that of the stone sill of the later starting line (see below), and it is quite likely that this sill, or another of the same width, was first laid down close to the original starting gate, thereby shortening the racecourse by about 1.25 m.

Whatever caused this interruption in the surfacing close to the triangular pavement, the next stage in the development of the starting device is unmistakable. A different kind of starting line is still partly preserved in its original position, 10.93 m. southeast of the first line. This is made of poros blocks of unequal length, 0.485–0.53 m. wide and 0.26 m. high, with the top approximately level with the race track. The stones have been cut down along the front, leaving a width of ca. 0.33 m. exposed. The sill is preserved to a length of 11.60 m., but only a length of six meters is undisturbed; the rest has been worn down on top and partly relaid. At the southwest end some pits dug below the Stadium floor (Pl. 24, a) have caused damage to the sill, and the Hellenistic Road (C) (above, p. 20, Pl. 9, c), which ran across the starting line, has worn down the surface to some extent. Nevertheless, what remains is sufficient to give a clear impression of its original condition (Pl. 24, b). The top of the sill is covered with cement. A single groove, triangular in section, 0.068 m. wide at the top and 0.041 m. deep, interrupted by plain areas 0.26–0.38 m. in length at each post hole, ran the length of the sill, at a distance of 0.13 m. from the exposed northwest edge. Seven post holes are now preserved, originally set with a heavy casing of lead (Pl. 24, c). The holes measure ca. 0.077 × 0.07 m. in area and extend through the thickness of the stones to a depth of ca. 0.26 m. As they are now spaced, three of the intervals seem to have their original length, but in one hole the lead is missing, so that the width of the lane cannot be measured accurately.

The following description of the sill (Plan VII) begins at the southwest end. Here a single block, broken at both ends, contains one post hole and part of one groove (Pl. 24, a, b, bottom). It cannot now be in its original position. The groove shows that it once formed a part of a lane, but the distance between the water channel and the first post hole is too short for the width of a lane. Nevertheless, it is probably now in the position it had while the Stadium was still in use. This is shown by the fact that both the top and the groove are aligned with those in the rest of the sill. Between the broken southwest end and the water channel there is now an interval of 0.20 m. At the other, northeast, end of this fragmentary block there was an irregular hollow, now filled up, of uncertain date (Pl. 24, a), which extended below the bottom of the sill. The next block begins at an interval of 1.16 m. and it too has been roughly cut off at the southwest end. This block now measures only 0.73 m. in length. It has one socket, not in the normal position, i.e. with its rear almost in line with the front edge of the groove, but more nearly in line with the bottom of the groove. The distance from this socket to that nearest to the water channel is 1.580 m. This is very nearly the same as the width of two other lanes that can be measured accurately, but since the first block has obviously been relaid, the space may not be exactly right. In the joint between this and the next block is one of the post holes in the regular position. Between the two holes in the second block is a short, 0.37 m., groove, both ends of which seem to be original. Then, after an interval of 0.18 m. a second groove, 0.63 m. long, begins and extends to the other end of the third stone. Here a different kind of block, measuring 0.59 × 0.43 m. in area and having no cuttings in the top (Pl. 24, b, e), has been inserted. Then follows another short block, fifth from the southwest end, with a groove 0.63 m. long. Its southwest end now abuts against the plain block, but before this block had been inserted, the adjoining blocks on either side met in a joint. This is shown by the positions of the sockets in these stones. The distance, axis to axis, of the two sockets, is now 2.18 m., and if we subtract from that the length, 0.59 m., of the plain stone, the resultant distance of 1.59 m. is the width of a normal lane. The next, i.e. sixth, block, which seems to be undisturbed, measures 1.83 m. in length; this contains two post holes, 1.59 m. apart. The next block, seventh from the southwest end, which is only 0.993 m. long, has no post holes, and after that follows a short, eighth block, only 0.515 m. long, with one post hole. The distance between the last two sockets is 1.60 m. The ninth block, which seems to have been ca. 1.47 m. long, had a post hole at the northeast end, but here the lead has been removed

(Pl. 24, e). Farther to the northeast the sill is too poorly preserved to yield accurate measurements. The two lanes where the sill is undisturbed measure 1.59 m. and 1.60 m. in width, giving a mean width of 1.595 m., which we may accept as the norm. This is only a little less than five feet of 0.3204 m., and a little more than 5¼ feet of 0.302, the shortened foot which we obtain from the length of the Later Stadium (below, p. 64).

Since the lanes, as shown by the intervals between the posts, are here *ca.* 0.55 m. wider than those on the earlier starting line, the number of runners that could be accommodated in each run must have been reduced. The width of the racecourse, measured between the inner edges of the two gutters, is 21.92 m. at the northwest end close to the basins, and it would have been slightly wider, *ca.* 21.96 m., at the second starting line. It is unlikely that the full width was utilized in the later starting line. There was probably an unused margin at either end and a blind lane in the middle. If we measure from the inner edge of the water channel to the first socket in its proper position, we obtain a length of 5.08 m., which would give us three lanes (4.785 m.) and an unused space, 0.295 m. wide, close to the channel. And, if the situation was the same at the other end, there would be room for 13 lanes (20.735 m.) with an unused space of 0.295 m. at each end, and with a blind space, 0.635 m. wide, in the center. It is more probable, however, that there was an even number of lanes, in that case 12 (below, note 67), and that the blind lane in the center was 2.23 m. wide. The reduction of starting gates from 16 to 12 might possibly indicate lessened interest and participation in the Isthmian Games, or a shift in popularity from the lighter events, such as running, to those of heavy athletics: boxing, wrestling, pankration. In the Later Stadium the lanes are only slightly narrower (1.51 m.), but the total length of the line is greater, so as to make room for 16 ordinary lanes and one blind space in the center.

The floor of the racecourse in the Earlier Stadium, as has been pointed out above, was surfaced with a coat of white earth.[58] It is preserved for a distance of only about 20 m. from the curved end of the Stadium; beyond that point the area was later occupied by buildings connected with the cult of Palaimon. The ground slopes gently toward the southeast for about 50 m. and then the slope becomes steeper. At the approximate middle of the Stadium, *ca.* 100 m. from the curved end, the modern ground level is fully three meters lower than the Stadium floor close to the starting gates. The racecourse itself would have sloped gently toward the southeast end, but not as steeply as that. It is obvious that the ancient ground level was here considerably higher than the modern level. The explanation for this change is to be sought in the construction of the Later Stadium, the spectatory of which was not far from the open end of the Earlier Stadium. At that point the present ground level is more than four meters below that of the earlier race track. The Earlier Stadium floor at the northwest end is at an elevation of 51.29 m. above sea level; the starting line of the Later Stadium is at 32.13 m., a difference of nearly 20 m. The lower, southeastern, half of the Earlier Stadium, which must have been raised by artificial fill, was presumably carted away and used for the embankment of the spectatory on the northwest side of the Later Stadium. This would explain the conspicuous difference in the present ground level between the curved end and the approximate position of the open end of the Stadium. Although there is now no possibility of finding traces of the lower end, the total length of the racecourse can be accurately calculated, as will appear below.[59]

The embankment for the spectators on the northeast side of the Earlier Stadium is supported by two parallel walls of solid and regular construction, running diagonally to the South and East Stoas of later date. The inner, i.e. southwest, wall begins 9.10 m. east of the Long Altar. The northwest end of the wall abuts against a large block, measuring 1.05 × 1.35 m. in area; this forms the north end of a short spur wall extending southward for a distance of 4.45 m. (Plan II, Pl. 24, d). The spur wall, which served as retaining wall for the northwest end of the embankment, does not seem to have extended any farther

---

[58] This kind of surfacing recalls the λευκὴ γῆ prescribed for the same purpose in the Xystos of the stoa above the Gymnasium at Delphi, *B.C.H.*, XXIII, 1899, p. 566; and Jannoray, *Le Gymnase*, pp. 35, 88.

[59] See also *Isthmia*, I, Appendix I, pp. 176–177.

toward the south, but its top is dressed off in such a way as to indicate that it had at least one more course of stones. The diagonal retaining wall, which begins at this large block, was 0.64 m. thick, but the preserved foundations are somewhat broader in places (Pl. 24, d). At a point 12 m. southeast of the corner, the wall was cut off by the construction of the second Altar of Poseidon, but the same wall reappears on the south side of the Altar foundation (Pl. 25, a). The builders of the Altar, as they came upon the wall, cut their trench diagonally through the earlier masonry instead of building on top of it (Pl. 25, b). By that time the ground level had probably risen to a height above the existing top of the wall. South of the Altar the same wall continues beneath the foundations for the rear wall of the East Stoa and of the Southeast Propylon (Plans II, VII). The "layer cake" foundation[60] for the enclosure around the second Altar of Poseidon, which is contemporary with the Altar, cuts diagonally through two courses of the inner of the two retaining walls of the Earlier Stadium. This wall continues southeast-ward to the modern road; it can be followed with one long interruption for a total distance of 78 m. The wall has buttresses on both sides. On the south side of the second Altar of Poseidon, where the ground sloped down toward the east, the existing top course has a drafted edge at the bottom and one beveled edge at each vertical joint. This indicates that the northeast face was intended to be exposed, whereas the other, inner face is uneven and was hidden by the embankment of earth.

Within the rectangle of the Southeast Propylon, where two courses of the inner retaining wall are preserved, the upper course has drafted edges both at the top and at the bottom. The missing third course was set back 0.035 m. from the drafted edge, as is shown by a well-marked setting line. Also the ends of the blocks in the third course are marked by scratch lines in the top of the existing course. The lowest course rests on earth, but in places where the ground was uneven there is a rough foundation of rather small, roughly squared blocks. The foundations of the Propylon, unlike those of the Roman Altar and its enclosing wall, extend over the Stadium wall, which continues at a slightly lower level south of the Propylon. The highest preserved course is here 0.78 m. high. The blocks are well finished on the exposed northeast side, but the edges are not drafted. In the rear the blocks are quite rough and uneven. The lowest course, which has a thickness of 0.83 m., projects on both sides of the upper course. Some of the blocks in this course, which have a drafted upper edge, appear to be re-used. At a distance of 6.60 m. from the east foundation of the Propylon the Stadium retaining wall breaks off, but the ancient surface was here leveled off, showing that the wall continued without interruption toward the southeast. At a distance of 16.65 m. from the point where the foundation breaks off, it is again preserved in its lowest course, which rests directly on virgin soil. The wall is here preserved for a length of 27.55 m. to a point near the modern road where it again breaks off. In some places only the lowest course is pre-served; elsewhere the wall extends to a depth of three courses. The bottom course at the northwest end of this long stretch is drafted at the top, as in the stretch south of the Roman Altar. There are buttresses at intervals on both sides of the wall, and in some places these actually tie in with the wall construction. In one place toward the southeast end of this stretch, the buttress on the outside is preserved in three courses to a height of *ca.* 1.50 m. Here, however, the blocks in the wall have been tilted over in a stream bed running roughly north to south. The drafted edges and smoothly finished northeast face of the wall just described indicate that this was intended as a single outer supporting wall for the embankment.

Probably at a somewhat later period, a second, outer wall was constructed parallel to the first; the distance between the two walls is *ca.* 3.02 m. at the highest preserved level. The courses in the outer wall, however, project out to an extent of 0.16–0.23 m. so that at the bottom of the foundation the distance from the outer, northeast face of the earlier, inner wall to the lowest course in the outer wall is 3.64 m. Here again the northeast face is straight and smoothly finished, and one edge of the vertical joint is beveled as in the inner of the two walls. The outer parallel wall, which was not continuous, began somewhere in the space now occupied by the foundation for the Roman Altar. At the southeast corner of the Altar, where five courses are preserved in place, the wall has been cut off diagonally by

---

[60] For an explanation of this term see below, pp. 72–74.

the Altar foundation; it does not reappear on the north side of the Altar. The foundation for the rear wall of the East Stoa crosses the Stadium retaining wall at a distance of only one meter from the Altar foundation. Unlike the earlier Roman foundation for the enclosure around the Altar, the builders of the Stoa laid this foundation directly on the blocks of the outer retaining wall of the Earlier Stadium. A little to the east of the East Stoa foundation this retaining wall of the Stadium is preserved to a height of four courses, some stones of which seem to have been re-used from earlier structures. Three of the blocks here have masons' marks on the exposed face, as shown in Plate 59, b, and one block in the second course from the bottom has a smooth drafting 0.075 m. high at the bottom. The upper two courses at this point have been cut through diagonally by the "layer-cake" foundation for the east wall of the Altar enclosure (Pl. 25, c). Where this outer retaining wall is interrupted by the north wall of the Southeast Propylon, 11.50 m. southeast of the Altar foundation, the three courses of the wall have been removed so that the Propylon foundation here rests on earth and on the rubble bedding for the earlier wall. The retaining wall reappears east of the Propylon and is here preserved in two courses. At a distance of 1.72 m. from the Propylon foundation and 16.70 m. from the southeast corner of the Roman Altar, this outer retaining wall makes a right angle corner with a crosswall that extends up to the earlier of the two parallel walls (Pl. 31, d). The actual juncture of this crosswall with the inner retaining wall was destroyed when the propylon foundation was laid. Most of the blocks in the retaining wall at this point seem to be re-used, and two blocks in the crosswall have cuttings for swallowtail clamps at the ends. The space between the two parallel walls and to the southwest was packed with stones and earth (Pl. 25, d).

Beyond the crosswall at this point there seems to have been no outer retaining wall for an undetermined distance. The southeast face of the crosswall is quite smooth and shows clearly that no wall abutted against it. From the crosswall just east of the Southeast Propylon, no part of the outer retaining wall has been uncovered for a considerable distance, and for part of that distance at any rate, none ever existed. The wall reappears at a distance of 29.00 m. from the crosswall (Plan II). At the point where it reappears, there are indications of later construction, which may have caused the removal of some parts of the wall. A rather indistinct wall bedding indicates that the wall extended at least 7.50 m. farther toward the northwest. The lowest course of the outer wall is here preserved for a distance of 3.85 m., and 2.18 m. from the preserved end a single course of a crosswall extends between the two parallel walls. The blocks of the crosswall are not tied in with either of the two parallel walls. The crosswall was probably laid when the outer wall was built, since the top of the two walls is here the same. At the southwest end of the crosswall, where the joint has been patched out with smaller stones, the top of the crosswall is at a level 0.09 m. below that of the inner retaining wall. From the southeast end of the short section just described, the blocks of the outer retaining wall have been removed for a stretch of 16.00 m. Here, however, it is clear that the wall had existed, because a rubble foundation still remains. At the end of this long stretch, where no blocks of the outer wall remain in place, there is another crosswall, built partly out of re-used blocks. From this point to the exposed southeast end of the outer retaining wall, a stretch of 6.50 m., the construction is different, and the outer wall has a slightly, ca. 2⁰, different orientation from that of the inner wall. The foundation here extends to a greater depth and two courses are preserved. Close to the crosswall, which rests on loose fill and is probably of later date, the outer wall forms an end, but no other wall abuts against it. This course is ca. 0.70 m. broad, and the outer edge is beveled. On the top surface is a raised part, 0.25 m. wide at the outer edge, on which no wall blocks rested. The inner part of the wall, ca. 0.43 m. wide, is very smoothly finished at a level 0.03 m. below the raised band at the outer edge. In this part of the top are setting marks for the missing next course. The existing wall blocks here, which formed a projecting socle, have a carefully cut drafting at the bottom, 0.10 m. high, and the vertical edges of the block have been drafted on both sides of the joint. This part of the outer wall is so different that it seems to have been built at another time and perhaps for a different purpose than the rest of the wall farther northwest.

The outer wall, in any case, was not continuous, but formed individual rectangular extensions, added perhaps at different times for the purpose of strengthening the construction rather than to increase the capacity of the spectatory. Possibly some sections of the inner wall, which are not battered like those in the outer one, collapsed or were damaged in an earthquake so as to require the addition of the second wall. Attempts to pursue the lines of foundations of the two walls on the south side of the modern road, where the ground level is lower, proved unsuccessful.

Not much has been cleared of the spectatory on the southwest side of the racecourse. The terrain here rose more steeply toward the southwest, making it unnecessary to construct an artificial embankment on that side. The bases of three monuments are preserved near the lower edge of the spectatory. At a distance of 2.20 m. from the southeast corner of the foundation for the Temple of Palaimon there is a large block, approximately one meter square in area and 0.40 m. high, which appears to be in situ (Plans IV, M[14], VII; Pl. 22, c). It is oriented parallel to the water channel of the racecourse. This may have been the foundation for a single seat of some official or for an altar, comparable to the Altar of Demeter Chamyne in the Stadium at Olympia.[61] Farther to the southeast there is a second base of larger dimensions, now preserved for a length of 4.89 m. At its southeast end it measures 2.36 m. in width but at its northwest end it is only 1.305 m. wide. At the southeast end a wing, 1.60 m. wide, projects 1.065 m. toward the racecourse. The northwest end of the base was broken up and removed when the later Palaimonion temenos wall was built, but a cutting in stereo north of this wall shows that there was a similar wing at that end, making a Π-shaped monument (Plans IV, M[15], VII, VIII; Pl. 25, e) with a total length of ca. 8.00 m. It may have held the seats of the judges or a proedria for honored guests.[62] The third monument (Plan IV, M[16]; Pl. 25, e, upper middle) is separated from the second by an interval of 4.35 m. It had a width of ca. 2.30 m. at the northwest end and it has been exposed for a length of 3 m., the southeast part being concealed beneath the modern road. This too was probably the base of a proedria or perhaps the reserved seats of the Hellanodikai.[63]

LATER STADIUM

The Later Stadium is still unexcavated, but its cardinal features were revealed in pits and tunnels and open trenches dug in 1960–1962. Although a final study of the Stadium as a whole must await complete clearing of the area, an immensely costly undertaking likely to be long delayed, it seems desirable to set forth here the results of our preliminary investigation in a more complete form than was done in the excavation reports.

The location of the Later Stadium, which is easily recognized by the configuration of the area, has never been in doubt.[64] Unlike the Earlier Stadium, which is situated on gently sloping ground, the Later

[61] Pausanias VI, 20, 9; Gardiner, Olympia, p. 8; Ludwig Drees, Olympia, p. 95, fig. 22.

[62] Its position on the right side, as one looks toward the open end of the racecourse, may be compared with that of the Hellanodikeion in the Stadium at Olympia (Emil Kunze, Olympiabericht, V, pl. 1; Ludwig Drees, Olympia, p. 94, fig. 21), which is, however, farther from the closed end.

[63] One of the two large foundations on the side of the Stadium may have supported the seats of the Athenian delegation, whose members enjoyed the traditional right of proedria in the Stadium at Isthmia. It was Theseus, who, according to Plutarch (Theseus, XXV, 5), accorded the Athenians this right. He stipulated that the extent of their reserved section should be equal in extent to the sail on the galley that had brought them across the Saronic Gulf.

[64] The Stadium is mentioned by Pausanias (II, 1, 7) and is referred to in the inscription in Verona, I.G., IV, 203, line 24. The Apostle Paul's allusion to runners ἐν σταδίῳ (I Cor. 9:24), though more general in sense, is probably made with reference to the Stadium at Isthmia, with which his Corinthian readers were well acquainted. W. G. Clark, who visited the place in the 1850s (Peloponnesus, pp. 49–51) so understood the reference in Paul's epistle. Leake (Travels in the Morea, III, p. 286) refers to "foundations of the wall which supported the rectilinear end." This wall, which is still there, is not ancient and is not at right angles to the main axis of the Stadium. Leake does not mention seats. The Stadium is shown in Monceaux's plan, Gazette Archéologique, IX, 1884, pl. 38, reproduced by H. N. Fowler, Corinth, I, p. 61, fig. 26. Frazer (Pausanias' Description of Greece, III, p. 9) says that some of the marble seats "are still in their places, hidden under a screen of brushwood." He probably mistook some scattered blocks of marble for Stadium seats in situ.

Stadium was constructed in a hollow at the lower end of a stream bed with steeply sloping sides (Pl. 26, a). The builders made use of this natural formation by leveling and broadening the bottom of the hollow for the racecourse proper and by shaping the sides of the ravine to provide space for the spectators. To meet the problems of drainage they diverted the water of the stream through a system of tunnels, dug in the sides of the Stadium and underneath the race track itself. These underground conduits have not been sufficiently investigated to make possible a description of the whole system.

After the building had fallen into disuse and the manmade outlet for the water had silted up, earth from the adjacent slopes washed down into the area until the ground level had risen about six meters at the upper, southwest, end and about two meters at the lower end of the Stadium. One half of the area, containing the closed end of the racecourse, is now a grove of citrus fruit trees, the other half is a plowed field, and the two slopes that formed the spectatory are planted with olives and other fruit-bearing trees. In the northeast half, where the accumulation of earth varies between two and four meters in depth, we dug a series of open trenches, seven on the northwest side and six along the southeast edge of the racecourse (Plan VI). One trench (A^5–B^6), 2.00 m. broad and 37 m. long, extended clear across the floor of the Stadium at a distance of 74 m. from the starting line at the open end. In the upper, southwestern half, where the earth fill above the Stadium floor reaches a depth of nearly six meters, we made our investigation through pits from which we ran tunnels to expose the vital features of the building. Only at the middle of the curved end, where few trees impeded our digging, were we able to clear a sizable section in a large open trench. Through these operations, which involved considerable difficulties and even danger, we learned that the Later Stadium is exceptionally well constructed and one of the best preserved buildings of its kind in Greece. The race track appears to be in nearly perfect condition. Only the east corner at the southeast end of the starting line has been washed away by the stream of water, which once again formed its own bed, after the building had ceased to be used and the drainage tunnels had been clogged up.

On each side of the racecourse runs a narrow channel which provided athletes and spectators with fresh running water (Pl. 60, Section A^5–B^6, and detail section). It is cut in poros blocks and lined with hard stucco, which covers also the side of the stones facing the spectatory. There are basins at intervals, projecting from the channel toward the race track.[65] Between the water channel and the foot of the spectatory there is a broad passage, designed to function also as drainage channel, with gravelly floor. A path, paved with poros blocks, extends across the passage from each basin to a stone curb at the foot of the spectatory. Both the water channel and the curb describe a gradual curve so that the racecourse at the widest point exposed in our trenches is 2.35 m. wider than at the open end and 2.46 m. wider than at the closed end. The water channels and the curbs do not run parallel; and the two passages are also wider in the middle than at the ends. The source of the water running through the channel was at the curved end of the Stadium, and the slope from one end to the other amounts to nearly one meter. The floor of the racecourse was fairly even, but nowhere in our trenches did we encounter any hard surfacing like the white earth used for the Earlier Stadium.

In the general plan of the Later Stadium (Plan VI), the trenches dug along the southeast flank are numbered A^1 to A^8, those on the northwest side are numbered B^1 to B^8. Since the latter are more revealing and the exposed construction is there in more nearly perfect condition, we shall begin our description on that side. Trench B^1 exposed the north corner of the racecourse and the northwest end of the starting line (Pl. 60). At the end of the starting line there is a rectangular base, 1.065 × 0.81 m.

---

[65] In the stadium at Epidauros, the basins are likewise turned toward the racecourse (Πρακτικά, 1902, pl. A; Gardiner, *Athletics*, p. 130, fig. 81). In the stadium at Olympia, however, the basins are turned away from the racecourse so as partly to obstruct the passage between the channel and the curb at the foot of the spectatory; Kunze, *Neue Deutsche Ausgrabungen*, p. 267, fig. 1. One basin at the Hellanodikeion completely blocks the passage; Ludwig Drees, *Olympia*, ground plan on inside of the cover and pl. XIV, and especially p. 94, fig. 21; cf. W. Zschietzschmann, *Wettkampf und Übungsstätten in Griechenland*, I, p. 57, fig. 6. The Delphic stadium has no passage and no basins or water channel. The same is true of the stadium at Athens in its present form.

in area, with a shallow cutting in the center, measuring 0.41 × 0.37 m., and 0.04 m. in depth (Pl. 26, b), probably for the insertion of the plinth of a statue. This must have been of bronze, for two smaller cuttings at the bottom of the sinkage seem to indicate the position of the feet. Part of the lead packing adheres to the stone in the corners of the cutting. The northwest end of the sill that formed the starting line fits closely to the edge of the base, and the two seem to be of one period. The beginning of the two starting grooves in the sill was exposed in our trench as shown in Plate 60. A water basin fits tightly against the southwest edge of the base, and the channel enters the basin in the west corner. From the northeast edge of the statue base a low curb, 0.22 m. wide and 1.68 m. long, forms the edge of the passage, which continues somewhat beyond the northeast end of the race track (Pl. 26, b). Here the passage measures 1.148 m. in width, and it is paved with large poros slabs which do not fit closely against the curb on either side. The slabs probably serve as cover of a drain. The curb on the other side, at the foot of the spectatory, ends 0.75 m. beyond the statue base, in a stone set at right angles to the passage and forming the lowest course of the analemma at the end of the embankment. The end of the stone is cut at an angle, showing that the analemma did not run at right angles to the axis of the Stadium.

In trenches B² (Pl. 26, c) and B³ both the channel and the curb were exposed, but nothing else of interest came to light. The passage in B³ had increased in width to 1.378 m. In trench B⁴, which was extended northeastward to include the second basin, the relationship of the different features is particularly clear. The inside of the basin measures 1.06 × 0.47 m. in area and 0.33 m. in depth. The stones in which the basin and the channel are cut have stucco on the side facing the spectatory (Pl. 26, d), and a paved walk extends from the stuccoed outer edge of the basin to the curb. Elsewhere in the trench the curb is *ca.* 0.43 m. high, too high for a single step; it is here only 0.25 m. high, so as to make the ascent to the seats easier (Pl. 27, a). This is clear indication that the spectators, as well as the athletes, used the water in the basins. The distance between the first and second basins is 29.25 m. Trench B⁴, which was extended up the slope of the spectatory, revealed three successively rising planes cut in the clay bank (Pl. 60, Section through B⁴); these would have been used as seats. They are rather irregular, both in width and height, and the possibility must be conceded that they had served as placements for seats. The latter alternative is not very likely, however, in view of the fact that stone seats would have required better underpinning, of which no traces were found in any of the trenches.

The masonry and stucco revealed in trenches B¹ to B⁴ are all of good Greek workmanship; nothing was found in them that would indicate alteration in Roman times. The three trenches B⁵–B⁷ farther to the southwest showed signs of later intrusion and rebuilding. In trench B⁵ the water channel and curb with the passage in between were again exposed. The curb was missing in the northeast half of the trench, and here a ramp-like flooring, making two low steps, descended across the passage to the edge of the water channel (Pl. 27, b). In the southwest half there is a curb, the top of which is higher than in the trenches farther to the northeast, and the bottom rests on earth, *ca.* 0.20 m. above the floor of the passage. Probably the original curb had here been removed and the "ramp" added to facilitate descent to the track level. Trench B⁵ was continued up the embankment for a length of 13 m. from the edge of the curb. Here, as in trench B⁴, the spectatory rises in a series of broad irregular steps (Pl. 60, Section through B⁵). The first three are of normal height for seats, and beyond the third level and slightly higher there is a passage (diazoma?), 2.90 m. broad, through which a deep narrow trench runs lengthwise. The latter was found filled with building debris, among which was a marble torch flame (Pl. 26, e). Farther up the slope the seats continue, very uneven both in height and width. The area covered by this trench seems to have undergone some changes in Roman times and possibly even later.

In trench B⁶ we uncovered the third basin at a distance of 45.30 m. from the second basin.[66] The passage here is 1.78 m. wide, and at the foot of the embankment is a curb of normal height and made like the curb revealed in trenches B¹ to B⁴. Resting on this curb and set back slightly from the edge is a much heavier course of poros stone (Pls. 27, c, 60, Section through A⁵–B⁶), the joints of which are

---

[66] This is exactly 150 feet of 0.302 m.; see below, pp. 63–64.

filled with lime mortar, clearly a Roman addition. Beyond this course the slope is stepped up as in the previously described areas. Trench B[6] is the north end of the long trench dug clear across to the other side of the racecourse and joined with trench A[5].

The last of the open trenches, B[7], on the northwest side in the northeast half of the Stadium, is 86 m. from the open end of the racecourse and only *ca.* 5 m. from the midpoint between the two ends. Here the late disturbances are even more obvious. As in all the trenches, we found the water channel intact here, but the curb has been rebuilt with large blocks, and from it a spur wall juts out at right angles, nearly closing the passage. Another wall, parallel to the first, extends over the channel a little farther toward the southwest. These crosswalls, built of large squared blocks, rest on no solid foundations. The explanation for these late changes must await the final excavation of the Stadium.

On the opposite, southeast flank of the racecourse, the situation is similar, but the original construction is here less well preserved. Our exploration began here in 1960 with a large trench in the very east corner of the Stadium. We encountered some large building blocks at a depth of *ca.* 3 m., and at a depth of nearly seven meters below the modern ground level we reached hardpan, without finding anything *in situ* that could be identified as being part of the Stadium. Later, in our more extensive exploration, we discovered that the stream of water from the gully above the Stadium had formed an outlet there washing away the ancient construction and digging itself down to a level far below that of the Stadium floor.

The following year, 1961, when we returned to the Stadium for further investigation, we opened a larger trench, A[1], farther to the northwest, where we exposed four and a half of the blocks that formed the sill of the starting line. We were prevented from uncovering the whole line by a much-used cart road that forms the only access to an orchard and several grain fields to the east of the Stadium. The accumulation of earth here is slightly less than two meters above the ancient level.

The stone sill of the starting line (Pl. 27, e) is 0.46 m. wide, made with large blocks, *ca.* 1.50 m. long but of slightly varying lengths. The two grooves shown in Plate 60, Section B–B, are V-shaped, but the rear (away from the racecourse) edge is more nearly perpendicular than the front edge. The distance between the two, measured at the bottom, is 0.13 m. Each pair of grooves is *ca.* 1.20 m. long. Post holes, *ca.* 0.07 m. square, with lead lining, are set at intervals of 1.50–1.52 m. The whole line, except the last stone at the southeast end, seems to be in good state of preservation. It can be restored to a length of *ca.* 25.00 m. The exposed lanes, as indicated by the post holes, measure on the average 1.51 m. in width. The sill probably had 16 lanes plus a blind space in the middle. The two grooves partly exposed in trench B[1] at the northwest end of the line indicate that the space at the end, between the statue base and the nearest post hole, was used by runners.

If all the lanes were of equal or nearly equal width, there would be room for 16 lanes and a blind space, 1.48 m. wide, in the middle, but there was probably more irregularity than is indicated by the three completely exposed lanes. This is shown by the situation at the southeast end of the line, where one stone of the sill and the statue base are missing. If we restore a statue base of the same size and in the same relative position as the base at the other end, the combined width of the last two lanes was 2.70 m.; and if the next to the last lane had normal width, the lane close to the base was only *ca.* 1.19 m. wide. This probably was the case. Inasmuch as the statue would have been set back somewhat from the edge of the base, the actual space between the post and the statue would have been nearly the same as in the other lanes. Theoretically then, the starting line may be restored as follows: $(14 \times 1.51) + (2 \times 1.19) + 1.48 = 25.00$ m. Thus the number of lanes was probably intended to be the same as in the first starting gates of the Earlier Stadium,[67] but the lanes in the Later Stadium are *ca.* 0.46 m. wider. The center lane, though nearly of the same width as the others, was probably blind.

---

[67] I believe that ancient stadia were designed to have an even number of lanes, and that normally there would have been a blind lane in the middle. There is clear evidence that this was the case in the first form of the starting line in the Earlier Stadium at Isthmia (above, p. 50), which had 16 lanes and a blind space in the middle. At Olympia there are

One very puzzling feature came to light near the southeast end of the starting line. There is a large block, measuring 1.26 × 0.55 m. in area, set flush against the inner face of the starting line with its top slightly below that of the sill. It has a complicated set of cuttings in the top (Pls. 27, d, 60, Section A–A), and the inner edge of the sill has been roughly cut away opposite the cutting in the stone. It is not clear to me whether this stone is part of the original construction or a later addition, but the latter alternative is the more likely. Nevertheless it fits so neatly against the sill of the starting line that it must have been placed in its present position while the Stadium was in use. For attempted explanation of this stone and the functioning of the starting devices, see Appendix II, pp. 140–142.

In trench A² we found a basin opposite the second basin on the northwest side. The basin in A² is much worn at the top and the outlet at the northeast end has been broken away (Pl. 28, a). A paved walk extended from the rear of the basin toward the spectatory, but the curb is here missing. Where it should have been is a narrow channel cut in the virgin soil; obviously the area has been disturbed. In the next trench, A³, both the channel and curb are preserved, and the passage here measured 1.79 m. in width, slightly more than the width of the channel on the northwest flank at the same distance from the end.

Trenches A⁴ and A⁵ were first dug close together and were then joined after the long trench A⁵–B⁶ had been opened up (Pl. 60, Section through A⁵–B⁶). The water channel and the curb are in place in both trenches, and at the edge of A⁵ a basin and paved walk across the passage were partly exposed (Pl. 28, b). Here too the passage is wider, 1.80 m. as compared with 1.78 m. in trench B⁶. The last trench in the northeast half of the Stadium is A⁶, and there too the original curb and channel are preserved. The passage measures 1.815 m. in width, again slightly more than in the corresponding trench B⁷ on the northwest side, where it is 1.80 m. wide.

Just beyond trenches A⁶ and B⁷ a row of tall cypress trees forming the boundary between two adjoining properties divides the northeast from the southwest half of the Stadium (Pl. 26, a). From there to the southwest end and slightly beyond, the deep soil covering the Stadium supports a grove of mature citrus fruit trees. For this reason we were not able to investigate the closed end of the Stadium as fully as would have been desirable. We dug one pit and short tunnel A⁷, on the southeast flank, at a distance of 150 m. from the starting line (Plan VI, Pl. 61, a). The situation here is very different from that revealed in the other trenches. There is a passage, 1.751 m. wide, with the water channel and a basin in the normal relationship to each other, but from the ends of the basin a seat, 0.38 m. wide and 0.216 m. high above the top of the channel, is set close to the front of the latter. How far it extends toward the northeast and southwest we were not able to discover in the limited confines of the trench. The curb, probably also used as seat, on the other side of the passage is 0.40 m. high above the floor of the passage and 0.35 m. wide. There are two more rows of seats, 0.21 m. and 0.252 m. high, and there may be others at still higher levels. These stone seats are set down on the sloping side with strips of earth separating each row from those above and below. Since no seats of this kind were found in any of the other trenches, it seems most probable that this is a section of special seats of honor, perhaps the Hellanodikeion. Its position, on the right side as one looks toward the open end and *ca.* 32 m. from the finish line, is comparable to that of the Hellanodikeion in the stadium at Olympia, but it is considerably closer to the end of the racecourse. In the Earlier Stadium at Isthmia, as we have seen, there are foundations for two similar features in a comparable relationship to the closed end of the racecourse.

We were successful in locating the two ends of the finish line in trenches A⁸ and B⁸, from which we dug long tunnels in search of the two vital points. All the work here had to be done under extremely difficult circumstances, especially in trench A⁸, where we operated at the end of a curving tunnel 20 m.

---

now 24 lanes in the west line and only 18 in the east. The sills of both lines have been much disturbed; they may have been designed for 20–24 lanes. At Epidauros there are 11 lanes, but there too there seem to have been changes. The second starting line in the Corinthian Agora has footholes for 16 runners and a wide blind spot in the middle. At Priene there were 8 lanes and a wide middle lane, at Miletos 12. It is probably more than a coincidence that in most cases the number of lanes is a multiple of four. Were the races sometimes run in heats of four runners?

from the descent, at a depth of more than 5 m. below the surface in the orchard. At the south corner of the racecourse there has been a certain amount of disturbance of the ancient construction, but we were finally able to expose the end of the finish line, with a small section of a single starting groove, a statue base close to the end of the starting sill, and one end of the adjacent water basin. This was enough to show that the arrangement here was very similar to that at the northwest end of the starting line at the open end of the Stadium (Trench B¹). The stone curb on the outer side of the passage here curves rather more abruptly than at the other end of the Stadium. A narrow water channel coming from the southeast brought water to the first basin at this end.

A very surprising discovery in trench A⁸ is a well-preserved retaining wall of Roman construction standing to a height of 1.487 m. At the top is a profiled coping, shown in Plate 61, b; this will be discussed in our description of trenches B⁸ and A–B. It is important here to observe that the distance from the inner, profiled face of the retaining wall to the inner edge of the water channel that lined the racecourse on the southeast side is *ca.* 6.60 m., more than twice as far as on the other side in trench B⁸.

From trench A⁸ we ran a second tunnel toward the north, and at its inner end at a distance of 5.50 m. from the inner, profiled face of the retaining wall we found a bench, carved in hard limestone, with a back and profiled front, as shown in section, Plate 61, a, right. So far as could be determined in the narrow tunnel, this bench follows the curve of the sphendone, probably abutting against the curb at the foot of the spectatory on both sides of the racecourse.

Trench B⁸ was laid out with the aim of discovering the west corner of the racecourse. At the time of digging, however, we did not know the length of the Stadium, and our trench fell short of the corner by nearly five meters. Later we dug a tunnel in order to reach the northwest end of the finish line. In trench B⁸ we reached the top of the retaining wall 2.25 m. above the floor of the passage. The profile is the same as in trench A⁸, but here the wall is much closer to the edge of the racecourse, its inner face being only *ca.* 2.63 m. from the inner face of the water channel (Pl. 28, c) as compared with 6.60 m. in trench A⁸. The retaining wall, built in two courses with a combined height of 1.50 m., rests on a heavy foundation projecting somewhat from the face of the wall (Pl. 28, e). Both this foundation and the retaining wall itself are quite clearly of Roman construction. And, whereas the face of the wall and probably part of the foundation were meant to be exposed toward the racecourse, on the other side, toward the spectatory, only *ca.* 0.35 m. at the top of the wall was exposed (Pl. 61, a, Section through B⁸). There was probably a diazoma at that height, which is very nearly at the same level as the broad passage observed in trench B⁵.

Before reaching the level of the water channel in trench B⁸, at a height of 0.57 m. above the floor of the passage we came upon a row of cover tiles, running approximately north-south (Pl. 28, c, right). They seem to have served as cover over a conduit in use after the Stadium had been abandoned for its original purpose. At the bottom of the trench at a depth of over five meters below the modern surface, we found the curb and the water channel in perfect condition and apparently undisturbed by later alterations. The passage here measures *ca.* 1.46 m. in width. At the farther end of a tunnel dug along the channel toward the southwest, we exposed a water basin at the end, and, abutting against its southwest end, a rectangular base with a cutting in the top for the plinth of a statue. The top of the base is 0.883 m. above the base at the north corner of the racecourse. A narrow water channel lined with good Greek stucco brought water to the basin. The channel crosses the passage at right angles, then continues under the curb toward the southwest. The northwest end of the finish line is in place, tightly fitted against the southeast side of the base. Nothing here seems disturbed, and the relative positions of the basin, statue base, and end of the finish line are the same as at the north corner of the Stadium. Here, however, we found no trace of a groove for the feet of the athletes, but at the northeast edge of the sill, a short distance from the end of the line, there is a cutting, 0.45 m. long, which resembles the cutting near the southeast end of the starting line, opposite the stone described above on p. 59. The crowded space in the tunnel and imminent danger of a cave-in prevented further investigation in this area.

The large, open trench A–B was dug at the sphendone, most of it to the south of the long axis of the Stadium. In a well dug here more than thirty years ago, the owner of the orchard had come upon some ancient water channels, considerably below the level of the Stadium seats. Our excavations revealed a paved corridor, *ca.* 1.62 m. wide, bordered on one, i.e. the inner, side by the rear face of the Roman retaining wall, and on the other by a second retaining wall 1.17 m. high, at the foot of the spectatory, which here has permanent stone seats. The upper part of the second retaining wall has a delicately carved moulding with a broad fascia at the top above a large cyma recta with plain fillets above and below the kymation (Pl. 61, b, middle profile). A single seat block still in place has its front face recessed below a broad plain fascia (Pl. 61, b, right profile). These mouldings are smoothly carved with an accuracy that contrasts sharply with the carving on the profiled face of the Roman retaining wall (Pl. 61, b, left profile). The difference is so striking that we may with confidence assume that the second, outer retaining wall and the seats are earlier, part of the original Greek construction, and that the inner retaining wall was added during some reconstruction in Roman times. It was probably at that time that a stairway was cut through the Greek retaining wall (Pls. 28, d, 61, b, Section through A–B), facilitating descent from the upper tiers of seats to the corridor. The steps, in any case, are not part of the original construction. The floor of the corridor, paved with poros slabs of different shapes and sizes, is also later than the Greek retaining wall. The corridor decreases gradually in width from 1.72 m. near the main axis of the Stadium to 1.61 m. at its farthest exposed east end, a distance of 7.00 m. The decrease in width of the corridor here is too gradual to account for the unsymmetrical position of the Roman retaining wall, which, as shown above, is nearly four meters closer to the curb at the northwest end of the finish line than at the southeast end. The reason for this anomaly is not apparent. In the original construction the curving retaining wall seems to have been placed symmetrically in relation to the axis of the building.

Extensive remains of Roman reconstruction can be observed a little to the southeast of the main axis. Here, behind the original retaining wall and presumably below the seats of the spectatory there is a fountain (Plan VI), placed off axis and with a slightly different orientation from that of the Stadium. The inside of the reservoir measures 2.20 × 1.70 m. The walls, still standing to a maximum height of 1.60 m., were stuccoed and decorated with paintings of marine life. On each of the two long walls (Pl. 62, a, b) is a single panel within painted frames. The stripes at the top of the paintings run horizontally for a distance of 1.26 m. from the outer corners, i.e. the end farthest from the racecourse; then turn down to form a vertical stripe, 0.46 m. long, which ends at a second horizontal stripe extending to the front, i.e. northeast wall. On both flank walls the top of the panels steps down in this fashion. The reason must be that the top of the walls in the fountain followed the descending tiers of seats, which did not leave room enough in the northeast part for panels of full height.

The water entered the reservoir through a large opening in the rear, southwest wall. Only part of that wall is now preserved, but at the southeast end of a large block, still in place at the northwest end of the wall, the border stripe on the face turns the corner and extends along the edge at the end of the block (Pl. 62, b, left). This shows that it was not a joint but the edge of an opening covered with stucco and at least partly painted. Since the rest of the wall is missing, the size of the opening is unknown, but it must have been at least 0.88 m. high, and probably large enough to permit a man to enter, whenever it became necessary to clean the reservoir. The northeast wall, which had no painting, is in the form of a parapet, 0.55 m. high, with a low "step" on the inside (Pl. 62, b, right, and a, left). This is in line with the Greek retaining wall, here cut down to form the front wall of the fountain over which the water could be reached from the corridor. The parapet is only 0.30 m. thick, and at the bottom is a large hole through which the water issued (Pl. 28, f). Presumably the opening could be regulated so that some of the water would run through a covered channel across the corridor to the basins at the southwest end of the Stadium, while the rest of the water remained and could be drawn from over the parapet in the front wall. An accumulation of building debris, including some large marble blocks, prevented further digging in this area.

The floor of the reservoir is made with small diamond-shaped bricks in a herringbone pattern (Pl. 28, f). In Corinth and elsewhere at Isthmia this kind of flooring is late Roman (e.g., Late Roman Cistern, below, p. 96), and it is likely that the existing floor in the reservoir is later than the paintings on the walls. The walls are built in ashlar style with well-fitted blocks and no mortar in the joints. They are probably from the original Greek construction of the Stadium, in spite of the different orientation of the fountain. A reservoir would have been necessary from the beginning to provide a constant source of water flowing to the basins on the sides of the racecourse. At that time the reservoir would have been concealed beneath the seats in the sphendone, but when it was rebuilt in Roman times it may have been left partly unroofed. The walls would hardly have been decorated with paintings, had the fountain not been accessible to the public. Before the existing plaster of lime was applied, the original Greek stucco would have had to be removed and the underground reservoir would then have been turned into an open air fountain. These tentative conclusions need to be verified by complete excavation of the building.

When first exposed the walls were covered with a very hard lime deposit, some of which was removed with great difficulty. The surface of the plaster has in many places been damaged by the water, and horizontal streaks in the paintings show the level of water standing to the height of the parapet. Above this level the paintings are better preserved.

At the bottom of the walls was a low dado in the color of the stucco, set off from the painted panels by broad (*ca.* 0.032 m.) bands in a deep maroon color (Pl. B). These stripes also run vertically in the corners. On the inside, between the maroon bands and the painted panels, runs a white stripe, *ca.* 0.008 m. wide. The background, in mottled marine green and a somewhat darker bluish green, is a convincing rendering of water in which fish and crustacea are represented swimming. The largest and best preserved panel on the right, northwest wall, shows five marine animals, preserved in whole or in part (Pl. A, top). In the upper left corner is the end of a tail in red, apparently part of a lobster. Next to it is a fish of medium size, rendered in two shades of red, with splashes of white. Although the shape is not exactly right, the color is perhaps sufficiently characteristic to indicate that this is likely to have been meant as a barbouni (red mullet), a great favorite in the Greek fish market. To the right of it is a slightly larger fish painted in light blue and white with back and gills in red. It looks somewhat like a baka-laos, a variety of cod, different from the common cod of the north Atlantic. Below is a smaller, elongated fish, rendered in light blue and yellow, possibly intended as a chilou, a not very common fish of average size. To the left of it is a small lobster or crayfish, of the family of Palinuridae. The upper part of the panel is lost, and at the preserved upper edge is a graffito, –] C Y N K P I T Є C [– – –, with the beginning and the end missing. Unless the word is misspelled, this seems to be a superlative, ἀ] συνκριτέσ [τατος, formed from ἀσύγκριτος (incomparable), in itself a superlative in sense. It was probably preceded by the name of some athlete and scratched by a spectator with fine disregard for grammar or logic, at an exciting exhibition of athletic skill in the Stadium.

Of the panel on the southwest wall (Pl. B) very little remains, but the colors are particularly bright. At the top is a fish headed for the deep. Its back, fin, and edge of the gills are in maroon, like the color of the border; but the body is rendered in light gray, with vertical splashes of red. This may be intended as a steira, a very choice variety of fish seldom seen in the common fish markets. The thin tail of a fish rendered in grayish blue and white is preserved at the lower edge; this may be part of a safridhi, a common spiny fish of medium size.

Not much remains of the painting on the southeast wall (Pl. C), and only in the upper right corner are any figures preserved. The front part of a crayfish can be seen at the upper edge, and a little below it a complete figure, painted like the first described in two shades of red, and probably intended as a barbouni. Below at the right is the upper part of what seems to be a small fish, so nearly obscured as to make identification quite impossible. A large fish, with head pointed downward, is partly preserved at the upper left. It is painted in white with gills outlined in red. This too may be a bakalaos.

The figures of the marine animals are sketchily drawn, and this makes identification very difficult,[68] but the painter seems to have had a sure eye for color. In spite of cursory execution, he has succeeded in conveying a sense of motion and realism. If the parapet in the northeast wall still retains its original height, the painted figures were always above water level and only the figureless lower parts of the panels were submerged. The green and blue on the walls as seen below the surface of the fountain would have lent their own color to the water and created the illusion that the fish were actually swimming in the deep.

The date of the paintings can only be surmised on the basis of the rebuilding of the Stadium in Roman times. During the hundred years between Mummius and Caesar when Corinth was largely unpopulated, the Stadium, like the other buildings at Isthmia, must have fallen into disrepair. We have seen elsewhere that the Sanctuary was not rebuilt till near the middle of the first century after Christ. By the time the Isthmian Games were returned to Corinthian management, the Stadium and the Theater would have headed the list of buildings to be reconstructed. It was probably then that the first rebuilding of the Stadium took place. Among the debris in and near the fountain there are some architectural members of marble, and many small chips from inscribed Ionic architrave and frieze blocks came from the same area. The letters were large, 0.072–0.08 m. high, and all apparently Latin. The only word that can with some probability be restored is some form of the word "sacerdos." Monumental inscriptions in Latin, at Isthmia as in Corinth, are more common prior to the reign of Hadrian than later.[69] To make the Stadium usable for athletic contests, the builders had to restore the waterworks, and it is probable that the remodeling of the original reservoir into an outdoor fountain dates from this reconstruction.

LENGTH OF THE RACECOURSE AND ANCIENT FOOT MEASURES

After this description of the two stadia we can now turn to the problem of the length of the racecourse as determinant of the foot measures involved. The matter has been discussed at greater length in Appendix I of *Isthmia*, I, a brief summary of which is presented here.

Because, according to published accounts, no two stadia had previously been found with racecourses of the same length, it has generally been assumed that the foot measure in use by the ancient architects cannot be deduced from the length of the stadia.[70] This conclusion disregards the fact that the word "stadion" was primarily a measure of length equal to six plethra, 100 fathoms (ὀργυιαί), or 600 feet. The paradox is more apparent than real. The figures given for the length of several stadia are based on calculations. The stadia in Greece with race track of known length are few and these fall into three specific groups. The two stadia at Isthmia provide the key to this very baffling problem.

The length of the racecourse in the Later Stadium, measured from the front edge of the post holes of the starting line at the open end to the middle of the sill of the finish line, is 181.20 m. This is very nearly the same as the length of the present racecourse in the stadium at Epidauros, 181.31 m.[71] From this

---

[68] Colored copies of the paintings from the fountain were examined by the Corinth fish-dealer Constantin Thomas, who kindly offered his opinion about the identifications, which can by no means be considered certain. The names given in the text are of course not scientific terms but names commonly used by Greek fishermen.

[69] *Corinth*, I, iii, pp. 18, 19.

[70] Dinsmoor, *AAG*, pp. 250–251.

[71] The length varies somewhat in the published accounts. Slight discrepancies, amounting to less than an ancient foot, may be due to several causes. The measurements are not always taken at the same point on the starting and finish lines. The two lines are rarely strictly parallel (on the stadium at Epidauros see P. Kavvadias, Τὸ Ἱερὸν τοῦ Ἀσκληπιοῦ ἐν Ἐπιδαύρῳ, pp. 108–109, who found a difference in length of 0.22 m. as measured along the two flanks of the racecourse), and in some places the stones of the two sills may be slightly out of place. Allowance must also be made for minor inaccuracies on the part of the architects, ancient and modern.

length, 181.20 m., we derive a foot length of 0.302 m. The correctness of this foot unit is further corroborated by the width of the lanes, indicated by leaded post holes on the starting line; these measure 1.51 m., exactly five feet of 0.302 m., from axis to axis. This, then, we can confidently accept as the unit of length in use when the Later Stadium was built.

Of the Earlier Stadium only a small part is preserved at the closed end. The open end has been completely destroyed, as shown by the fact that the present ground level in that area is some four meters lower than the level of the track at the closed end. The two starting lines at the closed end are 10.93 m. apart, measured from front to front of the post holes in each starting line. The earlier of the two is the row of sockets for upright posts on the sill in front of the triangular pavement. Thus the original length of the racecourse was shortened by about 34 feet of 0.3204 m. (see below) before the Earlier Stadium was abandoned and the Later Stadium was built. This removal of the Stadium from the immediate vicinity of the Temple of Poseidon to a place outside the sacred enclosure may have been done in connection with Alexander's visit and his plan to make Corinth the capital of the Greek world.[72] If the distance of 10.93 m. is added to the length of the Later Stadium, the total length, 192.13 m., is only 0.15 m. less than the length of the racecourse in the Stadium at Olympia, 192.28 m. The difference is so slight that we may assume that the two stadia originally had the same length, *ca.* 192.20 m. This would make a foot length of 0.3204 m., a unit of measure which can be verified by the length of the stylobate in several Peloponnesian temples.[73]

The stadium at Delphi, rebuilt by Herodes Atticus, has a racecourse of only 177.55 m., which results in a foot length of 0.2959 m.[74] This is the short Ionic foot in common use in Greece during Roman imperial times. The length of the stadium at Athens is unknown, since only one starting line was found. It too was rebuilt by Herodes Atticus, but we do not know whether it was laid out according to the same short foot as at Delphi or to the longer Attic foot of *ca.* 0.326 m., which it presumably had in its earlier reconstruction in the fourth century B.C.

Summarizing the conclusions reached by this study we can now establish five distinct foot lengths: a long, Olympic or Peloponnesian foot of 0.3204 m., derived from the stadium at Olympia and the first phase of the Earlier Stadium at Isthmia; a shortened Hellenistic foot of 0.302 m. used for the second phase of the Earlier Stadium at Isthmia, the Later Stadium at Isthmia, and the stadium at Epidauros; an Ionic-Roman foot of *ca.* 0.296 m. attested by the stadium at Delphi; a longer foot, which might be called the Attic, of *ca.* 0.326 m., deduced from the Perikleian monuments on the Athenian Acropolis; and the very long Philetairan foot of *ca.* 0.35 m. of Asia Minor.[75] There may well have been other standards of measure in use elsewhere, and when more stadia in Greece have been excavated it should be possible to corroborate or modify these conclusions. The importance of our study of the foot length is the inevitable conclusion that the length of the racecourse in the stadia constitutes the most reliable evidence for the different measures of length used in Greece throughout ancient times.

---

[72] The Later Stadium may be part of the extensive building program that resulted in the rebuilding of the Theater (third Greek period) and the establishment of the textile industry on the Rachi; Chrysoula Kardara, *A.J.A.*, LXV, 1961, pp. 261–266. It is tempting to refer these grandiose changes to the time of Alexander, when Isthmia assumed world significance as the intended meeting place of the United World. For a discussion of this event and its effect on the architecture of Corinth see O. Broneer, *Corinth*, I, iv, pp. 98, 157. Carl Roebuck (*Cl. Phil.*, XLIII, 1948, p. 76, note 19) has discussed the chronology and succession of events. The building program probably continued after the death of Alexander. A new impetus would have been given under Demetrios Poliorketes at the end of the century when a short-lived attempt was made to revive the League organized by Philip and Alexander.

[73] For further proof of this calculation see the full discussion in *Isthmia*, I, Appendix I, referred to above.

[74] *Ibid.*, p. 175, notes 5, 7.

[75] *Ibid.*, note 4.

CHRONOLOGY OF THE STADIA

The stadia described above are the only agonistic buildings so far excavated at Isthmia; they range in date from the formative years of the Isthmian Games to their closing in the early Christian era. Comparison between Isthmia and Olympia is particularly instructive in connection with the form and chronology of the stadia. In both places the earliest stadium was partly within the restricted precinct of the major deity; only later, as the purely athletic character of the Games increased in importance at the expense of religious aspects, were the stadia removed from immediate connection with the area and buildings devoted to specifically religious exercises.

How far back we should date the earliest Stadium at Isthmia is largely a matter of conjecture. The complete absence of datable pottery from the stone fill of the spectatory makes it impossible to assign a specific date to the meager remains of the Archaic Stadium. The reorganization of the Games in the 49th Olympiad (584–580 B.C.)[76] is perhaps the most likely upper limit for the building of the Archaic Stadium. As soon as the recurrent performance at Isthmia had evolved from a local or regional gathering of predominantly religious character into a fully organized festival of Panhellenic status, the staging of athletic contests would have required the construction of a race track for the training and performance of the athletes. The archaeological evidence shows that the Sanctuary included a structure of this kind, but gives us no information about its size and appearance or about the length of its existence.

The Earlier Stadium was rebuilt at two different occasions, both probably within the fifth century B.C. The inner of the two parallel walls, constructed as support for the spectatory, overlies the sacrificial area of the archaic period; consequently it would have been put up after the destruction of the Archaic Temple. The enlargement of the Stadium and the construction of the first starting gates may have been undertaken in connection with the rebuilding of the Temple ca. 470–460 B.C., or not much later.[77]

The second or outer of the two walls, which was not continuous, may have been built at different times.[78] It is not clear just what purpose it was intended to serve. When the debris from the fire that damaged the Temple of Poseidon in 390 B.C. was dumped out and the level of the temenos was raised toward the east, the outer face of the second parallel wall was buried to a height above its present preserved top, which is the fourth course from the bottom. The evidence is not sufficient to show whether the triangular pavement together with the sill with starting gates was then covered over and a new starting line laid close to the earlier sill. Whenever the change took place, the racecourse was then shortened by a little more than one meter.

In the more radical alteration of the Earlier Stadium, when a new starting device was made, the racecourse was shortened by about thirty-four ancient feet. The new line, which has a single groove and post holes lined with lead, shows much greater wear than the sill of the earlier starting gates and was probably in use over a long period. Perhaps it goes back to the time of reconstruction following the fire of 390 B.C. It must have continued to function as long as the Earlier Stadium remained in use. This is shown by the fact that the surfacing of the race track covered the other two starting lines. Before the Stadium was abandoned, the sill with leaded post holes and a single groove was partly relaid, and some

---

[76] Julius Solinus (VII, 14) states that the Isthmian Games, which had been interrupted under Kypselos, were restored to their former importance in the forty-ninth Olympiad, i.e. 584–580 B.C. Since the Games were held in even years before the time of Christ, this would presumably mean 582 or 580.

[77] The fill close to the wall produced very few datable sherds, and the Roman building activities in the area—the early Roman temenos wall, the East Stoa, the Southeast Propylon—left little of the fill undisturbed. In 1956 a small fragment of Attic black-figure (IP 1175) was found within the Propylon foundation, below the top of the Stadium retaining wall. This would of course be earlier than the construction of the wall.

[78] Close to the outer wall foundation, at a depth just above the bottom, was found a lamp (IP 3288) of Corinth type VI, dated to about 400 B.C. This may be taken as a *terminus post quem* for the outer wall. Since the debris from the fire of 390 B.C. was packed against the northeast face of the wall, a likely date for the outer wall at this point would be the decade before or the decade after 400 B.C.

of the original lanes, *ca.* 1.60 m. wide, were curtailed and the stones of the sill disarranged. Finally, after the Earlier Stadium proved inadequate and its position unsuitable, the Later Stadium was constructed at a considerable distance from the Temenos of Poseidon. The costly construction of a new Stadium with greatly enlarged space for spectators must have been occasioned by some decisive event in the history of the Isthmian Sanctuary. This may have been the choice of Corinth as the capital of the new world empire created by Alexander. In Corinth as at Olympia, Philip and Alexander inaugurated a building program on a vast scale; the Later Stadium could well be the result of these grandiose schemes by the Macedonian conquerors. After being remodeled, probably in the first century of our era, this building remained in use as long as the Isthmian Games continued to be held.

THE SANCTUARY IN ROMAN TIMES

TEMENOS OF POSEIDON

INTRODUCTORY COMMENTS

The conquest of Corinth by the Romans in 146 B.C. resulted in the devastation and all but total depopulation of the city. The men, at least all of military age, were slain and women and children were sold as slaves. But the buildings were not all destroyed; the temples of the gods were presumably not molested, and the personnel connected with these religious establishments were allowed to continue their services.[1] The Isthmian Games, which were held in conjunction with worship of the gods, were not discontinued; but since Corinth was virtually without inhabitants, they could no longer be managed from that city. The Sikyonians not only assumed management of the Games, but at one time they may actually have transferred them to Sikyon. About 140 years later the Games were administered from Corinth.[2] It is obvious that the Isthmian Sanctuary suffered much during the time that Corinth was very nearly an abandoned city.

How far can we trace the effect of these unhappy events in the material remains of the Isthmian Sanctuary? One unambiguous change, which I have discussed in an earlier connection (above, p. 21), was the removal of the Long Altar and the making of a cartwheel road that crossed the area in front of the Temple of Poseidon.[3] The long and frequent use of the road, as shown by deep wheel ruts in the Altar foundation, is telling testimony to the neglect, if not total disruption, of the cult of Poseidon

---

[1] Strabo, VIII, 6, 23; Pausanias II, 1, 2; 2, 2; VII, 16, 1–10. The history of Corinth is briefly sketched in Harold N. Fowler's introductory chapter in *Corinth*, I, pp. 13–17. A very useful bibliography on Corinth and Isthmia is found in Georges Roux, *Pausanias en Corinthie*, pp. 18–23.

[2] Only Pausanias (II, 2, 2) refers to the fact that the Isthmian Games came under Sikyonian management. He does not say that they were held at Sikyon, but this seems to be a likely inference. Among the agonistic inscriptions collected by Luigi Moretti in *Iscrizioni Agonistici Greci* there are only four that may have a bearing on the problem. His no. 51, pp. 131–138, which he dates *ca.* 135–130 B.C., i.e. a decade or more after the destruction of Corinth, records 36 contests in pankration and wrestling by a certain Menodoros from Athens. The list includes victories at Olympia and Nemea, among many others. Isthmia is conspicuously absent, and the author refers to an article by Sterling Dow (*Hesperia*, IV, 1935, p. 86) in which he suggests that the Isthmian Games may have been temporarily interrupted after 146 B.C. Menodoros nevertheless had the title of periodonikes. Somewhat later, about 100 B.C., Sokrates of Epidauros won nine victories at Epidauros, Nemea, and other sites, but none at the Isthmus (Moretti, p. 140, no. 53). In the first century B.C. a runner by the name of Drakontomenes of Halikarnassos won the "hippic" race for men (ἄνδρας ἵππιος) at the Isthmian Games, but the inscription (Moretti, p. 144, no. 56) does not say specifically that his victory was won at the Isthmus. The games would still be called Isthmian, even if held at Sikyon. The same is true of Philippos, son of Asklepiades (Moretti, p. 149, no. 58) who won an Isthmian victory in boxing about 25 B.C. Not much later a runner from Miletos (Moretti, p. 151, no. 59) won a race in armor in the Isthmian Games. At some time between 7 B.C. and A.D. 3 during the agonothesia of L. Castricius Regulus, the Isthmian Games were returned to Corinth. This follows from an inscription at Corinth in which Castricius is said to have been the first to have staged the games at Isthmia under the administration of the Roman colony of Corinth: *agonothete Isthmion et Caesareon qui Isthmia ad Isthmum egit primus sub curam Col. Laud. Iul. Cor.* The phrase *ad Isthmum*, it seems to me, can only mean that the games had been held elsewhere previously. The inscription is fragmentary, but this part of the text is beyond doubt; *Corinth*, VIII, iii, pp. 70–72, no. 153. To these references should be added a statement by Strabo (VIII, 6, 20, C 378) in which he speaks of the games at Isthmia in a past tense, as if they were no longer held: καὶ ὁ Ἰσθμιακὸς ἀγὼν ἐκεῖ συντελούμενος ὄχλους ἐπήγετο.

[3] Cf. *Isthmia*, I, pp. 98–99.

during those years. The colony named after Julius Caesar *Colonia Laus Julia Corinthiensis* was established in 44 B.C., but the formidable task of repairs and rebuilding took many years to accomplish. The most pressing measures had to do with the reinstatement and functioning of the administrative apparatus of the city. The rebuilding of Isthmia had no priority, and for some forty years after the colony had been planted, the Isthmian Games, including the Caesarea instituted in honor of Julius Caesar, continued to be in Sikyonian hands.

For the first celebration of the Games at Isthmia, the immediate concern would have been the reconditioning of the athletic buildings, in particular the Stadium. That some changes were made in the Later Stadium in Roman times has been pointed out above (pp. 57–61), but without further excavations it is not possible to show at what period each alteration was made. The Temple of Poseidon would also have been repaired; and presumably an altar was erected, or possibly part of the earlier structure remained standing. None of these changes have left any recognizable traces in the existing ruins. It is only in the area and vicinity of the Palaimonion that we can follow to some extent the order of events in the reconditioning of the Sanctuary. There, the first sacrificial pit (A) goes back to the period of Augustus, and the second pit (B) is only a little later. These will be described in the chapter on the Palaimonion (below, pp. 99–112).

LOWER TERRACE WALL

The ground level in the area of the Earlier Stadium had by that time been raised by at least 0.55 m. above the level of the racecourse, but it was still 0.85 m. below the level of the area east of the Temple of Poseidon. The descent from the north was along the line of the ramp that originally led down to the Stadium. To the east of the ramp, the enclosures around pits A and B (below, pp. 100, 101) served as retaining walls, and west of the ramp a broad terrace wall (Plans II, VII, Pl. 29, a) was built with steps leading up to the higher level south of the Temple.

The foundation for this wall is oriented north to south, roughly in line with the columns of the façade in the Temple of Poseidon. It begins 8.10 m. south of the southeast corner of the Temple. At its north end it had steps providing ascent to the higher area toward the west. It is not clear how far south the steps continued; but the foundation at any rate extended farther south than the existing remains of the wall. The line of the wall can be traced for a distance of about 18.00 m. in a shallow bedding in the Stadium floor, indicating that the wall crossed the triangular pavement of the starting line at the starter's pit. The lower of the two steps, preserved to a length of 6.85 m. at the north end of the wall, has a tread of 0.39 m. and a riser of *ca.* 0.18 m. The top, which is weathered along the front part and has traces of a setting line, shows the amount of overlap of the second step block over the first. At one point there is a dowel embedded in lead along the line of the second course. The upper step is 0.33 m. high and the blocks are 1.28 m. wide. The end block, which is re-used, has a cyma reversa at the end (Pl. 29, a, center right). The top of this block shows no weathering or setting line for a third step. It probably marks the original height of the stepped terrace, which at this point is approximately level with the surface to the west of it. Farther south, where the ground level is lower, the foundation of the wall would have reached down to greater depth.

This stepped terrace wall antedates the early Roman temenos wall which extends across it, but it is later than the destruction of the supporting wall along the west side of the ramp leading down to the Earlier Stadium. The lower of the two steps extends over the bottom course in the wall of the ramp (Plan VII, Pl. 29, a). The foundation extended down to the level of the earlier racecourse, which of course had by then been abandoned and covered over with earth.

Although earlier than the Temple of Palaimon, the stepped terrace is most likely of Roman date. It may be approximately contemporary with pits A and B. When the wall was built, the area later occupied by the Palaimonion complex seems to have been unencumbered by buildings or monuments other than the sacrificial pits with their small enclosures. The purpose and nature of construction of the wall south of the steps cannot be determined. It seems to have served chiefly as a formal division of the terrain with steps providing communication from the lower area on the east to the higher level on the west. In the pre-Roman era the "Polygonal Wall" farther west served the same purpose (above, p. 14).

SOUTHEAST HOUSE

Northeast of the Palaimonion a small area has been excavated, extending some ten meters east of the rear wall of the East Stoa and eleven meters south of the Southeast Propylon. This corner was occupied by a house (Plan II, Pl. 29, b), part of which was uncovered in our excavation. The exposed foundations measure 7.92 m. from north to south and 5.80 m. from east to west. Unlike the other Roman structures in the area, the house is not oriented according to the cardinal points of the compass, but rather SSW to NNE. The foundations are slight, only ca. 0.45 m. broad, and constructed with small stones embedded in earth mortar. The walls were built with large stones set at wide intervals and with small, roughly rectangular stones used for the rest of the construction. Walls of two rooms have been laid bare, and others probably exist in the unexcavated area to the south and east. The northernmost of the two rooms measures 3.67 m. from east to west and 3.60 m. from north to south on the inside. The second room farther south measures 3.50 m. from east to west and 3.25 m. from north to south. In the area occupied by this house were found large quantities of painted plaster, mostly red, white, black and green, with lines of brown on a few of the pieces. The fragments of plaster came from some loose debris on which the foundations of the house are bedded; consequently the plaster cannot have come from the walls of the house. In the same layer were found fragments of marble and pieces of stone which have crumbled from heat. The plaster is fairly heavy, having a total thickness of 0.017 m. It is made with a hard lime mortar of coarse substance, covered with a thin coat of stucco on which the colors were applied. The building to which the plaster belongs is not known; the rubble containing plaster fragments was probably dumped in this area at the time of reconstruction of the Sanctuary in the early Roman period.[4] The Southeast House is clearly earlier than the Southeast Propylon, the foundations of which cut into the foundations of the house. Because of its location close to but not within the Temenos of Poseidon, we may conjecture that it served as residence for officials associated with the cult.

FIRST ROMAN TEMENOS OF POSEIDON

TEMENOS WALLS

During the time between Mummius and the first reconstruction under the Romans, considerable damage would have been caused by neglect and decay of monuments in the Sanctuary. Not only was the Long Altar demolished, but the monuments on the north side of the Temple and presumably the East Gateway were pulled down. Many architectural pieces of earlier buildings found their way into the foundations for the earliest of the temenos walls of the Roman era. The sacred precinct of that period was comparatively small. On the north and south sides, the clear space between the Temple foundation and the temenos wall was about nine meters, and in the west it was less, only 8.60 m. At the east end, the distance from the Temple foundation to the east temenos wall is nearly 24 m. (Plans II–IV).

The foundation for the north temenos wall (Pl. 36, d) measures ca. 0.80 m. in width, with some variation. No part of the wall itself has been preserved, but the coping stones, to be described below,

---

[4] Similar fragments of plaster were found in large quantities in the ruins of a building partly uncovered in the 1970 campaign farther east, in the excavations conducted by the University of California at Los Angeles.

indicate a wall thickness of about 0.52 m. On the north face the wall had buttresses at intervals of 6.60–6.85 m. The subfoundation consists of rubble masonry, with stones and tiles and many fragments of architectural members imbedded in lime mortar. The upper part of the foundation, as well as the wall itself, was probably here built with poros blocks, as on the west and south. This is shown by the fact that an open trench now marks the line of the wall. It was found partly filled with loose rubble thrown in after the building blocks had been removed at the time of the general destruction in post-Classical times. In the eastern half of the north wall, where the rock level is high, the foundation trench was sunk down in the hardpan. Here, in most places, not only is the wall missing, but the foundation itself has been largely removed. Had the stones been removed when the temenos was enlarged in the second century after Christ, there would have been a packed floor over the foundation. It is unlikely, however, that any parts of the wall above the foundation remained in place after the enlargement of the temenos in the second century after Christ. Nowhere along the whole length of the first Roman temenos walls are any stones left in place above the ancient ground level. A water pipe (below, p. 91) runs close to the south face of the north foundation (Pl. 36, d), but does not cross it anywhere; this is either contemporary with the wall or later.

Toward the west end of the temenos, close to the large clay pit (below, p. 93), the foundation breaks off and the level surface of the temenos extends clear across the line of the wall. From there to the northwest corner of the temenos, a distance of 24 m., all traces of the north wall have disappeared. The same is true of the north half of the west temenos wall, but there the foundation trench, filled with earth of different consistency, is readily distinguishable from the hard road surface on either side. It is very obvious in this part of the temenos that nothing of the early wall survived in the western part after the reconstruction and enlargement of the temenos in the second century after Christ. When the West Stoa was built, the ground level west of the Temple of Poseidon was raised about 0.25 m. (see elevations in Plan II). The earlier temenos level has been exposed along the north edge; the rest of the foundation trench is buried under the later fill, and a large monument, M[11], was built above the foundation of the temenos wall.

The above description pertains to the northern half of the west temenos wall. Approximately at the axis of the Classical Temple, where the surface of the rock had been cut down prior to the construction of the Archaic Temple, the west temenos wall was laid directly on the rock without foundation. Where the rock surface was lower, a foundation for the wall was made of large, well-cut poros blocks resting on rock or virgin soil. These stones have a setting line for the next course, 0.13–0.20 m. from the east edge of the foundation, and the line continues on the smoothed surface of the rock. There is no corresponding setting line for the rear, west face of the wall; and it is likely that the ground level west of the early Roman temenos was somewhat higher, so that the lower part of the wall would have been partly hidden. The foundation for one buttress is in place; it is 0.76 m. wide and projects 0.50 m. from the rear face of the wall, and there were probably others. In the southwest corner of the temenos the situation is unclear (Pl. 30, a). There is no trace of foundations, either for the south end of the west wall or for the west end of the south wall, and the ground level here is *ca.* 0.75 m. above that of the early Roman temenos. A rough trench cuts across the corner diagonally. This looks as if it had been made for a water channel, but it may have held a slight retaining wall against which the west and south temenos walls abutted. There are some smaller cuttings in the surface of the rock at the higher level south and west of the corner, and it is possible that an area was left unaltered when the temenos wall was built because it contained some altar or other monument that had to be respected.

The temenos south of the Temple (Pl. 30, a) presents an unclear picture. The west end of the wall for a distance of 3.50 m. was omitted for reasons stated above. Farther east, where the foundation for the wall is well preserved for a length of 11.25 m., it consists of large poros blocks of unequal length and varying in width between 0.75 m. and 0.87 m. These are bedded in a trench cut in the rock. In the top of the blocks are pry holes for the setting of the wall blocks in the next course. Farther east, the existing level of the precinct is higher, and here and there the living rock projects to a height well above that of the precinct level at the east and west ends of the temenos (see elevations on Plan II). This higher surface begins 9.00 m. east of the west end of the Temple foundation. This area now retains the approximate level established in the period of the South Stoa, and the hard surface of the temenos extends across the line of the first Roman temenos wall. Where the foundation for this wall would have crossed over Water Channel II (Plans II–IV), which supplied the reservoir in the Earlier Stadium, the foundation of the temenos wall is missing for a distance of 11.00 m.; then, farther east, a stretch of 9.50 m. is preserved. The top of the existing foundation is here *ca.* 0.50 m. below the highest point of the living rock. Here too it is made of large blocks and has buttresses on the south side. The wall would have been removed at the time that the South Stoa was built; this is shown by the fact that the hard-packed ground level of the later temenos extends clear across the foundation trench of the early Roman temenos enclosure. East of the north-south "polygonal" terrace wall (the north-south arm of the upper terrace wall) of earlier times (Plans II–IV), the foundation for the south temenos wall is preserved and continues from there all the way to the east end of the temenos. It is made of large poros blocks, which rest on a sub-foundation of rubble similar to that of the north temenos wall. At the ramp leading down to the Earlier Stadium, the poros foundation ends and only the rubble foundation exists farther east (Pl. 29, a). There are clear traces of eight buttresses spaced at intervals of *ca.* 6.50 m. on the south face, and there were probably five more similarly spaced along the whole length of the wall. At the junction of the south and east walls, the rubble masonry of the foundation is uniform and turns the corner without break, showing that the two walls were laid at the same time. The east temenos wall, of which only the rubble foundation exists, crosses over the inner of the two parallel retaining walls of the Earlier Stadium (Pl. 25, a, lower right). This earlier wall, here preserved in the lowest course, was not cut through by the Roman foundation as was done southeast of the Roman Altar. Foundations for five buttresses are preserved on the east face of the wall (Plan II), and there may have been one more near the south end.

Within the area enclosed by the four temenos walls there is only one foundation for a monument, M[13], a small base at the southeast corner of the Temple, that could have existed in the early Roman period, and in its original use even this is probably earlier. Although the temenos wall had been removed, this restricted area close to the Temple remained unoccupied even after the temenos had been enlarged in the second century of our era.

Nothing but foundations and subfoundations now remain *in situ* of the early Roman temenos wall. The wall itself would have been removed in the second century after Christ, when the temenos was enlarged and stoas were constructed on three sides of the rectangle. Presumably the whole earlier temenos wall was built with poros blocks of large size. This we may conclude from the use of such blocks in parts of the foundation, in the top of which are pry holes for the first course of wall blocks. Many coping blocks (Catalogue, 1–15) have been found in different sections of the temenos, and it is probable that these had been used in the crowning course of the wall (Pl. 63, a, b). The lower part, which is rectangular in section, measures 0.223 m. in height and 0.522 m. in width. Above this part there is a setback on either side, and the upper part, which is 0.44 m. wide at the bottom, is rounded on top. This is slightly more than a semicircle in section. The total height is *ca.* 0.436 m. The length of the blocks varies between 1.388 m. and 0.74 m. There are some slight variations in other dimensions, but it is obvious that all these blocks come from one wall or system of walls. All the blocks are made with an exaggerated anathyrosis at either end (Pl. 29, c). The middle of the joint is gouged out in such a way as to leave a wide opening at the top. This was presumably filled with lime mortar. One block (4, Pl. 63, b) is peculiar in having three such joints, one at either end and one on the side. A block with the same profile would have extended out at right angles to the existing block. Two coping blocks of the same series are built into the north tower (Plan I, 19) of the Northeast Gate in the Fortress.

It would be difficult to find any other place for these coping blocks except on the early Roman temenos wall. The block with a joint on the side (4, Pl. 63, b) cannot have come from a corner, but presumably from a place where the wall was strengthened with a buttress. A short block would have extended from the third joint perpendicularly over the buttress. The areas where the blocks came to light also favor such an explanation. Of eleven blocks that have been found, six came from the south side of the temenos. Four had probably been built into the heavy foundation for the colonnade of the South Stoa, and when this was broken up, the coping blocks were left unused since they could not readily be fitted into a stone wall without recutting. On some of the coping stones the rounded top has, in fact, been squared off for re-use in a wall of stone masonry. Three blocks now lie in the northeast corner of the temenos, where they seem to have been built into the Northeast Gate (below, pp. 75–78). Two came from the northwest corner of the temenos, and four from the vaulted tunnel (below, p. 81). These had probably been intended for use in the massive foundation for the later north temenos wall (below, pp. 82–83) and were later left lying in the tunnel. In any case, the place of finding shows that they are earlier than the later north temenos wall.

At the east end of the temenos, an area 17.50 m. wide from east to west and 35.42 m. long, north to south, was added as a separate enclosure around the Roman Altar. From the southeast corner of the larger quadrangle, the south wall of the extension runs eastward. It does not continue in a straight line with the south temenos wall, but veers slightly to south (Plans II–IV, VII, VIII). Furthermore, the foundation is built in a different style of masonry, with alternating layers of rough stones and lime mortar. This "layer cake" technique (Pl. 30, b) is found only in the extension surrounding the Roman Altar and in the L-shaped wall on the south to be described below.

The foundation for the south wall of the Altar area appears between the two parallel walls of the Earlier Stadium, and the poros blocks in the inner of the two walls have been cut through diagonally by the trench for the Roman foundation (Pl. 25, d, right). The juncture between the south and east walls is missing, but where the east foundation crossed the outer of the two parallel terrace walls, the line of the Roman foundation is shown by a broad diagonal cutting through the two courses (Pl. 25, c). The bottom course was not cut through, however. North of the southeast corner of the Altar area, the foundation of the east wall was sunk to a depth of 2.50 m. below the early Roman ground level. In a deep pit directly east of the Altar, the west face of the wall foundation has been exposed, and here the alternating layers of mortar and stones, four of each, are very clearly indicated. Between this pit and the East Gateway, a stretch of 6.50 m., the line of the east wall is visible at the surface. The upper part of the foundation appears in a trench south of the Gateway (Plan V, Section B–B). North of the East Gateway, a late Roman cistern (below, pp. 96–97) covers the foundation for the east wall. It reappears north of the cistern, but here it does not reach down to solid ground, but rests on earth fill to a depth of about one meter. A parallel foundation here obscures the west face of the east wall foundation. At a distance of 8.40 m. north of the cistern, the east wall of the Altar area made a right angle with the north wall. Here, however, the latter continues westward only for a length of 2.80 m., and is then interrupted by a large block from one of the buttresses for the rear wall of the East Stoa. Somewhere along the line of the Stoa wall, the north wall of the Altar area must have formed a jog (Plans III, IV). From the Stoa wall to the point where it abuts against the early Roman east temenos wall, a length of 13.70 m., the foundation for the north wall of the Altar area is set 0.91 m. farther north. The abutment is formed by a large poros block (Pl. 30, c, right center), lying in its original position in the foundation of the north wall of the Altar area. The block measures 1.50 × 0.67 × 0.43 m., and a circular hole, 0.14 m. in diameter, apparently runs through the length of the block. Because of its small diameter it was possible to clear it only to a length of 0.70 m. from its east end; the west end is blocked by the foundation of the east temenos wall. This tubular opening through the stone is large enough for a small waterpipe.

The construction in the two sets of foundations is very different. All four walls of the first Roman temenos had buttresses at intervals of about seven meters; there are no buttresses in the enclosure around the Roman Altar. Furthermore, the very distinct "layer cake" technique appears only in the latter, whereas foundations below the stone work of the temenos walls appear as a solid mass of rubble construction without striations. This is enough to show that the walls surrounding the Roman Altar were not originally planned as an integral part of the first Roman temenos. The latter was intended to terminate toward the east with the buttressed east wall, *ca.* 6.00 m. west of the Roman Altar. Thus, both the Altar and the walls surrounding it on the south, east, and north would have been added later, though probably not much later. The temenos walls, as has been shown above, were finished with coping stones of which many have been found in various parts of the excavations north and south of the Temple of Poseidon. No such blocks have come to light south and east of the Roman Altar, and it is likely, though not certain, that the walls of the Altar enclosure had no coping of this kind.

Since the Roman Altar is outside the first Roman temenos, it can hardly have existed before the addition was made at the east end. An Altar of Poseidon must have existed elsewhere. The plan may have been to rebuild the Long Altar, and part of it, south of the Hellenistic Road (D), may have been standing and could have been reconstructed. Some of the moulded blocks, which we have found reasons to ascribe conjecturally to the Long Altar, preserve two coats of stucco; the thick layer of plaster in the outer coat is of a kind more characteristic of Roman than of Greek work.[5]

ROMAN ALTAR

The construction of a new Altar of Poseidon probably followed hard upon completion of the first post-destruction temenos wall. After the eastward extension had been made, the original east wall of the temenos no longer served any purpose and must have been wholly or partly removed to provide access from the temple area to the Altar. A great part of this area west of the Altar, where the sacrifices took place, had a pavement of hard-packed earth or macadam, which was at about the same level as the area in front of the Temple. The Altar is located near the southeast corner of the new rectangle at the east end of the temenos. Its foundation (Plan V, Pl. 25, a, upper left), which is made of irregular stones and hard lime mortar, measures approximately ten meters from north to south and 8.20 m. from east to west. On the east side, where the original ground level was low, the foundation reaches a depth of over two meters. At the southeast corner it runs across the outer supporting wall of the Earlier Stadium. Instead of merely pouring the rubble masonry over the retaining wall, the builders cut through the courses and removed the stones of the wall all the way to the bottom (Pl. 25, b). Thus the northwest end of the outer retaining wall was cut off and does not reappear on the west side of the Altar; it must have stopped somewhere within the area now covered by the Altar foundation (above, p. 54). The inner of the two parallel walls, which extended farther toward the northwest, reappears on the west side of the Altar (Pl. 25, a, b). Here again the blocks of the retaining wall were roughly cut away when the Altar foundation was laid. As we have seen above, these retaining walls were similarly cut through by the east and south walls of the Altar Terrace, but not by the buttressed east wall of the temenos.

Of the Altar itself (Plan V) only a single course of large blocks is preserved on the east and west sides and at the south end; at the north end nothing but the concrete foundation remains. At the level of the first course of stones, the Altar measures 7.61 m. from east to west and *ca.* 9.00 m. from north to south. These stones are 0.53 m. high at the southeast corner, but only 0.45 m. at the southwest corner. On the west face, the preserved course also decreases in height toward the north end from 0.45 m. to 0.43 m., and the blocks on the east face show a corresponding decrease in height. The difference is due to the fact that the foundation on which these stones rest was finished with a perceptible downward slope from northwest to southeast. The blocks vary both in length and width. The largest block on the south side is 1.77 m. long and 0.615 m. wide, and one block on the east flank measures 1.95 m. in length. There is a well-marked setting line in the top of the course, 0.45 m. from the outer edge on the east flank and at the south end and 0.435 m. on the west flank. The missing second course set along this line has left impressions on the edges of the concrete core, which extends to a height 0.60 m. above the top of the poros blocks. This core, like the foundation, consists of uncut stones and rubble laid in hard lime mortar.

---

[5] The blocks are described and illustrated in *Isthmia*, I, p. 99, fig. 72.

Built into this masonry are also a number of re-used blocks and fragments. The existing course of stones with the setting line on the top is the bottom step, and there would have been a second step above that. The Altar proper would then have measured *ca.* 4.91 × 7.20 m. in area. No stones have been recognized as coming from the superstructure.

The identification of this foundation as the Roman Altar of Poseidon rests partly upon its location, east of the Temple but off axis toward the south. Had it been placed on axis it would have blocked entrance through the East Gateway, now rebuilt on the earlier foundation. No other structure has been found that could have served as an altar in the Roman period, and the surrounding quadrangle with its hard pavement west of the Altar, i.e. on the side toward the Temple, is a further indication that this was the later Altar of Poseidon. This Altar too was destroyed while the other buildings of the Sanctuary were still standing. Before the East Stoa was constructed, the Altar had been demolished down to its present level. A shallow trench was then cut in the top of the concrete core along the line of the colonnade of the East Stoa (Plan V); and at the north end, where all the blocks have been removed, the foundation for the colonnade extends over the edge of the Altar foundation (Pl. 30, d). This shows that the Altar had been dismantled before the East Stoa was erected. A late water channel which crosses the south end of the Altar foundation cuts through the rubble core and the poros blocks on the east and west flanks. This channel (WCh VI) will be described later (p. 94) in the general description of the waterworks and conduits of Roman times.

No suitable successor for this Altar has been discovered, unless it be the small monument base, M[12], a little to the northwest of the Altar. This base, which measures only 1.60 × 1.25 m. in area, consists of four roughly fitted poros blocks in a single course laid directly on the earth floor of the rectangle without foundation. It seems altogether too small and poorly built for an Altar.

The south and east foundations of the quadrangular precinct enclosing the Altar are clearly distinguished by the "layer cake" technique of construction described above (p. 72). This rectangle is probably not much later than the first Roman temenos wall. From the south end of the Altar Terrace, and 2.20 m. east of the southeast corner of the temenos proper, a heavy wall extends 5.57 m. toward the south, then turns the corner and runs westward for a distance of 3.55 m., and there terminates against the northeast corner of the enclosure surrounding the two smaller sacrificial pits of the Palaimonion (Plans VII, VIII). This L-shaped retaining wall is built with a single course of heavy blocks resting on a "layer cake" foundation similar to that of the Altar area and probably of about the same date. The area to the south and east of this wall would have been at a somewhat lower level than on the west and north. The addition here, outside the space required for the sacrificial rites in front of the Altar, was probably conceived as a formal passage connecting the two cult areas of Poseidon and Palaimon.

EAST GATEWAY, ROMAN RECONSTRUCTION

The main approach to the Temple area was probably from the east both in Greek and Roman times. The original East Gateway (M[17], Plan III, above, pp. 15–16) may have survived the destruction by Mummius in some form or other, but after more than a century of devastation it would have been in need of repairs or rebuilding. That a Gateway existed or was planned to be built in the early Roman era, in the same place as before, is indicated by the position of the Roman Altar so far to the south of the east-west axis of the Temple and temenos of Poseidon. Had the Altar been placed more nearly on the axis, it would have blocked direct passage from the Gateway to the façade of the Temple. In fact the building seems to have undergone two alterations, both of them earlier than the construction of the East Stoa. At first the "layer cake" foundation for the east wall of the rectangle enclosing the Roman Altar was laid with its west face contiguous to the east face of the south wing of the Gateway foundation, its north end abutting on the central part of that foundation. The distinctive type of striated masonry of the wall foundation is particularly prominent here (Plan V, Section B–B, left). Since the same wall continued north of the Gateway, we may assume that the contact of its foundation with the Gateway substructure was similar on the north side, where the construction of the Late Roman cistern has obliterated the abutment.

The Gateway itself was probably rebuilt, this time with an archway over the entrance. Beneath the foundation for the colonnade of the East Stoa, a little to the south of the Roman Altar, was found a well-preserved two-faced voussoir of poros (IA 389, Pl. 64, a) that may have been part of such an arch. It comes from the spring of the arch, as is shown by the angle of the joints, one of which is perpendicular to the vertical edge; the other side makes an acute angle. The two faces are almost identical, with three fasciae surmounted by a projecting moulding which consists of a cyma reversa and a broad fillet at the top. The diameter of the semicircle of the arch would have measured *ca.* 2.87 m., which would fit an opening between walls resting on the outer edges of the central part of the Gateway foundation. The north-south precinct wall would have abutted against the outer faces of the piers supporting the arch at the east end of the two parallel east-west walls of the Gateway. The west façade may have had two columns between antae, as we have assumed to be the case in the pre-Roman Gateway. The sketch plan and elevation shown in Plate 64, b are presented, not as factual restorations, but merely as suggestions for the kind of Gateway that may have existed prior to construction of the Stoas.

At a later period some additional foundations were laid along the south and presumably also on the north flanks of the Gateway. At the southeast corner there is a rubble foundation of small, unshaped stones laid in earth mortar (Pl. 7, b, left). It measures 1.80 m. in length, east to west, and *ca.* 1.20 m. in width. Its west end abuts against the east face of the "layer cake" foundation of the east wall of the Altar area, which in turn abuts against the central part of the foundation for the pre-Roman Gateway. It does not reach down to solid ground, but is only 0.90 m. deep and rests on loose earth fill (Plan V, Section B–B). A corresponding foundation, hardly more than a stone packing, lies west of the Hellenistic foundation and in line with the rubble filling in the southeast corner. It seems unlikely that such unsubstantial foundations were designed to support any part of the stone construction in the Gateway, the major part of which rested on the solid stone masonry of the earlier building. They may be nothing more than stone packings for a broad platform on the two façades of the Roman Gateway.

LATER ROMAN TEMENOS OF POSEIDON

EAST STOA AND THE NORTHEAST GATE

The last enclosure around the Temple of Poseidon is represented by the Stoas, originally planned for all four sides of the temenos. In the course of construction, however, the plan for the North Stoa was discarded and a precinct wall was constructed on the north side of the temenos. The East, West, and South Stoas were apparently completed. Today only the foundations remain, and in many places they too have been largely removed; only some rubble subfoundations or cuttings in the rock are left to show the lines of the Stoa walls. The front foundation for the East Stoa runs parallel to the façade of the Temple of Poseidon at a distance of 31.90 m. The overall depth of the Stoa, from the west face of the front foundation to the east face of the rear foundation, is 7.60 m. The north end of the foundation is in such poor condition that it is impossible to tell whether that part of the Stoa was completely finished (Pl. 31, a). Presumably it was. The foundations extend to a point just north of the east end of the north temenos wall to be described below.

The Northeast Gate (Plans II–IV) is located 12.50 m. south of the north end of the Stoa. Here the rubble foundation for the colonnade is interrupted by a massive stone construction that measures 6.87 m. in length, north to south, built of large poros blocks extending down to bedrock. There were two heavy piers, one on either side of the opening. The north pier is 2.24 m. long, the south pier is 2.14 m. long; both have a thickness of *ca.* 1.24 m. The distance between them, representing the width of the opening through the Gate, is 2.50 m. The Gate is now blocked to a height above the preserved tops of the piers with large poros blocks that are obviously a late addition. The east-west road (H) ran north of the first Roman north temenos wall through this Gate. Where it would have passed through the rear wall of the Stoa, nothing but subfoundations are preserved, but there, too, there must have been a gate corresponding to the West Gate at the other end of the temenos (below, p. 80). The road metal, with a downward slope toward the east, is preserved over part of the area. The road crossed over the east corner of the Northeast Altar Terrace (above, p. 31), and here a water pipe ran along the north side of the road, apparently bringing water into the Roman cistern (Plans II, IV, Pl. 55, a). This road was probably a main thoroughfare which the East Stoa would not have been permitted to block. It is hardly accidental that the outer stairway of the Theater is placed directly opposite the Northeast Gate (Plan I). Through it there was easy communication between the temenos and the Theater, which was functionally part of the cult place of Poseidon.

South of the southern pier of the Northeast Gate, only the rubble foundation for the façade of the East Stoa remains (Pl. 30, c). It extends down to the rock or virgin soil. At a distance of 4.15 m. south of the Gate, the Stoa foundation crosses the early terrace wall (above, p. 17), which was cut through for the later foundation. North of the second Altar of Poseidon, where the foundation reaches a depth of over two meters (Plan V, A–A), it is made largely out of broken-up wall blocks from the Archaic Temple. The builders of the Stoa would have encountered these in the large trench dug for the foundation. The whole area here had been filled up with debris from the Archaic Temple and, at a higher level, from the fire of 390 B.C. (Pl. 31, b). The stones at the bottom of the trench are laid in a rubble construction without the use of mortar, but near the top mortar was used. The foundation for the colonnade extended over the foundation of the Roman Altar, where the step blocks have been removed at the north end (Pl. 30, d), and the concrete core of the Altar has been leveled off along the line of the Stoa foundation. This shows clearly that the Altar had been demolished before the foundations for the Stoa were laid (above, p. 74). The bedding on the Altar foundation is *ca.* 1.00 m. below the stylobate level in the West Stoa, which was probably the same as that for the East and South Stoas. South of the Altar, the Stoa foundation does not extend down to bedrock, but rests on a layer of earth *ca.* 1.50 m. deep. At the very south end, where the East and South Stoas meet (Plan VII), the top of the foundation for the former, for a stretch of 4.00 m., is made with large, roughly hewn blocks laid as headers. The stones are uneven on top, and there are no remains of mortar in the joints.

The foundation for the rear wall of the East Stoa is built in a variety of techniques. Because of the slope of the ground, it starts at a lower level than the foundation for the façade. At the north end, from the northeast corner of the building, as far south as the Northeast Altar Terrace (above, pp. 31–33), on a length of 16 m. not much is left of the rear foundation (Pl. 31, c), which here measures 1.08–1.25 m. in thickness. It is made with small stones and tiles laid in lime mortar. It turned the corner at the north end, but only slight traces of a foundation for the end wall remain (Plan II). There were probably buttresses at the corner, both on the east side and at the north end, but no part of them is preserved. But *ca.* 7.00 m. south of the corner, there is a foundation for a buttress east of the wall. It is 1.10 m. wide and projects 0.95 m. from the rear face of the Stoa foundation.

Along the west face of the rear wall there is an additional foundation, also built of rubble and lime mortar and having a thickness of *ca.* 0.50 m. It extends from the northeast corner of the Stoa southward for a distance of 13.85 m.; farther south it is now missing for a length of 14.00 m. Its construction is much like that of the Stoa foundation and is probably contemporary with it. It is mere strengthening of the rear wall foundation, the eastern portion of which would have been of stones too short to reach across the full thickness. This is shown by a section farther south, where the course of stones is preserved.

Where the rear wall of the East Stoa crossed over the Northeast Altar Terrace, the Stoa foundation has been largely removed over a length of 10.00 m. The destruction probably took place in late Roman times when building blocks from the Altar Terrace were removed. Beginning at the south corner of the Altar Terrace, the Stoa foundation is better preserved. Here, the exposed top is made with large poros blocks arranged as stretchers and resting on a rubble foundation of rough stones laid in lime mortar. For a stretch of 6.00 m. only one course of stones is preserved; beyond that there is a second course where the stones are arranged as headers (Pl. 30, c, lower right). This continues for a length of 6.50 m. to the north edge of the late Roman cistern. The poros blocks, however, are only *ca.* 0.75–1.00 m. long, and an addition was made along the west edge of the poros blocks so as to broaden the foundation to 1.35 m. The buttresses in the rear, here built with large stones resting on rubble foundations, are *ca.* 8.25 m. apart. In a pit dug between the west face of the foundation for the East Gateway and the Stoa foundation, the south face of such a buttress was exposed (Plan V, A–A). The Stoa foundation was removed for a length of 7.75 m. when the late Roman cistern was built. South of the cistern, where the Stoa foundation reaches a depth of 2.50 m., there is a short stretch, *ca.* 3.00 m. long, where the masonry somewhat resembles the "layer cake" technique of the early Roman temenos walls. This may be part of the reconstruction of the East Gateway in the first century after Christ. The west foundation of that structure was later incorporated into the foundation for the rear wall of the East Stoa. The evidence for these changes, however, is not altogether unambiguous.

From the south edge of the cistern, the existing top of the Stoa foundation is approximately level, and it continues so with no interruption to the south end of the Stoa. In some places the rubble masonry extends all the way down to stereo; elsewhere there is only a thin shell of masonry, *ca.* 0.50 m. or less, resting on earth. There were probably twelve buttresses in the rear wall of the East Stoa, nine of which are sufficiently preserved to be shown on the plan. The distances vary between 6.80 m. and 9.00 m. At the south end of the Stoa, i.e. at the juncture of the rear walls of the East and South Stoas, the masonry of the two foundations continues uninterruptedly, showing that the two Stoas were constructed as a unit. The upper part of the foundation between the late Roman cistern and the south end of the East Stoa must have been constructed out of large building blocks resting on the smooth bedding on top of the existing rubble foundation.

SOUTHEAST PROPYLON

In the second Roman period, after the East Gateway had been blocked by the East Stoa and its superstructure demolished, the principal entrance into the temenos was through the Southeast Propylon. The plan shows a rectangular building divided by a north-south crosswall into two sections. The rear, west wall of the Propylon is the same as the rear wall of the East Stoa. Nothing now remains except the foundation; not a single block of the walls is left *in situ*. The building measures 8.40 m. in width from north to south on the foundations, and 10.45 m. in length, measured from the rear foundation of the East Stoa to the east edge of the Propylon. The foundations, which have a thickness of 1.25 m., are very solidly constructed out of small stones laid in hard lime mortar. Everywhere they reach down to virgin soil. They are preserved in places to a height of 1.65 m. They extend across the two parallel terrace walls of the Earlier Stadium, which were cut through and removed to make room for the Propylon (Pl. 31, d). The foundations, as they now exist, were prepared to support a structure of large building blocks. The east foundation, at a level of −2.965 m., is completely smooth on top, and the north and south flanks continue at the same level for a distance of *ca.* 4.00 m. They are then stepped up to a height of *ca.* 0.52 m., approximately the height of a single course of large building blocks. From the jog between the two levels, the two side walls continue at the higher level as far as the crosswall. There they step up again the height of a single course of stones and continue at that level to the rear wall of the East Stoa. The east face of the crosswall is 7.45 m. from the east edge of the Propylon and only 3.10 m. from the rear of the East Stoa. Its foundation is less heavy than the other foundations, measuring only 0.90 m. in thickness. The north and south foundations of the Propylon terminate at two buttresses on the east face of the Stoa foundation (Plans II, VII). The abutments show that the Propylon, or at least its foundations, were constructed after the Stoa foundations had been laid, although the two buildings were probably planned together.

The shape and size of the Propylon foundations permit us to reconstruct a building with four columns on the façade, or possibly with two columns *in antis*. The two flanks were presumably solid walls, each terminating toward the east in an anta. The cross foundation would have supported the doorway, presumably with double doors. There were probably two columns between antae in the rear, supported on the Stoa foundation (Plans III, IV, VIII). Inasmuch as the east foundation of the Propylon is at a level more than 1.50 m. below the floor of the East Stoa, we must assume that there was somewhere a series of steps leading up to the higher level, but no foundation for steps now exists. Presumably the roof over the building was also at two levels, as is indicated in the perspective restoration in Plate 65. From what remains of the Propylon, it is not possible to restore the building in greater detail; we do not even know the order of the columns. In the southwest corner of the Propylon, and hidden beneath the floor, was a distribution basin from which terracotta pipes extend toward the north and east (Pl. 31, d). These will be described in connection with the waterworks of the Roman period.

The Southeast Propylon gave entrance into the East Stoa and, through its colonnade, into the temenos of Poseidon. It was presumably here that Pausanias entered the precinct.[6] The row of statues which he saw along the road from the Stadium to the Temple may have been supported partly on the foundations of the two parallel walls of the Earlier Stadium. These, however, were largely dismantled in early Christian times when the buildings of the Sanctuary were torn down to provide material for the Isthmus fortifications. No foundations or statue bases have been found that can be related to the statuary seen by Pausanias.

SOUTH STOA

The foundation for the South Stoa ties in with that of the East Stoa. This is plainly visible in the unified masonry at the southeast junction of the two buildings. The foundation for the colonnade of the South Stoa shows certain differences in construction. At the east end, the topmost preserved part of the foundation consists of massive blocks, most of them laid as stretchers at the two faces of the foundation, the intervening space being filled with smaller stones, some of which show evidence of re-use (Plan VII, Pl. 32, a). The stones in the two rows are very large, some having a length of well over 2.00 m. and a width of 0.90 m. They are roughly hewn and laid in the foundation very much in the form they had as they came out of the quarry, without being dressed in any way. Where the foundation is uneven at the top, it has been patched out with tiles and small stones in mortar, so as to make a fairly smooth bedding for the course above. This heavy course of stone rests on earth and in some places on a rubble subfoundation. The South Stoa foundation is here *ca.* 2.55 m. thick, which is 1.20 m. more than the thickness of the foundation for the colonnade of the East Stoa at the south end. It is difficult to account for this difference in the foundations of the two buildings in view of the fact that the two are tied in together at the corner and thus formed a single unit. If the East and South Stoas were intended to have the same depth, the north foundation of the South Stoa would project *ca.* 0.65 m. in front and rear of the stylobate. At the east end, the top of the foundation for the South Stoa is now 0.18 m. below that of the foundation for the East Stoa. There is no apparent reason for this difference in level, which would have been evened out in the upper courses. The stylobate, also of poros, was at a level *ca.* 1.45 m. above the surface of the existing foundation.

The broad foundation described above continued westward from the east end of the South Stoa for a distance of at least 25.50 m. and probably as much as 36.50 m., that is, to the northwest end of the Earlier Stadium. A short stretch of the subfoundation, where it crossed over the Stadium floor, was removed in the course of the excavation in order to expose the whole length of the balbides sill (Pl. 22, d). West of the Earlier Stadium, where the level of the foundation trench rises 1.30 m. above the Stadium floor, the Stoa foundation was entirely removed in antiquity for a length of about 35.00 m.; all that remains is a trench cut in rock to a maximum depth of 0.40 m. and a width of only 1.30 m. Since no

[6] Pausanias, II, 1, 7.

rubble foundation is here preserved, it is likely that the building blocks were laid directly on the bottom of the rock-cut trench.

In the western part of the Stoa, for a length of 44.50 m., the lower courses of the foundation remain in their original position, here laid in a trench cut in rock and virgin soil. In the west part of that stretch (Pl. 32, b), the existing foundation forms a series of "piers" that indicate the approximate spacing of the columns in the façade. Between the "piers" nearly all the foundation blocks have been removed. This indicates that the columns were still standing while the foundation blocks in the intercolumnar spaces were removed. On some of the "piers" there is a sinkage in the top, marking the position of the square marble plinth cut out of the same block as the column base. By calculating the average distance between these "piers" we arrive at the axial spacings of 3.37 m. This would allow for 37 columns with 36 axial spaces in the colonnade over a distance of *ca.* 122 m. At the west end of the foundation, at the juncture of the South and West Stoas, the corner block of the foundation is in place, and a single "pier" of the first space is preserved in the foundation for the West Stoa (Pl. 32, c, left of center). Although no exact measurements can be made on the basis of a single intercolumnar space at the corner, the distance indicates that the spacing of the columns was probably the same in the South and West Stoas.

The foundation for the rear wall at the east end of the South Stoa has a thickness of 1.35 m., which is slightly greater than that of the foundation for the rear wall of the East Stoa, here 1.25 m. The two foundations, which are constructed in the same way out of small stones laid in mortar, form a unified whole. On the preserved length between the east end of the South Stoa and the northeast end of the Earlier Stadium, the masonry is comparatively smooth on top, and there the upper portion of the foundation must have been constructed out of building blocks which have been removed. The top of the rubble foundation is here *ca.* 2.50 m. below the stylobate level of the Stoas. Like the rear wall of the East Stoa, the South Stoa foundation has buttresses in the rear, somewhat unevenly spaced, 7.20–7.70 m. apart. These were continued on the walls, above the level of the foundations; this is shown farther west where the wall blocks were laid on solid rock, without foundation. The rear foundation extended clear across the starting line of the Earlier Stadium, where the sills for the balbides were broken up and removed when the Stoa foundation was laid (Pl. 22, d, top). West of the Stadium where the ground level rises more than two meters above that of the racecourse (Plan II), the stone construction rested partly on solid rock. The trench both for the foundation and for the buttresses is shown by cuttings in the rock. At the west end of the Stoa, where the edge of the rock recedes and the crumbly crust of rock was partly cut away, the resulting vertical cutting has been patched out with masonry. Little remains here of the original foundation for the rear wall. Late retaining walls built along the line of the rear wall after the Stoa had been demolished have obscured the earlier construction. At the very west end, however, the rock was solid enough for support of the Stoa masonry (Pl. 32, d, center).

WEST STOA AND THE WEST GATE

North of the "pier" near the south end of the West Stoa, the foundation for the colonnade has been removed for a distance of 25.00 m. It extended over the West Waterworks, which of course had been destroyed and filled up before the West Stoa was built. A big water pipe that ran along the west side of the foundation was still in place (Pl. 33, a); this was removed at the time of the excavation in the area of the West Waterworks. At one point, 4.00 m. north of the West Waterworks, the foundation for the colonnade is preserved for a length of 5.55 m. What remains here is a single course, which is the stylobate itself, made of poros blocks laid as headers (Pls. 11, b, 36, c). They are much worn on top, partly by wheel traffic, and the stones are largely covered with hard road metal. The existing part of the foundation is very nearly opposite the West Gate in the rear wall, but there is no evidence for a gate here in the colonnade analogous to the Northeast Gate in the East Stoa. Here, the ground level east of the colonnade was about the same as within the Stoa, and the road probably passed over the stylobate between two columns. About 7.00 m. north of the preserved length of stylobate, two stones of the Stoa stylobate are left in their original position, forming a "pier" like those in the South Stoa. A marble base of the colonnade with its attached plinth, which now lies on the stylobate (Pl. 34, d), is not *in situ*, but it was found close to the "pier" and had probably stood on it originally. The rubble subfoundation can be followed northward for another 2.50 m., but the original ground level sloped down sharply toward the north, and there are no traces of the Stoa foundation beyond this point.

We return now to the southwest corner, where the rear walls of the South and West Stoas rested on beddings in solid rock, some 2.00 m. above the Stoa floor. The West Stoa has an overall depth of 7.50 m., measured from the west edge of the rear wall to the east edge of the foundation for the colonnade. This is so nearly the same as the depth of the East Stoa that we may assume that the two were designed to have the same depth. The South Stoa seems to have been slightly deeper. For the first 17.40 m. from the southwest corner there was no foundation for the rear wall of the West Stoa, and the wall itself up to a height of 2.00 m. consists of a vertical scarp cut in the rock (Pl. 32, d). Above the rock-cut part there is a horizontal bedding, 0.83 m. wide, for the blocks in the upper part of the wall. In the vertical face of the rock are two rows of small cuttings, *ca.* 0.12×0.12 m. in section and extending into the rock, 0.28 m. or less. The lower row has only three cuttings, *ca.* 0.80 m. above the Stoa floor. The upper row, in which there are six cuttings rather irregularly spaced, is 1.20 m. above the floor. These cuttings may have held brackets to support shelves for storage or display of merchandise. They resemble the kind of cuttings found elsewhere as anchorage for roof beams in lean-to sheds; for such a purpose, however, the cuttings in the wall of the Stoa are too far apart and too close to the floor level.

At a distance of 17.40 m. from the southwest corner, the high rock-cut part of the wall drops down to just above floor level, and from there on northward for a length of 11.80 m., the wall and its foundation were constructed with building blocks (Pl. 33, b, center). Farther north the wall blocks of the Stoa were laid directly on the hard native earth, here consisting of *kymilia*, only a little above the Stoa floor. The rear wall is here only *ca.* 0.65 m. thick, but behind it is a massive foundation of rubble, 2.25 m. broad, built against the rear face of the Stoa (Pl. 33, b). This may have been added at a later period, perhaps as strengthening for the wall after an earthquake. The west wall interrupted the early channel (WCh I) which brought water to the temenos in Greek times (above, p. 26). The channel appears on both sides of the west wall and is again interrupted by the foundation for the colonnade of the West Stoa.

Very nearly on the axis of the Temple of Poseidon, but slightly to the south of it, there was a gate in the rear wall of the Stoa, which appears to have been rebuilt several times (Pl. 33, b). The total width of the doorway was 2.94 m. In this opening now lie some building blocks, which show wheel ruts and marks of the plow on top. These were probably inserted as a late blocking or raising of the doorway similar to that found in the Northeast Gate, permitting wheel traffic to pass through the Gate at a higher level. North of the West Gate, a spur wall juts out toward the west for a distance of 3.10 m. This is made largely of small stones laid in lime mortar, but with larger blocks at the west end. From the west end of the spur wall, another thinner and less solidly built wall runs 5.00 m. toward the west, then turns a right angle and extends two meters north, and there disappears in the unexcavated area. This westward extension probably had no direct connection with the West Gate. From the spur, another solidly built wall extends 1.30 m. toward the south and there ends in a large building block. This short wall is tied in with the masonry of the spur wall in such a way as to indicate that the two were constructed at the same time. There may have been a corresponding spur wall south of the Gate, where the broad, heavy foundation described above ends in a straight line. If this was the case, the two east-west spur walls, together with the north-south crosswall, formed a small court measuring 1.45 m. from east to west and 2.85 m. from north to south, in front of the West Gate. The south spur wall, the existence of which is conjectural, probably did not have a north-south crosswall corresponding to that projecting from the north spur wall. If such a crosswall had existed, it would have closed the

Gate to wheel traffic, leaving only a gap 0.75 m. wide for pedestrians. These walls are all shown in Plan II, but the whole area has been so much altered that the original form of the West Gate is quite uncertain. It may have been a simple doorway as indicated in Plans III and IV. In view of clear traces of wheel traffic, both on the late wall in the Gate itself and on the stylobate of the colonnade, it seems unlikely that the roadway was ever closed to wheel traffic. The road that existed here goes back to a very early period. Only a little farther north, the archaic road, observed at a lower level north of the temenos of Poseidon, passed westward, and this route continued with no great change of level in classical times and throughout the Hellenistic and Roman periods.

The line of the west wall of the Stoa has been exposed north of the West Gate, and at the end of the extant foundation there is a large, carefully finished block, measuring 1.95 m. in length. Its top is approximately level with the Stoa floor (Pl. 33, b, lower left). At the north end of this block there is a cutting for a buttress, 1.20 m. wide and projecting westward 1.24 m. This is the only buttress of the west wall that has left clear traces in the ruins. Beyond this large block, the foundation trench has been uncovered for a distance of 5.00 m., up to the north edge of the excavated area. The hard road metal of the earlier roadways was cut through when the trench for the Stoa foundation was dug. The ground beyond that point sloped rapidly down toward the north, into a deep gully which has now been filled up with earth from the excavations. Thus, the north end of the West Stoa has completely disappeared, and nothing remains to show how the east-west temenos wall on the north side was fitted to the north end of the Stoa.

PROJECTED NORTH STOA AND THE NORTHWEST TUNNEL

The architectural reorganization of the temenos resulted in the construction of stoas on three sides. The plan, which included the addition of a stoa on the north flank, was altered before the foundation was completed. The northwest corner of the temenos is now buried under deep earth fill, so that the west end of the North Stoa foundation has not been exposed. Farther east, however, beginning at the northwest corner of the first Roman temenos, this fill has been removed, and a very heavy foundation, ca. 2.50 m. broad and still preserved in places to a height of over 3.00 m., has been exposed (Plan II). It is this foundation that was intended to carry the colonnade of a stoa facing south toward the Temple. The original ground level here sloped so steeply down toward the north that it was necessary to construct such a very heavy foundation. At the northwest corner of the excavated area, the foundation crosses over the earlier terrace wall described above (p. 9). In order to reach the level of the temenos, the foundation for the façade would have reached a depth of 7.00 m., and the foundation for the rear wall would have started at still greater depth. It was probably the great amount of work and expense connected with this construction that caused the builders to abandon this project, even after a large amount of the work had been done, but other causes may have contributed toward this change of plan.

The planners, realizing that the North Gully in times of rain became a rushing torrent,[7] in order to protect the foundation built a vaulted passage diagonally underneath the Stoa foundation. The two ends of the tunnel have been destroyed, but the vault is still preserved for a length of 14.50 m. (Pls. 33, c, d, 66). The width of the passage at the bottom is 1.20 m., and the height to the top of the vault is 1.92 m. The lower parts of the walls are constructed with large, squared poros blocks. The vault itself is constructed with voussoirs at the two ends, and in the middle it is built with small stones imbedded in a very hard lime mortar. The floor of the tunnel is paved with poros slabs, which had been laid down before the walls were built; this is shown by the fact that some wall blocks rest partly on the floor slabs. Inside the tunnel, at the southwest end, we found five coping blocks (visible in Pl. 33, c) of the kind assigned to the top course of the early Roman temenos wall (11–15, Catalogue, pp. 123–124). Two of the stones are broken, so that originally there may have been only four. Since these blocks would

---

[7] Due to more recent man-made changes in this area, no great amount of water now comes down the gully, the upper end of which has been filled up with earth from our excavations.

not have been brought into the tunnel after its construction, it is clear that this type of coping block is earlier than the tunnel, and consequently, earlier than the projected North Stoa.

The heavy foundation for the colonnade continues from the still unexposed northwest corner of the temenos for a distance of *ca.* 73 m. toward the east, and there comes to an end in an uneven line at the northeast corner of monument M⁵. At that point, a loosely constructed crosswall, which extends northward from the corner of the monument, overlies the east end of the heavy foundation. There is every reason to believe that the Stoa was planned for the whole length of the north flank, but the foundation for the colonnade was not carried eastward beyond that point. In the northeast corner of the temenos there is a light wall, only 0.47 m. thick and preserved for a length of 6.50 m., in line with the south face of the heavy foundation (Plan II). It is of such light construction, however, that it is unlikely to be connected with plans for the North Stoa.

There are less substantial but unmistakable traces also of the foundation for the rear wall of the unfinished North Stoa. At the northwest corner, *ca.* 5.00 m. to the north of the northeast end of the vaulted passage, there is a foundation, 1.20 m. wide and preserved for a length of 3.00 m., built of large poros stones (Plan II, Pl. 34, a). This lies on the north side of the gully. The distance from the north face of this piece of foundation to the south face of the massive foundation for the colonnade is 9.00 m.; this was the overall width planned for the North Stoa at foundation level. The four Stoas were designed to have very nearly the same depth. In line with this piece of foundation and 44.50 m. farther east there is a deep cutting in rock, 1.40 m. wide and 7.00 m. long (Plan II, Pl. 52, a). It is cut down to a maximum depth of 0.77 m. below the rock surface. This is a foundation trench for the rear of the Stoa. The rear wall would have passed so close to the pre-Roman North Propylon that the north corner of the Propylon has been cut back on a bias to make room for the Stoa foundation. At a distance of 14 m. east of the rock-cut bedding there is a stretch of rubble subfoundation approximately in line with the rear wall of the Stoa. This is only 1.00 m. wide and preserved for a length of 4.50 m. Its west end abuts against a somewhat heavier north-south foundation which extends northward from the east end of the unfinished North Stoa foundation for a length of 9.00 m. At the very northeast corner of the temenos, where the rear wall of the East Stoa turns the corner to form the north end, the construction indicates that the North Stoa was planned to form a unit with the East Stoa.

NORTH TEMENOS WALL

After the North Stoa project had been abandoned, a temenos wall was built to form the northern boundary of the temenos. Only its south edge is supported on the north edge of the broad foundation; the north half of the wall rests on loose fill in the rear. The south face of this temenos wall, preserved in places to a height of 0.70 m., is smoothly finished, but the rear face is less even. The ground level was probably somewhat higher on the north side of the wall than within the temenos. The exposed south face of the wall is constructed out of small squared blocks, with the joints smoothly filled with mortar. Since this wall is not built directly on the broad foundation, but rests only on the rear edge of it, it is clear that the foundation was not intended as support for the temenos wall. The thickness of the unused portion of the foundation, measured from its south edge to the south face of the temenos wall, is only a little less than 2.00 m. The top of this part of the foundation is *ca.* 0.25 m. below the level of the Roman temenos (Pl. 34, b).

At the east end, the North Temenos Wall terminates in a large poros block (Pl. 34, c), measuring 0.90 m. in length, 0.75 m. in width, and 0.44 m. in height. Its south face projects 0.07 m. from the face of the rest of the wall. In the rear of the wall, 0.40 m. from the east end of the terminal block, a buttress consisting of a single large stone projects 0.64 m. from the rear face of the larger block. There is a setting line on the south face of the large wall block, in line with the east face of the buttress; this probably marks the actual eastern limit of the wall. The projecting part of the stone east of the setting line forms a terminal buttress of the temenos wall. This comes close to the west façade of the East Stoa.

Neither at the west end nor at the east end are the foundations sufficiently well preserved to show how the North Temenos Wall tied in with the construction of the East and West Stoas, the foundations of which project at the east some eight meters north of the temenos wall.

RESTORATION OF THE STOAS

The construction of the three stoas marks the last major alteration in the architectural ensemble of the Sanctuary. To the same construction program we may attribute the rebuilding of the Palaimonion and the construction of the circular Temple to Palaimon. So far as it is possible to date the buildings, the first half of the second century after Christ seems to be the most likely period. Perhaps the program was initiated under the Emperor Hadrian in whose reign many sanctuaries and cities of Greece were rebuilt. It is unlikely, however, that the whole program was finished during his reign; the major part of the construction may have lasted well into the period of the Antonines. It would then coincide with the last great rebuilding of the Theater which, like the original plan of four stoas, was never carried to completion.

It is not possible to restore the Stoas with certainty in all details. Apart from the scarcity of building material on which to base the restoration, the difficulty is aggravated by the fact that in parts of the temenos the surface before our excavations began was lower than the ancient ground level. In the better preserved West Stoa, and in the western part of the South Stoa where the stylobate is partly preserved, it appears that the stylobate and presumably the floor level of the Stoas were approximately at our zero level, as shown in Plan II. In the eastern part, however, where the foundation for the East Stoa colonnade crossed the concrete foundation of the Roman Altar, the highest preserved level is approximately one meter below that of the Stoa stylobate. The rubble core of the Altar foundation here was visible above the ground when our excavations began. In the southeast corner, at the juncture of the colonnades of the East and South Stoas, the existing foundation is ca. 1.50 m. below stylobate level. At the Northeast Gate, the road level was well over two meters below the stylobate level of the East Stoa. The road here passed through a slype that interrupted the foundation for the Stoa colonnade. In view of the lowering of the ground level at the east end of the temenos since Roman times, so much of the East Stoa has been removed that little remains on which to base a reconstruction. We may safely proceed, however, from the likely assumption that the stylobate level of all three Stoas was the same.

The interaxial spacing of 3.37 m., as explained above (p. 79), can be determined by the extant "piers" at the western end of the South Stoa, although this does not agree with the distribution of the lion's head spouts on the simas. Such spacing allows for thirty-seven columns in the South Stoa and twenty-four in the West Stoa. It is likely, however, that the northernmost column as orginally planned was omitted and its place taken by a massive pier at the west end of the North Temenos Wall. The East Stoa had the same length, or was intended to have the same length, as the West Stoa, but three of the columns were probably omitted where the Northeast Gate interrupted the colonnade. There is no indication how this was handled at the corresponding point in the West Stoa where the stylobate is partly preserved. Although the gate through the rear wall of the West Stoa is preserved at foundation level, there is no foundation of a gateway through the colonnade, the intercolumniation of which was wide enough for cart traffic to pass between two columns. Access to the temenos from the east, on the other hand, where there was a very direct connection with the Theater, could be closed off by a gateway in the colonnade of the East Stoa, but at a level far below that of the stylobate. Since the wagon road was here more than two meters below the Stoa floor level, there were probably some retaining walls on either side of the road, but no foundations for such walls now exist.

What remains of the superstructure of the three Stoas is all from the façade. The stylobate was of poros and without doubt the rear walls were of the same material. A single, almost completely preserved column base (16, Pls. 34, d, 68, a) from the West Stoa indicates a lower diameter of 0.58 m., but this is the diameter not of the shaft itself but of the fillet at the bottom, which was ca. 0.06 m. larger in diameter than the greatest diameter of the shaft above the fillet. There was certainly considerable variation in the diameter of the columns. A small fragment from the lower end of a column (**19**, Pl. 68, b) shows a lower diameter of 0.5972 m. at the fillet, and of the shaft itself, 0.531 m. This piece was found at the corner of the South and West Stoas and could have come from either building. One large piece of a column shaft from the South Stoa (**20**, Pls. 21, c, center, 22, d, upper right) which does not preserve the bottom of the column, shows a diameter of 0.587 m. The existing base and numerous small fragments of column bases from the Stoas are all of white or very light gray marble, contrasting strongly with the color of the marble for the column shafts, which are of variegated marble, having bluish gray, green, and white striations. On three small fragments the diameter from the tops of columns, below the moulding, varied from 0.4871 m. to 0.5049 m., and to that is to be added the moulding at the top, which increases the diameter by 0.01 m. to 0.065 m. This moulding consists of a plain fillet surmounted by an ovolo, but the profile varies no less than the diameter (Pl. 69, b).

The capitals, like the column bases, were of white marble, and these too show considerable variation in design (Pl. 69, a). The largest fragment (**32**, Pl. 35, a) was found not in the excavations but in the debris from the trans-Isthmian wall, more than a mile to the northwest. There can be little doubt, however, that it belongs to the Stoas because at least seven smaller pieces from our excavation show the same design and workmanship and have the same dimensions (Pl. 35, b). The diameter, as indicated by the sinkage at the bottom of the column capital, fits the top of the column shaft. The design of the capital retains the conventional form with three eggs and darts between the volutes, the corner egg being partly covered by the leaves of the corner palmette. Another large fragment (**44**, Pl. 35, c) has the same dimensions, but differs radically in design. Instead of the usual corner palmette with four leaves at the level of the egg and dart moulding, this fragment has two leaves with upturned ends springing from the top of the volute and covering only the upper part of the corner egg and dart. The volutes differ also, not in design but in the form of the central eye, which here is in the same plane as the ridges of the volute, whereas on the other fragments there is a central boss raised above the plane of the rest of the volute. It is conceivable that **44** comes from another building, but because of its dimensions and provenance in the southwest sector of the excavation, it is more likely to have formed part of the colonnade either in the South or the West Stoa. Possibly this shows the form of capital in the East and West Stoas, and the other variety, represented by **32** and many smaller fragments, would then have been used exclusively in the South Stoa. These are mere conjectures which cannot be verified from existing remains (cf. restored capitals, Pl. 69, a).

There are enough pieces, small as they are, from the architrave-frieze to restore the profile with certainty, as shown in Plate 71. The architrave, with a total height of 0.335 m., was divided into three fasciae, increasing in height from the bottom up. The moulding at the top which separates the architrave from the frieze varies in profile from an almost uniform curve (Pl. 71, left) to a more angular design (Pl. 71, right). The frieze, carved in the same block as the architrave, has the usual cyma recta profile below a rather carelessly carved top moulding. The total height of the architrave-frieze blocks is 0.595 m. The dimension has been obtained through a combination of several fragments with overlapping profile.

The cornice and the sima were carved out of a single block, as shown in Plates 35, g, h, 70, a, b. Here too we find considerable variation, both in the size of the dentils and in the carving of the mouldings. The two completely preserved blocks, **55** and **54**, differ in total height as much as 0.017 m. (Pl. 70). The carving is careless and the design of the lion's head spouts in most cases is grotesque (Pl. 35, d–f). A very large number of these lions' heads were found in the areas covered by the Stoas, some in the southwest corner of the Sanctuary, others in the northeast corner. Surprisingly enough, many came from the trenches in the Temple of Poseidon, but their similarity with lion's head spouts found in the Stoas leaves no doubt that they all came from the same buildings. Stylistically the heads fall into two groups, one of which (Pl. 35, e) was found to be chiefly from the southwest area and would thus have come from the South or West Stoa; the others (Pl. 35, d, f), which were concentrated in the northeastern part of the temenos, are likely to have come from the East Stoa. The spouts were spaced approximately 0.69 m. apart, but on one completely preserved block (**55**, Pls. 35, g, 70, a) the distance between two of the heads is 0.58 m. This block seems to have come from the corner between the South and West Stoas, and the contraction here is probably due to its position in the building. The eaves gutter, carved in the top of the sima blocks, is so shallow that only a very small part of the water from the roof could have collected in it and poured out through the lion's head spouts. Furthermore, the channel was not continuous from block to block. This may have been done by design to prevent leakage through the joints of the marble. The roof would have been of terracotta tiles, many pieces of which were found in the debris from the Stoas. They are too small to permit restoration of their dimensions. Presumably there were antefixes and ridge palmettes, but of uncertain design, and these have been omitted in the restored drawing of Plate 72. In Plate 67, an attempt has been made to arrange the extant members of the Stoas according to dimensions and design into two groups assigned to their respective buildings, but the assignation is quite uncertain.

In many details the Stoas show inferior design and workmanship, but the effect of these colonnades on three sides of the temenos would have been very imposing (cf. Pl. 65). The North Stoa was omitted after a massive foundation of great depth had been constructed for the western part of the building. The omission of the Stoa, as suggested above, was probably an economy measure, but it is not unlikely that this barrier on the north side was omitted also in order to prevent obstruction of the view toward the mountains in the north (Pl. 2, a). In any case, after the plan had been curtailed, a temenos wall was constructed along the north side, resting partly on the abandoned foundation of the Stoa and partly on earth. The quadrangular area surrounding the Temple of Poseidon was now effectively separated from the area dedicated to the worship of Palaimon. The ornamental entrance into this quadrangle was at the southeast corner, through an imposing Propylon, and the road to this entranceway led past the Later Stadium, which had also been rebuilt and remodeled in Roman times. The wagon road that passed through the temenos north of the Temple now led through gates in the East and West Stoas.

AREA AROUND THE TEMPLE OF POSEIDON

After the construction of the three Stoas and the north precinct wall, the temenos had assumed the final form that it retained until early Christian times. The space east of the Temple of Poseidon, which was the cult area par excellence, now extended 34.50 m. from the Temple façade to the colonnade of the East Stoa; and its north-south dimension, from the temenos wall in the north to the façade of the South Stoa, measured 69.50 m. The total east-west length of the quadrangle, not including the depth of the Stoas, was 109.80 m. The second Altar of Poseidon, which was in use during the early Roman period, had been demolished and the colonnade of the East Stoa ran over it. The stone and mortar masonry of the inner core is here preserved to an elevation of −1.057 m., which is only slightly higher than the level in front of the Temple. No foundation for a new altar has been discovered. The only monument base in this area, M^{12} (Plan IV, Pl. 31, b), is altogether too small for an altar. It consists of four poros blocks in a single course, resting on earth fill to a depth of 1.45 m. above the hard surface of the archaic period. The base now measures 1.55 m. from north to south and 1.23 m. from east to west. It might have been larger originally, but that is unlikely; in any case, it seems too flimsy a construction for the base of an altar. Another possibility is that an altar was constructed on the foundation of the Long Altar, perhaps at the south end where the foundations have been removed over a length of 12.60 m. (Pl. 65). One other monument that may have been standing in the east area is represented by the small base M^{13}, at the very southeast corner of the Temple of Poseidon. Originally, it had an overall length of ca. 2.00 m. and a width of at least 0.97 m. At some time the top was cut away so as to form a rough basin. Neither the shape nor the purpose of this small monument can be determined.

On the south side of the temenos (Pl. 32, b), the space between the façade of the South Stoa and the south flank of the Temple of Poseidon is 20.50 m. wide. The ramp leading down into the Earlier Stadium and the two north-south retaining walls as well as the foundation of the early Roman temenos wall (Pl. 29, a) now lay buried beneath the ground level established in front of the South Stoa. There are no monument bases on the south side of the Temple of Poseidon that can be assigned to this late period. At a distance of 12.00 m. south of the flank of the Temple of Poseidon and 19.50 m. west of its façade, the highest point of the native rock, +0.45 m., may have projected above the ground level. There is a rough north-south cutting in the rock at this point, which may have been made for the bedding of a monument base of some kind, but no stone of the base itself remains. In the southwestern part of the temenos, the rock projects to a height of +0.355 m. This too may have been partly exposed at the surface of the temenos. There are slight traces of cuttings in the rock surface, and all over are scratches made by the plow so that the earlier cuttings have been largely obliterated. A small vertical cutting 0.23 × 0.19 m. in area extends to a depth of 0.27 m.; this may be an anchorage for a mast.

At the west end, the space between the Temple of Poseidon and the West Stoa façade is 23 m. wide. There is one large monument base, M^{11}, in this area that clearly belongs to the late Roman period. It is situated a little to the north of the axis of the Temple, and its east end overlies the foundation for the early Roman temenos wall. The base, which measures 3.50 m. from north to south and 3.75 m. from east to west, is now preserved to a height ca. 0.35 m. above the rock level, but only a little above the temenos level of the late Roman period. It consists of small stones with many fragments of tiles laid in a matrix of hard lime mortar. The base is large enough and of suitable construction for an altar, but it is unlikely that the Altar of Poseidon was transferred from the east to the west end of the Temple.

Few monuments of late Roman times have left their traces in the area north of the Temple. The clear space of the temenos here measures 24.50 m. in width from the north flank of the Temple to the south face of the temenos wall. In the western part of the area, opposite the opisthodomos of the Temple and 8.20 m. from the north flank, there is a poros base (IA 1365, Plan II) measuring 1.06 × 1.01 × 0.38 m. Both the top and the sides are much weathered and defaced. On the upper surface is a rectangular cutting 0.22 × 0.22 m. in area at the top, but narrowing toward the bottom and extending to a depth of 0.33 m. This base rests partly on the foundation for the early Roman north temenos wall. It has traces of stucco on the east side, and it seems to be a re-used block from the Temple of Poseidon; consequently it would belong to the post-destruction era. At a distance of 6.00 m. east of the poros base and 12.00 m. from the north flank of the Temple, there is a rectangular pit (Plans II, IV), the floor of which is ca. 0.70 m. below the late Roman level of the precinct. The pit measures 3.25 m. from north to south and 4.06 m. from east to west. Its floor is lined with roof tiles which measure 0.60 m. in length and 0.43 m. to 0.46 m. in width. On the walls of the pit are similar roof tiles set on end. When the pit was discovered, it was filled to a height of 0.25 m. with pure clay, and it is obvious that it had been used for dissolving clay for some purpose. Water would have been obtained from a manhole at the southeast corner leading down to a large drain of Roman times, to be described later (p. 95). It is unlikely that the clay had been used for making tiles or pottery, since there is no other evidence for ceramic manufacture in the vicinity; more probably it was used for the making of clay mortar.

Most of the area between the Temple and the North Temenos Wall was occupied in late Roman times by an east-west road, the line of which changed somewhat from time to time (Plan IV). Where the clay pit is located, the road made a slight northward bend to avoid the pit; this would be an indication that the pit was in use at the same time as the road. The Roman road (H), which will be described in a separate chapter (pp. 87–89), nowhere encroached upon the area between the early Roman north temenos wall and the north flank of the Temple. At the west end of the area, the late Roman road made a sharp bend close to the northwest corner of the early Roman temenos, then turned sharply southward and made a wide S-curve toward the West Gate of the Stoa. The fact that the road avoids the area of the early Roman temenos would seem to indicate that the space enclosed by the early Roman temenos wall on the north was still respected even after the wall had been removed and thus continued as an inner sacred precinct after the construction of the Stoas and of the later North Temenos Wall. The evidence is inconclusive however, because here, as everywhere within the temenos, the earth above the temenos level was turned over when the buildings were demolished and the building stones carted off to be used in the Early Christian Fortress. At a distance of 13.85 m. east of the clay pit, there is another rectangular block, M[10], measuring 0.854 × 0.73 m. in area and 0.22 m. in height. It rests on a foundation of smaller stones, showing that it is now lying in its original position. In the top are four small, shallow drill holes *ca.* 0.027 m. in diameter and extending to a depth of only 3 mm. The block probably supported a monument of some kind, but the period of its use is uncertain.

At a point 7.50 m. west of the east end of the temenos, there is an L-shaped structure abutting against the North Temenos Wall (Plan II, Pl. 5, a, upper right). It measures 5.00 m. from north to south and 5.16 m. from east to west. It was probably larger originally, since the west end is roughly broken away. At the southeast corner there seems to have been a solid base, or perhaps a single block, 1.00 × 1.20 m. in area, which is now missing. This base extended into the southeast corner of the structure, and here is preserved an L-shaped block, measuring 0.65 m. from east to west and 0.77 m. from north to south, which would have fitted against the northwest corner of the missing base. The broad foundation for this base, on which the walls also rest, and the massive type of masonry indicate that the building served some important function. The walls are 0.72 m. thick, constructed very much like the North Temenos Wall, but with somewhat larger stones on the outer face. The inner face is also carefully finished, with its joints pointed up with the trowel. Where the east wall abuts against the south face of the Temenos Wall, some stones are missing, and it seems clear that this structure was partly demolished when the North Temenos Wall was built. Presumably it extended farther north, and its north end was removed to clear the space for the later wall. There is no indication how far it extended toward the west in its original period, since no west wall is preserved. At a point 5.80 m. west of the eastern arm of the L-shaped structure, a large building block extends at an acute angle into the North Temenos Wall, which covers part of the block (Plan II). It measures 1.10 × 0.80 m. in area and 0.50 m. in height. In the center of the stone is a rectangular hole, 0.12 × 0.14 m. in area and 0.30 m. deep. Something was inserted in this cutting that presumably served some permanent purpose, since the stone was not removed when the wall was built. It is not clear whether this block had any direct relation to the L-shaped structure, the south arm of which runs parallel to the North Temenos Wall. The east arm is not perpendicular, but forms a slightly acute angle with the south arm. There is nothing to indicate the original form of the L-shaped building nor to suggest what purpose it served. All that we can say for certain is that it is earlier than the North Temenos Wall. Since it was left and is still preserved to a height of 0.50 m. above the temenos level, it probably continued in use after the Temenos Wall had been constructed. Possibly it had served as a pen for animals brought to the Isthmus for sacrifice or for transportation.

ROMAN ROADS

After the three roads (D), (E), and (F) that crossed the Long Altar foundation had been abandoned, probably at the time when the early Roman temenos wall was constructed, the area east of the Long Altar was raised slightly and covered with a layer of tamped earth and stone chips. Within the area enclosed by the early Roman temenos wall, there are no traces of roads other than the pre-Roman roads at the east end that have been described in an earlier chapter (pp. 20–22). After the construction of the temenos wall, all the roads going from east to west seem to have been shifted to the north side of the temenos, that is to say, to the area between the early Roman north temenos wall and the later North Wall constructed partly on the foundation of the projected North Stoa. This area, which at that time was outside the restricted sacred precinct, shows evidence of having been occupied by roads over a long period. Although they shifted lines over a broad terrain, they are in reality one single roadway (H), (I) going from east to west. Before the construction of the East Stoa, the level of this east-west road in the western part of the temenos was about one meter below our zero point, but where it crossed over the Altar Terrace in the northeast corner of the Sanctuary, its level was nearly 2.00 m. lower. In most places the roadbed consists of the rock surface itself, but the hollows are filled with hard road metal. The road ran across the monument bases M^1 and M^5–M^7, in the top of which are well-worn wheel ruts (Pls. 5, a, c, d, 6, a).

After the East Stoa was constructed, the east-west road probably shifted slightly southward and passed through the Northeast Gate (Pl. 31, a), which provided communication with the Theater. The opening in the Gate measures 2.50 m. in width; consequently it had ample room for carts to pass through. There would have been a corresponding opening in the rear wall of the Stoa, but there all the stones have been removed and only subfoundations exist. The Northeast Gate is now blocked by a low wall of late date which shows no marks of wheel traffic at that height. Unless the colonnade of the East Stoa had been demolished by that time so that the wheel traffic passed farther north, we must assume that the road was at a height nearly a meter above the earlier road level. In the eastern part of the area, between the early and late Roman temenos walls, the roads (H), (I) followed approximately the same route, about halfway between the two walls. The road continued with a slight northward bend as far west as the west façade of the Temple. It runs north of the large clay pit, which probably was in existence in late Roman times while the road was in use. To judge by the type of tiles used for the floor and walls, the pit must have been made comparatively early in Roman Imperial times, in any case not later than the second century after Christ.

West of the Temple of Poseidon the road ran approximately 18.00 m. north of the Temple foundation. Here the late Roman roadbed, which was above the dump from the destruction of the Archaic Temple, was partly removed when we excavated the area. A section of the Roman road has been left in place at the west end, and it is here at a level of *ca.* 1.00 m. below our zero level. At the now missing northwest corner of the early Roman temenos, the road again turned southward rather abruptly. It is traceable at various levels, and here, as in the eastern half of the area, the road seems to have wandered over a wide terrain. In the early period, however, before the construction of the West Stoa, it continued its westward course some five meters north of the West Gate. After the construction of the Stoa, it was routed farther south through the Gate. The stylobate of the Stoa has been worn down by wheel traffic, and within the Gate itself and west of the Stoa there are clear traces of the road. The opening of the Gate was more than two meters wide; it probably had the same width as that of the Northeast Gate. In the West Gate, too, the opening was blocked up in later times with a rough wall, the top of which now is scored and worn by wheel traffic. The ancient remains in this area were barely covered by the modern fill, so that the relationship of the road to the gateway and the dating of the road in its several periods become a matter of conjecture.

From this description of the roads along the north side of the Sanctuary we may draw some conclusions about the east-west lines of communication in the Roman era. The arch built into the gate at the northeast corner of the Early Christian Fortress (Plan I) is datable to early Imperial times, and this must mark the line of the main route from Athens to Corinth in use at that period. It is presumably the same road that has left its marks in the area between the early and late Roman temenos walls north of the Temple of Poseidon. To the south of the West Foundation, nearly two miles west of the Sanctuary (below, p. 122), we discovered traces of a road that was in use in late Roman times but may have existed earlier. This was probably the road that connected the Sanctuary of Poseidon and the city of Corinth.

All the roads that we have followed, from the early archaic road at the north edge of the Sanctuary to the late Roman thoroughfare that passed through the Northeast and West Gates, served fundamentally the same purpose, being part of the communication system between Attica and Megara on the east and the Peleponnesos on the west and south. At one time after the abandonment of the Earlier Stadium but before the first Roman reconstruction of the Sanctuary, the road was shifted to the south side of the temenos through the area later occupied by the Palaimonion. The bifurcation of the two roads would have been somewhere to the east of the Sanctuary of Poseidon. During the two centuries after the destruction of Corinth in 146 B.C., the road changed direction again so as to pass along the north-east edge of the spectatory in the Archaic Stadium and then over the foundation of the demolished Long Altar. After the construction of the first Roman temenos, the road was shifted back to the area north of the Temple.

HYDRAULIC WORKS

TERRACOTTA PIPES

The terracotta pipes and water channels[8] that crisscrossed the Sanctuary at all levels are all of Roman times and later. These are described in the following paragraphs. Some are now almost entirely missing, having cracked and disintegrated since the time of excavation. Others that appeared at a high level had to be removed in order to make it possible to excavate the ancient buildings farther down. Most of them were found at the level of the ancient temenos, so near the modern surface that they were easily reached by the plow. Whatever was in place at the time of excavation is recorded in the actual state plan (Plan II); and in the restored plan (Plan IV), most of these, but not all, are again indicated. In some cases where the course of a given conduit is certain, it has been partly restored in the plan.

It is not possible to establish the relative date of all the numerous terracotta pipes, especially those of which only short pieces are preserved; and their absolute dates are even more difficult to determine. The pipes vary considerably in size but are otherwise similar; and since the same forms have been in use down to modern times, before pipes of cement and metal were introduced, the dating of ancient terracotta pipes with no help from stratification is quite impossible. If, however, a given pipe is preserved for a considerable length, its relation to the buildings as well as to the other water pipes in the same area is of paramount importance. The direction in which the water flowed can always be determined by the way the sections of the pipe fit into each other. At the lower end there is a narrow neck that fits into the collar of the next section. The joints are filled with a hard white substance which appears to be pure lime.

Probably the earliest of the water pipes in the western part of the Sanctuary is pipe *a*, which has been exposed at the northwest corner of the foundation for the Temple of Poseidon (Pl. 11, c, upper right). From here it runs northeastward for a distance of 7.00 m., but it does not appear in the excavated area west of the Temple. The sections have an effective length of 0.58–0.60 m.,[9] and the outside diameter measures 0.125 m. What is preserved lies on the hard virgin soil at a level considerably below that of the near-by pipe *c*, which rests on earth, *ca.* 0.10 m. above the surface of the rock.

Close to the southwest corner of the South Stoa two pipes, *b* and *c*, start from the same point and run almost parallel for a short distance. Pipe *b* continues straight north close to the west edge of the foundation for the West Stoa colonnade, while pipe *c* turns northeastward and runs diagonally across the west end of the Sanctuary toward the northwest corner of the Temple foundation. At the point where the two pipes begin (Pl. 36, a), close to the south wall of the South Stoa, there seems to have been a distribution tank or clearing basin. One block remains on the west side, with a heavy incrustation of lime deposit on its east face. Neither the floor nor the other three sides of the basin are preserved; they seem to have been destroyed when pipe *c* was laid. Pipe *b* begins 1.00 m. to the north of the clearing basin, with which it may have originally been connected. It lies at a slightly lower level than *c*

---

[8] In this description of the waterworks, the terracotta conduits that are circular in section are labeled water pipes and designated by the letters of the alphabet on Plan IV. Other conduits, which are approximately rectangular or semicircular in section, whether covered or open, are referred to as water channels and numbered with Roman numerals. Unless otherwise specified, the references are all to Plan IV.

[9] Henceforth, except in certain specific cases, only the effective length of the sections is recorded. The total length includes the narrow neck at the lower end of each section, which fits into the pipe below.

and is doubtless the earlier of the two. It was laid *ca.* 0.30 m. below the floor of the Stoa, and since it runs parallel and very close to the foundation it is not earlier than the Stoa, but may be contemporary with it. The sections are *ca.* 0.40 m. long and the outside diameter is 0.17 m.; but here, as in all the terracotta pipes, the sections vary considerably both in length and diameter. Pipe *b* ran across the West Waterworks at a level 0.70 m. above the floor of the main area (Pl. 33, a). A few sections of the pipe had to be removed when the building was excavated. From the distribution tank at the west end of the South Stoa, where it begins, the pipe can be followed to the north for a distance of 51 m. It has not been completely exposed, but wherever it appears it is well preserved. Where the pipe breaks off at the north end the ground slopes toward the North Gully, and here the foundations of the West Stoa are missing. Pipe *b* probably turned the corner at the north end of the West Stoa colonnade, then extended eastward on the north side of the late Roman North Temenos Wall. At the North Propylon, where a small area has been excavated just north of this wall (Plan II, Pl. 36, b), a terracotta pipe was exposed running parallel to the wall from the west to east. The sections here measure 0.37–0.40 m. in length and *ca.* 0.165 m. in diameter. Since these are the approximate dimensions of pipe *b*, where this runs below the floor of the West Stoa, it is probable that the sections exposed at the North Propylon are parts of the same pipe. Another stretch, 2.50 m. long, appeared 7.00 m. to the east of the North Propylon in the area now covered by the excavation dump (Plan II). At the east end of the north temenos wall this west-to-east line of pipe has again been exposed for a distance of 3.00 m. The sections are here smaller, measuring only 0.32–0.34 m. in length and 0.15 m. in diameter. At the east end of the temenos wall the pipe turns southward (Plan II) in the general direction of the large Roman Northeast Reservoir, into which it probably poured its water.

Pipe *c* is clearly later than the Stoa foundation. Its south end is preserved, and here a short section of smaller diameter was inserted into the first section of normal diameter. A hole was cut in the top of this smaller section and a vertical piece of pipe, still left in place, inserted in the hole (Pl. 36, a). Directly above this point a rubble foundation juts out 0.65 m. beyond the north face of the South Stoa wall at a height of 1.50 m. above the level of the pipes. This foundation, which is only 0.40 m. deep and rests on earth, cannot be part of the construction of the Stoa proper, but must be later. It may have been made as a subfoundation for a later wall, preserved farther east; or, possibly the rear wall of the Stoa was cut through and a stairway made for descent from higher ground on the south. It is unlikely that pipe *c* was in use when this foundation was laid, since the vertical section of the pipe would have been cut off by the foundation. Presumably the vertical piece was laid close to the South Stoa wall, and at a level above the natural rock it would have connected with a horizontal pipe extending through the Stoa wall. It is conceivable that both pipes *b* and *c* were designed to take water collected from the roof in the rear of the Stoa.

It is clear that pipe *b* is earlier than *c* and that it belongs to the period of the clearing basin. At a later period the clearing basin was destroyed and pipe *c* laid at a higher level. Where this pipe extended through the foundation for the columns of the South Stoa, a poros block still *in situ* has been trimmed off at its southeast corner, and a channel was cut through the foundation for the pipe. North of the South Stoa foundation, the line of pipe *c* is preserved for a distance of six meters. The sections of the pipe measure 0.145 m. in diameter on the outside and 0.41 m. in length, including the neck that fits into the collar of the next section. The effective length of the sections varies between 0.34 m. and 0.37 m. From the southwest corner of the temenos, pipe *c* ran northeastward, crossing the early Roman temenos wall (Pl. 36, c). At the point of crossing, the pipe is not preserved, but on the east side of this wall it reappears and continues northeastward, skirting the northwest corner of the Temple (Pl. 11, c). It makes a wide curve, then turns and continues straight eastward, just inside, i.e. on the south side, of the early Roman temenos wall. There the pipe is wider, having an outside diameter of 0.172 m., and the length of the sections is here *ca.* 0.40 m. When the pipe was laid, the line of the north temenos wall was probably visible, since the pipe follows very close to the south edge of the foundation (Pl. 36, d). The wall itself can hardly have been standing. Pipe *c* is preserved to a point 6.00 m. east of the east end of the Temple, but is there made with smaller sections with a diameter of only 0.115–0.135 m. and a length of 0.35–0.38 m. It is clearly later than the two roads crossing the north end of the Long Altar. Somewhere between the north end of the Altar and the Northeast Reservoir, pipe *c* must have crossed over to the north side of the early Roman temenos wall. From the point where it breaks off near the north end of the Altar it cannot be traced with certainty toward the east. The whole area was here turned over and disturbed when the East Stoa was built in Roman times. Another short stretch is preserved 35.00 m. farther east and at a lower level, and here the sections measure *ca.* 0.42 m. in length and 0.16 m. in diameter at the joints. The pipe here crossed the Northeast Altar Terrace diagonally with a perceptible downward slope toward the east (Pl. 55, a). Although the connection is not preserved, it seems likely that this pipe also brought water to the large Roman Northeast Reservoir, which has been partly excavated to the south of the Northeast Cave. Whether the stretch of pipe preserved near the reservoir is actually part of the long west-to-east pipe *c* is a matter of conjecture, but it is probable. The great variation in diameter and length among the sections may be due to the re-use of old material, and may also indicate that the pipe was repaired from time to time and would thus have been in use over a long period.

The two pipes *b* and *c* would have formed the main inflow to the Roman reservoir; and since they came from the same place in the southwest corner of the Sanctuary, it is likely that they tapped the same water source. Pipe *b* may have become irreparably damaged where it crossed the gully at the northwest corner of the Sanctuary, and this would have necessitated the laying of pipe *c*, which for much of its distance ran inside the small, earlier enclosure surrounding the Temple. Thus, the distance was considerably shortened and the pipe could then be laid on firm ground close to the foundation of the temenos wall, where it was less likely to be damaged. At the northeast corner of the Sanctuary, where pipe *b* turns southward, there is a short section of another pipe (shown in Plan II) only 0.13 m. in diameter and made with sections measuring *ca.* 0.40 m. in length. It runs from northwest to southeast and is preserved for a stretch of only *ca.* 1.00 m. This is probably part of an earlier system, the source or destination of which cannot be determined from the scanty remains.

We return to the northwest corner of the Sanctuary. There pipe *d* (Plan IV) runs from north to south for a distance of 9.00 m. The sections are small, *ca.* 0.32 m. in length and 0.12 m. in diameter. This pipe probably crossed the gully at the time when the North Temenos Wall was preserved to its full height and the vaulted tunnel took the water that collected in the stream bed. In a rock-cut channel north of the gully, traces of pipe *d* were found. At its south end it seems to have emptied into the large north drain to be described later. Initially this may have been designed to bring fresh water to the area east of the temenos, but it was later converted into a drainage canal.

In the area between the south flank of the Temple of Poseidon and the South Stoa the modern ground level was only slightly higher than that of ancient times, and in some places the rock projected above the surface of the plowed field. Thus the plow would have caused damage to any terracotta pipes that existed there, and some have doubtless disappeared completely. Here and there over the area were found sections of pipes mixed with the earth, and some pieces are still lying on the surface left in the excavation. It is not always possible to tell whether such fragments now lie in their original position. Where parts of two sections are found with the joint preserved, we may assume that they are *in situ*. Some of the shorter sections of pipes do not merit description, and these are not rendered on the restored Plan IV.

Near the southwest corner of the Temple of Poseidon a stretch of pipe *e*, 8.00 m. long, runs from southeast to northwest. The sections vary in length from 0.31 m. to 0.39 m., and in diameter from 0.145 m. at the south end to 0.11 m. at the north end of the preserved stretch. No part of pipe *e* is preserved south of the early temenos wall. Farther east, pipe *f* runs from west to east along the north face of the early stone curb for a distance of thirteen meters. The sections are 0.39 m. long and 0.11 m. in diameter. In the same area, farther east was revealed pipe *g*, first running southwest to northeast about eight meters, then continuing 33 m. more straight eastward. There are traces of other pipes running approximately from southwest to northeast, and some of them possibly joined pipe g, which runs parallel to the Temple between the curb and peristyle foundation of the Temple. One small pipe, h, appears at the edge of the trench for the early Roman temenos wall a little farther east. It came from the southwest, and then, after crossing the curb it ran west to east, close to pipe g. At one point close to the southeast corner of the Temple, pipe h, which is later than g, crossed over the latter. One pipe, not shown in the plans and preserved only to the extent of two sections, ran from north to south, unlike all the other pipes in this part of the temenos, which run from west to east or southwest to northeast. This north-south pipe may have taken water from the roof of the Temple and emptied it into the extensive west-to-east system of the larger pipes, i–k.

South of the southeast corner of the Poseidon Temple two pipes, i and j, ran approximately from southwest to northeast. These are later than the demolition of the early Roman temenos wall, the foundation of which they crossed over at the ramp of the Earlier Stadium. A little east of the south end of the Long Altar, the two pipes came together and continued toward the northeast as a single conduit. Pipe i is probably earlier and had to be replaced by j. Both i and j are later than pipe k, which ran in somewhat the same direction. Pipe k is partly imbedded in the hard flooring west of the later Altar, where another pipe comes in that may have been a repair of pipe k. It seems to be later than the destruction of the East Stoa. Six meters north of the second Altar, it ran across the foundation for the façade of that building.

In addition to the pipes described above, there were traces of others, too poorly preserved to be entered on the restored Plan IV. Some of these have been rendered on the actual state Plan II. Most of them ran well above the ancient level of the precinct, and probably have no direct connection with the Sanctuary. Their direction from southwest to northeast indicates that they brought water to the fields below the Theater, and there, too, several terracotta pipes were found above the Roman ground level.[10] In the area of the Palaimonion where the fill was deeper, there were many pipes and some water channels at high levels and consequently of late date. Most of these have been removed. Water pipe l ran diagonally over the Temple foundation toward the southeast; then a section of 17 m. was missing, but it reappeared over the south room in the middle compartment of the Palaimonion.

At the east end of the Sanctuaries of Poseidon and Palaimon, three water pipes brought water from south to north. The earliest is pipe n, which dates before the construction of the Southeast Propylon. It is a large pipe, the sections of which measure 0.14–0.16 m. in diameter and 0.395–0.415 m. in length. Its south end was cut off by a projecting corner of the Southeast House. From there it is preserved as far as the south wall of the Southeast Propylon. The foundation for this wall caused the removal of the pipe for a distance of 1.25 m., but on the north side it continues within the Propylon for 3.30 m. more, a total distance of over ten meters. It is thus earlier than both the Southeast House and the Propylon. Pipe m, which was probably intended to replace n, has approximately the same diameter, but most of the sections are slightly shorter. South of the Propylon it is preserved with some interruption for a distance of about 27 m. and is broken off at the south end where it may have connected with a poorly preserved settling basin. At the very southeast corner of the excavated area close to the modern road, a short stretch of a pipe running from west to east has been exposed. Its sections measure ca. 0.40 m. in length and 0.16 m. in diameter. Its west end is broken off. At the east end it turns sharply toward the north but was here cut off by a north-south wall of unknown purpose east of the Palaimonion area. From the sharp curve at the east end it would seem to follow that this pipe is the same as the south-to-north pipe m, which, as will be shown below, is contemporary with the Southeast Propylon. Thus pipe m ran outside the Palaimonion and parallel to its south wall; then at the southeast corner it turned and continued northward outside the east Palaimonion wall. Thus it provides evidence for the continued existence of the early Palaimonion precinct wall after the Propylon was constructed, probably in the second century after Christ. Pipe m goes clear through the south and north concrete foundations

---

[10] Gebhard, *Theater at Isthmia*, pp. 126–127.

for the Southeast Propylon and thus would have been laid when the Propylon was built, since it is embedded in its foundations. Near the southwest corner of the Propylon the pipe runs through a distribution tank (Plan II, Pl. 31, d) cut out of a single poros block. The north-south crosswall overlies the west edge of the tank, which apparently existed before the Propylon was built. The tank measures 0.475 × 0.46 m. in area and 0.37 m. in depth. Perhaps it was intended to serve as a settling basin or to facilitate cleaning of the pipes rather than for the purpose of distribution. Some sections of the pipe have holes cut in the top, which would have been made to help clean out the silt. Although all the terracotta pipes were used as conduits for fresh water rather than for drainage, it is obvious that much trouble was caused by sediment and lime deposit within the pipes. Nearly all the pipes are now completely filled with a fine sand and dried mud. Some of that probably found its way in after the partial destruction of the pipes, but even while these were in use there would have been a considerable amount of sediment.

On the south side of the tank, pipe m entered through a hole cut in the stone, and on the opposite side the pipe has been inserted in a similar hole through which the water flowed toward the north. The two holes cut for the pipe are roughly circular and the sections of the pipe are carefully fitted into these openings. In the east wall of the tank there are two very irregular holes, which do not seem to have been connected with any water pipe. A similar irregular cutting goes through the north wall near the top. North of the tank, pipe m, which ran below the floor of the Propylon and through the foundation for the north wall, had to make a curve to avoid an outcropping piece of rock. It continues northward into the unexcavated ground east of the second Altar of Poseidon. It may have brought water to the large Roman reservoir south of the Northeast Cave or continued down to the Theater area.

A third south-to-north pipe (o, Plan IV) was exposed within the Propylon and to the north of it. It is smaller than the other two; its sections measure only 0.11–0.125 m. in diameter and 0.51–0.53 m. in length. On the south side of the Propylon in the area of the Southeast House, no trace of the pipe has appeared; on the other hand it seems to have been cut through by the north foundation of the Propylon and is thus to be dated before the construction of both these buildings.

One very small pipe, p, runs through the Propylon from west to east. The sections measure only 0.085–0.10 m. in diameter and 0.38–0.40 m. in length. The length of the pipe preserved within the Propylon area is 4.35 m. Of its eleven sections exposed within the Propylon, all but two have holes in the top for cleaning (Pl. 31, d), and the patches over two of these were found in place. Pipe p, which antedates the construction of the Southeast Propylon and was cut off by the east foundation, has lately been exposed for a length of 7.40 m. east of the façade of the Propylon.

WATER CHANNELS

In addition to the terracotta water pipes, which are circular in section, there are a number of conduits more or less rectangular in section, which for the sake of distinction are here called water channels. To this class belong the early cement-lined channels, I–III, that brought water to the temenos of Poseidon and to the Stadium in pre-Roman times. These channels have been described in an earlier chapter, pp. 24–27.

To a later period belong several conduits made of terracotta and shaped like troughs. The sections taper toward the lower end, and at the upper end is a collar where the next tile fits in. Although several of these conduits are of very late date, there are some remains of earlier ones. On the north side of the Temple, west of the large clay pit, one such conduit (Plan IV, WCh IV) brought water from west to east. There are slight traces of this conduit close to, but outside, the northwest corner of the early Roman temenos and a longer stretch, 3.50 m. long, was found just west of the clay pit. The sections are ca. 0.555 m. long, 0.10 m. wide at the upper end and 0.07 m. at the lower end, measured on the inside, and the depth is 0.075 m. At the lower end of each section the sides and bottom are thinner where the two sections overlap. WCh IV was cut off by the northwest corner of the large clay pit and consequently is earlier than the pit. East of the clay pit, WCh IV continues below the macadam floor of the Roman temenos. It shows a considerable decline toward the east at a level which indicates a date prior to the construction of the North Temenos Wall. A short stretch of a conduit running from south to north was encountered in the area of the North Propylon, but at a level well above the existing foundations. Although the connection is not preserved, it seems likely that this is a continuation of WCh IV. It would have been cut off by the construction of the foundation for the unfinished North Stoa and is thus earlier.

A little to the north of the Southeast Propylon, WCh V has been exposed for a length of 5.00 m. The sections are 0.56 m. long, 0.11 m. wide at the upper end, 0.07 m. at the lower end, and 0.07 m. deep. The cover consists of square bricks measuring 0.25 m. on the side. The channel ran west to east, parallel to the north wall of the Propylon, but turned slightly southward at the northeast corner as if to avoid the Propylon foundations. This being the case, WCh V is probably later than the Propylon, but in view of the fact that no part of it has been preserved farther west, it is not clear how it may have connected with any of the existing pipes or water channels in the area.

The best preserved of the channels is WCh VI (Plans II, IV, Pl. 32, b), which runs approximately parallel to the South Stoa, *ca.* 4.00 m. north of the façade. At the west end, where a stretch of 9.00 m. is preserved, the conduit is cut in poros blocks of varying lengths, some of which seem to have been building blocks from the Temple of Poseidon. The channel is *ca.* 0.12 m. wide and 0.10 m. deep and is covered with pieces of tiles laid in lime mortar. It is clearly of very late date and was probably laid after the destruction of the buildings in early Christian times. In a post-destruction building west of the Temple of Poseidon (below, p. 97) are built in at least seven sections taken from WCh VI. Another very late house extending partly over the south foundation of the Temple of Poseidon was constructed partly out of blocks from the channel. About a dozen pieces are here preserved (Pl. 37, c). Thus the channel was destroyed when these two late foundations were laid. As now preserved, only the western part of the channel was cut in poros stone. Beginning at a point 42.50 m. east of the West Stoa façade, WCh VI is made with terracotta sections, 0.79 m. long, laid end to end. The channel itself, which is not rectangular but curvilinear in section, measures 0.075–0.10 m. in width and 0.08 m. in depth. It is covered with pieces of bricks which measured *ca.* 0.30 m. in width and 0.40 m. in length, but most of them are cut in half. They show finger marks on both sides, making an X in the middle. The channel cut through the early north-south "polygonal" terrace wall, and here it veers slightly toward the north. Near the south end of the Long Altar of Poseidon, WCh VI cuts through the foundation for the early Roman temenos wall. Here a clearing basin was constructed, measuring 0.28 × 0.30 m. in area and 0.60 m. in depth. The channel continues eastward for a total length of nearly 100 m. across the excavation, cutting through all the existing foundations, including that of the second Altar of Poseidon. Here a channel was cut through the west and east poros walls and clear through the inner core of concrete; sections of terracotta were then laid in the channel and covered with stones. This shows that WCh VI is post-destruction in date. East of the Altar foundation, where the ground level drops rapidly toward the east, there is no further trace of the channel.

Another late conduit, WCh VII, which has been largely removed, is shown in the actual state Plan II, and in Plate 37, a, left, but not in the restored Plan IV. It ran just below the surface of the plowed field. It first appeared at the northwest end of the Stadium reservoir, and here a short stretch, 10.00 m. long, is still left in place. From there it continued almost due east for a distance of 70 m. and then disappeared into the unexcavated area. Where it crossed the semicircular monument, which we have identified as an ornamental portal into the Palaimonion, a short branch turned southeastward, while the main channel continued eastward as far as the Southeast House at the edge of the unexcavated area. A stretch of 10.00 m. has been left in place at the east end. The top of the channel is here only 0.20 m. below the present surface. A short section of the same channel was found at the retaining walls of the Earlier Stadium and near the modern road, making a total length of *ca.* 95 m. This unnumbered water channel is made with field stones laid in lime mortar and is floored with roof tiles of the kind still used locally. The sections vary considerably in length from 0.44 m. to 0.50 m. The sides of the channel, which are built of small stones, rise to a height of 0.14 m. above the floor of the channel. The width at the top is ca. 0.15 m. Because of its high level and the nature of the construction, it must be very late, probably modern.

The very latest of the conduits, WCh VIII, was found just below the surface, a little to the north of the foundation for the Palaimon Temple; it is shown in Plan II and Plate 37, a, center, but it has not been entered on the restored Plan IV. It was preserved for a distance of 15.00 m.; the rest of it, both to the east and west, had been removed before our excavations began. The section that crossed over the area of the balbides was removed in our excavations.

These very late west to east conduits, probably bringing water from the fountain at the west edge of the modern village, are a direct continuation of the hydraulic works of ancient times which have been described above. Other channels of recent date and still in use run along the modern road, bringing water from wells west of the village to orchards in the vicinity of the Later Stadium and the housing development of the Corinth Canal Company in the village of Isthmia. The many conduits that cross the excavations from west to east and the reservoirs constructed to collect ground water show that the water problem was always very important at Isthmia. They were probably intended primarily to serve the needs of the large crowds of visitors with their beasts of burden attending the Isthmian Games. But the water may have been used also for irrigation, as it is at the present time.

NORTHEAST RESERVOIR (ROMAN CISTERN)

The Northeast Reservoir (Pl. 55, a) is located ca. 3.00 m. east of the east corner of the Northeast Altar Terrace, and 5.00 m. south of the stairway to the east chamber of the Northeast Cave. The preserved top is approximately level with the area originally occupied by the entrance courts in front of the cave. When the reservoir was made, the area of the courts was partly cut away. Only parts of the north and west walls of the reservoir have been exposed; the rest is still buried under late Roman fill. Although the west wall has not been fully exposed, its south end was reached through a tunnel at a distance of 5.57 m. from the north end. The east-west dimension is well over six meters, but the fill in that part was too loose for tunneling, and this made it impossible to obtain exact measurements. The preserved depth of the reservoir is 2.70 m. The west wall is standing to a height of 1.60 m. The lower part up to a height of 1.15 m. is made with bricks, and the upper section is built with large poros stones. The north wall is preserved still higher, to a total height of 2.60 m. The vault, only a small part of which is preserved on the north side, was also made with brick and rubble masonry, and some of the fallen vault now lies on the floor. The vault begins at a height of 2.40 m., and the north wall is stuccoed up to that height; the vault itself was not stuccoed on the underside. The floor is made with a hard cement. The reservoir probably remained in use throughout the Roman period. It was found filled to the top with building debris of late Roman times, dating from the time of the destruction of the Sanctuary.

GREAT NORTH DRAIN

North of the early Roman temenos wall and at a distance of 10.00–11.00 m. to the north of the Temple of Poseidon, there is a large underground drain, reached through several manholes (Plans II, IV). The first manhole from the west is located 15.50 m. northwest of the northwest corner of the Temple foundation. The mouth was blocked with two large building stones projecting 0.35 m. above the level of the road; this is an indication that the manhole and the channel had been in use after the road had been abandoned or had perhaps only been diverted slightly toward the north. At a depth of a little over 1.00 m. below the road level, terracotta water pipe d (above, p. 91) entered the manhole. This is rectangular in section, measuring 0.90 × 0.41 m. It is built of squared blocks to a depth of 2.50 m.; below

that depth it is oval and cut in the hard native marl. It extends down to a depth of 8.60 m. From th
first manhole the channel runs westward for a distance of 1.40 m., then stops abruptly. Here it measure
0.70 m. in width at the bottom and 1.85 m. in height. Neither the manhole nor the drainage channel a
this point contained much pottery, and the few sherds found in it indicate a date in the late Roma
period.

East of the first manhole the drain continues eastward 30 m. to a second manhole, which is circula
in section. It is located at the southeast corner of the clay pit, 1.50 m. north of the foundation for th
early Roman north temenos wall. The third manhole is 29.60 m. east of the second one and 61 m. fron
the west end of the passage. The mouth was found covered with re-used blocks, including one larg
piece of a lion's head spout from the roof of the Temple of Poseidon. The shaft was empty to a dept
of 6.85 m., almost to the top of the channel, the floor of which is here 8.40 m. below the level of th
temenos. The channel here measures 0.50 m. in width and 1.50 m. in height; it has been cleared to th
bottom for only about 1.00 m. to the east and west. The fill, consisting mainly of dried mud, contained
three Roman bricks with grooves in the top, two diagonal and one parallel to the sides of the brick
These are of a type usually broken in two and encountered in late Roman wall building and as cover
for water channels. At the bottom of the large drain is a tiled water channel, 0.20 m. wide and 0.10 m
deep. The fourth manhole is 30 m. farther east and only 2.00 m. west of the northeast corner of the earl
Roman temenos. It was found covered over with two large poros blocks (Plan IV). Here the depth to th
bottom of the drain is 8.40 m. The tiled channel at the bottom is 0.24 m. wide and 0.115 m. deep belov
the floor of the rock-cut channel. From the fourth manhole the channel continues almost due east fo
a distance of 16.70 m., then turns *ca.* 30⁰ to the south and continues 18.50 m. to a fifth manhole which
is also covered with two large stone blocks visible from below. Some 10.00 m. beyond this point th
roof is caved in, and it proved impossible to penetrate farther without digging down from above. Eas
of the fourth manhole the channel has not been entered on Plans II and IV.

Whatever was the original date of the channel, the fill shows that it continued in use until late Roman
times and probably until the destruction of the buildings in the early Christian era. At that late date
the channel must have been in use as a drain to carry off rain water that had collected in the temenos
north of the Temple. Originally, however, it seems to have been designed as a water conduit; this is
indicated by the brick-lined smaller channel at the bottom of the rock-cut tunnel. The fact that water
pipe *d* emptied its contents into the channel at the first manhole is a further indication that it was no
originally intended for drainage.

POST-DESTRUCTION BUILDINGS

Late Roman Cistern

North of the foundation for the East Gateway and partly resting upon that foundation is a late
Roman cistern (Plan V, Pl. 37, b) with an inside measurement of 5.96 m. from north to south and
slightly over 5.00 m. from east to west. The whole east end has been destroyed so that the east line o
the floor cannot be measured accurately. The walls are heavy, *ca.* 0.85 m. thick, and made of stone
laid in a hard lime mortar. On the inside the walls are plastered with a thick, watertight stucco, and th
floor is made with small diamond-shaped bricks in a herringbone pattern. There is a raised cushion o
hard cement added at the bottom to prevent leakage along the edges. The floor is heavily incruste
with lime. The cistern is clearly later than the destruction of the East Stoa. The foundation for the rea
wall of the Stoa was partly removed before the cistern was built. Furthermore, the northwest corner o
the cistern cuts into the line of the Stoa foundation, and the orientation is somewhat different from tha
of the Stoa. The floor of the cistern was at a level at least 1.60 m. below that of the East Stoa. The
brick flooring is of a kind in common use in Corinth as late as the fourth and fifth centuries after Christ
and it is to that general period that the cistern must be dated.

HOUSE AT THE SOUTHEAST CORNER OF THE POSEIDON TEMPLE

One small house built after the destruction of the Temple of Poseidon was found at the south edge of the Temple foundation, 17 m. from its east end (Pl. 37, c). Its scanty remains were removed when the Temple was excavated; now only a cutting in stereo marks its location. The building was not oriented like the Temple, but more nearly northeast to southwest. The overall dimensions of the house were *ca.* 4.60 × 3.24 m. The walls consisted largely of re-used blocks resting partly on stereo and partly on the rubble from the demolished Temple. The southeast wall, which rested entirely on rubble fill from the Temple foundation, was made largely out of poros blocks from WCh VI. The highest preserved part of the house was on the northwest side, where the wall had a height of 0.81 m. Two blocks built into this structure are from the corner block of the geison of the Temple of Poseidon,[11] and other fragments likewise came from the Temple. The doorway was probably in the northeast wall, where the foundation was missing for a stretch of nearly 2.00 m. The earth floor sloped slightly down from north to south. In the north corner was a fireplace containing ashes, surrounded by stone slabs set on end. Close to the northwest wall and equidistant from the two ends of the room was a small bin made with stones set on edge. Near the bin lay half a millstone. The fireplace and the bin indicate that the house had been used for living quarters, but its haphazard construction shows that it was probably intended for temporary use, perhaps by the workmen demolishing the buildings of the Sanctuary and carting materials to the Fortress and the Isthmian wall.

WEST HOUSE

Some nine meters west of the southwest corner of the Temple of Poseidon is a small structure (Plan II, Pl. 30, a, center) measuring 3.84 m. from southeast to northwest and 3.47 m. from northeast to southwest on the inside. The walls are made of poros blocks of various sizes, many of them taken from a water channel similar to WCh VI still preserved in front of the South Stoa (above, p. 94). There seems to have been an opening 0.96 m. wide for the door in the southwest wall of the house. The walls are too thin and poorly constructed to have supported a proper roof, and it is quite possible that both this tiny hut and the small house built over the debris from the demolished south foundation of the Temple of Poseidon are temporary shelters hastily constructed for the wrecking crew.

SOUTHWEST HOUSE

South of the building just described there is a slightly better constructed building (Pl. 32, b, top center), measuring 7.00 m. from east to west and 5.65 m. from north to south on the outside. The walls, which are 0.58–0.70 m. thick, are made of coarse field stones and re-used blocks laid in earth mortar, with many marble fragments from the ancient buildings built into the masonry. The latter include recognizable fragments from the Temple of Poseidon; others probably came from the demolished South Stoa. Since the building is wholly within the area of the Stoa, it is obviously later than the destruction of the Sanctuary. Built against the east wall of the room is a small cubicle with an inside measurement 1.37 m. square. The walls are all smooth on the inside and quite rough on the outside. When this small structure was built, the floor level of the larger room was about 0.75 m. above the floor of the Stoa. The walls are constructed much like those of the larger room with small stones, here, however, laid in a hard lime mortar. The same type of mortar is also used at the northeast corner in the east and north walls of the large room. Possibly part of the outside walls were rebuilt in more permanent technique when the cubicle was constructed against the east wall. East of the east wall of the house and running parallel to it is a second north-to-south wall. The space between the two walls is only 0.80–0.90 m. The east wall is built with much larger blocks, re-used from the demolished ancient buildings, and here, too, several fragments of marble have been built in. This wall perhaps served as a retaining wall for a higher area to the east; since it does not tie in to any other wall, it does not form part of a building. West of the

[11] *Isthmia*, I, p. 130, fig. 123, p. 135, pl. 22, e.

Southwest House there is a very rough east-to-west wall *ca.* 6.00 m. long and constructed largely out of marble blocks. This seems to be a retaining wall built after the south wall of the South Stoa had been demolished. Among the marble blocks in this wall are many fragments of columns and cornices from the Roman Stoa.

Northwest Structure

In the northwest corner of the temenos, only 3.50 m. north of the Temple foundations, there are two very rough walls forming an L-shaped structure (Plan II), which is certainly later than the destruction of the classical buildings. The walls are thin, only *ca.* 0.45 m. thick. The north-south wall is preserved for a length of 2.40 m. and the east-west wall is 1.75 m. long. The walls, made of medium sized stones laid in a mortar of earth, rest directly on the temenos floor, without foundations. A small Doric capital of a late, debased design was found close to the east-west wall.

PALAIMONION

INTRODUCTORY COMMENTS

One of the few buildings at Isthmia mentioned by Pausanias is the Temple of Palaimon, which he saw "Within the peribolos on the left."[1] He entered the Sanctuary from the Stadium, presumably through the Southeast Propylon and, after a description of the Temple of Poseidon and its statuary, he proceeded to the Palaimonion. There he saw within the Temple statues of Poseidon, Leukothea, and of Palaimon himself, but he gives no further description of the building. His attention was drawn to an underground structure, the Adyton, in which oaths were administered. His description of the Palaimonion is so imprecise that scholars have assumed that the Adyton was a building separate from the Temple.[2]

The general location of the precinct of Palaimon became clear as soon as we had discovered the Temple and temenos of Poseidon. Guided by Pausanias' account, we dug a trial trench in the area, but what we first encountered was the triangular pavement of the Earlier Stadium with its puzzling starting pit and radiating grooves (above, pp. 47–55). Above the stone pavement we came upon a roughly square foundation of Roman concrete with very little of the outer shell of poros stones left in place. We had expected to find a very ancient cult place of Palaimon;[3] the findings in our trenches did not fit this conception of the shrine. It was only later that we realized how wrong these preconceived ideas had been; all the material remains of the Palaimonion turned out to be of Roman date. Moreover, all the references to the cult of Melikertes-Palaimon at Isthmia are from writers, Latin and Greek, of Roman imperial times.[4]

It would doubtless be wrong to infer from the late date of the evidence that no cult of Palaimon had existed at Isthmia prior to the Roman era. The cult of the hero would not have originated at so late a date. Mythology ascribes the origin of the worship of Melikertes-Palaimon to Sisyphos, whose statue was later erected in the Palaimonion (the base supporting the statue of Sisyphos can be seen in Pls. 22, d, 23, c). Somewhere in the area of the Earlier Stadium there was probably an earlier cult place, consisting perhaps only of an altar or a minor monument marking the traditional burial place of the boy hero. Enough of this probably survived the years of desolation to keep alive the tradition of the boy's death by drowning and the discovery and burial of his body by Sisyphos that resulted in the founding of the Isthmian Games.[5]

---

[1] Pausanias, II, 2, 1.

[2] J. G. Frazer, *op. cit.*, pp. 14–15; and Will, *Korinthiaka*, pp. 177–180, 184–187. Pausanias' text reads: ἔστι δὲ καὶ ἄλλο, Ἄδυτον καλούμενον, κάθοδος δὲ ἐς αὐτὸ ὑπόγεως, which might be rendered: "And there is also another (structure), called Adyton, and an underground descent into it," etc.

[3] Will, *Korinthiaka*, pp. 168–180, 210–212; W. R. Ridington, *The Minoan-Mycenaean Background of Greek Athletics*, pp. 52–53; Jack Lindsay, *Clashing Rocks*, pp. 234–235, 449, note 102; L. B. Farnell, *Hero Cults*, pp. 40–42.

[4] John G. Hawthorne, "The Myth of Palaimon," *T.A.P.A.*, LXXXIX, 1958, pp. 92–98, where the literary references are collected. Cf. Will, *Korinthiaka*, pp. 172, note 1, and 184.

[5] The myth is told in varying versions by ancient authors, mostly of late date; Apollodoros, *Bibl.*, III, 4, 1–3; Pausanias, II, 1, 3; Philostratos, *Imag.*, II, 16; Hyginus, *Fabulae*, II, 5, III, 4, IV, 1–2, 5; Ovid, *Metam.*, IV, 416–431; *Fasti*, VI, 485–550. The story of Ino is briefly related by Euripides in a choral ode in *Medeia*, lines 1282–1289. These references are collected and discussed in an unpublished term paper by Richard J. Wright, a copy of which was kindly sent to me by his professor at the University of Chicago, John G. Hawthorne.

After the destruction of Corinth by Mummius, the area originally occupied by the Earlier Stadium continued to fill up with sand and mud washed down from above. If we are correct in our conjecture that an early cult place of Palaimon had existed in the early period somewhere near the closed end of the Stadium, it is likely that the cult continued after the destruction of Corinth. We may assume that the Temple of Palaimon, which represents a late stage in the architectural development of the Palaimonion, owed its location to the existence of an earlier cult place, however insignificant it may have been. The area east of the Temple, as will be shown below, was found strewn with lamps and other cult objects, many of which are of earlier date than the Temple itself; and these were found at levels below that of the later precinct level (below, note 13).

FIRST AND SECOND PERIODS

Whatever cult building had existed prior to the rebuilding of the Isthmian Sanctuary, the earliest existing structures that we can plausibly connect with the cult of Palaimon are three sacrificial pits. Pit A is located a little to the east of the basin at the northeast end of the balbides sill (Plans II–IV, VII, VIII). Its floor is sunk to a depth of 1.30 m. below the level of the sloping ground of the spectatory. The pit measures 3.70 m. in length and 2.00 m. in width. On the north side it was lined with a rough wall, the stones of which have crumbled and cracked from intense heat; the three other sides consist of natural rock (Pl. 37, d). When the pit was discovered it was filled to a height of 0.80 m. with ash and burnt animal bones, together with some pottery and lamps (Pl. 38, a) that date the fill in the first half of the first century after Christ.[6] The area surrounding the pit was enclosed within a wall of stone masonry, enough of which remains to make it possible to determine the approximate dimensions of the enclosure (Plans VII, VIII). The north wall and the north ends of the east and west walls are still partly preserved (Pl. 37, d, upper right, behind marble pile), and the length of the enclosure from east to west is 9.60 m. No trace of the south wall survived after the foundation for the façade of the South Stoa was laid, but it is possible to calculate the north-south width at about eight meters. The west wall rests on earth fill to a height of 0.55 m. (Pl. 37, d, top center), showing that when the pit was in use the ground level had risen to that height above the Stadium floor. There is some evidence for a doorway in the north wall where there are no large blocks but only a foundation of small stones for a length of 1.75 m. (Plan VII).

At a somewhat later period pit B was dug some three meters to the southeast of the first one. This measures 3.80 m. from east to west and more than 2.40 m. from north to south. Only the southern part is well preserved; the rest was destroyed when the South Stoa was constructed. Like pit A, the second pit was sunk below the floor of the Stadium, here within the area of the race track. The east, south, and west walls were lined with stone masonry, which has crumbled from the heat even more than the stone wall in pit A. The north wall is missing. We do not know exactly where the ground level was when pit B was in use, but it was at least 1.20 m. above the floor of the pit. The preserved part of pit B had a deposit of ash, animal bones, and pottery, which show a date somewhat later than that from pit A,

---

[6] The vases from pit A shown in Plate 38, a are: bowls, IP 2153 and 2148; beakers IP 1998 and 1999; lamp IP 1911. The predominant type is a bowl, 0.158–0.164 m. in diameter, which tends toward hemispherical form. Most of them have plain rim, and the surface is covered with a dull coat of mottled red and gray color. There were also one-handled beakers of thin fabric, fragments of two gray-colored unguentaria, and some jugs of coarse ware with tall vertical neck and wide horizontal rim. Fragments of similar jugs came from pit B (see note 7). The complete lamp of Corinth type XVI (Pl. 38, a) came from the top of the fill. The vases range in date between the beginning and the middle of the first century of our era. The pit would have been filled up close to A.D. 50. For the dating of the pottery from this and the other sacrificial pits, I am indebted to John W. Hayes, who, while a member of the British School of Archaeology in Athens, made a thorough study of the pottery and left notes on his findings.

still within the first century after Christ (Pl. 38, b).[7] Only on the south side, however, was this fill found undisturbed. After the construction of the second pit, a much larger enclosure was made surrounding both pits A and B (Plans III, VII, VIII). The original north wall was utilized and an addition made toward the east and south. The south wall of the enceinte around pit A was probably removed when pit B was constructed. The new enclosure, no two walls of which are parallel, measures 16.25 m. from east to west along the north wall and 18.50 m. on the south. The length from north to south is 19.70 m. on the east side and 17.35 m. on the west. The doorway in the north wall of the earlier enclosure probably remained the principal entrance after the sacred area had been enlarged.

At one point along the line of the west wall there is a small irregular foundation, measuring 1.20 × 1.00 m. in area and made out of two rectangular blocks and some smaller stones. This foundation is sunk below the floor of the racecourse, its top being approximately level with the surfacing of white earth. It lies on the line of the broad stripe of dark earth, which we have interpreted as a foundation trench for a second starting line (above, p. 50). Possibly when the trench was dug, the hard virgin soil was found disturbed at this point, and the stones were inserted to fill an existing depression. The stones, however, are not oriented according to the direction of the stripe of dark earth, and they are too high to have supported a sill for the starting line. If such a sill existed, the stone fill was inserted after the sill had been removed. A shallow trench, 0.50 m. in width and only a few centimeters deep, extends southward for a distance of 8.50 m. from the southwest corner of the larger precinct (Pl. 21, c, lower right). This is at a much lower level than the bottom of the west wall of the enclosure around the pits. There is, however, a similar cutting exposed for a length of 2.20 m. at the west end of the south wall of the larger enclosure. This cutting seems to extend eastward below the existing south wall, which now rests on an earth fill, 0.35 m. deep, above the floor of the Stadium. The eastern part of this foundation trench, however, is filled with small stones. Possibly, when the wall was built these trenches were dug down to the level of the Stadium floor through the white earth used for surfacing and were later partly filled up with earth and small stones to save material for the walls. It is conceivable, however, that earlier walls had existed along the lines of the precinct walls, both on the west and the south, before the accumulation of earth had risen to the height indicated by the existing walls. But the shallow trench which extends southward from the southwest corner of the enclosure cannot have been part of the enclosures around the pits. It was probably a rough terrace wall, at the east edge of an area of higher level. This would explain why it stops dead at the south end without turning a corner to the east or west.

The irregularly quadrangular precinct that encloses pits A and B seems to indicate that pit A continued to be used after pit B had been constructed. The relationship of the various walls within the Palaimonion area tends to show that this single enclosure, with its two sacrificial pits and whatever cult objects may have existed in the area of the later Temple, constituted the whole cult apparatus of the Palaimonion in early imperial times.

THIRD PERIOD

At a later period the Palaimonion was rebuilt and the larger sacrificial pit C was constructed some fifteen meters southeast of pit B (Plans III, VIII). This is oriented east to west. The area enclosed by the precinct wall then constructed covers 782 square meters; its total east-west length, measured on the

---

[7] Plate 38, b contains pictures of bowls IP 1979 and 2171; Palaimonion lamp IP 2187. The pottery from pit B appears to be only a little, perhaps 20 years, later than that of pit A, but clear evidence for its exact date is lacking. Color-coated bowls predominate, but they are more open than those from pit A, and most of them have concentric grooves on the inside and a groove below the rim on the outside. One (Pl. 38, b, left) has a rouletted band below the outside groove. Jugs like those from pit A occurred, but no beakers of thin fabric. Pit B contained some Palaimonion lamps of an early phase (Pl. 38, b, right). The pottery clearly follows in development that from pit A, and there is no doubt about the relative date of the two pits. The fact that they were enclosed within a single enceinte after pit B had been made tends to show that pit A was not abandoned immediately after pit B began to be used.

inside, is 41.60 m. It was divided by two north-south walls into three parts, two large rectangles at either end and a smaller compartment in the middle. The latter was further subdivided by an east-west crosswall. The eastern division, which is the largest of the three, measures 18.25 m. from east to west, and about 19.00 m. from north to south. Approximately in the center of this rectangle, which was wholly unroofed, is the large sacrificial pit C (Pl. 38, c, e, upper right), measuring 4.05 m. from east to west and 3.57 m. from north to south. Its walls, preserved to a height of 1.10 m., consist of the native rock to a height of 0.24 m. above the floor of the pit, their upper parts being constructed out of stones laid in earth mortar. The stones in the walls are even more disintegrated by fire than is the case in sacrificial pits A and B. Attempts to protect the stone walls are shown by traces of clay mortar preserved in a few places. The east wall seems to have crumbled completely from the heat, and there a second wall, 0.75 m. high above the bottom of the pit, was then constructed, largely out of bricks. The bricks too are blackened and cracked from the heat, showing that the pit continued in use for a considerable time after the wall had been patched. When the pit was discovered, it was filled to a height of *ca.* 0.75 m. above the floor with ash and burnt animal bones and with large quantities of lamps and vases (Pl. 38, d),[8] the latest of which bring the date down to the middle of the second century after Christ.

West of pit C the ancient ground level rose slightly in a series of roughly indicated, low steps (seen in Pl. 38, c, beyond the pit), which may have supported movable seats for the dignitaries watching the ceremonies centered around the pit. Along the south side, the area close to the pit is now filled with stones and earth, probably brought in for the purpose of raising the surface to the level of the rest of the temenos (Pl. 38, e). An irregular stone packing of the same kind is found in the northeast corner of the precinct. From the southeast corner of the pit, a very rough foundation extends eastward toward the east temenos wall (Plan VII); this may be part of a retaining wall for a slightly higher area toward the north.

The east wall of the precinct is preserved for most of its length; its foundation extends somewhat below the level of the Stadium floor. At the north end, the wall now begins 1.20 m. south of the southeast corner of the South Stoa, and there a large buttress of the Stoa meets the end of the wall. Only the difference in building technique shows where the precinct wall ends and the Stoa buttress begins. The latter is built with lime mortar, the precinct wall with earth mortar. Originally the precinct wall probably extended a little farther north. From the north end, the foundation for the east precinct wall runs south for a distance of 17.70 m. It measures *ca.* 0.78 m. in thickness and is preserved to a maximum height of 0.70 m. It is built of rather small irregular stones laid in a mortar of earth. If there was a wall of better construction at a higher level, it is nowhere preserved. On the east side the foundation has a series of buttresses with intervals of *ca.* 3.75 m. Only three are preserved, one at the very south end of the wall and slight traces of two more.

---

[8] The vases shown in Plate 38, d are: bowls with offset rim, IP 1051, 1420; mugs of coarse fabric, IP 1028, 1085; Palaimonion lamps, IP 1033, 1032. The contents of pit C fall into two chronologically differentiated groups. In the deposit of the lower level the bowl is the predominant shape. These are smaller than the bowls from pits A and B, and the rim is vertical and sharply set off from the body. These bowls, which are imitations of late Arretine bowls, occur only in the lower stratum of pit C. For the shape cf. bowl from Athens published by Henry S. Robinson, *The Athenian Agora,* V, *Pottery of the Roman Period,* p. 47, pl. 8, no. H8. With the bowls were some Palaimonion lamps of a shape transitional between the larger form found in pit B and the very small lamps from the upper stratum of pit C. The upper stratum of this pit contained fragments of some seven hundred one-handled mugs of coarse, dark gray fabric and numerous small Palaimonion lamps of the same coarse clay and dark gray color as the mugs. There were some bowls, larger than their counterparts from the lower level. For the earlier contents of the lower level, Mr. Hayes suggested a date about 75–125 after Christ. The vases and lamps of the upper level would come down to about A.D. 150. To the same period belongs a large lamp of Corinth type XXVII, with figures of Kybele and Attis on the discus; *Hesperia,* XXVII, 1958, p. 34, no. 54, pl. 16, a. The fragments were found scattered along the north edge of the pit. The contents from the upper stratum of pit C represent the latest phase of the Palaimonion pottery and lamps. All three pits contained much ash and many burned bones of sacrifical animals, all cattle, in some cases at least young bulls, which had been burned whole. This is of interest as confirmation of Philostratos' statement (*Imagines,* II, 16, 3) that black bullocks were sacrificed to Palaimon. For information about the bones I am indebted to Professor Nils-Gustaf Gejvall of the University of Stockholm.

The south wall is only 0.44 m. thick, but it rests on a broader foundation measuring 0.72 m. in thickness. In some places the wall is preserved to a height of 0.78 m. above the foundation. In the eastern part the ground level was the same as the Stadium floor or lower, but farther west the projecting foundation on the north side shows that the surface had risen to a height of about 0.47 m. above the race track (Pl. 39, a). On the south side the foundation does not project beyond the face of the wall. The relationship of the many walls in this area can best be followed by comparing the actual state plans, Plans II and VII, with the restored Plans III and VIII.

Of the west foundation only a stretch of four meters and a single buttress are preserved south of the Temple of Palaimon (Plans VII, VIII); the rest would have been removed when the foundation for the Temple was laid. The north wall disappeared when the foundation for the rear wall of the South Stoa was constructed. The distance from the south face of this foundation to the north face of the south precinct wall measures 18.90 m. at the east end of the precinct. This, then, was the approximate north-south dimension of the precinct in the time before the construction of the Temple of Palaimon.

The middle of the three divisions is the smallest, having an inside width of 6.25 m. The two parallel walls which bounded it on the east and west are built in the same technique as the outer walls of the temenos, i.e. with small stones laid in earth mortar, and with somewhat larger blocks interspersed in the masonry. They contain some stones that have been burnt and blackened in fire; these had probably been built originally into one of the sacrificial pits. These two walls, which do not run quite parallel to the east wall of the large eastern division, form an angle of 87°50′ with the south wall. This slight deviation from a right angle, which may have been made by error, determined the axis of the semicircular structure of the next stage in the architectural development of the Palaimonion. The east wall of the middle division (Pl. 38, c, middle) has a thickness of ca. 0.77 m., and near its south end, where it abutted against the south precinct wall, it is still preserved to a height of 0.85 m. above the Stadium floor. When the wall was constructed, the ground level was about the same as the race track. The juncture of this wall with the south precinct wall has been covered over with lime mortar masonry of a later period, so that it is not apparent whether the two walls were bonded together. At the north end (Plan VII), it appears as if the foundation for the east wall had been cut through by the foundation for the south wall of the enclosure around pits A and B, but this cannot be the case. The pottery from pits A and B is earlier than that of pit C, and we may assume that the walls encircling the three pits are similarly related chronologically. The situation seems to be as follows. The builders of the north-south east wall of the middle division ran their foundation up to the east-west foundation of the earlier enclosure, which they did not remove, but built their wall over it. That part of the north-south wall which overlay the earlier east-west foundation has been removed, and this gives the false impression, more so on the plan than on the ground, that the north-south wall is the earlier. The east wall of the middle division has here been interrupted by the construction of a semicircular foundation (below, p. 105) of somewhat later date (Pl. 39, b, center). It reappears, however, on the north side of the semicircular wall and extends almost to the rear wall of the South Stoa. The interrelations of the various walls at this vital juncture are further obscured by the fact that one of the buttresses behind the South Stoa wall was placed very nearly in line with the earlier north-south wall (period plan, Plan VIII).

The west wall of the middle division is partly covered over by the later foundation for the peribolos wall surrounding the Temple of Palaimon (Plans VII–IX). The south end of the wall is entirely missing for a distance of 2.50 m., but farther north, where some large building blocks are built in among the smaller stones (Pl. 38, c, center), the wall is preserved to a height of 0.70 m. above the racecourse. Like the east wall of the middle division, the west wall has been interrupted by the foundation for the semicircular monument. The foundation for the south wall of the enclosure around pits A and B is here covered over by the broad semicircular foundation. Farther north, within the Semicircle, the west wall of the middle division reappears and is here preserved to a height of one meter above the Stadium floor (Pl. 39, b, left center). This section of the wall shows that the floor level of the semicircular structure was at least one meter higher than the level of the racecourse. The foundation of the west wall of the middle division extends northward to within 0.70 m. of the rear wall of the South Stoa. Approximately along the line of the Stoa foundation we may postulate the existence of an earlier wall forming the north side of the whole precinct in the period prior to the construction of the Stoa. The two north-south partition walls described above would have been bonded into, or abutted against, this no longer existant east-west wall.

This middle division was further subdivided by an east-west crosswall into two rooms, a smaller one on the south and a larger on the north. The wall separating these two compartments is built in the same technique as the parallel north-south walls and has a thickness of 0.54 m. At the east end its foundation abuts against the foundation for the east partition wall, but at its west end the crosswall appears to be bonded into the west partition wall. The larger, north room had an inside length from north to south of 13.20 m. and a width of 6.25 m. The floor level in the two compartments was probably now considerably higher than the Stadium floor. This appears from the fact that no trace of a doorway is preserved in the east wall. Judging from the arrangements of the earlier precinct walls, we may conjecture that the entrance was from the north through the larger of the two compartments. Although the east-west partition wall in one place is preserved to a height of 0.70 m. above the Stadium floor, it has no threshold or trace of an entrance. If one existed, it must have been at a higher level. In the period plans, Plans III and VIII, we have restored a doorway in the partition wall and another in the southeast corner of the smaller room, giving access to the eastern compartment of the South Building. It is possible, though unlikely, that the smaller compartment was entered from the south and was unconnected with the larger one. The latter, which was probably entered from the north, would have provided communication between the two larger divisions to the east and west, as was almost certainly the case in the later period.

The west division of the precinct, which is only slightly smaller than the east division, measures 15.80 m. from east to west on the inside, the north-south dimension being approximately the same as that of the other two divisions. The floor level in front of the Temple, as stated above, was nearly half a meter above the surface of the racecourse, but south of the peribolos the ground level was probably lower. The small section of the west wall that appears south of the Temple of Palaimon rests on an earth fill, here 0.30 m. above the level of the earlier east-west road (C) (above, p. 20). The rest of the west wall as well as the wall on the north side is missing, and the west face of the wall separating the middle compartment from the large western division is hidden beneath the foundations for the later peribolos wall. No structure apart from the enclosing walls remains in the western division to indicate what purpose it served. The large number of lamps of several kinds found at different levels in this division shows the ritual importance of the place. On the analogy of the arrangement in the later period, we may conjecture that the cult place proper of Palaimon existed somewhere in the area later occupied by the Temple. It may have been an altar or small shrine with a cult statue around which the ceremonies centered.

FOURTH PERIOD

The next structure to have been built in this area is a lime-pit set against the west face of the east partition wall, ca. 2.00 m. south of the rear wall of the later Stoa. The pit (Pl. 39, b, center right) measures 1.38 m. in length, 1.12 m. in width, and it has a preserved depth of 0.74 m. It is lined on all four sides and at the bottom with terracotta roof tiles, measuring ca. 0.70 × 0.58 m. Some of them have the characteristic beveled edges of Greek roof tiles; others are typical Roman tiles (Pl. 39, c). They had probably been made as replacements for Greek tiles in some large building, perhaps the Temple of Poseidon. No stamps have been found on any of the exposed sides of the tiles. The pit was first dug below the floor of the Stadium and was then lined with plaster and the tiles set on end in wet lime against the sides. Lime was also found on the inside of the pit, adhering to the surface of the tiles, thus indicating what the pit was used for. The southeast corner of the pit was cut off when the foundation for the semicircular monument was made; this shows that the lime-pit is earlier than this foundation. When the Semicircle was constructed the ground level, as shown above, was at least one meter, and probably more, above the floor of the Stadium, and the lime-pit at that time would have been buried beneath the floor of the building. Nothing was found in the pit other than the tiles to indicate the period of its use. It may have been made while the precinct of Palaimon was in a process of reconstruction, and after its use it was filled up and allowed to remain below the ground level.

Next in sequence of construction is the semicircular foundation which cuts across the two walls of the middle division of the precinct. The building, which opened to the north, had an inner diameter of *ca.* 10.00 m. The existing foundation, which measures 0.80–1.00 m. in thickness, is built with lime mortar and small stones. It is sunk in a trench 0.25 m. below the floor of the Stadium, and on top it has been evened off with fragments of roof tiles laid in mortar. The tiles seem to be of the same kind as those used for the lime-pit. The top of the foundation is now 0.44 m. above the Stadium floor, but the floor level inside the building was considerably higher. In the rear, the foundation is straight, being much wider at the ends than in the middle. The length of the straight section, 7.60 m., is the same as the outside width of the middle division of the precinct. Apparently one or both of the two parallel walls of this division were still standing when the semicircular building was constructed. The two ends of the semicircular wall extended slightly to the north of the rear wall of the South Stoa, and the distance from a line joining the two ends to the rear wall of the Semicircle is approximately 5.50 m. on the foundation. Thus, if allowance is made for the thickness of a wall, the interior is very nearly a half circle. The two ends of the wall were broadened into two massive piers, both of which were largely cut away when the South Stoa was built. Because the two parallel walls of the middle division do not form a right angle with the south wall of the precinct, the axis of the semicircular structure, which was determined by the orientation of the parallel walls, does not make a right angle with the rear wall of the South Stoa. Although the ends of the semicircular foundation were cut off by the foundation for the rear wall of the Stoa, it is likely that the Semicircle, whatever purpose it served, continued in use after the construction of the Stoa. If so, it would have been reached from the north through a doorway in the rear wall of the Stoa.[9] In our reconstruction we have assumed that the semicircular building formed the principal entrance into the Palaimonion complex (period plans, Plans III, VIII). Prior to the construction of the South Stoa, the façade would have consisted of the two piers with broad antae facing two columns that flanked the central passage. Two stones from the foundation for the east column are still left in their original position, and a cutting in the ground was found for the removed west foundation. In the final period the approach to the semicircular entranceway was through a door in the rear wall of the South Stoa.

This ornamental gateway[10] provided direct and ceremonial communication between the temenos of Poseidon and the cult place of Palaimon. Within or in front of this portal stood a statue of a certain Nikias who had distinguished himself both as an orator and agonothetes. The statue base, which seems too large and heavy to have been moved very far from where it had been standing, was found in the area of the removed rear wall of the South Stoa at the very north edge of the semicircular foundation. The statue supported by the base had once, according to the epigram, been set up within the pronaos

[9] Similarly, the Bouleuterion in Corinth, which was elliptical in form and entered through openings in the rear wall of the South Stoa; *Corinth*, I, iv, pp. 129–132, pls. III, XVII, XXI.

[10] In the Roman reconstruction of the theater at Corinth three such semicircles provide communication between the large court in the rear and the stage; see Richard Stillwell's reconstruction in *Corinth*, II, pp. 99–105, pl. VII, a. In several theaters of Roman times the regia is semicircular with doors in the center opening on the stage: the large theater at Pompeii, Margarete Bieber, *The History of the Greek and Roman Theater*, p. 172, fig. 607; the theater of Pompey in Rome, *ibid.*, p. 184, fig. 640; theaters at Orange, *ibid.*, p. 200, fig. 675; Merida, *ibid.*, p. 202, fig. 680; Dugga, *ibid.*, p. 204, fig. 689; and cf. wall painting from Pompeii, *ibid.*, p. 232, fig. 775.

(prodomos) of the Temple of Poseidon, but it must have been subsequently moved to the place where the base was discovered.[11]

South of the middle division, the South Building, consisting of two large compartments, was added, the walls of which extend southward underneath the modern road. The westernmost of the three north-south foundations, which measure 1.15 m. in thickness, has been exposed for a length of 6.30 m.; of the middle foundation a length of 5.30 m. has been uncovered, and of the eastern, 3.50 m. The west and middle foundations of this south building are the better preserved, and they have been smoothly finished off on top with fragments of roof tiles. The masonry is very similar to that in the foundation for the Semicircle, and the two buildings are probably of contemporary construction. All three foundations (Pl. 25, e, top) are very solidly built with the use of smaller stones and large blocks laid in a hard lime mortar. They are broad enough to have supported walls with vaulted ceiling, and some pieces of a rubble vault were found in the area. Since the southern part of the South Building is still concealed beneath the road pavement, the extent of the walls in that direction is unknown. From the construction of the north wall, which also formed the southern limit of the small compartment in the middle division, it becomes clear that the floor level within the two rooms was at least 0.70 m. above the floor of the Stadium. There is evidence for a door leading from the small compartment into the east room of the South Building. A threshold block of hard limestone lies on the wall close to the place where it was discovered. At the west end of this block there is a pivot hole and a rectangular cutting, but the other end of the block has been broken away. The rear or north edge of the block has been cut with a saw. In the later period the floor level of the small south room in the middle division was probably about the same as that of the two rooms in the South Building, approximately one meter above the Stadium floor. Fragments of a marble arch were found within the south compartment of the middle division, and it is not unlikely that this arch formed part of the doorway (Pl. 39, d). The arch, made in two large blocks with a vertical joint at the middle, was framed by three successively receding fasciae with a kymation at the top. A similar kymation extended horizontally above the arch and vertically on either side. In the corners are carved rosettes. A restoration of the archway is shown in Plate 74, a. No part of the impost has been preserved, but it is conjecturally indicated in the drawing. The rear of the marble arch was plain, except for a very low cyma reversa on each side, which presumably was carried across the top.

The foundations considered so far within the area of the Palaimonion, except those of the Semicircle and of the South Building, which are all later than the main complex, have one characteristic in common: all are made with stones laid in earth with no use of lime mortar. Some parts of walls preserved above the foundations are constructed in the same technique. The later walls, to be described below, are made with lime mortar above their foundations. This difference in the type of construction forms a useful criterion for determining to which period a wall or set of walls belongs.

FIFTH PERIOD

The Precinct

In the final reconstruction of the Palaimonion, the western part was rebuilt, but the large eastern division surrounding sacrificial pit C probably remained with but slight changes as long as Palaimon continued to be worshiped at Isthmia. In its northwest corner the construction of the semicircular entrance-way had encroached slightly upon this area. The east wall of the middle division was at least partly demolished, and what remained became buried as the ground level was raised. In the area to the south and west of sacrificial pit C and in the northeast corner of the precinct there are large quantities of

---

[11] Inventory No. IΣ 358. The text, which is published in *Hesperia*, XXVIII, 1959, pp. 324–326, will be included in the definitive publication of the inscriptions of Roman times from Isthmia, by Daniel J. Geagan.

rough field stones, some of which may have been brought in to raise the floor level; others, however, lying at a higher level, apparently have come from the tumbled precinct walls. Because of the disturbances made in the stratification in the early Christian era when the buildings were demolished to provide building material for the Fortress, it is not possible to determine where the ground level was in all parts of the area; but the stone packings at the lower levels would not have protruded above the surface, nor was the ground level raised in the later period over the whole area here, as was the case in the large western division. Consequently we may conclude that the eastern division remained largely unencumbered by later structures. In any case, the sacrificial pit C remained in use through the subsequent period, after the construction of the Temple.

The western part of the Palaimonion was rebuilt in the final reconstruction, and now for the first time a Temple was erected. At this time the area of the western division became the peribolos of the Temple, enlarged toward the west by an extension of 10.40 m. The ground level was raised so as to form a level space surrounding the Temple on all sides. The east partition wall of the middle division was no longer visible above ground, and the smaller compartment on the south received a new set of walls built in the later technique. The double crosswall between the north and south compartments of this middle division is of two periods. The north wall, described above (p. 103), is the earlier of the two. In the later period the ground level here had risen to more than 0.80 m. above that of the Stadium, and the threshold in the east-west crosswall would have been at a level above the preserved top of the wall. The larger north room, which probably continued to be entered from the north through the Semicircle, must have had doors giving access to the small compartment on the south and to the peribolos of Palaimon on the west. The smaller room now probably had two doors in the south wall, each communicating with one of the two compartments of the South Building.

The new crosswall on the south side (visible in Pl. 38, e, right center) between the north and south compartments of the middle division has a foundation of small stones and earth mortar, but the wall proper, partly preserved at the west end, is built with lime mortar like all the walls of the later period. The same is true of the new, inner wall on the east side of the small compartment. There, too, the foundation up to a height of ca. 0.80 m. above the Stadium floor is built with stones and earth, but in the wall proper, as shown at the south end, the stones are laid in lime mortar and the wall is there bonded into the foundation of the contemporary south wall of the compartment. Consequently the two inner walls on the north and east sides of the small compartment are clearly to be dated in the last period of the Palaimonion. There is a broad, irregularly L-shaped hollow in the north and east part of the small compartment, sunk to a depth of ca. 0.30 m. below the Stadium floor. The foundation for the inner east wall extends all the way to the bottom of the hollow, but the inner north wall rests on earth fill to a height of 0.68 m. Nevertheless, the two walls are doubtless of the same period and they seem to be bonded together at the northeast corner of the room.

There must have been some compelling reason for doubling the wall on the north and east sides of the room, in spite of the fact that the earlier walls are still standing to a height of nearly one meter above the Stadium floor. After the two inner walls had been constructed, the double walls had a joint thickness of ca. 1.20 m. The earlier west wall of the room is now missing for a distance of two meters at its south end. Where preserved, its thickness together with that of the later east peribolos wall is ca. 1.00 m., and the south wall of the small compartment was ca. 0.90 m. thick. The explanation for this heavy construction is probably that the small room in the later period had a vaulted ceiling. Many lumps of masonry with stucco were found in the area, and some of these are arched. On the east face of the later north-south wall, which here forms the partition between the small compartment and the peribolos to the west, there is a patch of stucco made with coarse lime mortar, the surface of which was smoothed and seems to have been divided by red stripes into panels. Only a small part of the vertical stripe, 0.023 m. wide, is preserved. Pieces of rubble masonry with stucco came from the fill in this part of the building, some of which retain colors of wall decoration, and many fragments show graffiti scratched on blue or white plaster.[12] The painted wall plaster would have been in a roofed part of the building.

Both rooms of the middle compartment in this final building period must have had a ground level more than a meter above the Stadium floor, as shown by a gateway foundation extending westward toward the Temple from the later east wall of the western division (below, p. 109). Since we have found reasons to conclude that the original ground level surrounding the sacrificial pit in the eastern division remained at about the level of the Stadium floor, there would have been steps or a ramp leading from that level to the higher ground level in the peribolos east of the Temple of Palaimon. There are no traces of a foundation for a stairway, and a ramp is the more probable alternative.

The peribolos walls surrounding the Temple are best preserved on the south side. When the wall was built, the ground level here had risen to a height of 0.75 m. above the Stadium floor. A trench having the approximate width of the foundation was dug through this fill and a subfoundation constructed out of small stones and earth. Above this fill the wall construction begins, here built with stones laid in lime mortar (Plan IX, Section C–D; Pl. 40, a). Up to a height of 0.53 m. above the subfoundation the face of the wall is less smooth and left unstuccoed; only the interstices were smoothly filled with mortar. This lower part of the wall forms a projecting socle, 0.56 m. thick, whereas the wall proper, beginning at a level *ca.* 1.30 m. above the Stadium floor, is set back from the face of the foundation 0.02–0.04 m. on both sides and is only about 0.53 m. thick. The two faces of the wall are built with roughly rectangular poros stones, 0.20–0.35 m. long and about half as wide, laid in irregular courses. On the south or rear face of the wall (Pl. 38, e, lower right) the joints are smoothly pointed up with lime mortar, but there is no stucco. There are three buttresses made with larger blocks bonded into the wall at intervals of 3.38 m. and 3.46 m. The foundations of the buttresses, like that of the wall itself, extend all the way down to the floor of the Stadium. The north face of the wall toward the peribolos is covered with lime plaster, *ca.* 0.015 m. thick, above the level of the projecting socle. This may have been applied at some later time. Had the plaster been intended from the beginning, it would have been better technique to have roughened the mortar with which the joints were filled. The plaster is preserved over a large area of the wall, but nowhere are there any colors other than the natural white of the plaster. The space between the south face of the later peribolos wall and the north face of the earlier precinct wall (Pl. 39, a) is slightly over 2.00 m. wide. What is still standing of the earlier wall was probably concealed completely below the ground level established when the later peribolos was constructed.

The length of the peribolos from the east to west was 25.53 m., measured from the inner faces of the walls. Of the west wall only a very small piece remains, but enough to mark the western limit of the precinct. West of this wall the ground has been tested with trial trenches, and it is clear that there was no further extension of the peribolos in that direction. On the north side the earlier precinct wall may have been standing for a time after the construction of the Temple; later the rear wall of the South Stoa would have formed the northern limit. The clear inside width of the peribolos from north to south was then *ca.* 16.50 m.

The foundation for the east wall separating the peribolos from the two rooms of the middle compartment is constructed like that of the south wall, though here the ground level seems to have been only *ca.* 0.56 m. above the Stadium floor when the wall was built. The rubble of the subfoundation is intact throughout, and the socle above this level is preserved to a height of 0.52 m., i.e. 0.95 m. above the Stadium floor. No part of the stuccoed wall face remains here.

Built against the west face of the east wall but not bonded into the wall construction are two foundations, the tops of which are now 0.70 m. above the Stadium floor level (Plans VII–IX, Pl. 38, e, center). The smaller of the two, measuring 1.60 m. in length from north to south and 0.88 m. in width, begins slightly less than four meters from the southeast corner of the peribolos. At a distance of 1.67 m. from

[12] Daniel J. Geagan, who is making final study of the graffiti, has kindly provided me with his copy of the texts. The larger pieces appear to be lists of names and in one case the list is dated by the office of some official.

the north end of the smaller foundation there is a large platform (Pl. 39, b, lower center) measuring 2.22 m. in length and having about the same width as the smaller foundation. The larger of the two foundations, which is nearly on the axis of the Temple of Palaimon, probably supported the principle entranceway into the later peribolos from the east (Plan VIII and Frontispiece). The smaller foundation may mark a side entrance into the peribolos; or possibly it served as support for a small altar or stone table used in the nightly cult rites of Palaimon.

Among the marble fragments from the area of the middle division were many pieces of a large Ionic column (**78**, Catalogue p. 128), the capital of which could be restored as seen in Plate 74, b. It is made of white marble, probably Pentelic, and the diameter of the sinkage for a column measured 0.85 m. This then would be the diameter at the top of the column shaft, including the moulding. Tiny fragments of a large Ionic base came from the same vicinity, and within the semicircular foundation was found a small fragment of a column shaft of blue marble (**79**, Catalogue p. 128) with a diameter of *ca.* 0.70 m. The dimensions indicated by these fragments show that they probably belong to the same column, which by normal proportions would have had a height of more than seven meters. There is no building in this area large enough to have had columns of that size, and it seems likely that the fragments came from a free standing pedestal for a statue or monument of some kind. This would have required a heavy foundation, but no such foundation has been found in the area of the Palaimonion. Possibly it stood somewhere south of the Palaimonion in the area covered by the modern road.

In the eastern part of the peribolos the ground level as now left by the excavations is perfectly level since it consists of the floor of the Earlier Stadium. The western part, however, rises perceptibly where the spectatory of the Earlier Stadium began. The foundations for the Temple of Palaimon rest partly on this higher ground and partly on the level area of the racecourse (see east-west section, Plan X). What remains *in situ* of the Temple is merely the rubble core of the foundation, all the stones except a few on the south and north sides having been removed. When the Temple was constructed the ground level had risen to a height of 0.60–0.85 m. above the level of the racecourse, but in the rear the ancient ground level was considerably higher (Plan X), and the accumulation of earth correspondingly less deep. The builders of the Temple dug through this fill down to the level of the Stadium floor. On the north side the Temple foundation rests partly on the southwest half of the balbides sill. Here the stone slabs were not removed as they were when the rear foundation for the South Stoa was laid. We were thus able to tunnel under the rubble foundation of the Temple so as to expose the full length of the balbides sill and the triangular pavement with the grooves. The Temple is not situated in the center of the later peribolos but toward its west end. The distance from the front edge of the Temple foundation to the east peribolos wall is 12.20 m., whereas the space in the rear between the Temple foundation and the west peribolos wall is only 5.30 m. Between the south edge of the Temple and the south peribolos wall there is a space of 4.47 m.; the corresponding space on the north side was *ca.* 4.00 m. The greater area to the east of the Temple would have been used for functions of the cult. Here we found large quantities of lamps (Pls. 40, b, c), both the larger types without handle (Pl. 40, d, top row), which were probably set out on small pedestals or on the ground, and also the small portable types carried in the hands of the worshipers.[13]

THE TEMPLE OF PALAIMON

The Temple foundation (Plans II–IV, VII–IX; Pl. 41, a, b) in its present form measures 8.80 m. from east to west, *ca.* 8.00 m. from north to south, and it is standing to a height of about 2.00 m. above the floor of the Stadium. What remains is chiefly the concrete core, which would have been faced with stone masonry on all sides. The lower part, however, had no such facing. Two small blocks, which seem to

---

[13] From the large number of lamps found in the Palaimonion, it becomes obvious that these played an important role in the nocturnal mystery rites in the worship of the hero. The lamps, which comprise many types, will be published in final form in another volume of the Isthmia series.

be in their original position at the northeast corner, and six blocks along the south face of the foundation permit us to estimate the size of the foundation above ground. A succession of setbacks in the front and rear and also on the two flanks show the position of some blocks that have been removed. The overall dimensions at the preserved height show that the foundation was not quite square, the length from east to west being *ca.* 0.80 m. greater than the width.

In the main axis, a broad passage, now *ca.* 1.70 m. wide, runs through the foundation, beginning two meters from the east end. At a point close to the center of the foundation, this passage turns at an angle of 35⁰ toward the north. The passage, which is now preserved to a height of 1.80 m., was originally lined with poros blocks reducing the actual width to 0.73 m. at the east end and 0.63 m. at the west end. Only the bottom row of stones now remains in place, but the impressions of individual blocks in the upper courses show clearly on the concrete walls on both sides (Pl. 22, a). The descent at the east end was from a platform *ca.* 1.38 m. wide and 0.85 m. above the floor of the passage. On each side of the entrance is a very rough depression (Pl. 41, b) which might mark the existence of a door jamb. There are no steps from the platform to the passage, a height of nearly one meter; presumably there was a wooden stairway of four or five steps. The bend of the passage comes exactly above the water basin at the southwest end of the balbides sill. Before this basin was excavated, it was filled to the top with stones and hard lime mortar (Pl. 22, b). The walls and bottom of the passage are covered with a heavy, 8–20 mm. thick, watertight stucco which contains particles of crushed bricks. This continues as far as the northwest corner of the foundation. At that point the passage was joined to the southeast edge of the Stadium reservoir (the juncture is shown in Plan VIII and Pl. 41, c). From there on toward the northwest, the original Greek stucco of the reservoir is preserved. This stucco is very different from that in the passage through the Temple foundation. The Greek stucco, which is lighter in color, consists of the hard natural cement, mixed with coarse-grained sand, commonly used as lining in waterworks of pre-Roman times. At a distance of 2.40 m. from the corner of the Temple, the original reservoir had been closed with a stone slab held in place against two upright stone posts (above, p. 27, Plan VIII). The sluice for controlling the flow of water was destroyed when the Roman temple was built. The two periods of construction are here clearly distinguishable. The extant stone pier on the south side, which is still standing to a height of 0.87 m. (Pl. 13, b, lower right), had its corners trimmed off and the exposed edge has been resurfaced with the kind of stucco found in the passage under the Temple. This is considerably darker than the Greek stucco and has a bluish tinge on the surface. The fact that the walls and the floor of the passage under the Temple were covered with watertight stucco shows that it was intended to hold water, although it is unlikely that water was drawn from this source either within the foundation of the Temple or outside. Obviously the water was meant to serve some other purpose.

In spite of the almost total destruction of the building, it is possible to restore the superstructure from the foundation with the help of coins on which the Temple appears (Pl. 42, a, b).[14] They reproduce the details with remarkable clarity. They show a circular Temple with Corinthian columns, set on a podium

---

[14] The coin of Caracalla shown in Plate 42, a, b was found in 1971 some hundred meters east of the Palaimonion. I am indebted to the Director of the excavations, Professor Paul Clement, for the photograph and permission to reproduce it here. Three coins, one of M. Aurelius, one of Geta, and one of Caracalla, showing the Temple of Palaimon, are reproduced in Imhoof-Blumer and Gardner, *Numismatic Commentary on Pausanias*, pl. B, I, XI, XII, XIII, but none of these is of the same issue as the coin found at Isthmia. One poorly preserved coin of Hadrian from the Corinth excavations (*Corinth*, VI, pl. III, no. 111) shows the statue of the boy on the dolphin within the circular temple with only five equidistant columns showing. The tree is not visible, nor is the arched entrance to the crypt indicated. This seems to be the earliest of the series showing the Temple. The coins differ in several details. In two of them the statue of the dolphin and boy is omitted; all but one show the opening to the crypt in the Temple foundation, two show a sacrificial bull; and on two of them a tree appears as it does on the coin found at Isthmia. In one case there are two trees, one on either side of the Temple. The tree was probably regarded as essential to the cult. It may represent the tree that Pausanias saw on the shore, where the body of Palaimon was discovered by Sisyphos. The tree close to the Temple would have been planted there in Roman times. On the architecture of monopteros monuments, like the Temple of Palaimon, see Wolfgang Binder, *Der Roma-Augustus Monopteros auf der Akropolis und Sein Typologischer Ort*, Stuttgart, 1969.

and with a domed roof. On none of the coins are walls indicated, but in the center of the open colonnade there is a statue of Palaimon lying prostrate on the back of a dolphin. The statue is mentioned in Pausanias' description of the building. All but one of the coins indicate an opening on the façade giving access into the passage. On the evidence of these coins and of Pausanias' description, we have restored the circular Temple shown in Plate 73. In our restoration we assumed that there were eleven columns, with a somewhat larger space on the axis of the east façade. Such a disposition of columns would show the statue to better advantage from the front. The circular structure, with an outer diameter of *ca.* 6.90 m., rested on a square base measuring 7.00 m. on the side. In the rear and on the flanks there would have been a single step, but in front, where the ground level was lower, we have restored four steps below the base. Since the opening into the passage was on the axis, there would have been no access to the interior of the colonnade at that point; those who wished to enter the colonnade would have approached from the southeast and northeast corners.

A few other details of the building can be recovered with the help of the coins and fragments of sculpture and architecture found in the area surrounding the foundation. At the eaves of the roof the coins show a kind of akroterion, apparently in the form of a dolphin. The marble piece with floral design shown in Plate 41, d, which was found close to the Temple foundation, would be suitable for an akroterion on such a building. It is conceivable that figures of dolphins alternated with akroteria of this kind. At the peak of the roof was a finial of some kind. In addition to the statue of the boy on the dolphin, Pausanias mentions statues of Poseidon and of Leukothea in the Temple of Palaimon. These may well have stood within the colonnade, but on the coins only the statue of Palaimon is shown. A large number of fragments of marble statuary came from the area; most of them, however, are so small that the identity of the figures cannot be determined, with one exception. This is a figure of Pan playing the syrinx (Pl. 42, c). Only the face, one foot, and the hand holding the instrument are preserved.

The identification of this foundation as the Temple of Palaimon leaves no room for doubt. Pausanias saw the Temple on the left as he entered the temenos of Poseidon, and in his description of the building he mentions the underground passage in which inviolable oaths were administered, presumably to athletes and officials of the Sanctuary. It is not obvious from Pausanias' account that this crypt was part of the Temple, and prior to our excavations in which the foundation of the Temple was revealed, it was frequently assumed that Pausanias' "adyton" was in a separate building. Now that the whole building complex has been uncovered, we know that no such crypt existed anywhere else, and the passage underneath the floor of the Temple, as indicated on the coins, fits Pausanias' description perfectly. From the foundation we can estimate the free height of the passage at *ca.* 1.90 m., enough to permit a man of average stature to stand upright. The bend at the very center of the foundation probably has some significance other than structural convenience. Since this passage, as well as the earlier reservoir to which it is joined, was completely underground, the light would not have penetrated into it beyond the bend, and of course the entrance could be closed to shut out light from there. If the athletes took their oaths in this place, there would be good reason for such an arrangement. They had to stand in total darkness and in water up to their knees, while the officiating priest pronounced the ancient formula[15] of the oath with threats of dire consequences to perjurers. This would be calculated to strike fear into the minds of young athletes and to impress them with the sacredness of their oaths. Although the athletes, and presumably the officials of the games, probably had to swear first on the Altar of Poseidon,[16]

---

[15] Pausanias' statement, II, 2, 1, ὃς δ'ἂν ἐνταῦθα ἢ Κορινθίων ἢ ξένος ἐπίορκα ὀμόσῃ implies, but does not specifically say, that it was the athletes who took their oaths in the crypt. Its wording is reminiscent of a passage in an epigram in honor of an orator and agonothetes by the name Nikias, whose sterling qualities were held up as examples to the young, citizens and foreigners alike: Νικία, ὦ μέγα χάρμα πολῇ τε καὶ τεκέεσσιν Ἄστοις καὶ ξείνοις, ὡς μέγ' ὄνειαρ ἔφυς, *Hesperia*, XXVIII, 1959, p. 325.

[16] The initiatory sacrifice was made to Poseidon, according to Xenophon (*Hell.*, IV, 5, 2). On the question of oaths and 'Schwurgötter' see Ulrich von Wilamowitz-Moellendorff, *Der Glaube der Hellenen*, I, p. 226, II, p. 391; Nilsson, *Op. Sel.*, I, pp. 447–448.

the most awesome oath was the one they had to take in the crypt of the Palaimonion. The tradition, which had no basis in fact, that the founding hero lay buried beneath this Temple was of course intended to enhance the solemnity of the occasion.

Perhaps the crypt also served as manteion. We know of the existence of such a place from an inscription on the base of a statue of a certain Blastos, the Prophet,[17] but no other information is available on the subject. Within the peribolos, a little to the northeast of the Temple, was found another base which had supported a statue of Sisyphos, the mythological ruler of Corinth and reputed founder of the Isthmian Games. The king's name is inscribed on the front in large Greek letters of Roman imperial times and again on the back of the base in somewhat smaller letters of the same period. A third base of the same kind, now in the epigraphical collection at Ancient Corinth, records the dedication of a statue to Iuventianus, the Priest. This is the great donor and High Priest of Poseidon who built and restored many of the buildings at Isthmia, among them the Palaimonion.[18] In modern times this base had been brought to New Corinth together with other stones from Isthmia, and from there it was brought to Ancient Corinth.

The circular Temple and its peribolos were apparently the latest additions to the cult place of Palaimon. The actual remains give no clue to the exact date of construction. The comparative lateness is shown by the fact that the ground level, as indicated by the foundations, had risen to a height of *ca.* 0.75 m. above the Stadium floor. Among the coins depicting the Temple, there is one of Hadrian[19] that differs from the later issues by omitting the podium with its entrance into the crypt. This is the earliest coin of the series, and it is just possible that it was issued to mark the opening of the Temple. Such a date would fit the other evidence from the Palaimonion. It would then have been built after sacrificial pits A and B had been abandoned and filled up, while pit C, with its more elaborate enclosure, served the sacrificial needs of the cult.

We know that the Temple of Palaimon was standing and in use as late as the time of Pausanias' visit to Corinth, probably between 155 and 170 of our era.[20] Strangely enough, there is no archaeological evidence for the continued existence of the cult beyond the middle of the second century. The latest phase is represented by the lamps and vases from the upper stratum of pit C. It is unlikely that the worship of Palaimon was discontinued at that early date, but some change must have occurred to account for the disuse of pit C. Possibly the answer to this question will come from further study of the buildings in the area farther east, where the excavation campaigns of 1970 and 1971 brought to light some objects of later date that point to cult connections of some kind.

[17] The inscription IΣ 293 reads: Βλαστὸς μάντις; *Hesperia*, XXVII, 1958, p. 22.
[18] *Corinth*, VIII, iii, p. 89, no. 201. His full name and title, Π(όπλιος) Λικίνιος Π(οπλίου) υ(ἰὸς) Αἰμ(ιλίᾳ) Πρεῖσκος Ἰουουεντιανός, ἀρχιερεὺς διὰ βίου, appears in the inscription in Verona (*I.G.*, IV, 203,), which lists his benefactions at Isthmia. Other inscriptions in which his name occurs are *Corinth*, VIII, iii, nos. 199, 200, 306.
[19] Above, note 14.
[20] On this question, see Georges Roux' thorough discussion in his *Pausanias en Corinthie*, pp. 27–29.

THE SACRED GLEN

One adjunct to the Sanctuary of Poseidon was known as the Sacred Glen (Ἱερὰ Νάπη), within which were located sanctuaries of Demeter and Kore, Dionysos, Eueteria (Good Seasons), Artemis, and Kore. Apparently there were two cult places in which Persephone received worship, one in conjunction with her mother and one as a separate goddess. Pausanias does not refer to the Sacred Glen and he probably does not mention any of the sanctuaries in this area. We know of their existence only from the inscription *I.G.*, IV, 203, now in the Lapidario at Verona. The approximate location of the sanctuary (Plan I) became known some years ago through the discovery of two dedications to Demeter. One is a large relief krater, the fragments of which came from a well in the property of the late Nikolaos Papatheodorou, some 300 m. west of the temenos of Poseidon. This unique vessel, IP 384, is practically complete. The figures, in appliqué technique—a drunken Herakles facing a female figure (probably Methe), a satyr, four maenads—are drawn from Dionysiac revels, but the vase is a dedication to Demeter (Pl. 42, d) rather than to the god of wine who, however, also had a cult place in the Sacred Glen. The dedicatory inscription incised on the inside of the rim, ΣΟΦΑ ΔΑΜΑΤΡΙ, is written in Doric Greek, in letters of the fourth century B.C. John L. Caskey, who published the vase,[1] dates it and most of the other objects from the well in the fourth century B.C., probably in the third quarter. The second dedication is on a statue base, IΣ 316, of blue marble (Pl. 43, a)[2] found some 150 m. farther west in an orange grove belonging to the brothers Antonios and George Papatheodorou. It carries the inscription ΚΛΕΩ: ΘΑΣΙΔΟΣ: ΔΑΜΑΤΡΙ. In the top is an oblong sinkage for a statue, and together with the base was found a fragmentary statue representing a young girl holding a goose in her lap. This is presumably intended as a representation of Kleo, the dedicator, and her gift to the goddess. The plinth of the statuette fits exactly the cutting in the top of the base; consequently there is no doubt that the two belong together. These two dedications must have come from the sanctuary of Demeter and Kore mentioned in the inscription in Verona.

The area round the well in which the vase was found is now bare rock, with no recognizable cuttings of ancient buildings. Since it is more likely that the statue with its inscribed base was found near the place where it had been set up, we undertook in 1960 an investigation of this area. The field had by then been planted with citrus fruit trees; consequently the excavation had to be limited to a comparatively small area at the southwest corner of the field, where the base and the statuette were said to have been found. By that time a number of T-shaped poros blocks had been turned up by the plow among the orange trees, and this discovery gave us further reason for investigating the area. We had hoped to find traces of some of the sanctuaries mentioned in the Verona inscription, but what our excavation brought to light does not seem immediately related to any kind of cult place. The three structures found in this area are more appropriate to some industrial establishment. The first of these is in the form of a stuccoed channel or reservoir (Pls. 43, c, 75, a, 76, a), measuring 11.00 m. in length and *ca.* 0.60 m. in width. The floor slopes down from the north end where the depth is only 0.71 m. to the south end where the channel measures 1.335 m. in depth. The total decline at the bottom is 0.125 m. Originally the whole

---

[1] *Hesperia*, XXIX, 1960, pp. 168–176.
[2] O. Broneer, *Hesperia*, XXVIII, 1959, p. 326, no. 1.

channel seems to have been roofed over, except for an opening at the south end. Two of the cover slabs are still preserved *in situ*, and there was probably one more farther south. The south end, for a distance of 1.30 m., was left uncovered. The cover slabs are rectangular stones, 0.41 m. wide, *ca.* 0.76 m. long, and 0.22–0.23 m. thick. The remarkable thing about this cement-lined receptacle is a series of twenty chutes at the east edge (Pls. 43, b, c, 75, a, 76, a) extending down at an angle of *ca.* 45⁰ into the interior. As shown by the existing slabs, the chutes were cut through the cover slabs, and the lower part is cut in the wall of the channel. Only in the southern half are the chutes nearly intact, but enough is preserved of the others to show that they extended all the way to the north end. The chutes, like the walls and the floor of the channel, are covered with hard cement, but this has not been applied to the underside of the cover slabs. The chutes begin 1.40 m. from the south end and extend all the way to the north end. In the open part of the channel, at the south end, there are steps in the walls of the channel, one on the west side and two on the east (Pl. 76, a).

Before we attempt an explanation of this puzzling structure, it is necessary to describe the T-shaped stones (Pls. 43, d, e, 75, b, c) referred to above. Five such stones are completely preserved and there are fragments of two others from the same area, some found within the cement-lined receptacle, others in the vicinity; and two came from the fill of the small eastern cistern to be described below. The tops are saddle-shaped, and underneath, the stones narrow down to a width of a little more than half that of the upper part. The top, the front, and the two sides of all the blocks are covered with a hard stucco, similar to that found in the chutes and on the walls and floor of the channel. Only the bottom and the rear end of the T-shaped blocks are unstuccoed and roughly finished. The stones are of two varieties, similar in profile at the top, but differing somewhat in the vertical part. The first variety (Pl. 75, b) has a broad top and a short, thick stem. The second form is rather tall and slender, and the front half of the stem has been cut away up to a height of 0.06 m. (Pl. 75, c). The height above this cutting is about the same as the full height of the first variety, so that in the front parts all the stones are about equally high. From the shape of these stones, it seems fairly clear that they were set out upright in a row with the rear, unstuccoed ends abutting against a wall or some structure that concealed that part of the stones.

We return now to the east edge of the cement-lined channel. The chutes, which are rather irregular in shape, vary in width between 0.12 m. and 0.23 m. The spaces between the chutes, 0.21–0.29 m. in width, are not covered with stucco; something stood there that has been broken away. Since the stems of the T-shaped blocks correspond roughly in thickness to the spaces between the chutes, it is fairly obvious that they belong here. The difference in the two types of stones is due to the fact that the cover slabs are of unequal length. Thus the first type of T-shaped block stood on the top of the longer cover-blocks, and the second variety rested only with the front part on the shorter cover-blocks and the taller rear part of the stem reached down below the top of these slabs. If set out in this fashion, the tops of the T-shaped blocks would be in a straight, horizontal line, and the stones would have been set free from each other, with open spaces of 0.05–0.09 m. between them (Pl. 43, e). Thus the interspaces between the tops of the stones would come directly above the chutes. One can only draw the conclusion that these stones formed the seats in a large public latrine, conveniently near the Sanctuary, but not near enough to be offensive to visitors.

An ancient well is located two meters east of the south end of the channel. The well curb (Pl. 44, a) is a carefully carved, circular drum, having an outside diameter of 0.95 m. and rising to a height of 0.33 m. Carved in the same block is a square plinth measuring 0.98 m. on the side. On one side of the wellhead the smooth circular edge of the drum comes straight down to the plinth; on the other side there is an ovolo moulding at the base. Both the moulding and the top of the base on that side are covered with hard cement. The other side is unstuccoed. The less carefully finished side was presumably turned toward some permanent structure that concealed these details. The well-shaft at the top is only 0.46 m. in diameter, but farther down it grows to a width of 0.87 m. The well curb and the stucco that adheres to it have the characteristics of Greek workmanship, but the well, which extends down to a depth of 12.37 m., contained a mixture of Greek and Roman objects. Only the upper part of the fill to a depth of two meters had suffered contamination in 1914, when, according to a village resident, the well was partly opened and again filled up. Among the small objects from the fill of the well are two rolled pieces of lead, apparently intended as curse-tablets, but not pierced with nails as is usual in such objects. One shows no trace of letters; the writing on the other is very fine and difficult to read.[3]

At a distance of 17.00 m. east of the cement-lined channel with the chutes, a small area (Pl. 76, b) was excavated that seems to have been occupied by a commercial establishment. In the northern part is a cistern (Pls. 44, b, 76, b, 77, a), measuring 4.15 m. in length, *ca.* 1.35 m. in width, and with a preserved depth of 1.25 m. The north and west walls are carved out of native rock. The east and south walls are built with stones cut into rectangular shapes and laid in horizontal courses. The masonry is of the careful type characteristic of Greek classical times. The walls were covered with a watertight stucco, much of which has peeled off. At the west end of the cistern is a large inlet, measuring 0.60 × 0.28 m. across, and 0.90 m. in depth. The south half of the area (Pl. 44, c) is rather irregular and appears to have been altered. At the east end the floor level is approximately the same as that of the cistern, but in the southeast corner the native rock extends to a height of 1.30 m. above the floor. The east wall of the cistern continues in a straight line clear across the southern half and abuts against a vertical cut in the native rock. Here two walls, one running east-to-west and the other north-to-south, are preserved to a height of 1.27 m. above the floor. These walls are built partly out of re-used blocks of Greek workmanship and partly out of small uncut stones and tiles. One of the re-used blocks is a basin, set on edge (Pl. 77, a), the inner cavity of which measures 0.80 m. in length, 0.46 m. in width and 0.25 m. in depth. One of the blocks in the east-west wall is a roughly cut Doric capital with the abacus measuring 0.67 m. on the side. At the higher level in the southern part are the remains of a floor made of hard cement resting on a layer of small stones (Pl. 44, c, right). Close to this floor there was an ash pit, 0.77 × 0.43 m., with some of the ashes still left on the bottom. Other small piles of ash were found in the vicinity. The establishment resembles the fullers' shops excavated on top of the Rachi,[4] but it is not so well preserved and lacks the two circular vats that are characteristic of the Rachi units. The pottery found in the area was chiefly of the fourth century B.C. Considerable quantities of roof tiles and loomweights of types dated in the fourth century were also found. Eight meters to the east of the area described above, a smaller cistern (Pls. 44, d, 77, b) was discovered which is oriented nearly north to south. At its north end a stairway of five steps leads down to a small landing from which there are three more steps down to the floor. The cistern measures 8.00 m. in length, including the descent, and 0.89 m. in width. It was covered with slabs, two of which were found *in situ*. The depth from the bottom of the slabs to the floor of the cistern is 1.85 m. The steps and all the walls were covered with watertight cement. This small reservoir seems to be unconnected with any building. It was probably made to receive the water from the roof of some building in the vicinity, perhaps to supplement the limited amount of water collected in the larger cistern.

The two dedications to Demeter would seem to indicate that the sanctuaries mentioned in the inscription in Verona were located somewhere between the ancient well in which the relief krater was discovered and the area excavated by us at the southwest corner of the Papatheodorou fruit orchard, where the inscribed statue base and the statuette of Kleo were turned up by the plow. Small soundings which we carried on among the trees of the orchard brought to light a few pieces of roof tiles and some fragments of architecture, but nothing that could be remotely associated with an ancient temple. It is quite likely that the sanctuaries were located in the area just north of the modern road which is now occupied by

---

[3] Michael H. Jameson, who has succeded in reading some of the text, has kindly sent me the results of his study. He finds the word EYAMΩN, apparently the name of a daemon, repeated to form a pattern, arranged so that one letter is omitted at the beginning of the word each time the name is repeated until at the end only the last letter N remains. The tablet will be published in another volume dealing with inscriptions from Isthmia.

[4] See Chrysoula Kardara, *A.J.A.*, LXV, 1961, pp. 261–266.

modern houses of the village. The three excavated areas can hardly have been directly connected with any of the cult places in the Sacred Glen. The buildings uncovered are either parts of some small commercial establishment or perhaps even private houses. For the time being, the exact location of the sanctuaries must remain unknown. To excavate the whole area between the road and the North Gully, now mostly occupied by the citrus fruit orchard, would be costly, and the probabilities of finding anything of importance are not promising. The congeries of religious establishments in the Sacred Glen were probably loosely connected with the Isthmian Sanctuary. They can hardly have been of major importance since Pausanias ignores them completely. It has been suggested that the sanctuary of Artemis mentioned in the inscription is referred to by Pausanias in II, 2, 3, but this is not very likely. His mention of this sanctuary does not follow his account of the sanctuaries of Poseidon and Palaimon but is inserted with his description of the two harbors of Corinth. For this reason it seems more likely that he saw the Artemis sanctuary near the harbor of Kenchreai, which he describes after his reference to the temple of Artemis.

THE WEST FOUNDATION AND THE HIPPODROME

A t a distance of *ca.* 2.00 km. southwest of the Temple of Poseidon a monument has been exca-vated which probably was somehow connected with the Isthmian Sanctuary (Plan I, inset). It was discovered in 1960 when the owner of a field, Alekos Goumas, reported that there had been some illicit digging in a low mound on his property. The Ephor of Antiquities in the Corinthia at that time, the late Nikolaos Verdelis, suggested that we investigate the mound. We found ample evidence of fresh disturbance of the soil above the outcropping of an ancient wall of good classical construction. In 1961 we laid bare the whole foundation.

The principal structure is a longer than wide rectangular foundation (Pls. 45, a, 78, 79) with a projecting wing at each end of the façade structurally tied in with the main part of the foundation. The monument is oriented very nearly according to the cardinal points of the compass and faces the south. The foundation, which is 1.80 m. broad, measures 25.49 m. in length from east to west on the euthynteria, and somewhat over 16.00 m. from north to south, not including the wings. A second, less broad founda-tion, which runs parallel on all three sides, is unconnected with the former. At the west end two courses in the broad east-west foundation are preserved; at the east end, where the original ground level was lower, the foundation is four courses deep. Most of the euthynteria is preserved, except at the east end. It is constructed with headers on the south side backed by a row of stretchers on the north. The stones vary somewhat in length and width, but the approximate size is 1.20 × 0.60 m. in area and 0.385 m. in height. In the course below the euthynteria there is a row of stretchers on the south side and headers on the north, but the masonry of this course is somewhat less regular than that of the euthynteria. The foun-dation for the east wall, which has the same thickness, extends northward for a distance of *ca.* 17.38 m., including the southeast porch and measured on the setting lines for the next course (Pl. 79). It comes to an abrupt end at the north, but one rather irregular block measuring 0.87 × 0.70 m. in area buttresses the end of the wall. This stone is so rough on the top that no other blocks can have rested upon it. On its lowest course, the east foundation measures 18.20 m. in length; the corresponding north-south foundation at the west end, which is less deep at the south end, has a total length of 17.40 m. These dimensions include the foundations of the two wings but not the buttresses at the north ends. Two smaller stones have been inserted as buttress at the north end of the west wall. The euthynteria course is preserved except at the southeast corner, and four blocks of the first course above the euthynteria are still *in situ* in the west wall. In the north part of this wall, where the native rock rises to a higher level, there was no separate euthynteria course, but the rock has been dressed down to the proper level. That the topmost course preserved on all three sides (except for the four blocks of the west wall) is the euthynteria is indicated by setting lines at a distance of 0.13–0.17 m. from the outer edge of the foun-dations. On the east foundation there are some cross scratches indicating the exact length of the blocks in the course above. Three of the blocks so indicated vary in length from 1.205 to 1.21 m.[1] In the top of the euthynteria course are pry holes (Pls. 45, c, 78), which indicate that the course was started in the middle and laid from there toward the two ends. The foundation for the wing at the west end

---

[1] With a foot length of 0.304 m., which came into use in the fourth century B.C., the blocks measure *ca.* 4 × 2 feet in area. See above, pp. 63–64, and *Isthmia*, I, Appendix I, pp. 176, 180.

(Pl. 45, b) measures 3.03 m. in length from east to west, exclusive of the lowest course, and 1.50 m. in width. The foundation for the corresponding wing at the east end (Pl. 45, a), here preserved at a lower level, measures 3.15 m. in length and 2.22 m. in width. The difference in the dimensions of the two wings is due to the fact that the foundation at the southeast corner goes deeper and the courses are stepped back toward the top. The structures that rested on the two foundations were certainly alike.

Not a single fragment was found that can be identified as coming from the superstructure supported on these broad foundations. It is quite certain that there was no colonnade. Had columns existed, some small pieces from the capitals or from the arrises would have broken off and would have been found in the fill of the area. This becomes all the more apparent when we consider the remains from the foundation of a parapet that surrounded the monument on three sides, south, east, and west. At the west end, where the natural rock is higher, there is no outer foundation. The blocks of the parapet base were laid in a rock-cut trench, 0.90 m. wide. This runs parallel to the broad west foundation at a distance of 1.13 m. The trench for this outer foundation of the west parapet apparently proved too wide, and a rough packing of undressed field stones was inserted between the foundation and the east edge of the trench. The west face of the outer wall is marked by setting lines cut in the rock, showing that the wall had a thickness of only 0.42 m., leaving an unused space, 0.20 m. wide, at the outer edge and a broader space, *ca.* 0.30 m. wide, along the inner face, where the stone packing is now left. At the north end, the west parapet wall terminated against a nearly vertical cutting in the rock (Pl. 45, d) slightly farther north than the north end of the inner broad foundation. The outer foundation on the south side (Pl. 45, a, left) is made with poros blocks of the same size as those used in the broad inner foundations. Only the southern part of the top course has been smoothly dressed on a width of 0.78 m.; this bedding is slightly narrower than the trench cut in rock for the outer west foundation. Setting marks and the weathering on the south foundation show that the wall that rested on these blocks had approximately the same thickness as the parapet wall at the west end. The outer edge of the south parapet foundation was 3.55 m. (3.65 m. at the east end) from the outer face of the wall on the inner broad foundation. The corresponding distance of the west parapet is only *ca.* 2.28 m., *ca.* two-thirds the distance at the façade (Pl. 79). At the west end the outer south foundation is only one course deep; in the east half of the same foundation there were four courses, the upper two of which are now missing. The south parapet foundation extends 2.13 m. to the east beyond the east face of the inner broad foundation, but the south end of the outer east foundation for a length of at least 3.50 m. has been removed. Farther north where the top of this foundation is preserved, there are setting lines indicating that the east face of the outer wall was 2.11 m. east of the outer face of the east wall that stood on the broad east foundation. This shows further that the two flank walls of the monument, which had approximately the same dimensions, were also at about the same distance from the inner wall. At the north end the outer east foundation extended only a little farther north than the inner east foundation.

The outer foundations carried a profiled parapet (Pl. 80, a), numerous fragments of which were all along the foundations on the east, south, and west sides. Two kinds of mouldings from the front of the parapet were found in large numbers. At the base was a large torus surmounted by a cyma reversa; above that a slight setback, and then a plain wall surface is to be restored. The total height of the moulding at the base is 0.145 m. The second type (Pls. 45, e, 80, a) is in the form of an Ionic geison with a cavetto and plain fillet above the hawksbeak and a blunt drip at the bottom. The moulding at the base of the soffit very nearly repeats the profile at the top of the corona. The tops of these pieces are concavely curved. Two other types of moulding, found in much smaller number in the same context, are almost certainly from the rear of the same parapet. One of these (IA 941), shown in Plate 80, b, has two surfaces at an angle of 95⁰ to each other, with one corner cut away concavely so as to form a cavetto; at the lower corner is a rectangular cutting. The one surviving fragment of this kind was discovered in the southwest corner, together with numerous pieces from the front of the parapet. The second variety, of which there are three small fragments, IA 936 (Pl. 80, c), 790, 934, has a double setback, the combined depth of which is almost the same as that of the rectangular recess on the first kind. These two varieties of mouldings seem to fit well on the back of the parapet, as shown in Plate 80, a, lower right. Thus the parapet would have had an ornate side with mouldings at top and bottom projecting far toward the front, and a plainer rear side. When the parapet was broken up and the material re-used, the mouldings on the face which projected too far were cut away. This is the reason why so many pieces of the mouldings from the front were found, while only a few small fragments of the less deeply profiled rear survived. The parapet is carefully carved in fine-grained poros stone but was not covered with stucco. The pieces show but little weathering, an indication that the monument was demolished at a comparatively early date. The height of the parapet may be estimated at about one meter to give proper proportion to the mouldings.

In addition to the solidly built broad foundations and the equally well-built foundations for the parapet, there is a wall preserved for a length of 17.00 m. directly north of the broad south foundation (Pls. 46, a, 78, Section A–A). Its maximum height is 0.75 m. It is built in a distinctive technique, with large blocks set upright at unequal distances and the spaces between these blocks filled with polygonal masonry of smaller blocks. This wall clearly antedates the broad south foundation and has a slightly different orientation. At the west end its face was cut back to make room for the missing courses that stood on the broad foundation. Near the east end the earlier wall makes a northward curve so that the two walls at one point are 0.30 m. apart. The south face of this earlier wall is smooth and was intended to be seen; in the rear the wall is quite uneven. It was thus constructed as a retaining wall for the higher area to the north.

The area enclosed by the three broad walls and the hillside in the rear presented a bewildering picture of uncut stones of different sizes thrown up in heaps to a maximum height of 1.20 m. above the ancient ground level (Pls. 46, b, 78, Section B–B). Originally nearly all the space north of the south foundation was occupied with piles of stones of this kind. Along the south side and in the center of the area the stones were removed in the course of our excavation down to the ancient ground level, which is only a little below the euthynteria course of the broad foundation. In the area thus cleared north of the earlier wall, and almost midway between the east and west ends of the monument, is a shallow pit (Pl. 46, c) measuring 2.60 m. from north to south and 2.35 m. from east to west. The pit, which had been dug to a depth of 0.40 m. below the ancient ground level, was filled to the top with ash and carbonized wood. A few metal objects that came from the fill are so corroded that in most cases their shape cannot be determined. The only other objects of interest from the pit and from the earth directly above the layer of ash are a few droplets of glass and some very fragile laurel berries and laurel leaves, apparently from a crown made of bronze and plated with a thin cover of gold. The pit contained a few animal bones, but no recognizable human remains. Surrounding the pit there was a ring of stones, nearly circular, but measuring 9.20 m. in diameter on the outside from east to west and about 8.70 m. from north to south (Pl. 46, d). The inner diameter is ca. 6.25 m. The stones had not been laid carefully but thrown in helter-skelter, making a ring ca. 1.20 m. broad that was bedded in a shallow trench, dug to just below the ancient surface. There may have been an entrance on the east side, where the stones are missing for a length of 1.00 m. The stone circle is now preserved to a height of only some thirty centimeters above the ancient ground level; originally it was probably much higher. It is earlier than the early east-west retaining wall, which cuts into it on the south side (Pls. 46, d, 78). From these observations we obtain the following relative chronology. The stone ring with the ash pit in the center is the earliest. The polygonal east-west retaining wall follows next in order, and the heavy parallel foundations are the latest. Presumably the parapet was built at the same time as the broad foundations or not much later.

Before our excavations, the area around the circular stone wall was filled to a height of 1.25 m. above the ancient ground level with piles of stones and earth. Here and there in this fill were found several spear points and a few spear butts of iron, and many strigils, all in very poor condition. Some of the spear points seem to have been covered with a thin coat of silver and are in an excellent state of preservation (Pl. 47, a);[2] others are completely corroded by rust. A few other objects of interest from the area include four iron rings pierced with a large bolt and nails (Pl. 47, b); these may have been used as metal trimmings for the legs of a wooden table. There was also some pottery, the bulk of which can be dated about the middle of the fourth century B.C. (Pl. 48, a).[3] The earlier pieces found in the fill are so few as to have no direct bearing on the date of the monument. A few fragmentary terracotta figurines, some broken roof tiles, and pieces of basins or perirrhanteria came from the fill among the stones. Carbonized wood and ash appeared at various levels throughout.

Although it is possible to establish the relative order in which the various parts of the monument were constructed, there seems to be no great chronological difference between them. The fragments from the parapet, which are very numerous, seem to be of approximately the same date as the pottery found among the stones in the rear.[4] The masonry of the broad foundations is of a type attributable to the middle of the fourth century, and the east-west retaining wall appears to be of the same date or only a little earlier. Thus the remains of the monument and the objects found with it point to a uniform date approximately 350 B.C.

Since no part of the structure that rested on the inner broad walls was found, the nature of the building can only be conjectured. Reasons have been adduced above for the assumption that it did not carry a colonnade or other elaborate structure. The form of the superstructure was such that it could be entirely removed without being broken up into small pieces. This contrasts with the parapet, which was completely shattered, thus leaving numerous fragments from which to restore its profile. If a superstructure with delicate mouldings had stood on the broad foundations, it would have suffered a like fate and in any case some fragments would have been broken off. The most likely form of monument supported on the broad foundations is a large exedra facing the south and flanked by two wings. We may thus restore a single course of stones above the existing euthynteria. This seems to have projected slightly beyond the north edge of the foundation, as indicated by the fact that the south face of the earlier retaining wall has been cut back. The setting line along the south edge shows that the euthynteria there projected somewhat beyond the line of the course above. Consequently this course had about the same width as the foundation, ca. 1.80 m. At the rear edge we may reconstruct a plain wall, probably 0.60 m. thick and rising to a height of at least 1.50 m. In front of this wall there would have been a bench, approximately 0.45 m. wide, leaving a space of 0.75 m. by which the occupants could reach their seats. The parapet would have been sufficiently low so that the spectators seated in the exedra, which was at a higher level, could see over it. The bedding for the sill of the parapet is ca. 0.75 m. below the toichobate level of the broad inner foundation. If we assume that the course on which the seats rested had the same height as the sill of the parapet (it was probably somewhat higher), the eye level of the spectators

---

[2] These, together with the arms and armor from the main excavations, are being studied by Alaster Jackson of the University of Manchester; they will be published in another volume of the Isthmia series. Though the final study has yet to be made, Mr. Jackson has reached the following tentative conclusion regarding their date: "The probabilities point to Classical, perhaps fourth century date for the West Foundation weapons, but they can not be certainly dated in themselves."

[3] The carafe on the left in Plate 48, a belongs to a relatively rare type of pottery found both in Corinth and in Athens (*Hesperia*, XXXI, 1962, p. 25, no. 22). Recently fragments of similar vases were found in the area east of the Sacred Spring in Corinth; Charles K. Williams, *Hesperia*, XXXVIII, 1969, pp. 57–59, figs. 8, 9, pl. 18, a–d; XXXIX, 1970, p. 5, nos. 5, 6, pl. 1. The red-figure lekythos on the right in Plate 48, a can be dated to the approximate middle of the fourth century B.C. (*Hesperia*, XXXI, 1962, p. 25, no. 23).

[4] A date in the second half of the fourth century is based on a single monument from Greece. There are only three profiles that closely resemble those from the coping of the parapet. They are all from the epikranitis course in the Temple of Zeus at Stratos (Lucy T. Shoe, *Profiles of Greek Mouldings*, pl. LXI, 21–23), which has been dated in the 320s. So W. B. Dinsmoor (*AAG*, chart opp. p. 340) and Lucy Shoe (*loc. cit.*). D. S. Robertson (*Handbook of Greek and Roman Architecture*, p. 330) gives 330 B.C. as the probable date. Among the mouldings from Italy an anta capital from Kaulonia in the Reggio Museum comes nearest to ours in profile, but the resemblance is not very close. Lucy T. Shoe (*Profiles of Western Greek Mouldings*, pl. VIII, 6) assigns it to "probably late fourth century."

would have been 1.50–1.75 m. above the parapet sill, and the parapet would have been perhaps one meter high.

There are only slight traces of later occupation of the site. In the northeast part of the area a tile grave was found (Pls. 47, c, 78) containing a skeleton in very poor condition and no other objects. Four complete tiles have been put together out of the fragments from the grave. They are clearly of Roman date, but the type is somewhat unusual. They measure 0.54 m. in length and 0.44 m. in width at the upper end, narrowing down to 0.395 m. at *ca.* 0.075 m. from the lower end, where the raised edges terminate. The overlapping part at the lower end has the corners cut back to a width of only 0.353 m. so as to fit between the raised edges at the upper end of the tile below, as seen in Plate 47, d. There are no stamps on any of the tiles. The grave seems to be an isolated burial unconnected with the purpose of the monument, which may already have been destroyed when the burial was made. In the fill above the foundations at the southeast corner, some fragments of Roman pottery were found and with them a bronze coin of Marcus Aurelius. These late objects may date the destruction rather than the use of the monument. It seems unlikely that the destruction took place in mediaeval or modern times. Only at the southeast corner, where the mixed, partly modern fill extended down to a greater depth, some of the blocks in the foundation had been removed more recently. Workmen from the village of Kyras Vrysi informed us that stones had been removed from the foundation at this point some twenty-five years ago to be used in a culvert in the vicinity.

There are several features of this isolated monument that invite comments. If, as I believe, the inner road foundation supported an exedra facing the south, there would have been something to occupy the spectators' attention in that direction. This was probably the hippodrome, and from the configuration of the terrain one would suppose that the foundation is located somewhere near the turning point or the finish line of the racecourse. This would sufficiently explain the position of the grandstand at this point. But the monument was more than an exedra. The pit, filled with ash and surrounded with a stone circle, points to some cult practice in this area. A likely explanation is that the mound in its original form was a heroon; but since no human bones were found in the pit, it was probably not the burial place of some historical figure. The scrappy fragments of a metal wreath culled from the ashes of the pit and the numerous spear points and strigils that lay scattered among the stones are probably dedications to some hero worshiped at this place. If he was, as is probable, a mythological figure, there would have been no actual burial, and the large amount of ash in the pit would not be the remains of a funeral pyre but of sacrifices to the hero.

In his description of the Isthmian Sanctuary in the second book, Pausanias does not mention the hippodrome, but we know from victory lists that horse races of various kinds formed part of the Isthmian festival program. Moreover, in his later description at Olympia, Pausanias states that in the hippodrome at Isthmia there was a monument of Taraxippos, whom he identified as Glaukos, the son of Sisyphos.[5] In the Olympia hippodrome Pausanias saw an altar of Taraxippos, whom the periegete there took to be none other than Poseidon. The function of this hero, whose cult place was situated at the critical point in the racecourse where the charioteers had to negotiate the dangerous turn, was to throw the horses into panic. Presumably sacrifices were made to this malevolent hero in order to forestall such catastrophes. If the monument unearthed in our excavations was sacred to him, it is remarkable that the metal objects found in the mound seem more suitable as dedications by athletes than by charioteers or owners of the horses. The facts that these objects lay scattered in various parts of the mound and that most of the strigils had been twisted out of shape can be explained on the ground of later disturbance of the mound. Although the ash pit itself gave no appearance of having been ransacked, the whole area round about had obviously been turned over in illicit digging in search for objects of value. The better preserved objects would have been carried away. The strigils may perhaps have been used in grooming of the horses after the races, but spear points belong in the pentathlon. Although

[5] Pausanias, VI, 20, 19.

there is no other evidence for such a practice, we might perhaps conjecture that spear throwing here a Isthmia took place in the spacious hippodrome rather than in the restricted space of the Stadium, wher stray throws would have been a danger to the spectators.[6]

The area in front of the West Foundation is comparatively level, with only a thin cover of soil abov the solid rock. A late east-west road runs *ca.* 13 m. south of the monument. The wheel tracks, whic show a wheel base of *ca.* 1.40 m., have been traced in cross trenches for a distance of 65 m. toward th west (Pl. 81). To judge by the depth of the ruts in the rocky surface (Pl. 48, b), the road must have bee in use a long time. It is, of course, impossible to determine how early the road came into use. It ma be even earlier than the hippodrome and could have been in use throughout ancient times. The Isthmia Games, being held for only a few hours every two years, need not have prevented road traffic throug the hippodrome, which had no permanent seats or embankments for spectators. The few pottery frag ments found directly above the roadbed indicate that the road was still in use in late Roman and earl Christian times. From the direction of the road, it seems likely that it is the same main thoroughfar between Isthmia and Corinth that ran through the Sanctuary of Poseidon (above, p. 18). Some 240 m east of the West Foundation and a little to the south of its façade, we found traces of what seem to b the same road, here with well-marked wheel ruts, in places 0.45 m. deep. The axle width indicated b these ruts is 1.40–1.45 m. In the area east of these road marks there is a rock-cut dike, which seems t have resulted from quarrying. The stone is of the same kind as that used in the West Foundation. It i clear that the hippodrome—if it existed here—cannot have extended farther east. The lay of the lan southwest of the West Foundation shows that the racecourse would not have extended more than abou 50 m. west of the monument. Thus the maximum length of the racecourse would be 240+25 (length o West Foundation)+50 = 315 m.[7]

---

[6] Accidents in spear throwing were probably common, e.g. Antiphon's defense (II, 2, 7) which had to do with th accidental killing of a boy, but this happened during practice in the gymnasion. Cf. Jüthner-Brein, *Athlet. Leibesüb.*, I p. 342. Cf. also Plutarch, *Perikles*, XXXVI, 3.

[7] Little is known about the length of the Greek hippodrome. At Olympia the hippodrome has been swept away by th Alphaios. Ludwig Drees (*Olympia*, English Version, p. 97) gives 384.56 m. as the length of the racecourse. This is calcu lated on the basis of two stades, with a foot length of 0.32046 m. The hippodrome on Mt. Lykaion has the approximat length of 240 m. The Athenian hippodrome, according to *Etym. Mag., s.v.,* Ἐνεχελιδώ, was 8 stadia, *ca.* 1,565 m. long but this has little likelihood of being correct. Gustave Fougères (*Mantinée et l'Arcadie Orientale*, p. 99) estimated th length of the hippodrome at Mantineia at *ca.* 400 m., and its width 200 m. What seems to follow from these largely un supported guesses is that the Greek hippodrome, unlike the stadion, had no fixed length. For a full discussion of th subject see K. Schneider, *R.E.*, VIII, 2, cols. 1734–1745.

CATALOGUE OF ARCHITECTURAL MEMBERS

EARLY ROMAN TEMENOS WALLS

Many coping blocks were found in various parts of the temenos of Poseidon. They are of poros and all have the same profile, height, and width (see **1**, Pl. 63, a), but vary considerably in length. Those that are well preserved have the two ends gouged back in the middle so as to form a very rough and exaggerated anathyrosis, which was presumably filled with mortar. One block, measuring 0.80 m. in length and trimmed on top and on one side, is built into the late closing of the Northeast Gate. Two others, not included in the catalogue, are built into Tower 19 of the Early Christian Fortress.

1. IA 1614. Pl. 63, a. Coping block, found on the foundation for the South Stoa colonnade, close to sacrificial pit B.

L. 1.334 m.; W. 0.52 m.; H. 0.455 m.

The lower part of the block, up to a height of 0.22 m. is rectangular in section; then there is a setback, 0.038 m. wide, on either side, and the upper part is rounded.

2. IA 1617. Pl. 29, c. Coping block like the preceding, found slightly north of the South Stoa, opposite the Semicircle.

L. 1.00 m.; other dimensions as in the preceding.

3. IA 1616. Short coping block like the preceding, found *ca.* 5.00 m. farther north.

L. 0.75 m.

The top has been scratched by the plow and is weathered.

4. IA 1615. Pl. 63, b. Coping block like the preceding, found on the foundation for the early Roman temenos wall, 4.50 m. west of the preceding.

L. 1.277 m.; W. 0.525 m.; H. 0.436 m.

The profile is the same as that of the other blocks, but on one side, 0.62 m. from the better preserved end, is a joint for a block extending at right angles to **4**. This joint would indicate that short blocks were put in at the buttresses, but no such block has been preserved (above, p. 71).

5. IA 1618. Short block like the preceding, found at the Northeast Gate, in the front foundation of the East Stoa.

L. 0.74 m.

The top has been chiseled away so as to square the block for re-use in some construction, probably in the late wall blocking the opening in the Northeast Gate.

6. IA 1618A. Block like the preceding, built into the late blocking wall and still in place in the Northeast Gate.

L. 0.80 m.

The block has been trimmed on the top and on the sides, but appears to retain the full length.

7. IA 1619. Coping block like the preceding, found slightly west of the Northeast Gate.

Pres. L. 1.33 m.

At one end the block has been roughly cut back diagonally, and the upper part is broken away; the other end is smooth and lacks the usual anathyrosis.

8. IA 1618B. Coping block like the preceding, built into the west wall of a small pit of late construction, between the south flank of the Temple of Poseidon and the early Roman temenos wall.

9. IA 1618C. Coping block like the preceding, built into the east wall of the same pit in which **8** is found. Both ends are broken away.

10. IA 1620. Coping block like the preceding, found in the debris of the foundation for the projected North Stoa in the northwest corner of the temenos.

L. 0.71 m.

On one side is a cutting 0.14 m. long, 0.15 m. high, and 0.11 m. deep, probably from secondary use of the block.

11. IA 1620A. Coping block like the preceding, found at the inner end of the vaulted passage in the northwest corner of the temenos.

L. 1.094 m.

12. IA 1620B. Coping block like the preceding and found in the same place.
L. 0.717 m.

13. IA 1620C. Coping block like the preceding, found in the same place, slightly farther toward the northeast mouth of the passage.
L. 1.388 m.

14. IA 1620D. Coping block like the preceding, found in the same place, farther toward the mouth of the passage. The end is broken away.
Pres. L. 0.60 m.

15. IA 1620E. Coping block like the preceding, found in the same place, farther toward the mouth of the passage. The end is broken away.
Pres. L. 0.50 m.

THE STOAS

Architectural members from the three Stoas are comparatively few in number, but sufficiently representative to enable us to restore the buildings with a minimum of conjecture. Most of the existing pieces and numerous fragments belong to the West and South Stoas; of the East Stoa only a few pieces have been found. As will appear in the description of the individual members, there is considerable variation throughout. Doubtless the Stoas were constructed over a long period of time, and the construction involved changes in marble-cutters and perhaps in architects as well. There is some evidence for the supposition that the East and West Stoas differed somewhat in detail, though not in general design, from the South Stoa.

16. IA 1626. Pls. 34, d, 68, a. Ionic column base of grayish, brittle marble with attached plinth; found in the northwestern part of the excavated area, probably close to the place where it had been set up in the West Stoa. It is now lying on an isolated piece of the stylobate, which may have supported it originally.
Plinth: 0.713 × 0.745 m.; H. *ca.* 0.095 m.; total H. of plinth and base: 0.286 m.; D. of base top: 0.58 m.

The base has a large torus at the bottom and a smaller one at the top, separated by a scotia. In the top is a roughly circular dowel hole, *ca.* 0.05 m. in diameter and 0.045 m. in depth; from it a pour channel extends to the edge. The carving is rather uneven and the top is roughly picked. The base is very nearly complete, with only two corners of the plinth and some of the upper torus broken away.

17. IA 349W. Fragment of column base with attached plinth, from the South Stoa.
Pres. H. 0.235 m.; H. of plinth 0.109 m.; H. of lower torus 0.087 m.

White marble. Marks of straight-edged chisel are visible on the torus and scotia; the plinth is finished with a toothed chisel.

18. IA 349L. Small fragment of Ionic base, found among the marbles from the South Stoa.
H. of upper torus 0.052 m.; no other dimension preserved.

White marble. Part of scotia also preserved. Probably part of same base as the preceding.

19. IA 352A. Pl. 68, b. Small fragment from the bottom of an unfluted Ionic column, found at the south end of the West Stoa.

Pres. H. 0.485 m.; D. including base fillet 0.5972 m.; greatest D. above base fillet 0.531 m.

Grayish white marble with prominent purplish gray and green streaks. The fillet at the bottom is 0.05 m. high, and projects 0.03 m. from the face of the shaft.

20. IA 352F. Pl. 21, c, center. Large fragment of unfluted column, broken at both ends, and found at the curved end of the Earlier Stadium.
Pres. H. 2.10 m.; greatest D. 0.587 m.; smallest D. 0.569 m.; diminution on a length of 2.00 m. *ca.* 0.018 m.
Mottled gray and purple marble with white streaks.

21. IA 352E. Small fragment found with the preceding and part of the same column.

22. IA 352C. Fragment of unfluted column, found in the crypt of the Palaimon Temple, toward the west end.
Pres. H. 0.80 m.; Pres. D. 0.513 m.
Conglomerate purple marble with many white parts.

23. IA 352D. Column fragment, apparently from same shaft as the preceding and found in the same place.
Pres. H. 0.64 m.; greatest Pres. D. 0.51 m.

24. IA 352B. Fragment of the upper part of an unfluted column, found in the South Stoa.
Pres. H. 1.03 m.; D. just below top moulding 0.478 m.; greatest D. one meter farther down 0.485 m.; diminution on a length of one meter *ca.* 0.007 m.

Mottled greenish gray, purple, and white marble. The top moulding has been neatly chiseled away and the other end cut off in a straight line; apparently the fragment was prepared to be used as a roller, but there are no holes in the ends.

25. IA 349C. Pl. 69, b, left. Small fragment from the upper part of an unfluted column, preserving a moulding at the top, found in the South Stoa about midway between the two ends of the building.

Pres. H. 0.28 m.; greatest Pres. D. below the neck moulding 0.4871 m.; D. including moulding at top *ca.* 0.541 m.

Mottled gray and white marble. The top moulding consists of a plain fillet surmounted by an ovolo *ca.* 0.05 m. high.

26. IA 349D. Pl. 69, b, center. Small fragment from the top of a column, found in the same place as the preceding.

Pres. H. 0.33 m.; D. of shaft below moulding 0.4928 m.

Mottled gray and white marble. The moulding is very low.

27. IA 352G. Pl. 69, b, right. Small fragment from the upper part of a column, found at the south edge of the foundation for the Temple of Poseidon, close to the post-destruction house (see text, p. 97).

Pres. H. 0.92 m.; D. 0.5049 m.

Mottled green, purple, and white marble. Moulding at the top is carefully carved.

28. IA 604. Small fragment from the upper part of a column, found in the Palaimonion.

Gray micaceous marble. The diameter seems to be the same as that of the preceding fragments. The carving is very rough, and the ovoloid top of the moulding is merely blocked out.

29. IA 352J. Small fragment of an unfluted column, built in a late wall east of the Southwest House.

Pres. H. 0.82 m.; greatest Pres. D. 0.475 m. (not complete D.).

Mottled purple, green and white marble.

30. IA 352K. Fragment of unfluted column, now built into a late retaining wall in the rear of the South Stoa near the west end.

Pres. H. 1.60 m.

Mottled purple and white marble which tends to flake lengthwise. The diameter is not obtainable without removing the block from the wall.

31. IA 352I. Circular, rough-hewn drum found built into the same wall as the preceding.

Pres. H. 0.47 m.; D. 0.67 m.

Mottled purple, gray, and white marble. The top has been cut with a saw, and at the edges are three rough cuttings which seem to indicate that the block in its present form had been used as a hitching post. In the top is a rough cutting which, if carried through, would

reduce the diameter to *ca.* 0.61 m. This seems to have been prepared for a column of the Stoa and rejected before being finished.

32. IA 1119. Pls. 35, a, 69, a. Fragment of Ionic capital found in the debris of the trans-Isthmian wall where the modern highway intercepts it.

Pres. L. 0.46 m.; H. exclusive of volute 0.19 m.; H. of the egg-and-dart moulding is 0.085 m.

White, fine-grained marble. Preserved are one end of the abacus, almost a complete volute, the corner palmette, and two eggs and darts. Although the fragment was found far from the excavations, it is almost certainly from the Stoas. This is shown by several other fragments of similar workmanship and dimensions. There were three eggs and darts, two of which were partly covered with the corner palmette, having four leaves with leaf stalk and heart from which the leaves spring. Three leaves turn down, and their top turns up and partly covers the egg. For the profile, see drawing in Plate 69, a. The eye of the volute is a rounded disc projecting from the plane of the volute.

33. IA 741. Pl. 35, b, right. Small fragment of Ionic capital found in the third manhole of the North Drain.

H. of egg-and-dart moulding 0.085 m.

White marble. Preserved are all three eggs and two darts, and parts of the two corner palmettes. The leaves are shaped somewhat like those in 32, but the stalk is less prominently rendered and the top leaf is less turned up. Also, the second leaf from the top partly covers the edge of the egg.

34. IA 560. Small fragment of Ionic capital, preserving one complete dart of the moulding and part of an egg; found at the east end of the South Stoa.

H. of moulding 0.085 m.

White marble.

35. IA 583. Pl. 35, b, left. Small fragment of Ionic capital, found toward the east end of the South Stoa.

White marble. Preserved are parts of the corner egg and two leaves of the palmette. Dimensions and design are almost identical with those in 32.

36. IA 703. Small fragment of Ionic capital, found between the early Roman temenos wall and the South Stoa. Preserved is one dart which shows that the fragment belongs to the Stoa columns.

White marble.

37. IA 564. Fragment of volute, found in the eastern part of the South Stoa. Carving is very similar to that of 32.

White marble.

38. IA 439. Small fragment of volute similar to the preceding two, found east of the Roman Altar. Because of its provenance it is likely to have come from the East Stoa.
White marble.

39. IA 565. Fragment of volute preserving central disc, found in trench for the South Stoa wall.
White marble. The carving is similar to that in the fragments discussed above. Pinhole in the center of the central disc.

40. IA 408. Small fragment of volute, found toward the east end of the South Stoa.
White marble.

41. IA 446. Small fragment of volute, from the same place as the preceding.
White marble.

42. IA 566. Fragment of volute, found at the west end of the South Stoa.
White marble. The carving of the volute is deeper and more carefully executed than the preceding, but because of its size and its provenance, it is attributable to the South Stoa.

43. IA 349U. Small fragment of a volute from the west end of the South Stoa.
White marble. The carving is rather similar to that of **42**.

44. IA 553. Pl. 35, c, 69, a. Fragment of Ionic capital, found at the west end of the South Stoa.
H. exclusive of volute 0.162 m.
Grayish marble. Preserved are most of one volute, part of the abacus, the whole corner palmette, and parts of two eggs and one dart. This piece is very different from those described above, but because of its provenance and dimensions, it seems appropriate to include it in the discussion of the West and the South Stoas. It is probable, however, that this does not belong to the original construction of the Stoas. The palmette here, consisting of only two upturned leaves and a two-leafed heart, comes directly below the abacus and so high up as to stand clear of the egg-and-dart moulding. The abacus, unlike that of **32**, has a vertical end. The central disc of the volute is on the same plane as the ridges of the volute. The cushion was decorated with a carelessly carved leaf design. This might be from a repair to the Stoa colonnades.

45. IA 349H. Pl. 71, b. Fragment of Ionic architrave found at the west end of the South Stoa.
Pres. L. 0.21 m.; Pres. H. 0.266 m.; Pres. W. 0.07 m.; H. of lower fascia 0.065 m.; of second fascia 0.098 m.
Light gray, brittle marble. The heights of the two lower fasciae are completely preserved, and part of the third. Very roughly finished with a toothed chisel, but a straight-edged chisel is used at the edges of the fasciae. For the profile, see Plates 67, 71, b.

46. IA 349A. Pl. 71, b. Fragment of architrave-frieze block found in the west part of the South Stoa.
Pres. L. 0.415 m.; Pres. H. 0.51 m.; Pres. W. 0.14 m.
Light gray, brittle marble. The fragment preserves the upper fascia, H. 0.104 m., the moulding above the architrave, H. 0.071 m., and most of the frieze except the top moulding. For the profile, see Plate 71, b.

47. IA 349J and 349E. Pl. 71, b. Two adjoining fragments from the upper part of the frieze from the west end of the South Stoa.
Combined Pres. L. 0.365 m.; Pres. H. 0.295 m.; Pres. W. 0.074 m.
The marble is light gray and brittle. The two fragments preserve the upper part of the cyma recta of the frieze, and the top moulding. For the profile, see Plate 71, b.

48. IA 349Q. Pl. 71, b. Fragment of the upper part of the architrave, found in the west end of the South Stoa.
Pres. L. 0.34 m.; Pres. H. 0.29 m.; Pres. W. 0.298 m.
Light gray, brittle marble. The fragment preserves the upper fascia, H. 0.105 m., and the moulding above the architrave, H. 0.074 m. The surface is roughly cut with a toothed chisel, but the edges of the fasciae are finished with a straight-edged chisel. For the profile, see Plate 71, b, right.

49. IA 353. Fragment of the upper part of the architrave, found in the west end of the South Stoa.
Pres. L. 0.21 m.; Pres. H. 0.275 m.; Pres. W. 0.066 m.
Light gray, brittle marble. The fragment preserves the height of the middle fascia, 0.097 m., and the left end of the block.

50. IA 349I. Small fragment of the architrave, found in the west end of the South Stoa.
Pres. L. 0.24 m.; Pres. H. 0.075 m.; Pres. W. 0.05 m.
Light gray, brittle marble. Preserved is the full height, 0.074 m., of the moulding above the architrave. It is finished with a toothed chisel, but a narrow, straight-edged chisel has been used on the edges of the moulding.

51. IA 349G. Small fragment of the lower part of the architrave, found at the west end of the South Stoa.
Pres. L. 0.17 m.; Pres. H. 0.103 m.; Pres. W. 0.046 m.
Light gray, brittle marble. The carving is similar to the previous pieces discussed. The fragment retains the full height, 0.061 m., of the lower fascia.

52. IA 349F. Fragment from the lower part of the frieze, found in the west end of the South Stoa.
Pres. L. 0.235 m.; Pres. H. 0.19 m.; Pres. W. 0.087 m.
Light gray, brittle marble. The fragment preserves the lower part of the frieze kymation and the height, 0.075 m., of the moulding above the architrave.

53. IA 349V. Small fragment from the upper part of the frieze, found at the west end of the South Stoa.
Pres. L. 0.19 m.; Pres. H. 0.145 m.; Pres. W. 0.15 m.
Light gray, brittle marble. The carving is similar to the preceding pieces discussed. The top is roughly chipped away with the use of a pick or a chisel.

54. IA 1627. Pls. 35, h, 70, b, 71, a. Cornice-sima block, completely preserved, found at the middle of the West Stoa; it is now set up on the preserved part of the Stoa stylobate.
L. 1.32 m.; H. 0.456 m.; W. not including lion's heads 0.87 m. Dentils: W. *ca.* 0.055 m.; W. axis to axis 0.082 m. Distance between lion's head spouts 0.675 m.
The marble is a gray, brittle variety. The sima is in the form of a very flat cyma recta. The surface is finished with a toothed chisel; only the edges of the mouldings have been finished with a straight-edged chisel. The ends have carefully finished anathyrosis, but the mouldings are not completely finished at the edges as if a final carving had been intended after the block was in place and had then been omitted. The lion's heads are roughly carved, but far more skillfully than most of the lion's heads from the South Stoa. In the top of the block is a rough channel near the front, 1.14 m. long, 0.045 m. wide at the top, and 0.055 m. deep. This was obviously made to receive the water which then ran out through the lion's head spouts, but the channel does not extend to the ends of the block, so that there was no continuous trough at the eaves, and it seems much too small to take all the water from the roof. In heavy rains the water would have splashed over the edge. For profile, see Plate 71, a.

55. IA 349. Pls. 35, g, 70, a, 71, a. Cornice-sima block, found at the southwestern corner of the temenos at the junction of the West and South Stoas.
L. 1.71 m.; H. 0.473 m.; W. 0.815 m. Dentils: W. 0.068–0.081 m.; W. axis to axis 0.108–0.115 m.
Grayish white marble. The block is broken in the middle, but the two pieces form a complete block. It was probably the last block at the west end of the South Stoa. The distances between the lion's head spouts are 0.578 m. and 0.677 m. There is a beam cutting, 0.32 m. long and 0.19 m. deep, in the rear of the block. There are no proper anathyroses and, in fact, the middle part of the block projects beyond that of the edge so that tight joints would have been impossible. The carving is much inferior to that of the preceding; the base moulding above the dentils is not an ovolo, but a flat beveled band, and the lower curve of the sima has completely disappeared and been displaced with a straight surface above a flat band, 0.037 m. high. The carving of the lion's head spouts, too, is very inferior. For profile, see Plate 71, a.

56. IA 368. Small fragment of the cornice, preserving five dentils of width *ca.* 0.055 m., found at the southwestern corner of the Temple of Poseidon.
Pres. L. 0.49 m.; Pres. H. 0.12 m.; Pres. W. 0.25 m.
Light gray marble.

57. IA 746. Small fragment of cornice preserving three dentils *ca.* 0.072 m. wide, found in northeastern part of Sanctuary.
Pres. L. 0.415 m.; Pres. H. 0.127 m.; W. 0.17 m.
The moulding above the dentils is a carefully carved cyma reversa. The surface is worn and weathered, probably from lying exposed in the field.

58. IA 440. Small fragment of the cornice preserving two dentils, *ca.* 0.055–0.058 m. wide, found in the eastern part of the South Stoa.
Pres. L. 0.185 m.; Pres. H. 0.13 m.; Pres. W. 0.15 m.
White, fine-grained marble. Moulding above the dentils is a carelessly carved ovolo.

59. IA 586. Small fragment of cornice preserving right end of block.
Pres. L. 0.18 m.; Pres. H. 0.085 m.; Pres. W. 0.155 m. Dentil: W. 0.06 m.
White marble. The moulding above the dentil is an ovolo.

60. IA 404. Small fragment from the cornice, found in the eastern part of the South Stoa.
Pres. L. 0.104 m.; Pres. H. 0.101 m.; Pres. W. 0.142 m.
Left edge of a block with anathyrosis preserved and part of the corona and the ovolo above the dentils.

61. IA 736. Fragment of a sima block, found in a field east of the temenos, but probably from one of the Stoas.
Pres. L. 0.96 m.; Pres. H. 0.18 m.; Pres. W. 0.165 m.
The left end is from a joint of the block. Preserved are one complete and one partially preserved lion's head spout. The approximate distance between spouts is *ca.* 0.615 m. The lion's heads resemble those on the blocks of the sima from the West Stoa.

62. IA 599. Pl. 35, f. Complete lion's head spout, found in the southwestern part of the temenos.
Gray marble.

63. IA 634. Pl. 35, f. Lion's head spout, all but the lower jaw preserved.
Bluish gray marble. Very coarse work.

64. IA 550. Pl. 35, d. Complete lion's head spout.
Gray marble. Coarse work.

65. IA 626. Pl. 35, d. Upper half of lion's head spout.
Gray marble.

66. IA 551. Fragment of a lion's head spout.
Gray marble.

67. IA 549. Fragment of a lion's head spout.
Gray marble.

68. IA 597. Small fragment from the top of a lion's
head spout.
Gray marble.

The following heads or fragments of heads were also
found in the same area. These could have come either
from the West or the South Stoas. IA 578, 554, 577,
598, 558.

69. IA 601. Complete lion's head spout, found in
middle part of the South Stoa.

70. IA 547. Fragment of a lion's head spout, found
in the Palaimon Temple.

71. IA 589. Fragment of a lion's head spout, found in
the middle part of the South Stoa.

72. IA 611. Fragment of a lion's head spout, found
south of the Temple of Poseidon.

All but IA 589 of the fragments found in the southwestern part of the temenos or in the South Stoa are
of exceptionally poor quality and may be attributed to
the same marble-worker or group of craftsmen. IA 589,
however, is of better quality and, although found in
the South Stoa, may perhaps have come from the
East Stoa, where heads seem to have been of slightly
better quality. The following heads or parts of heads
come from that part of the excavations. IA 744
(Pl. 35, e), 742 (Pl. 35, e), 737, 576, 721, 745, 667, 743,
731, 739.

PALAIMONION AREA

73. IA 593. Pl. 41, d. Floral akroterion found northeast of Palaimon Temple.
L. at top 0.17 m.; H. 0.40 m.; W. 0.165 m.
There is a row of three low acanthus leaves at the
bottom, and above that a single large leaf folded over
so as to be in profile on both sides. White marble.
Perhaps from the roof of the Temple of Palaimon
(above, p. 111).

74. IA 572. Pl. 82, a, lower left. Ionic column base of
red marble, broken into many fragments. Found
in the area of the Palaimon Temple.
H. 0.145 m.; D. at lower torus 0.483 m.; D. at top
representing lower diameter of column 0.336 m.
For profile, see Plate 82, a. In the top is a circular
dowel hole with traces of a pour channel. Small dowel
hole in the bottom, square in section, ca. 0.027 m.,
0.055 m. in depth.

75. IA 570. Pl. 82, a, lower right. Ionic column base in
fragments of red marble, found together with the
preceding.
H. 0.145 m.; D. of lower torus 0.51 m.; D. at the
top representing diameter of column ca. 0.356 m.
The profile is very similar to that of **74.** In the top
was a circular hole of uncertain diameter from which
a pour channel extends to the edge of the base. In the
bottom is a dowel hole, 0.025 m. square and 0.065 m.
deep.

76. IA 1422. Pl. 82, a, top. Ionic column base of red
marble, found in 1967 in the Fortress, just inside
Gate 14.
H. 0.138 m.; D. of upper torus 0.365 m.
In the bottom is a small, roughly circular dowel
hole, ca. 0.03 m. in diameter and 0.046 m. deep. In
the top is a large circular dowel hole, ca. 0.12 m. in
diameter and 0.058 m. deep. A pour channel extends
from it to the edge. Part of the lower torus and about
one-third of the top is broken away. The dimensions
are slightly different from those of **74** and **75,** but the
material is the same, and it is likely that all three come
from a single monument.

77. IA 1687. Pl. 82, b. Base of anta or pilaster, found
in the area of the Semicircle.
Max. L. 0.68 m.; H. 0.258 m.; W. 0.505 m.
At the bottom is a plinth, 0.10 m. high, and above
that there is a very flat torus, set off from an upper
rounded moulding (low torus) which is now largely
missing. The base is finished on three sides and rough
in the back. In the top is a circular dowel hole, 0.05 m.
in diameter and ca. 0.04 m. deep, and from it a pour
channel extends to the edge. Grayish blue marble
which tends to flake. Rather rough work. This may
have formed the anta of an opening in the rear wall of
the South Stoa leading into the semicircular entranceway (Plan VIII).

78. IA 617. Pl. 74, b. Several fragments of a large
Ionic capital, found scattered about in the middle
division of the Palaimonion.
White marble. For detailed description, above, p. 109.

79. IA 387. Fragment of large unfluted column shaft
found in the Semicircle.
Pres. L. 1.11 m.; Pres. D. 0.70 m.
Mottled blue-green marble with streaks of white.
Above, p. 109.

80. IA 618. Pls. 39, d, 74, a. Many fragments of
marble arch, found in the middle division of the
Palaimonion, mostly in the small south room.
Bluish gray marble with a tendency to flake. For
further description, above, p. 106.

SACRED GLEN

81. IA 1623. Pls. 43, d, 75, b. T-shaped block with ridged top, found at the cement-lined channel in the Sacred Glen area.

L. 0.37 m.; H. to top of ridge 0.405 m.; W. at the top 0.376 m.

Originally this and the next seven blocks of the same shape had thin, hard stucco on the top, flanks, and one end. One end and the underside are roughly finished and unstuccoed. The material is a fine-grained poros, smoothly finished except on the bottom and at one end where it is finished with a straight-edged chisel. Much of the stucco has peeled off.

82. IA 1624. Pl. 43, d. T-shaped block like the preceding, found in the same place.

L. 0.38 m.; H. 0.358 m.; W. 0.368 m.

Most of the stucco has disappeared, but enough remains to show that it was surfaced like the others.

83. IA 1621. Pl. 75, c. T-shaped block of the same general shape as the preceding, but not identical.

L. 0.344 m.; H. 0.462 m.; W. 0.291 m.

The part below the top is considerably narrower than that of **81**, and the total height is greater. However, there is a cutting at the bottom, reducing the front part to a height of 0.407 m., which is approximately the same as that of **81**. Pieces of stucco remain on all the finished surfaces.

84. IA 1622. T-shaped block like the preceding, found in the same place.

L. 0.336 m.; H. 0.431 m.; W. 0.30 m.

The top is slightly flatter than those of the preceding. Otherwise the shape is the same, and like those it is stuccoed on the top and on three sides. There is a cutting at the bottom which reduces the height in front to 0.397 m.

85. IA 1625A and 1625B. Two fragments of a stone like the preceding, with some parts missing.

Total H. 0.48 m.

A cutting at the bottom reduces the front part to *ca.* 0.399 m.

86. IA 1621C. Fragmentary block of the same type as the preceding.

L. 0.37 m.; total H. 0.471 m.; W. not preserved.

A cutting at the bottom reduces the height in front to 0.388 m. It differs from the others in having a horizontal band, 0.10 m. wide, on the top and slanting surfaces, presumably on both sides, but one side of the block is missing.

87. IA 540. T-shaped block like the preceding, found in the same place.

L. 0.345 m.; total H. 0.45 m.; W. 0.277 m.

A cutting at the bottom reduces the height to 0.41 m. The stucco is comparatively well preserved on three sides and at the top.

WEST FOUNDATION PARAPET

88. IA 923. Fragment of base moulding with part of a joint at the rear end preserved.

Pres. L. 0.265 m.; Pres. H. 0.159 m.; Pres. W. 0.145 m.

Above the bottom is a slight setback only 0.005 m. high, then a large torus, and above that a cyma reversa. Above that the stone is broken away. For the profile see IA 780, Pl. 80, a. Gray poros, with smooth carving showing horizontal streaks of chisel or rasp. No stucco.

89. IA 942. Fragment of base moulding.

Pres. L. 0.245 m.; Pres. H. 0.143 m.; Pres. W. 0.14 m.

Profile like the preceding. At the top of the cyma reversa was a setback 0.016 m. wide. Beyond that the stone is broken away. Poros stone and workmanship like the preceding.

90. IA 794. Small fragment of torus from moulding like the preceding.

Pres. L. 0.07 m.; Pres. H. 0.06 m.; Pres. W. 0.069 m.

This is from a corner piece, the two toruses making a sharp edge.

Other fragments from base mouldings of the same kind are IA 780, Pl. 80, a, lower left, 782, 783, 784, 785, 786, 789, 792, 795, 799, 901, 921, 922, 923 A–P, 925, 926, 933, 935, 937, 940, 952.

91. IA 791. Pl. 80, a, upper right. Fragment of coping in the form of an Ionic cornice, preserving the concave curve at the top and part of the drip.

Pres. L. 0.21 m.; Pres. H. 0.215 m.; Pres. W. 0.11 m. Fine-grained poros. No stucco.

92. IA 796. Fragment like the preceding, preserving part of the curving top, the moulding above the corona, the drip, and part of the soffit.

Pres. L. 0.23 m.; Pres. H. 0.17 m.; Pres. W. 0.09 m.

93. IA 943. Pl. 80, a, upper left. Fragment of coping like the preceding, but with somewhat gentler curve at top.

Pres. L. 0.19 m.; Pres. H. 0.175 m.; Pres. W. 0.125 m.

Preserved are part of the top, the moulding above the corona, and part of the soffit. The drip is broken away.

94. IA 943D. Fragment from the top of parapet preserving the full height of corona and the mouldings at the top. Also complete profile of the moulding underneath the soffit. From the west flank.

Pres. L. 0.295 m.; Pres. H. 0.19 m.; Pres. W. 0.12 m.

Most of the moulding at the top and the drip are broken away.

Other fragments from the top of the same coping are IA 781, 787, 788, 797, 798, 800, 927, 928, 929, 930, 938, 939, 943 A–C, 943E.

95. IA 941. Pl. 80, b. Small fragment from the rear of the coping, with a curved chamfer at the top.

Pres. L. 0.202 m.; Pres. H. 0.255 m.; Pres. W. 0.132 m.

The top has a slight downward slope but is not concavely curved like the front part of the coping. Gray poros, unstuccoed. The carving is not as fine as that on the fragments from the front part of the coping.

96. IA 941A. Fragment preserving part of the top, the concave chamfering and the full width of the fascia, 0.015 m. From the west flank.

Pres. L. 0.35 m.; Pres. H. 0.22 m.; Pres. W. 0.14 m.

Other fragment with the same profile is IA 941B.

97. IA 936. Fragment from the rear side of base of parapet with two recesses as shown in Plate 80, c.

Pres. L. 0.25 m.; Pres. H. 0.182 m.; Pres. W. 0.092 m.

The block is finished like all the others from the parapet.

Other fragments with the same profile are IA 934, 936A, 936B, 970.

ADESPOTA

98. IA 435. Pl. 82, c. Small fragment of Doric capital, found on the Rachi.

H. of abacus 0.08 m.

On the top is a relieving surface 0.056 m. wide. The surface is covered with two coats of fine stucco and in the top are traces of burning. This may be from the upper range of the interior order of columns in the Temple of Poseidon; cf. *Isthmia*, I, pp. 87–88.

99. IA 429. Pl. 83, a. Fragment of Doric capital. Provenance unknown.

Total H. 0.184 m.; D. at top on arris 0.2005 m., in flute 0.189 m.; H. of abacus 0.074 m.; restored W. of abacus 0.5095 m.

On the top is a relieving surface 0.045 m. wide, and on the bottom a narrow relieving surface and an axial scratch line. Traces of smooth stucco. Smooth, careful carving. Probably 4th century B.C.

100. IA 430. Fragment of Doric capital like **99** and probably from the same order. Found in the Earlier Stadium. Only about one quarter of the capital is preserved.

101. IA 619. Pl. 83, b. Fragment of Doric capital preserving nine complete flutes at the top and the total height. Found southwest of the Roman Altar.

H. 0.16 m.; W. of flutes at the top 0.052 m.; H. of abacus 0.067 m.; W. of abacus 0.428 m.

In the top is a rectangular dowel hole 0.032 × 0.035 m., and *ca.* 0.014 m. deep; there is a relieving surface at the edges. The bottom has a deep square empolion as shown in Plate 83, b. The surface is covered with fine stucco. Careful work, probably of the 4th century B.C.

102. IA 620. Fragmentary Doric capital resembling **101**, but of slightly different dimensions. Found southwest of the Roman Altar.

Total H. 0.165 m.; H. of abacus 0.066 m.; W. of abacus 0.433 m.

On the top are relieving surfaces, a small square dowel like that of **101**, and a small scratch line. In the bottom is a large double cutting like that on the preceding. Although the dimensions vary slightly, it is probably from the same order. The capital has been squared off for later use.

103. IA 538. Pl. 84. Doric capital of unfluted column. Found on the Rachi.

Pres. H. of capital 0.202 m.; D. at the top 0.383 m.; H. of abacus 0.081 m.; W. of abacus 0.475 m.

On the top are a relieving surface, which runs diagonally at the corners, and also several lines and scratches which are probably original. A large hole, 0.11 × 0.105 m. in area, runs through the full height of the capital. This is obviously from late use. The original work is careful, but the surface has been much pitted and scratched. There is now no trace of stucco.

104. IA 1149A and B. Two fragments of a capital like the preceding, and apparently having the same dimensions, found in the north part of the Sanctuary. Only about one-half of the capital is preserved.

105. IA 613. Pl. 85, a. Small part of a Doric capital of an unfluted column, found at the Cyclopean Wall. For dimensions and profile, see Plate 85, a.

On the top is a very prominent groove which seems to have run in the axis of the column. There were no annulets and apparently no necking band. Very poor, careless work, probably of Roman times.

106. IA 575. Pl. 48, c, left. Small fragment of Ionic column capital with volutes on both sides and a leaf pattern on the back, between the two volutes. Found in the southwest part of the Sanctuary.

107. IA 546. Volute of small Ionic column with a part of the corner palmette preserved. Found northwest of the Palaimon Temple. White marble.

108. IA 581. Pl. 48, c, right. Volute and corner palmette of some small column capital, apparently of unusual design, found in the race track of the Earlier Stadium.

So far as can be determined from the small fragment preserved, the abacus did not begin above the eye of the volute, but considerably farther over. It is likely that this was a column not of a building but of a pedestal supporting a tripod or some other monument. White marble.

109. IA 366. Pl. 48, d. Small Ionic capital, not from the excavations.

Abacus 0.328 × 0.325 m.; D. of top of column *ca.* 0.295 m.

In the sinkage on the underside there is a fine circle incised which is 0.195 m. in diameter. On the face between the volutes are the usual three eggs and darts and corner palmettes with three leaves, and the cushion has three vertical bands on either side. Careful Roman work. White marble.

110. IA 513. Small fragment of capital like the preceding, preserving only the eggs and darts and a small fragment of the corner palmette. Not from the excavations.

111. IA 710. Pl. 86. Part of a capital of a pier or anta, with three faces preserved, found in the Sacred Glen.

Pres. L. 0.265 m.; Pres. H. 0.174 m.; W. at top 0.28 m.; W. at bottom 0.22 m.

Below a plain band 0.027 m. high, there is a prominent hawksbeak with a total height of 0.055 m. and below that a plain fascia 0.087 m. high. The profile is the same on the front and on the two sides, but the middle part of the front, to a width of *ca.* 0.10 m., is rough and only partly finished. Fine early work, probably 5th century B.C. Surface covered with a smooth stucco.

112. IA 1394. Small piece of moulding like that of the preceding item and probably part of the same capital. Found at the north end of the West Stoa.

113. IA 594. Pl. 87, a. Pier capital with mouldings on all four sides, found in the southwestern part of the Sanctuary.

For dimensions and profile, see Plate 87, a.

There is a moulding at the top consisting of a cavetto, a hawksbeak, and below that two fasciae. The top is rather roughly finished and has a smooth relieving surface. Careful work, probably of the 4th century B.C. No stucco.

114. IA 716. Pl. 87, b. Pier capital finished on all four sides, found in the Sacred Glen.

For dimensions and profile, see Plate 87, b. The top edges are beveled to form broad relieving surfaces, and within this band the top is colored red. The lower part is divided into two fasciae, a very narrow one at the bottom and a broad one at the top. Careful work. No stucco.

115. IA 496. Pl. 88, a. Small fragment of anta capital with moulding poorly preserved on three sides. The lower part is in two fasciae. Found on the Rachi.

Pres. L. 0.19 m.; Pres. H. 0.19 m.; Pres. W. at top 0.17 m.

It appears to have been stuccoed. For profile, see Plate 88, a.

116. IA 569. Pl. 88, b. Fragment of a pier capital, found southwest of the Roman Altar, finished on all four sides.

L. at the top 0.205 m.; Pres. W. at top 0.95 m., but seems to have been square; at the bottom it now measures 0.16 m. in length, and seems to have had the same width; H. 0.106 m.

The moulding at the top consists of a plain band above a chamfered surface, with a roughly rounded edge at the top. In the top were three cuttings, probably for a tripod. One now contains some hard white substance that appears to be pure lime. The top is smooth, but the bottom is very roughly finished. Mottled pink and brown limestone with prominent veins.

117. IA 355. Pl. 89. Triglyph-metope block found in the North Gully.

For dimensions, see Plate 89.

Very fine work of the 4th or 5th century B.C.

118. IA 354. Pl. 90. Fragment of a Doric cornice found in the same place as the preceding and apparently belonging to the same building.

For dimensions, see Plate 90.

The hawksbeak above the corona has been broken away. Otherwise the block is in very good condition. On the fascia at the bottom of the block are clear traces of a meander pattern.

119. IA 614. Pl. 91, a. Triglyph block of poros found in the eastern part of the Palaimonion.

H. 0.345 m.; W. of the triglyph 0.223 m.; for other dimensions see isometric drawing in Plate 91, a.

The outer edges of the triglyph project on each side, showing that no metope was attached. Rather coarse work, which may have been covered by stucco, but the surface has been much pitted and defaced.

120. IA 648. Pl. 91, b. Fragment of Doric cornice preserving the full height, one complete mutule, and parts of two viae. Found in Northwest Reservoir.

Pres. L. 0.39 m.; Pres. H. 0.188 m.; Pres. W. 0.42 m.; L. of mutule 0.291 m.; W. of mutule 0.173 m.; Pres. W. of via 0.069 m.

The hawksbeak at the top and the drip are largely broken away. The cyma reversa at the base of the cornice is well preserved. The whole surface was covered with a fine, smooth stucco. Careful work, probably of the 4th century B.C.

121. IA 539. Pl. 49, a. Large fragment of Doric cornice, apparently from the same building as **120**. Not from excavations.

Pres. L. 0.85 m.; H. 0.172 m.; L. of mutule 0.29 m.; W. of mutule 0.173 m.; W. of via 0.075 m.

The preserved end has anathyrosis and on the top is a cutting for a T-clamp. Fine work, with thin white stucco.

122. IA 432. Small fragment of mutule preserving three of the guttae. This appears to be from the same building as the preceding two fragments.

123. IA 713. Small fragment of cornice, preserving part of the face and the width of one via, 0.077 m. Found in the Northwest Reservoir.

Pres. L. 0.385 m.; Pres. H. 0.13 m.; Pres. W. 0.225 m.

124. IA 702. Pl. 92, a. Small fragment of raking cornice, found in the Sacred Glen.

Pres. L. 0.23 m.; H. 0.15 m.; Pres. W. 0.26 m.

The moulding at the base of the soffit is well preserved. It may be from the same building as the preceding two pieces.

125. IA 714. Pl. 93, a. Small fragment of raking cornice of some small monument, preserving the apex of the gable. The left edge is preserved. Found in the Sacred Glen.

Pres. L. 0.20 m.; Pres. H. 0.08 m.; Pres. W. 0.32 m.

At the top is an ovolo, and underneath that a small vertical band. The lower edge seems to have come down in a sharp point but is now broken away. Top and bottom are roughly finished with a straight-edged tool, but the face is rather smoothly finished. No trace of stucco.

126. IA 645. Small fragment of Doric cornice preserving the top and face and part of one via at the joint. All the guttae and the bottom of the mutule have been broken away. Found in the northeastern part of the Sanctuary.

Pres. L. 0.22 m.; Pres. H. 0.16 m.; Pres. W. 0.24 m.

There is a relieving surface on the top 0.078 m. wide. The hawksbeak at the top is broken away.

127. IA 919. Fragment from the corner of an Ionic cornice. Found in the Later Stadium.

Pres. L. 0.28 m.; Pres. H. 0.19 m.; Pres. W. 0.27 m.

The preserved surface consists of a corona surmounted by a cyma reversa moulding, and a poorly carved ovolo moulding at the base. Finished with a toothed chisel, but a straight-edged tool used on the mouldings and along the edges. Light gray marble.

128. IA 1377. Pl. 93, b. Small poros fragment of what appears to be a cornice, but is probably part of a coping stone of some parapet. Found south of the Northeast Altar Terrace.

Pres. L. 0.195 m.; Pres. H. 0.13 m.; W. 0.155 m.

At the top is a projecting plain band with a very small hawksbeak moulding underneath, and then a corona and part of the soffit are preserved. Traces of very thin stucco. For the profile, see Plate 93, b.

129. IA 759. Pl. 93, c. Small fragment of a profiled member of uncertain purpose. Found at the Hexamilia Settlement.

Pres. L. 0.16 m.; Pres. H. 0.18 m.; Pres. W. 0.08 m.

The lower edge is preserved, but the upper edge is broken away. There was a plain vertical surface at the top and below that a projecting moulding which appears to have been in the form of two cyma reversas, one above the other. Then there is a plain band, 0.02 m. wide, and at the bottom a broad fascia 0.085 m. Fine work with smooth white stucco.

130. IA 621. Pl. 92, b. Fragment of some circular monument, probably from the top. Found in the north Palaimonion.

For dimensions, see Plate 92, b.

At the very top is a plain band, 0.048 m. high, and below that a cyma reversa, then a plain band 0.053 m. high, and at the preserved bottom a curving moulding like the echinus of a Doric column. The surface is rough and finished with toothed chisels, a finer one on the mouldings and a coarse one at the top.

131. IA 761. Pl. 94, a. Coping block, found at the Hexamilia Settlement.

For dimensions and profile, see Plate 94, a.

Beneath a rounded top was a prominent moulding, now largely missing, and underneath are two fasciae. In the top is a cutting for a hook clamp at either end. Very fine carving and smooth white stucco, preserved only below the moulding.

132. IA 918. Pl. 94, b. Fragment of a marble relief with the figure of a shield, found in the Later Stadium.

For dimensions and profile, see Plate 94, b.

Grayish white marble which tends to flake. The surface has been finished with a toothed chisel. Rather coarse, uneven work, probably Roman.

133. IA 946 + 917 + 909. Pl. 50, a. Three adjoining fragments from the top of a circular monument with a diameter of *ca.* 0.655 m. Found in the Later Stadium.

Pres. L. 0.37 m.; Pres. H. 0.17 m.; Pres. W. 0.12 m. There was a projecting band at the top, 0.05 m. wide, and underneath that an egg-and-dart moulding, and then bead-and-reel. Underneath the latter, the surface has been slightly cut back to form a plain drum. Rather uneven and poorly carved work of Roman times. Light gray marble.

134. IA 420. Boukranion in relief with the background missing. Found in the northwestern part of the Sanctuary.

Pres. L. 0.17 m.; Pres. H. 0.265 m.; Pres. W. 0.05 m. There are traces of a fillet depending from the horns and some floral design above. The eyes consist of roughly gouged-out sockets and there is a prominent groove through the middle. Light gray marble.

135. IA 409. Small fragment containing parts of a floral design, consisting of a half palmette at the left edge and presumably a complete palmette with tendrils at the bottom in the middle. The left side, which is roughly finished, is original. Place of finding unknown. White marble.

There is a wide variety of mouldings, some examples of which are illustrated in Plates 49–50, 85.

136. IA 633. Pl. 49, b, left. From east part of Sanctuary.

137. IA 651. Pl. 49, c, center. From Theater area.

138. IA 699. Pl. 49, c, left. From Theater Cave.

139. IA 672. Pl. 49, b, right. From eastern part of Sanctuary.

140. IA 625. Pl. 49, c, right. From eastern part of Sanctuary.

141. IA 349S. Pl. 49, d, center. From South Stoa.

142. IA 349T. Pl. 49, d, right. From South Stoa.

143. IA 698. Pl. 49, d, left. From Theater Cave.

144. IA 650. From Theater area.

145. IA 533. From north of Roman Altar.

146. IA 518. Pl. 50, b, left. Not from excavations.

147. IA 652. Pl. 50, b, right. From Theater area.

148. IA 762. From Theater area.

149. IA 519. Not from excavations.

150. IA 573. From area of Palaimon Temple.

151. IA 349P. Pl. 50, c, right. From South Stoa.

152. IA 750. Pl. 50, c, left. From northeastern part of Sanctuary.

153. IA 417. From Earlier Stadium.

154. IA 904. Pl. 50, d, right. From Later Stadium.

155. IA 905. Pl. 50, d, left. From Later Stadium.

156. IA 907. Pl. 50, d, center. From Later Stadium.

157. IA 754. Pl. 85, b. Piece of base moulding, found at the Hellenistic Isthmian Wall east of Hexamilia.

Pres. H. 0.212 m.; Pres. L. 0.305 m.; Pres. Th. 0.022 m.

At the base is a plain fascia, 0.108 m. high, at the top of which is a setback, and then a cyma reversa, and above that a torus. The slanting top surface, which is preserved to a width of 0.047 m., has a slight concave curve. The material is fine-grained poros. All the exposed surfaces are covered with a thin smooth stucco. At the bottom is a thin relieving surface, 0.012 m. wide.

APPENDIX I

CONTENTS OF THE LARGE CIRCULAR PIT

In an earlier chapter (pp. 22–24) I have described the Large Circular Pit, which proved to be by far the most productive area in the Isthmia excavations. Of pottery alone no less than 712 inventoried items came from there, in addition to prodigious quantities of sherds of lesser importance. Among the finds from the Pit there are also 260 pieces in the inventory of miscellaneous objects, which include terracotta figurines, bronze figurines, and other metal objects. There were a few inscriptions and fragments of sculpture, and some, surprisingly few, pieces of roof tiles. The following list is intended to show the approximate date of the fill, based chiefly on the pottery. The final study of the pottery, which is now being made by D. A. Amyx, has not yet been completed.

In the excavation reports,[1] I stated that the Pit had presumably been filled up from 480 to 470 B.C. It is now clear that such a date is too early. More likely the debris was thrown in after the middle of the fifth century.

The Pit was excavated during three seasons. In the autumn of 1957, when it was discovered, a limited area 1.55 × 3.60 m. was dug to a depth of 8.40 m. on the east side, and less extensive probings were made elsewhere to test the fill. The following spring, March 26 to April 18, 1958, work in the Pit was resumed in several sectors, eventually extending over the whole area of the circle. At a depth of 15.25 m. the work was discontinued because of the abundance of water and the collapse of a mass of earth and rock from the side of the Pit. It became clear to us then that the Pit would have contained water in fair amounts at the end of the rainy season, i.e. at the time of the Isthmian Festival. During the summer there was a conspicuous lowering of the water level. The following autumn, September 28 to October 28, work continued in the Pit until bottom was reached at a depth of 19.75 m. Because of the sticky consistency of the fill at the lower levels, the earth could not be properly searched for objects until it was dry. Whereas the major part of the finds came from depths accurately recorded, the gleanings from the pile of earth would of necessity be somewhat mixed. It is very probable that, except for about two meters at the top of the shaft, the contents had been dumped in at one time. The large amount of uncut stones from the fill are almost certainly from the Cyclopean Wall that ran diagonally, southeast to northwest, across the southwest corner of the later temenos of Poseidon (above, p. 7). All this points inevitably to a general clean-up and landscaping undertaken some time after the construction of the Classical Temple, not long after the middle of the fifth century B.C. The amount of pottery and other objects from the fill is so immense that this date, for which there is logical reason, cannot be far from correct. Certain discrepancies will be discussed below.

DEPTH

I.   0–2.20 m. Immense quantities of pottery (153 inventoried pieces), mostly archaic and classical, Greek and Roman, and a few prehistoric. The bulk of the pottery ranges in date from Mycenaean times to late fifth century B.C. There was a considerable admixture of later ware, especially fragments of Palaimonion lamps, no less than 15 pieces (above, pp. 104–109) from the first century after Christ.

[1] *Hesperia*, XXXI, 1962, p. 2; and cf. *Isthmia*, I, p. 12.

DEPTH

II. 2.20–5.00 m. 68 inventoried pieces of pottery, mostly sixth and fifth centuries B.C. with a few earlier fragments. A single fragment, not inventoried, is a handle of a Roman vase of the second or third century after Christ. Nothing else later than mid-fifth century B.C.

III. 5.00–8.40 m. Pottery less abundant, 25 inventoried pieces, ranging in date from eighth to mid-fifth century B.C.

IV. 8.30–13.00 m. Comparatively little pottery, only 31 inventoried pieces, mostly seventh to fifth century B.C. One sherd of ribbed ware, IP 1737, is later; it might be as early as the second half of the fifth century B.C. but could be fourth century.

V. 13.00–15.00 m. Much pottery, 83 inventoried pieces, mostly seventh and sixth centuries B.C. Latest datable piece *ca.* 500 B.C.

VI. 15.00–15.80 m. End of 1958 campaign. Much pottery, 69 inventoried pieces. They range in date from early seventh to fifth century B.C. A stamped amphora handle, IP 1692, is recorded as coming from fill at a depth of 15.25 m.[2]

The fill from 15.80 to the bottom of the Pit was doubtless thrown in at one time, as shown by the fact that sherds from the upper layers fitted pieces from the very bottom. After this discovery the pottery was thrown together to facilitate work by the potmenders.

VII. 15.80–19.75 m. Immense quantities of pottery, 283 inventoried pieces, mostly archaic, coming down to the middle of the fifth century B.C. or perhaps a little later. One box of pottery, recorded as coming from a depth of *ca.* 18.65 m., contained pottery of the fourth century B.C. and no less than seven loomweights, some of which are as late as the end of the fourth century. For several reasons it is unlikely, in fact quite impossible, that these objects came from such a depth in the well. Some confusion must have taken place when the pottery was being washed. With large quantities of pottery coming from different areas of the excavation and with not enough space available for spreading out the sherds, such an error is explainable. A gust of wind might have moved some of the empty boxes on which the depths were marked, and in this case pottery from the Pit must have been put into a box from some other area. *Haec mea culpa est.* The box in question also contained a fragment of modern glass, which cannot have been found so far down the well-shaft.

---

[2] This type of Rhodian stamp is dated in the first half of the second century B.C., V. R. Grace and M. Savvatianou-Petropoulakou, *Délos*, XXVII, p. 304, pl. 53, no. E 8. The notation of its discovery reads: "Work began at 7:25 A.M., salvaging sherds from the mud pile on the surface. Basket No. 14 contains material from this salvaging operation, i.e. from depths 15.05–15.25." The amphora handle is recorded as coming from basket 14. J. G. Hawthorne, April 18, 1958, p. 147. Since the rest of the pottery at this depth is all of early date, this late amphora handle must have found its way into basket 14 from elsewhere during the salvaging work. It may have come from earth fill higher up in the shaft. A nearly similar amphora handle, IP 1314, of the same date (Grace and Savvatianou-Petropoulakou, *op. cit.*, pp. 303–304, pl. 53, no. E 7) was found in the Pit at a depth of only 1 m. (Notebook of J.G.H., Oct. 22, 1957, p. 55).

APPENDIX II

ΒΑΛΒΙΣ, ΥΣΠΛΗΞ, ΚΑΜΠΤΗΡ

Architecturally the Greek stadium appears to be a simple structure, the principal features and the use of which can be readily understood. Actually both its construction and its functioning have given rise to many questions that still remain unanswered. The most difficult problem has to do with the lines and devices for regulating the start and finish of the various forms of foot races.[1] In spite of much study on the part of several competent scholars, it is still a matter of uncertainty what signal or mechanical operation gave the runners the cue for the start of the race at any given period. There is no single solution to this problem; the answer is contingent upon changes of time and place. The two stadia at Isthmia,[2] I believe, have brought the problem closer to its solution than all the other known stadia in Greece.

The question of starting devices has been extensively discussed in two recent publications, one by H. A. Harris, the other by Julius Jüthner and Friedrich Brein,[3] referred to in note 1. Both follow much the same line of reasoning, and both find the solution to the problem in the starting gates discovered in the Earlier Stadium at Isthmia. What they failed to take into account is that the intricate starting device represented by the *balbides* sill—both Harris and Brein call it *hysplex*—was discarded at an early date in favor of a different and presumably simpler method of starting runners on their way. When first discovered, the sill lay concealed under a smooth layer of white earth of the kind used in the surfacing of the race track. After the triangular pavement had been discarded and covered over in this way, a new starting line of a totally different kind was laid down, at first perhaps close to the original sill, then moved to a point farther from the end of the Stadium (above, pp. 49–52). We are thus faced with the task of explaining the operation of not one but two different kinds of starting devices. And here at Isthmia we are in a position to follow the successive changes that brought these mechanisms into existence.

There is no problem about the operation of the first starting gates in the Earlier Stadium (Pl. 95);[4] it is merely a question of nomenclature. Both Harris and Brein would apply the name *hysplex* to the

---

[1] There were three types of ordinary races: a) the stade (στάδιον), a single run of 600 ancient feet, starting at the open end and finishing at the closed end of the stadium; b) the double stade race (δίαυλος) of 1200 feet, starting and finishing at the closed end of the stadium; c) the long distance (δόλιχος), a run of from seven up to 24 stadia, starting and probably also finishing at the closed end. Other types of races are recorded: the "horse" race (ἵππιος δρόμος) of 2400 feet, the race in armor (ὁπλίτης δρόμος), and the torch race (λαμπάδηδρομία), a form of relay race. The last two, which generally had religious or commemorative significance, were usually run to some altar or shrine outside the stadium and thus had no fixed length. There were races for men, for youth (ἀνένειος), for boys, and for girls. There seem to have been also certain kinds of obstacle races, which were not part of the regular program of athletic events. The best description of the types of races is found in Jüthner-Brein, *Athlet. Leibesüb.*, II, i, Chapter VII, pp. 95–156; and see also Gardiner, *Athletics*, pp. 128–143; Harris, *Greek Athletes*, pp. 64–77.

[2] See chapter on the stadia, pp. 47–63.

[3] Other sources are: W. Zschietzschmann, *Wettkampf- und Übungsstätten in Griechenland*, I, *Das Stadion*, pp. 7–43; P. Roos, "The Start of the Greek Foot Race," *Opuscula Ath.*, VI, 1965, pp. 149–156. References to the pertinent literature can be found in the notes of Jüthner-Brein's monumental work.

[4] These are explained in the chapter on the Earlier Stadium (above, pp. 47–55); they have been published several times in the past: *Hesperia*, XXVII, 1958, pp. 10–15; *Report of the Third Session of the International Olympic Academy*,

form of starting line represented by the triangular sill, but this I believe to be incorrect. It must be admitted, however, that some ancient writers may in some cases have used the two names, *balbides* and *hysplex*, with much the same meaning. Both words appear to be of non-Hellenic origin. *Balbis* seems to be restricted to the stadium, though occasionally it is used figuratively in other connections to denote either the start or the finish of some undertaking.[5] It was a well-known term as early as the time of Aristophanes, in whose extant plays it occurs twice.[6] Spectators in the theater in Athens in the fifth century B.C. obviously knew the meaning of the word without explanation.

Hysplex is a term of wider application.[7] Its fundamental meaning is that of a trap or noose, something triggered to spring shut or to open at the touch of some form of detent. It was used in the hippodrome as early as the time of Plato's *Phaidros*,[8] but its occurrence in inscriptions and literature dealing with the stadium is comparatively late. Its first use in this sense seems to be an inscription from Delos dated in the third century B.C.[9] This is of utmost importance for our approach to the problem. There are good reasons for dating the triangular sill at Isthmia in the fifth century B.C., or at least in the first half of the fourth century, in any case more than a century earlier than the first extant use of the term for the stadium.

From the two stadia at Isthmia we know the relative dates of the various starting devices. The *balbides* is the earliest (Pl. 95, top), and it seems to have been discarded after only a short period of use, though it may well have existed later in other stadia that have not yet been excavated. The second starting line at Isthmia may be disregarded since we know nothing about its form, and even its existence remains in doubt (above, p. 50). The third starting line is sufficiently well preserved to give us definite information about its form. It is a broad sill, with exposed width of 0.32 m., and with a single groove in lengths of *ca.* 1.24 m., between leaded sockets (Pl. 95, bottom, and Section A–A) for posts, set *ca.* 1.59 m. apart. The southwest end has been patched and partly reset, and the northeast half is missing; but enough remains to show the spacing of the posts and the disposition of the groove for toe holds. Unlike the starting lines in other stadia, the two sides of the groove here have very nearly the same slope (Pl. 95, Section B–B). The whole sill, groove and all, was covered on top with hard cement. There is nothing to indicate how the gates, if there were gates, were opened or closed. Or should we suppose that there were no gates, but merely a rope stretched in front of the starting line? The posts cannot have been used in the same way as the more slender uprights in the earlier sill, which held wooden cross bars operated by cords from a starting pit (Pl. 23, c). Harris' statement[10] that "neither the pit nor the staple in the sill is essential to the working of the hysplex" is unacceptable. He would fix a staple to the post near the ground, then run the cord through a pipe (syrinx),[11] apparently lying on the surface. Without a starting pit the starter would have to operate the cord from the ground, a most inconvenient arrangement, and the number of pipes radiating from the starter's position would have caused intolerable annoyance to

---

1963, pp. 182–183, 187; *Tenth Session of the Olympic Academy*, 1970, pp. 94–99; and cf. *Isthmia*, I, Appendix I, pp. 174–181. My explanation of the *balbides* presented in these reports has been accepted by all the authorities on the subject. But Harris, *Greek Athletes*, pp. 68–70, misunderstood the actual mechanism of the cross bars by which the gates were closed and opened. In his drawings, figs. I and II, he turns the upright posts around so as to obtain a signal post like a railroad semaphore.

[5] See Liddell-Scott-Jones, *Greek English Dictionary*, *s.v.*; H. Frisk, *Etym. Wörterb.*, I, 1, 1960, p. 214. In Becker's *Anekdota Graeca*, I, p. 220, the following description of *balbides* occurs: ξύλα δύο τῶν δρομέων, ἀφ'ὧν σχοινίον τι διατέταται, ὁ καλεῖται βαλβίς, ἵνα ἐντεῦθεν ἐκδράμωσιν ἀγωνιζώμενοι. Cf. Aristophanes, *Knights*, 1159: ἄφες ἀπὸ βαλβίδων ἐμέ.

[6] *Knights*, 1159; *Wasps*, 548.

[7] For the etymology see H. Frisk, *Etym. Wörterb.*, I, 1, p. 975, who gives this explanation: "Auslösende Vorrichtung zum Entlassen der Wettläufer, zum Fangen von Vögeln und Tieren usw." "Aussehen (Schlinge? Stellholz? Seil?) unbekannt. Deswegen schwebt eigentlich die Etymologie in der Luft."

[8] *Phaidros*, 254 E: ὥσπερ ἀπὸ ὑσπληγος ἀναπεσών, here obviously used with reference to starting gates in the hippodrome.

[9] *Inscriptions de Délos*, nos. 1400, line 9; 1409, Ba II, lines 43–44.

[10] *Greek Athletes*, p. 70.

[11] The inscription from Delos lists items of expenditure for the *hysplex* of the stadium including two pipes (σύριγγες), a rather small number, if, as Harris believes, the cords operating the gates ran through pipes.

the runners unless they were buried in the ground. No traces of such pipes have been discovered. One would expect an improvement rather than such a patently inferior starting device. A further reason for rejecting Harris' explanation is the position of the post holes in relation to the groove. A horizontal bar extending from post to post would be almost in line with the groove, so that a runner with the toes in the groove would have had to stand stock straight or lean backward waiting for the cue, not an advantageous pose at the start of the race. And in other instances where there are two grooves in the sill the post holes come in the middle between the grooves[12] or in line with the outer groove.[13] Only one foot could then be placed in its groove before the gate opened. In these instances the posts cannot have been used for starting gates, unless we are to assume that the runners had to fumble for the toe holes after the bars were down.

Obviously, with the new kind of starting line some other mode of signaling the start was introduced, the exact nature of which is a matter of conjecture. The posts in any case must have served a new purpose. They are now heavier and set in square holes encased in lead (Pls. 95, 96, a, 97). They are, I believe, turning posts (καμπτῆρες), fastened in the sill so firmly that the runner could grab his post with his left hand and swing around with a minimum loss of time and momentum. Brein follows Harris in assuming that all the runners turned around a single post midway between the two ends of the line. Harris criticizes Gardiner, who "usually so shrewd in his judgement of these practical points fell into the error of supposing that each runner in the longer races turned round a separate post, and that this was the purpose of the sockets. This" Harris says, "would have caused the runner, if he was leading his left-hand neighbor, to collide head on with him as he rounded the post."[14] That seems to be Harris' only objection to separate turn-posts. Since the posts were five feet apart (at Olympia four feet), the objection seems pointless. On the other hand Harris admits the difficulties involved in the single turn-post, and he finds that "it is one of the many mysteries of Greek athletics that in the whole of Greek literature there does not appear to be any reference whatever to this problem."[15] The answer is, of course, that the problem, and so the mystery, did not exist. The posts, set in lead for safe anchorage, were surely *kampteres*. Had they merely been uprights intended to support a rope or piece of wood by which the gates could be closed, the expensive use of lead for fastening them to the sill would be an unwarranted increase in the cost.[16]

How then could the simultaneous start of several athletes be regulated? We know that in the fifth century a trumpeter signaled the start of the horse races. In contests of later times the trumpeter seems to have been a common official at the games, and contests in trumpeting were held at some of the games.[17] From two references from Aristophanes, it would seem that the start was announced by a herald shouting the signal, and in any case a herald would have called to the contestants to take their places at the starting line.[18] The actual start would then be announced by a blast from the trumpet or by some mechanically operated device.

---

[12] So at Olympia, Jüthner-Brein, *Athlet. Leibesüb.*, II, i, p. 59, fig. 9; and Delphi, *ibid.*, p. 60, fig. 10. In the gymnasion at Delphi the single groove in the starting line has the same relation to the sockets as in the third starting line of the Earlier Stadium at Isthmia. See Jannoray, *Le Gymnase*, pl. VII, 1 and 2.

[13] This is the case in the line at the closed end of the stadium at Epidauros (Pl. 97).

[14] *Greek Athletes*, p. 68.

[15] *Ibid.*, p. 71.

[16] At Olympia, where the sill is of hard limestone, there is no lead in the sockets. At Epidauros and Isthmia, third starting line in the Earlier Stadium and in the Later Stadium, the sill is of poros. This is too soft and fragile to resist the strain caused by the violent jerk exerted by the runner; hence the need for setting the posts in lead.

[17] Sophocles, *Electra*, 711; Luigi Moretti, *Iscr. Agon. Gr.*, p. 100; and cf. Harris, *Greek Athletes*, p. 66. Competitions of trumpeters are recorded in victors lists; Dittenberger, *Syll.*³, II, 667, line 45 (161–160 b.c.); III, 1059 II, line 20.

[18] *Knights*, 1159. In a race in armor at Delphi the herald's shout, οἱ ὁπλῖται παριόντων (Heliodoros, IV, 1) would not be the signal for the start but the call to the runners to come forward. Likewise the enigmatic command βαλβῖδα ποδὸς θὲτε πόδα παρὰ πόδα (Moeris, 193, 4-Becker) would be the equivalent of our "On your mark! Get set!"; the "Go!" signal would then follow by trumpet or by some mechanically operated gadget. Gardiner (*Greek Athletic Sports and Festivals*, p. 273) and Bruno Schröder (*Der Sport im Altertum*, p. 106) find support for the common use of the command ἄπιτε the

The Earlier Stadium at Isthmia was abandoned some time probably in the fourth century B.C., and the Later Stadium was built at a greater distance from the Temple of Poseidon. The starting line was now broadened to 0.46 m., and in place of the single groove the new line has a double groove with the side away from the race track much steeper than the other (Pl. 96, a, cf. Pls. 27, e, 60). The post-holes, heavily lined with lead, are similar to those in the later starting line of the Earlier Stadium (Pl. 24, c) and not very different in size, but they are now set closer together, *ca.* 1.51 m. as compared with 1.59 m. The difference probably has to do with the change in the foot length from 0.3204 m. to 0.302 m. In either case, the interval, axis to axis, was probably intended to be approximately five feet.[19] At Olympia it was only four.

Whatever instrument, trumpet or mechanical device, was used for signaling the start of the races, it was probably the same in the Later Stadium as that used in the final period of the Earlier Stadium. This too proved unsatisfactory and was replaced by a new device of intricate design. The evidence for this change is a large rectangular block with a series of cuttings on top and set close to the inner edge of the starting line in front of the second lane from the southeast end of the line (Pls. 27, d, 96, a). The stone is in its original position, but it was not part of the primary design of the Stadium. It is not fitted neatly to the edge of the starting line sill but is 0.065 m. from it, and its emplacement or the functioning of its mechanism required the cutting away of the edge of the sill close to the stone for a length of 0.43 m. and a width of *ca.* 0.10 m. The cutting is rough, but whatever was inserted in it formed an essential part of the mechanism anchored in the cuttings of the rectangular stone.

Were this a single phenomenon, it could be dismissed as a late and probably unimportant alteration. But, as we shall see, such stones with comparable if not similar cuttings are found in two other stadia. It is likely that there was a similar stone at the other, northeast end of the starting line; but this part of the line, being concealed beneath a much used agricultural road, was not disclosed in our investigatory trenches in the Later Stadium.[20] At the other end of the racecourse, we exposed the two ends of the finish line, but the narrow tunnel in which we had to operate did not permit clearing of a large part of the stone sill. Nevertheless, at the two ends close to the statue bases against which the sill abuts, there are cuttings in the inner edge of the sill somewhat similar to the cutting behind the rectangular stone at the southeast end of the starting line (Plan VI). Whether stones with similar profiles stood in front of the two cuttings in the finish line can only be revealed by more extensive excavation in the Later Stadium.

In the stadium at Epidauros there are stones in the same relative position. The starting line at the open end of the stadium is largely missing, but its position is quite clear, and when the building was excavated by Kavvadias in 1894 more of the sill was visible.[21] At the north end of this sill, a rectangular block with cuttings in the top lies close to the inner, i.e. toward the race track, edge of the starting line (Pl. 96, b). The cuttings are so badly weathered and worn that it is not clear whether they were similar to those in the stone of the Later Stadium at Isthmia, but what is still visible makes it likely that they were used for a similar purpose. The position too in relation to the starting line is very nearly the same. There were stones in the same position relative to the finish line at the east end of the race track (Pl. 97), and at the time of excavation, these stones were sufficiently prominent to elicit comments

---

direct equivalent of our "Go!", as a signal for the start, but Jüthner-Brein, *Athlet. Leibesüb.*, p. 90, note 175, very correctly point out that the command ἄπιτον in *Knights*, 1159 does not signal the actual start of the race, since the Demos in the second line below gives the command, θέοιτ'ἄν, to start the race. There were also contests of heralds; see Moretti, *Iscr. Agon. Gr.*, nos. 38 (*ca.* 250 B.C.), 70 (A.D. 140), 90 (*ca.* A.D. 253–257).

[19] *Isthmia*, I, Appendix I, p. 176.

[20] *Hesperia*, XXXI, 1962, pp. 12–13; and above, p. 58.

[21] P. Kavvadias, Τὸ Ἱερὸν τοῦ Ἀσκληπίου, pp. 96–118, fig. on p. 111. I am indebted to the former Director of Antiquities N. Yalouris and to the Ephor E. Deilaki for permission to make the drawings for Plates 96, b and 97 and for instructing the local guards to clean off the stones that had been partly covered over with earth and vegetation since they were first exposed by Kavvadias.

on the part of the excavator. The stones that now lie in a slanting position at some distance from the sill lack the elaborate cuttings in the top, but in each case the edge of the sill has been cut away behind the stones. They were obviously not a part of the original plans of the stadium.[22]

The racecourse in the Corinthian Agora[23] also has such a stone with cuttings in the top at each end of the later of two starting lines (Pls. 48, e, f, 98). The cuttings are not exactly like those in the stone of the Isthmia Stadium but sufficiently like them to indicate similarity of purpose. The stones in the Corinth race track do not lie in front of the starting sill, but are notched into the front part of its two ends. Here, too, the stones have clearly been inserted at a later period as an alteration of the original design. The sill is very broad, 1.23 m., and any mechanism set into the cuttings in the two stones would have stood in front of the toe holds in the sill. Thus their spatial relation to the position of the runners at the start would be much the same as at Epidauros and Isthmia.

The analogous form of these cuttings and the relative position of the stones in three different stadia make it clear that we are dealing with the introduction of a new feature which must have served some function in connection with the start of the races. All lie in front of the straight line of the feet of the runners, and in every case there is evidence of subsequent addition to the design of the buildings. The lateness of the change is shown by the absence of such stones in the stadium at Olympia and in the two existing starting lines of the Earlier Stadium at Isthmia. The stones are, at any rate, later than the changes that resulted in the abandonment of the Earlier Stadium and the construction of the new. The most likely time for that change is the period of Alexander, as has been shown in the description of the Later Stadium (pp. 65–66).

It may be of significance that this innovation has been found so far only in two stadia in the Corinthia and in the Asklepieion at Epidauros.[24] From an inscription at Epidauros[25] frequently referred to in literature on the ancient stadium, we learn that a Corinthian engineer by the name of Philon had been given the contract to install a *hysplex* in the stadium in the Asklepieion. Philon and his guarantor, a banker by the name of Nikon, likewise from Corinth, were fined for breach of contract and for failing to pay the fine within the stipulated time. One gathers from the inscription that the *hysplex* was actually installed, since half the payment for the work was subtracted from the fine. The inscription is dated in the third century B.C. This date agrees well enough, so far as our evidence shows, with the addition of the stones with the cuttings in the top inserted close to the starting lines in the three stadia. It seems probable that the stones were prepared for the starting mechanism. The name *hysplex* was given to these gadgets presumably because they were operated by means of a spring or torsion mechanism that could

[22] In Kavvadias' drawing of the terma (*op. cit.*, p. 112) two other stones are shown between the sill of the finish line and the slanting stones shown in our Plate 97. They had cuttings in the top comparable to those in the Later Stadium at Isthmia and since they were in the same relative position, they were probably intended to serve the same pupose. Further details appear in Πρακτικά, 1902, pp. 78–92, pls. Α–Δ. Here (pp. 85–86) Kavvadias speaks of an "Epidaurian foot" of 0.3022 m., which he said was otherwise unknown to him.

[23] Charles H. Morgan, *A.J.A.*, XLI, 1937, pp. 549–550, pls. XV, 2, XVI; cf. Jüthner-Brein, *Athlet. Leibesüb.*, II, pp. 62–63.

[24] Stones of somewhat similar form with cuttings in the top are found in the orchestra of some Greek theaters. In the theater at Sikyon there were two stones, one at either end of the orchestra gutter. Only one at the west end is still in existence, but the other was seen by the American excavators and entered into their drawings in *A.J.A.*, VIII, 1893, p. 394, fig. 14. See Heinrich Bulle, *Untersuchungen an Griechischen Theatern*, p. 193, pl. 42, and E. Fiechter, *Das Theater in Sikyon*, p. 26, figs. 16 and 17, pl. 2. Both stones had a large (diam. 0.13 m.) circular hole extending through the thickness of the slab, and smaller cuttings in the top, apparently for anchorage of a table-like structure, which Bulle and Fiechter interpreted as a water clock. A late water channel extends from the edge of the tank in the middle of the orchestra to the two stones. In the theaters at Megalopolis (Bulle, *op. cit.*, p. 107, pl. 18, E; Fiechter, *Das Theater in Megalopolis*, pp. 24, 26, pls. 1, 4) and Eretria (Bulle, *op. cit.*, pp. 90-91, pl. 13), some stones in comparable positions in relation to the orchestra have been interpreted as "mast shoes", presumably for suspension of the stage properties of some kind. Fiechter, *loc. cit.*, doubts that the stones in the Megalopolis theater could have been so used. It is unlikely that any of the stones in the theaters have any direct relation to those in the stadia, but if intended as anchorage for masts, they would have been used in somewhat the same way.

[25] Dittenberger, *Syll.³*, III, 1075.

be triggered by the release of a lever.[26] Philon may have been commissioned earlier to install similar contrivances in the racecourse of his home town and in the stadium at Isthmia. It is not unlikely that these stones with peculiar cuttings in the top found in the stadia at Isthmia, Corinth, and Epidauros are the very stones that he prepared as support and anchorage for his new starting device.

It would be desirable to be able to show how such a starting device operated, but the actual mechanism is probably beyond recovery. We may conjecture that it operated by means of twisted ropes that created torsion strong enough to raise a bar, or to lower or withdraw a rope stretched in front of the starting line.[27] Since there was one stone at either end of the line, each mechanism presumably opened half the gates, and if all the runners started at one time, the two *hyspleges* would have had to be operated simultaneously.

Having relegated the name *hysplex* to this comparatively late device, we are justified in retaining the name *balbides* for the earlier starting gates at Isthmia, as I have suggested in earlier reports. They were well known in Athens at the end of the fifth century B.C., but had perhaps proved too cumbersome to operate. One reason for the change may have been the installation of the individual *kampteres* in all the lanes. These posts, which became essential equipment of the stadium in all the longer races, provide explanation for the use of the lead in the stadia at Isthmia and Epidauros.

---

[26] See Epigram from Pergamon dated in the time of Attalos, adopted son of Philetairos (280–272 B.C.), in which the *hysplex* is referred to in connection with the hippodrome: ἀθρόα δ'ὕσπληξ πάντα (τὰ ἅρματα) διὰ στρεπτοῦ τείνατ'[τ'ἒ] χουσα κάλω. Moretti, *Iscr. Agon. Gr.*, p. 94, no. 37, translated the passage: "E tesa era la transenna tutti insieme i cocchi trattendo per mezzo di una fune ritorta." In the Olympic hippodrome Pausanias (VI, 20, 11) says that a cord was stretched across in front of the starting stalls instead of the *hysplex*, καλώδιον ἀντὶ ὕσπληγος. Cf. Josephos, *B.J.*, III, 5, 4. A scholion on Dionysios Periegetes, 121, shows that the *hysplex* was used to push away a bar in the racecourse: κυρίως τὸ μηχάνημα τὸ ἀποκροῦον τὸν κανόνα τοῦ δρομέως. This can not apply to the starting gates (*balbides*) in the Earlier Stadium at Isthmia, the cords of which were operated manually from the starting pit. I quote this line of Dionysios Periegetes from Liddell-Scott-Jones, *Greek-English Lexicon*, *s.v.* ὕσπληξ.

[27] The inscription from Delos referred to above, note 9, lists several items that went into the making of the *hysplex*: three elbows (ἀγκῶνας), four posts (παραστάδας) together with two columns (κίονας), and two pipes (σύριγγας).

INDEX

Fish Painting, Later Stadium, Northwest Wall (1 : 4)

Southwest Wall

Southeast Wall

Fish Paintings, Later Stadium (1 : 4)

PLATE 1

Isthmia, Aerial View

PLATE 2

a. Isthmia, View from South

b. Isthmia, View from North

PLATE 3

a. View of Temple Foundation, Looking East

b. Temple of Poseidon, Looking West, Acrocorinth in Background

PLATE 4

b. Retaining Walls NG² (below) and NG³ (above)

d. North Propylon, from South of West

a. Early Retaining Wall NG¹ (right) and Roman Foundation (left)

c. Debris from Archaic Temple above Archaic Road

b. Monument Bases M⁴ and M⁵, from Northeast

d. Monument Bases M⁵-M⁸, from Northeast

a. Monument Base M¹, from Southeast

c. Monument Bases M⁵-M⁷, from North of West

PLATE 6

b. North-South Terrace Wall, Upper Terrace

e. Threshold at North End of East Stoa

d. Debris from Northwest of Roman Altar

a. Monument Bases M⁶-M⁸, from East

c. East-West Terrace Wall, Upper Terrace, from West

PLATE 7

b. East Gateway Foundation, from Northeast

d. North End of East Stoa, Northeast Gate, from Northwest

a. Debris in Area North of Roman Altar

c. East Gateway Foundation, East Face

PLATE 8

a. Archaic Road (A), Looking East

b. Archaic Road (A), Looking West

PLATE 9

b. Building Blocks on Archaic Road, West Area

d. Retaining Wall West of Sanctuary

a. North Edge of Archaic Road above Gully, from Northeast

c. Area East of Palaimon Temple, Showing Road (C)

PLATE 10

c. Large Circular Pit, when First Discovered

d. Large Circular Pit, Seen from Above and Showing Trimmed Rim

a. North End of Long Altar, from North

b. Road (D) Crossing Long Altar, from Southeast

PLATE 11

b. Water Channels I (lower left) and II (upper left) at Stylobate of West Stoa

d. Detour of Water Channel I, North of M⁵

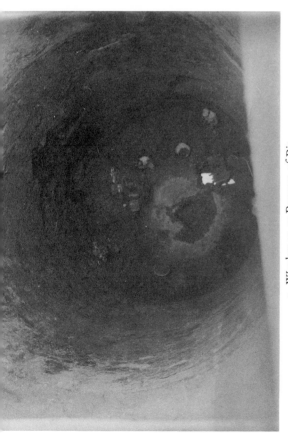

a. Workmen at Bottom of Pit

c. Water Channel I and Water Pipes *a* and *c*, at Northwest Corner of Temple

PLATE 12

b. West Waterworks, Water Channel III (lower right)

d. Water Channel II, with Cover

a. Junction of Water Channels II, III and Detour, from North

c. Water Channels II and III and Junction of Detour, from South

PLATE 13

a. Northwest End of Stadium Reservoir

b. Southeast End of Stadium Reservoir

d. Northwest Reservoir, East Corner of Clearing Basin

c. Stairway in Northwest Reservoir, from Below

e. Northwest Reservoir, South Corner of Clearing Basin

PLATE 14

a. Northeast Altar Terrace, Northeast Face

b. Northeast Altar Terrace, from East

c. Snake Vase, IP 363, from West Waterworks

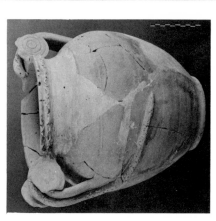

d. Thymiaterion, IP 1334, from Northeast Altar Terrace

e. Inscription on Wall of Northeast Altar Terrace

PLATE 15

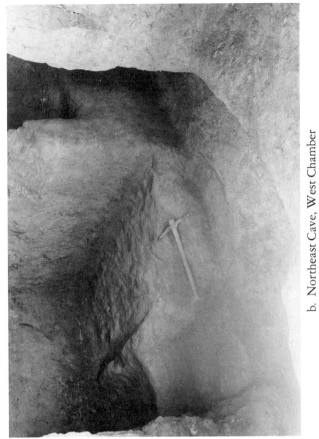

b. Northeast Cave, West Chamber

d. Northeast Cave, Foot of Stair and Covered
Pits in Passage

a. Northeast Cave, from South

c. Northeast Cave, Roman Supporting Wall in West
Chamber

PLATE 16

b. Northeast Cave, Late Wall across West Entrance

d. Theater Cave, West Chamber from North

a. Northeast Cave, Bronze Door Knocker, as Found Close to West Entrance

Supporting Piers at Entrance to East Chamber

PLATE 17

a. Theater Cave, Chute on North Side
   of Disposal Pit

b. Theater Cave, Table in Entrance Court,
   as Found

c. Theater Cave, Table in Entrance Court, with
   Pithos Removed

d. Theater Cave, Northwest Corner of Entrance
   Court, Showing Table and Pithos, Restored

e. Theater Cave, Pottery Pit, as Found

PLATE 18

b. Theater Cave, Kitchen Sink and Drain in Pantry

d. Theater Cave, East Court, Kitchen Area

a. Theater Cave, Kitchen in West Court, as Found

c. Theater Cave, West Chamber, Showing Vault and

PLATE 19

d. Theater Cave, Vases from Pottery Pit, Set out on the Kitchen Stove

b. Theater Cave, West Chamber, Cult Niche and Doorway, Partly Restored

a. Theater Cave, West Chamber, Cult Niche and Doorway, as Found

c. Theater Cave, Southeast Corner of East Chamber

PLATE 20

a. Stone Packing of Archaic Stadium (center), South of Roman Altar

b. Stone Packing of Archaic Stadium Close to Modern Road, from Southeast

PLATE 21

b. Water Basin and Four Stones with Sockets for Standards

d. Confluence of Parallel Water Channels

a. Earlier Stadium Ramp, Looking South

c. Earlier Stadium from the South

PLATE 22

b. Water Basin, Partly Excavated

d. Starting Gate Sill, Earlier Stadium, from Northeast

a. Water Basin in West Corner of Earlier Stadium

c. Later Starting Line, Water Channel and Base M14, Southwest Side of Earlier

PLATE 23

e. Triangular Pavement Covered with White Earth

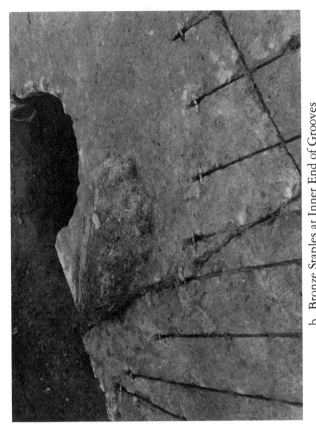

b. Bronze Staples at Inner End of Grooves

d. Starting Gates in Operation

a. Earlier Stadium, Starter's Pit

c. Starting Gates, with Posts and Strings Restored

PLATE 24

a. Southwest End of Later Starting Line, Showing Hollow

b. Later Starting Line from Southwest

c. Starting Line in Earlier Stadium, Showing Lead Socket

d. Northwest End of Inner Retaining Wall

e. Later Starting Line, from Northeast

PLATE 25

a. Parallel Retaining Walls Interrupted by Roman Altar

b. Inner Retaining Wall, West of Roman Altar

c. Outer Parallel Wall with Receding Courses

d. Parallel Walls and Stone Fill South of Roman Altar

e. Foundations M^{15} and M^{16} underneath Palaimonion Walls

PLATE 26

b. Later Stadium, Trench B¹

a. Later Stadium Hollow, Seen from the Rachi

e. Later Stadium, Marble Torch, IA 408, from Trench B⁵

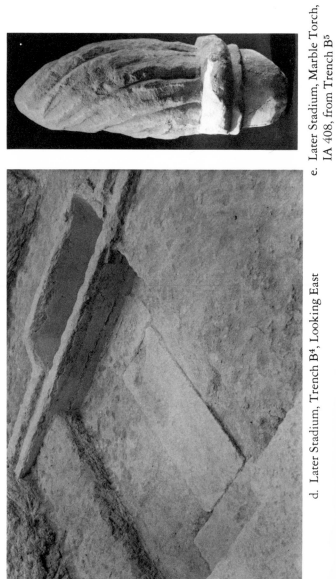

d. Later Stadium, Trench B⁴, Looking East

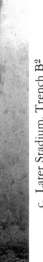

c. Later Stadium, Trench B²

PLATE 27

a. Later Stadium, Trench B⁴, Looking West

b. Later Stadium, Trench B⁵, Showing "Ramp"

c. Later Stadium, Trench B⁶, Looking West

d. Later Stadium, Stone with Cuttings, at East Corner of Race Track

e. Starting Line at Open End of Racecourse

PLATE 28

a. Later Stadium, Trench A²

b. Later Stadium, Trench A⁵

c. Later Stadium, Trench B⁸, from Above

d. Later Stadium, Steps Cut through Retaining Wall of Sphendone

e. Later Stadium Fountain, from South

f. Later Stadium, Parapet in Trench B⁸

PLATE 29

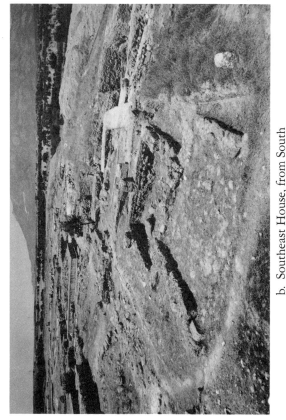

b. Southeast House, from South

a. North End of Lower Terrace Wall, Showing Re-used Block

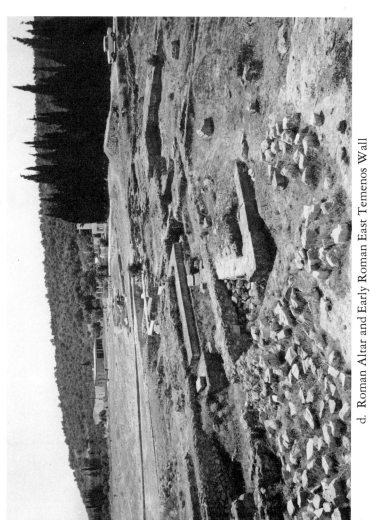

d. Roman Altar and Early Roman East Temenos Wall

c. Coping Block, 2, Showing Anathyrosis

PLATE 30

b. Foundation Showing "Layer Cake" Construction

d. Roman Altar Foundation, from North

a. Southwest Corner of First Roman Temenos, from Southeast

c. North of East Gateway, from East

PLATE 31

b. Base M¹², and Stratification East of it

d. Southeast Propylon, from East

a. North End of East Stoa, Showing Northeast Gate, from East

c. North End of East Stoa, from North

PLATE 32

b. West End of South Stoa, Showing Piers

d. Rock-cut Wall at South End of West Stoa, from Northeast, Showing Cuttings

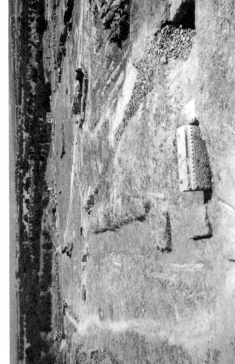

a. Foundations for East and South Stoa Colonnades, from East

PLATE 33

b. West Gate, from West of North

a. West Waterworks, Showing Pipe *b*

d. Outer End of Northwest Tunnel

c. Inner End of Northwest Tunnel

PLATE 34

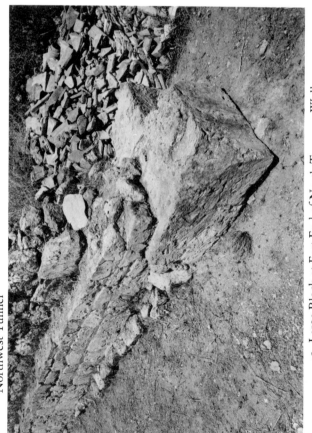

a. Stones from Rear Foundation of Projected North Stoa, and Mouth of Northwest Tunnel

b. Broad Foundation for North Stoa Colonnade, with Temenos Wall in the Rear (at Monument M⁶)

c. Large Block at East End of North Temenos Wall

d. Marble Column Base, 16, from West Stoa

PLATE 35

h. Cornice-Sima Block, 54, from West Stoa

g. Cornice-Sima Block, 55, from West End of South Stoa

d. Lion's Head Spouts, 64, 65

e. Lion's Head Spouts, IA 744, IA 742

f. Lion's Head Spouts, 62, 63

a. Fragment of Ionic Capital, 32

b. Two Fragments of Ionic Capitals, 35, 33

c. Large Fragment, 44, from West Stoa Capital

PLATE 36

b. North Propylon Area, from Northeast

d. Area North of Temple of Poseidon, Showing Water Pipe *c*

a. South Ends of Water Pipes *b* and *c*

c. West Stoa from South, Showing Pipes *b* and *c*

PLATE 37

a. Late Conduits WCh VII and VIII, North of the Temple of Palaimon

b. Late Roman Cistern, from Northeast

c. Late House at Southeast Corner of Temple of Poseidon

d. Pit A, from Southeast

PLATE 38

c. Palaimonion from East, Pit C in Foreground

e. Palaimonion, from Southwest

a. Pottery and Lamps from Pit A

b. Pottery and Lamp from Pit B

d. Lamps and Vases from Pit C

PLATE 39

a. Palaimonion, South Wall, First Period, Showing Projecting Foundation

b. Palaimonion, Semicircle, from Southwest

c. Lime Pit in the Palaimonion

d. Marble Arch, 80, from Palaimonion

PLATE 40

b. Lamps and Pottery, as Found, in Palaimonion

d. Six Lamps from Palaimonion

a. South Wall of Peribolos, Showing Construction

c. Group of Lamps, as Found, in Palaimonion

PLATE 41

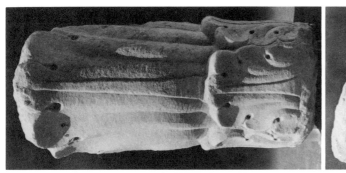

c. Crypt in Temple of Palaimon, Looking Northwest

d. Akroterion, 73, Face and Profile

a. Temple of Palaimon, from Southeast

b. Temple of Palaimon, from East

PLATE 42

a, b. Coin of Corinth, Found at Isthmia, Obverse and Reverse

c. Fragments from Figure of Pan, Playing the Syrinx

d. Relief Krater, IP 384, Dedicated to Demeter

PLATE 43

a. Statuette of Kleo, IS 254 + I Σ 316, Dedicated to Demeter

b. Stuccoed Channel, Showing Chutes and Cover Slabs

c. Stuccoed Channel in Sacred Glen, from South

d. Two T-Shaped Stones, **81, 82**

e. T-Shaped Stones, Indicating Original Arrangement in Sacred Glen Area

PLATE 44

b. Larger Cistern in Sacred Glen, from Southwest

d. Smaller Cistern in Sacred Glen

a. Well Curb in Sacred Glen

PLATE 45

b. West Foundation, from Southwest

e. Profile of Cornice from Parapet

d. North End of Rock-cut Bedding and Stone Packing of Parapet, West Flank

a. West Foundation, from East

c. Broad East-West Foundation, from East

PLATE 46

b. East Foundation, from Northeast

d. Stone Circle Surrounding Ash Pit

a. Retaining Wall North of Broad South Foundation

c. Pit, after Clearing

PLATE 47

b. Iron Trimming, Probably from Table Legs

d. Four Tiles, from Grave in West Foundation

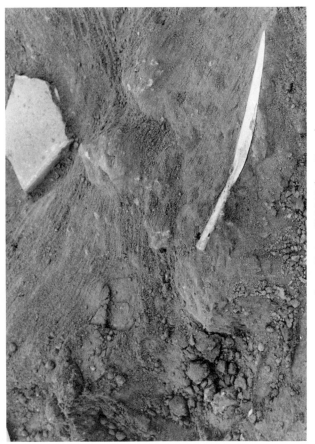

a. Spear Point, IM 3126, as Found

c. Late Grave, from West Foundation

PLATE 48

e. Starting Line in Corinthian Agora, South End

f. Starting Line in Corinthian Agora, North End

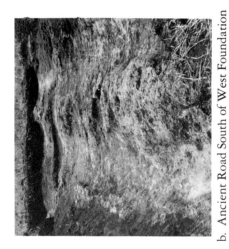

b. Ancient Road South of West Foundation

a. Two Vases, IP 2822, 2828, from West Foundation

c. Fragments of Ionic Capitals, 106, 108

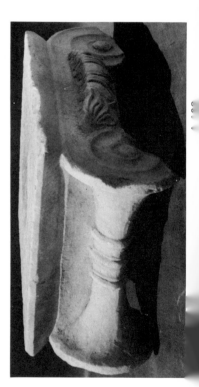

PLATE 49

a. Doric Cornice, **121**

b. Base Mouldings, **136, 139**

c. Base Mouldings, **138, 137, 140**

d. Mouldings, **143, 141, 142**

PLATE 50

a. Adjoining Fragments from Top of Circular Monument, 133

b. Mouldings, 146, 147

c. Mouldings, 152, 151

d. Decorated Mouldings, 155, 156, 154

PLATE 51

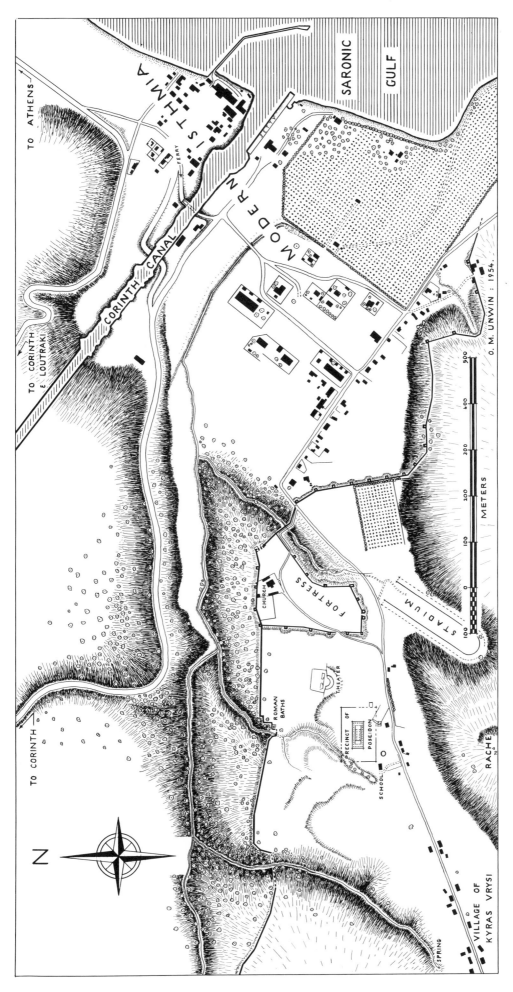

Isthmia, Physical Features

PLATE 52

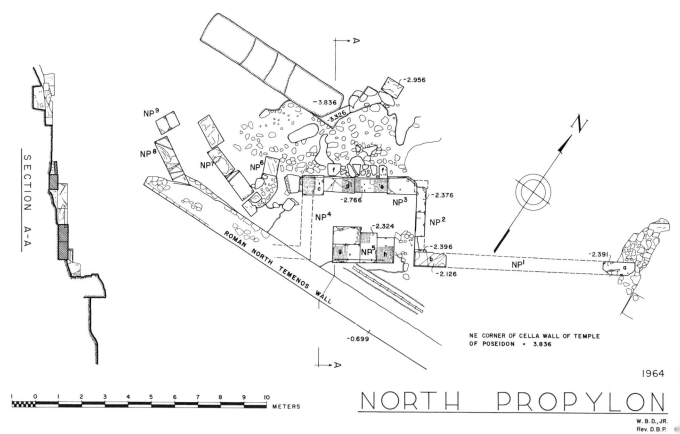

SECTION A-A

NP⁹
NP⁸
NP⁷
NP⁶
NP⁴
NP⁵
NP³
NP²
NP¹

ROMAN NORTH TEMENOS WALL

N

-2.956
-3.836
-3.326
-2.766
-2.376
-2.324
-2.396
-2.126
-2.391

-0.699

NE CORNER OF CELLA WALL OF TEMPLE
OF POSEIDON = 3.836

1964

NORTH PROPYLON

W. B. D., JR.
Rev. D.B.P.

| | 0 | 1 | 2 | 3 | 4 | 5 | 6 | 7 | 8 | 9 | 10 |
METERS

a. North Propylon

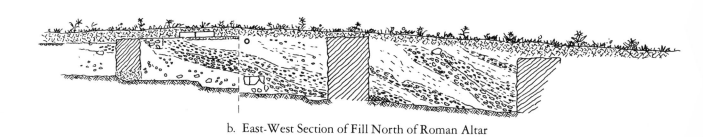

b. East-West Section of Fill North of Roman Altar

gyulid 1971

c. Conjectural Plans of East Gateway, Greek Period

PLATE 53

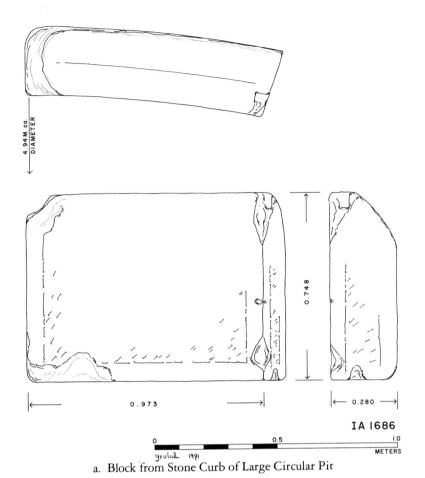

4.94 M. ca.
DIAMETER

0.748

0.973

0.280

IA 1686

0   0.5   1.0
METERS

grolich 1971

a. Block from Stone Curb of Large Circular Pit

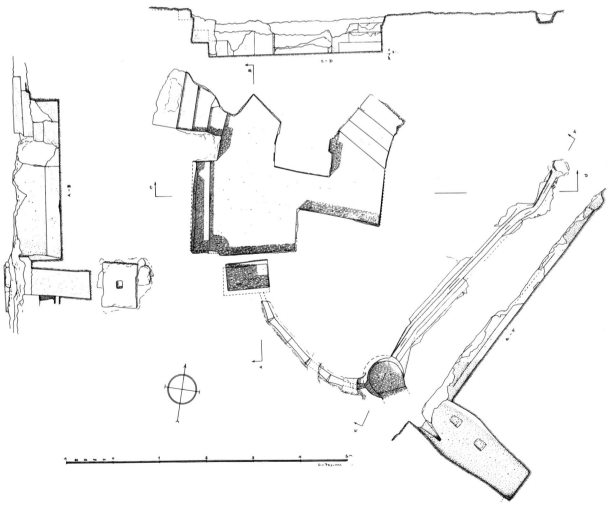

b. West Waterworks, Plan and Three Sections

PLATE 54

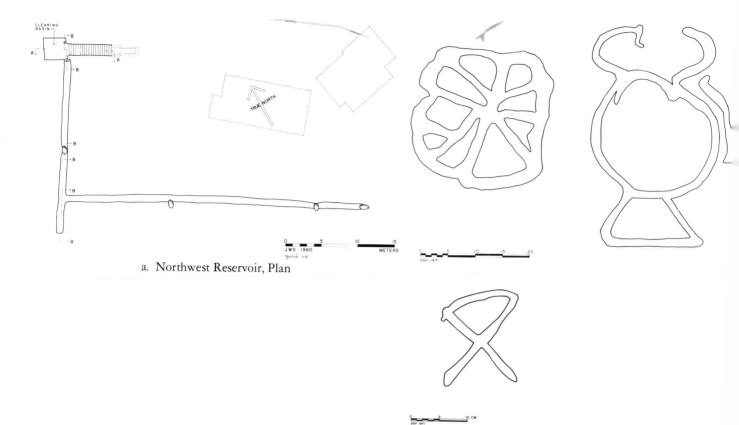

a. Northwest Reservoir, Plan

b. Designs Smeared on Stucco in Settling Basin

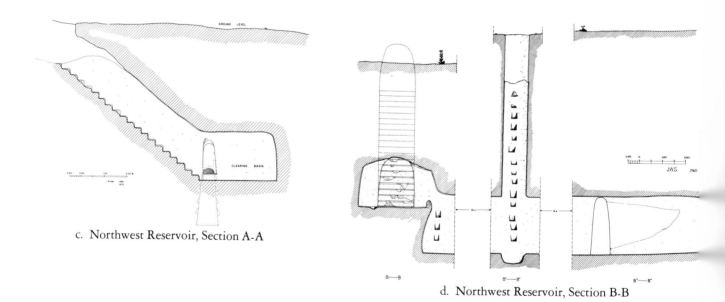

c. Northwest Reservoir, Section A-A

d. Northwest Reservoir, Section B-B

PLATE 55

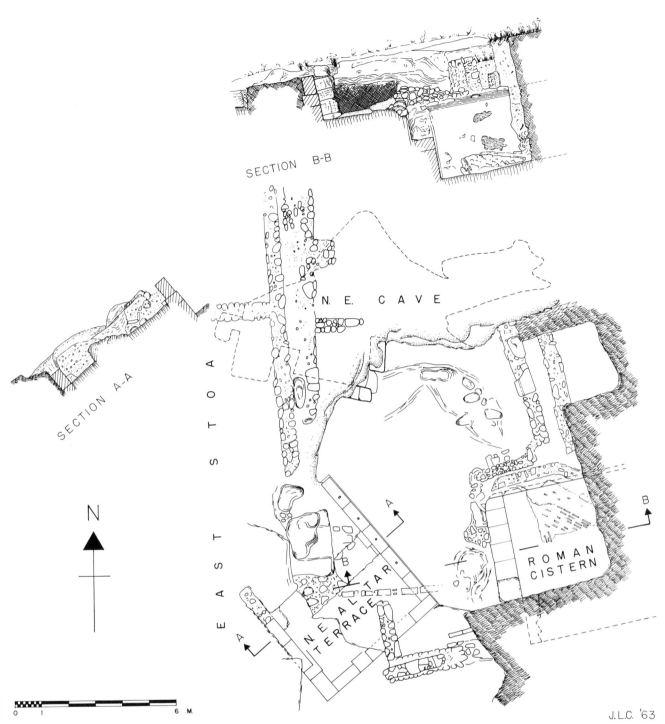

SECTION B-B

SECTION A-A

N. E. CAVE

E A S T   S T O A

N

ROMAN
CISTERN

N E   A L T A R
T E R R A C E

A

B

A

B

B

A

0   1   6 M.

J.L.C. '63

a. Northeast Altar Terrace and Surroundings, Plan and Sections

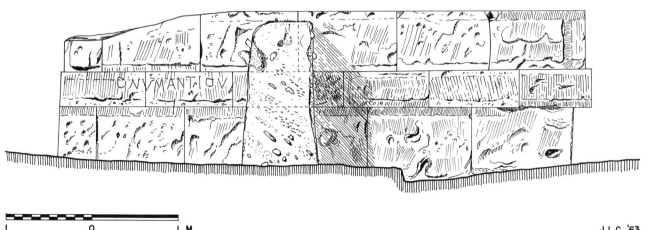

ONVMANTIOM

1   0   1 M.

J.L.C. '63

b. Northeast Altar Terrace, Inscribed Wall

PLATE 56

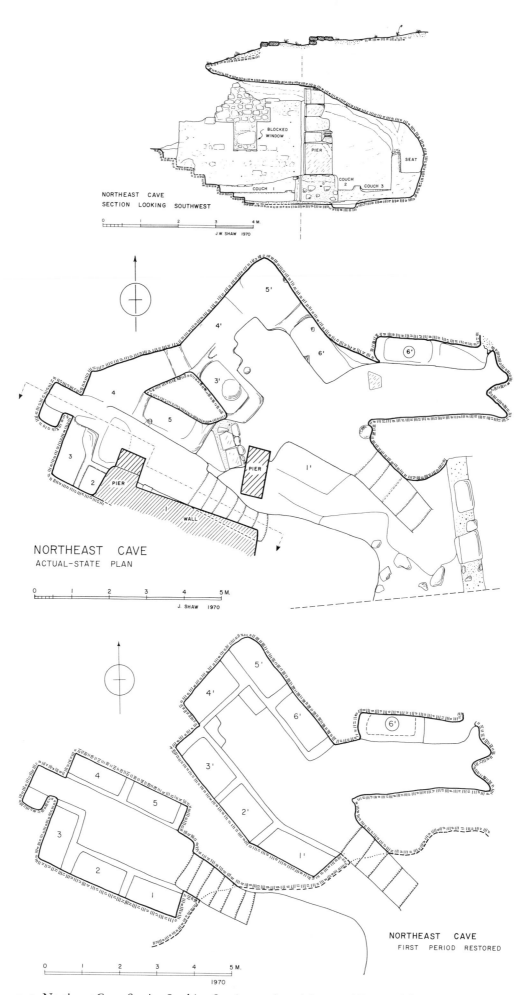

NORTHEAST CAVE
SECTION LOOKING SOUTHWEST

0   1   2   3   4 M.

J.W. SHAW 1970

NORTHEAST CAVE
ACTUAL-STATE PLAN

0   1   2   3   4   5 M.

J. SHAW 1970

NORTHEAST CAVE
FIRST PERIOD RESTORED

0   1   2   3   4   5 M.

1970

a.-c. Northeast Cave, Section Looking Southwest, Actual State and Restored (First Period) Plans

PLATE 57

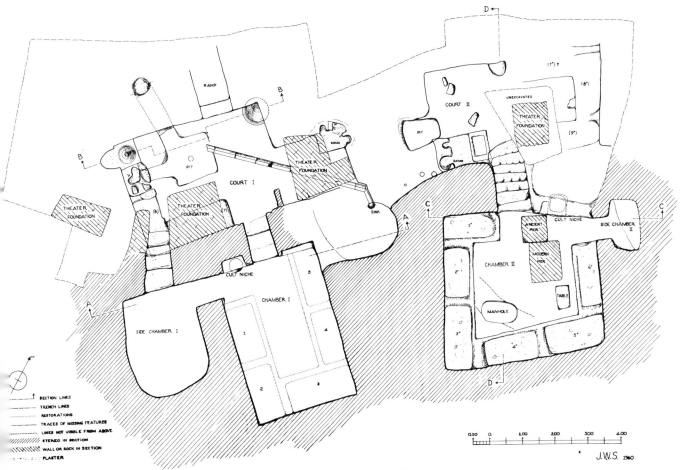

SECTION LINES
TRENCH LINES
RESTORATIONS
TRACES OF MISSING FEATURES
LINES NOT VISIBLE FROM ABOVE
STEREO IN SECTION
WALL OR ROCK IN SECTION
PLASTER

a. Theater Cave, Actual State Plan

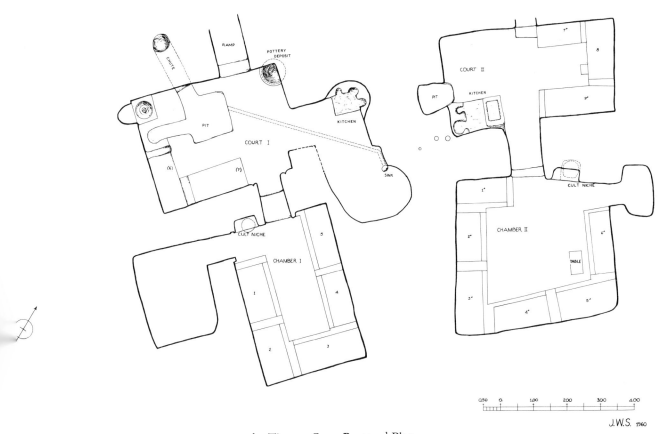

b. Theater Cave, Restored Plan

PLATE 58

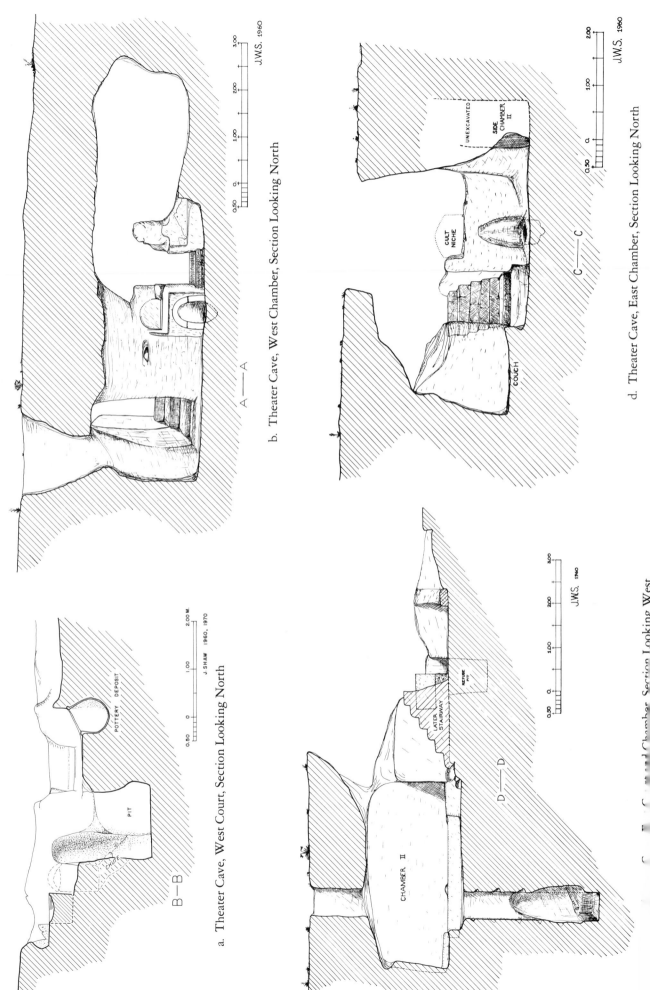

a. Theater Cave, West Court, Section Looking North

J. SHAW 1960, 1970

POTTERY DEPOSIT

PIT

CHUTE

B—B

0.50 0 1.00 2.00 M.

b. Theater Cave, West Chamber, Section Looking North

J.W.S. 1960

A—A

0.50 0 1.00 2.00 3.00

d. Theater Cave, East Chamber, Section Looking North

J.W.S. 1960

UNEXCAVATED

SIDE CHAMBER II

CULT NICHE

COUCH

C—C

0.50 0 1.00 2.00

CHAMBER II

LATER STAIRWAY

REFUSE PIT

D—D

J.W.S. 1960

0.50 0 1.00 2.00 3.00

PLATE 59

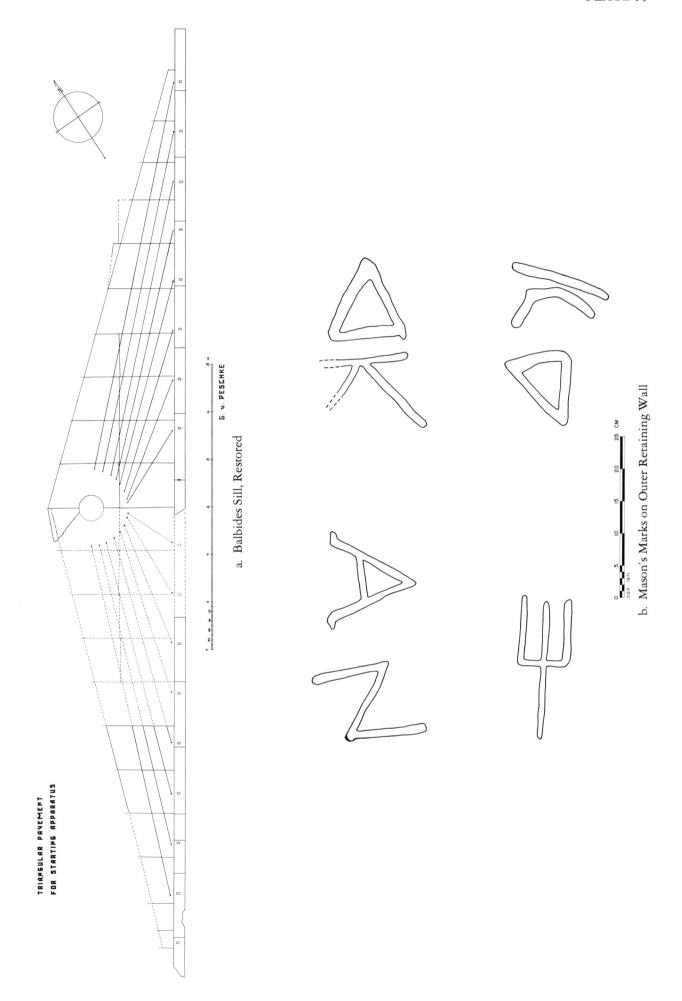

a. Balbides Sill, Restored

b. Mason's Marks on Outer Retaining Wall

PLATE 60

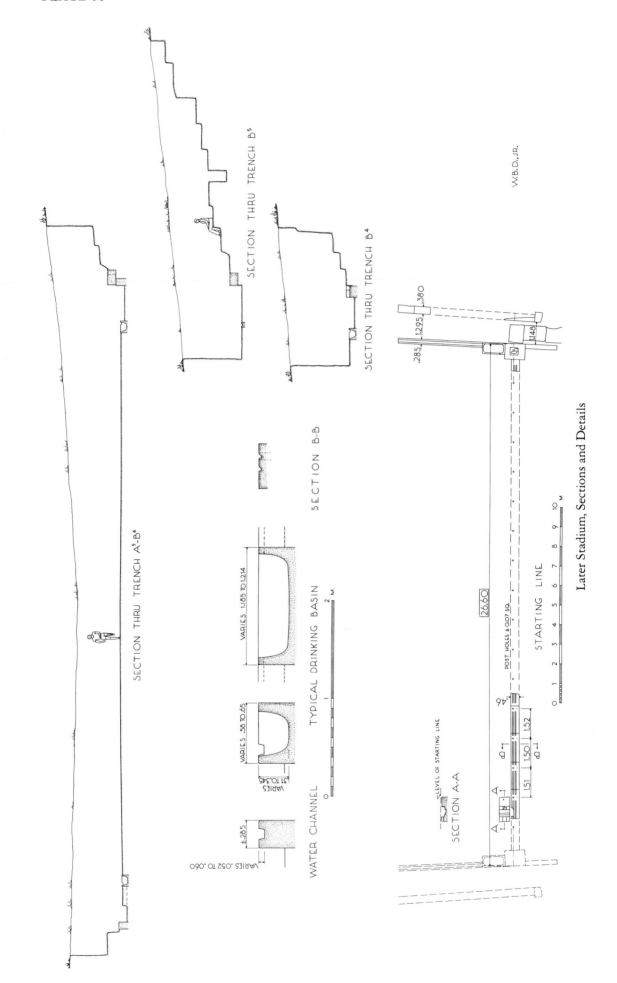

SECTION THRU TRENCH B⁵

SECTION THRU TRENCH B⁴

SECTION THRU TRENCH A⁵-B⁶

SECTION B-B

VARIES .58 TO.65

VARIES 1:1.85 TO 1:214

VARIES .131 TO.345

TYPICAL DRINKING BASIN

±.285

VARIES .052 TO .060

WATER CHANNEL

26.60

POST HOLES ± 0.07 SQ.

STARTING LINE

.46

1.52

1.50

1.51

LEVEL OF STARTING LINE

SECTION A-A

.285 1.295 .380

.148

W.B.D.,JR.

Later Stadium, Sections and Details

PLATE 61

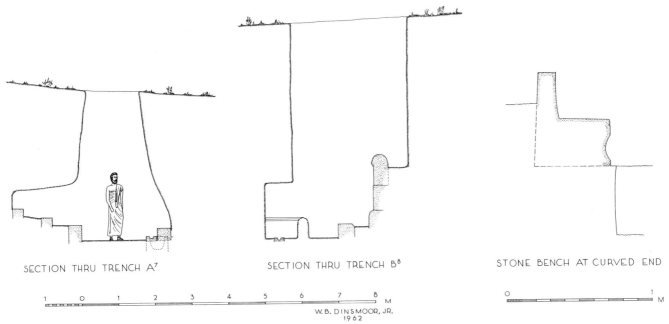

SECTION THRU TRENCH A⁷

SECTION THRU TRENCH B⁸

STONE BENCH AT CURVED END

W.B. DINSMOOR, JR.
1962

a. Later Stadium, Profiles and Sections at Sphendone

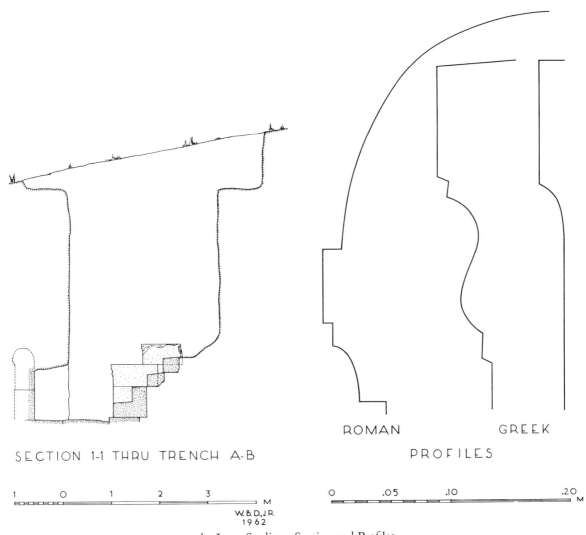

SECTION 1-1 THRU TRENCH A-B

ROMAN

GREEK

PROFILES

W.B.D., JR.
1962

b. Later Stadium, Section and Profiles

PLATE 62

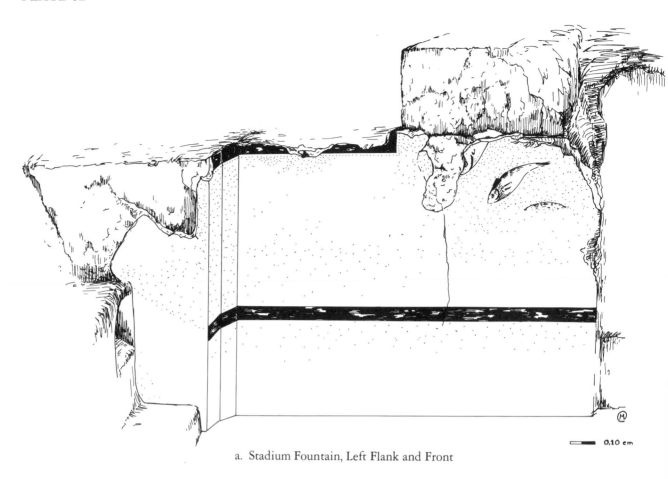

a. Stadium Fountain, Left Flank and Front

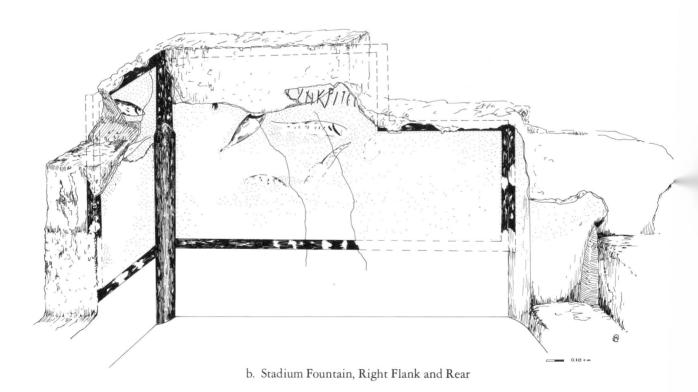

b. Stadium Fountain, Right Flank and Rear

PLATE 63

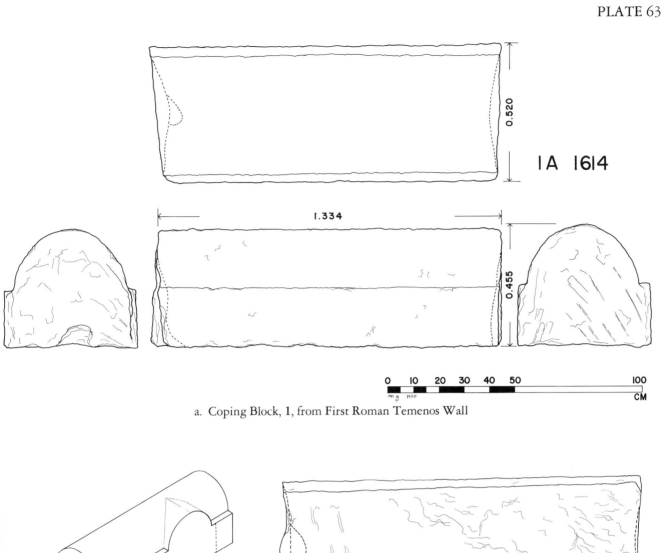

IA 1614

1.334

0.520

0.455

0 10 20 30 40 50 100

CM

m g 1970

a. Coping Block, 1, from First Roman Temenos Wall

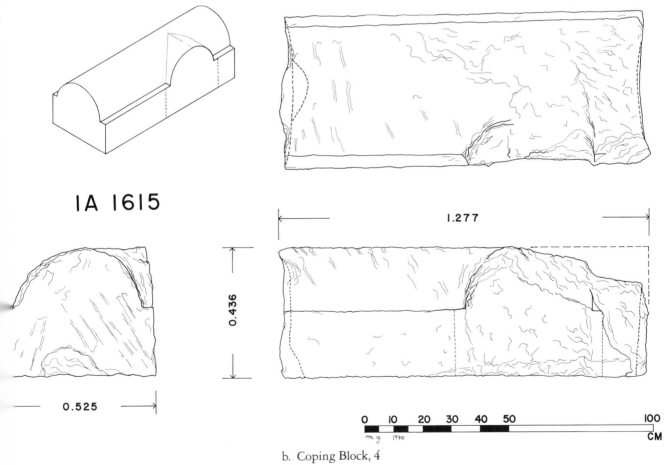

IA 1615

1.277

0.436

0.525

0 10 20 30 40 50 100

CM

m g 1970

b. Coping Block, 4

PLATE 64

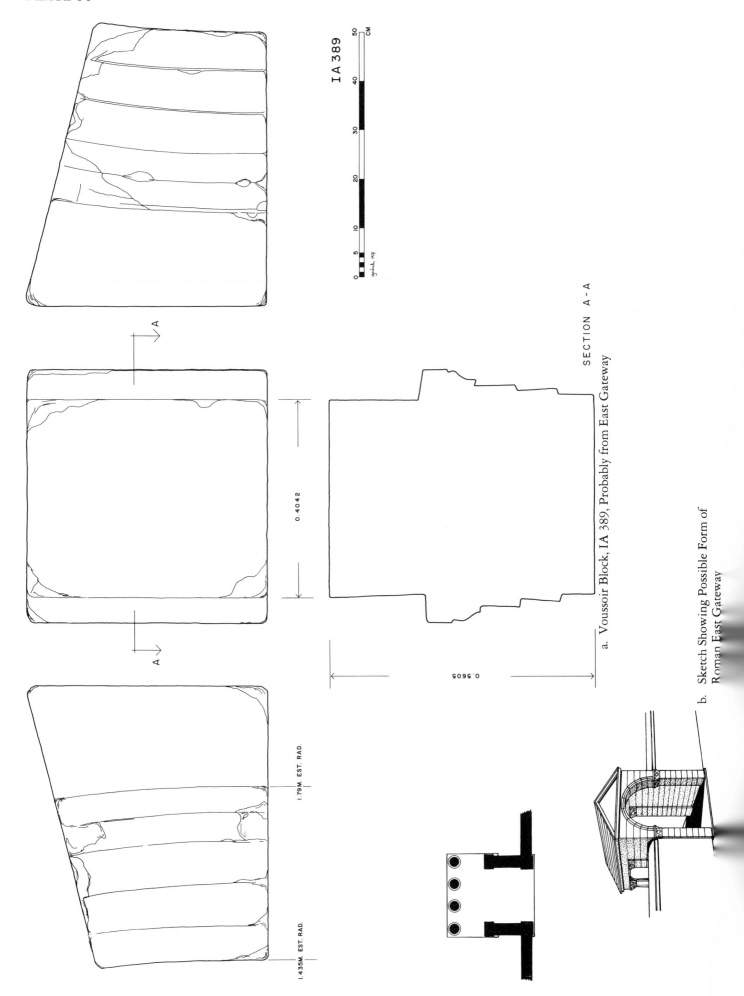

IA 389

SECTION A - A

a. Voussoir Block, IA 389, Probably from East Gateway

b. Sketch Showing Possible Form of Roman East Gateway

PLATE 65

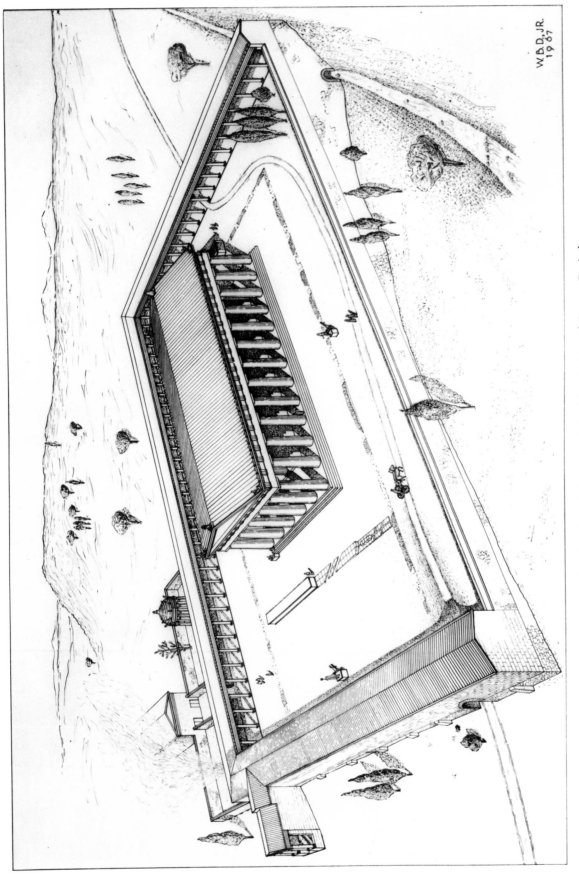

W.B.D., JR.
1967

Perspective Drawing of Temenos of Poseidon in Second Roman Period

PLATE 66

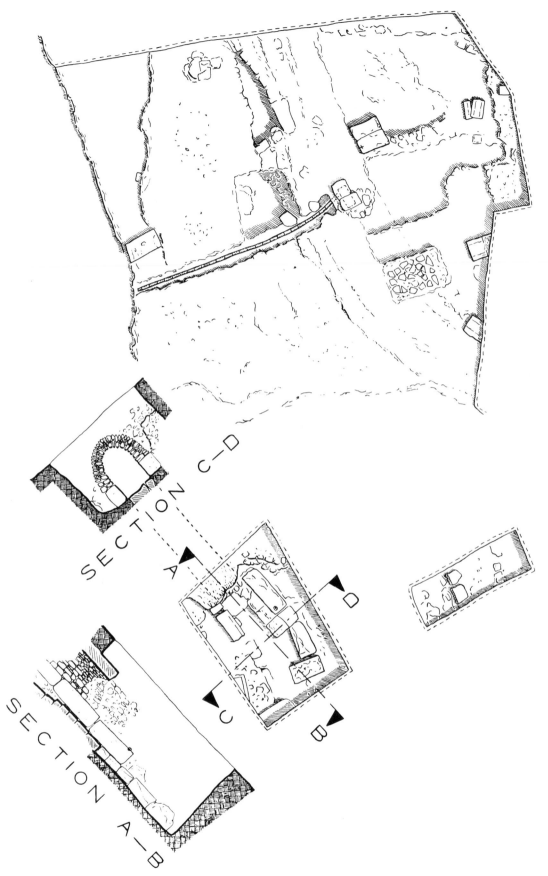

SECTION C–D

SECTION A–B

Plan and Sections of Northwest Tunnel

PLATE 67

ISTHMIA. ARCHITECTURAL DETAILS of STOAS

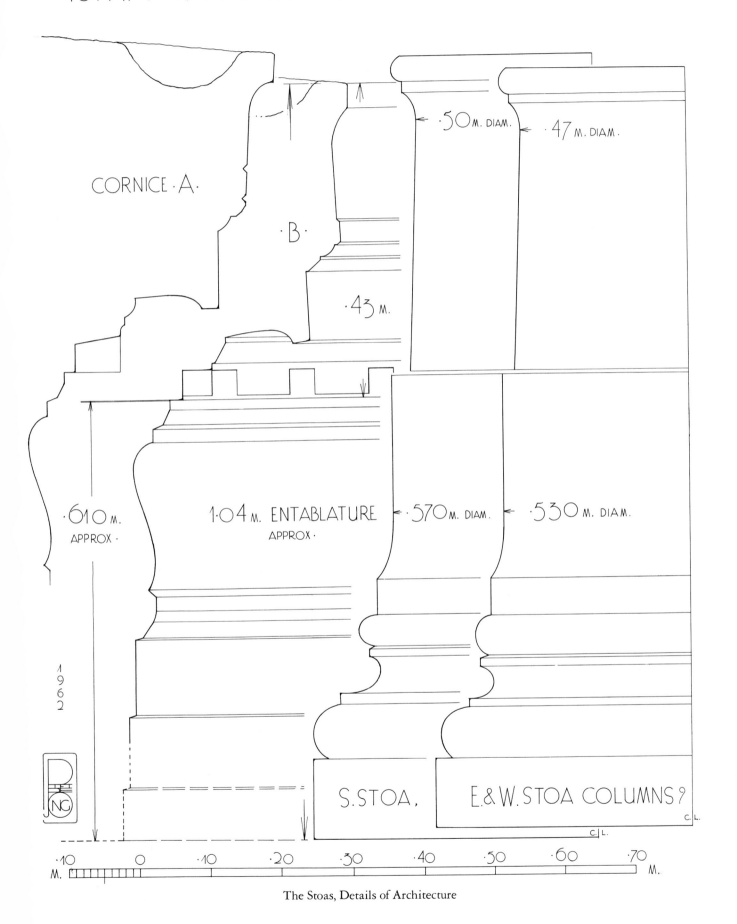

CORNICE ·A·

·B·

·50 M. DIAM.   ·47 M. DIAM.

·43 M.

·610 M.
APPROX·

1·04 M. ENTABLATURE
APPROX·

·570 M. DIAM.   ·530 M. DIAM.

1962

S. STOA,   E. & W. STOA COLUMNS?

C. L.

C. L.

·10   O   ·10   ·20   ·30   ·40   ·50   ·60   ·70
M.   M.

The Stoas, Details of Architecture

PLATE 68

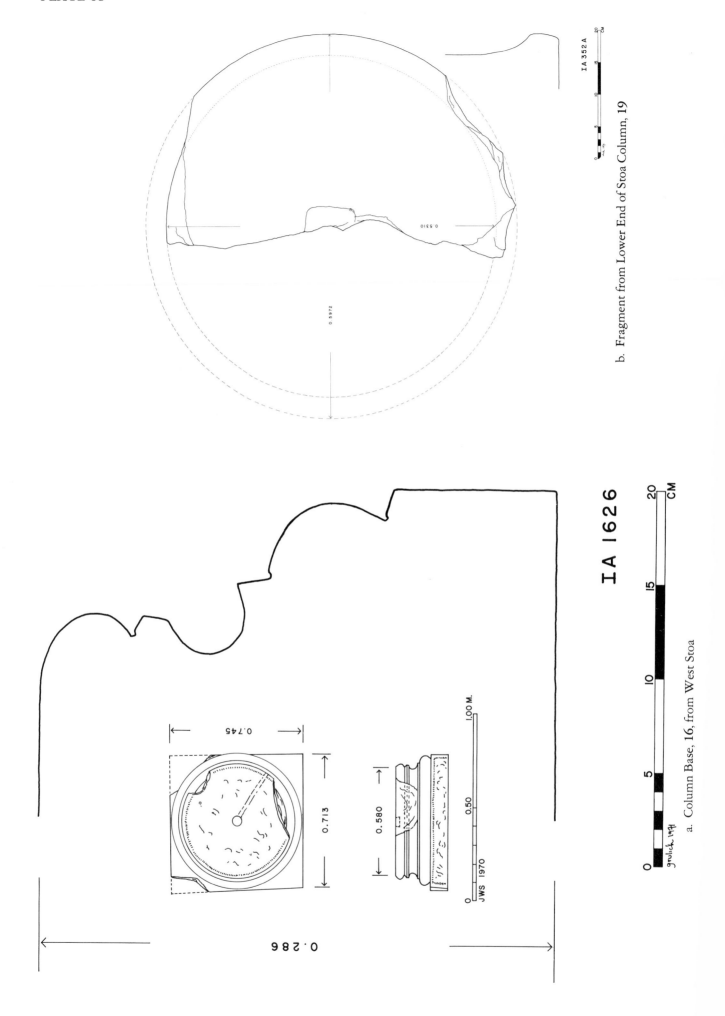

b. Fragment from Lower End of Stoa Column, 19

IA 352A

IA 1626

a. Column Base, 16, from West Stoa

PLATE 69

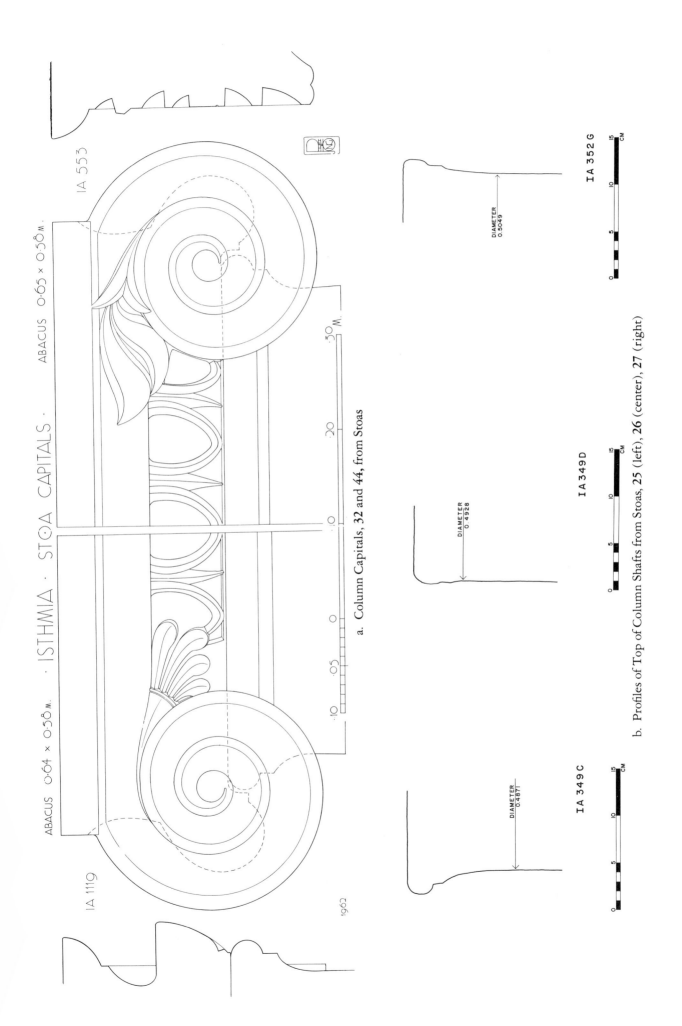

· ISTHMIA · STOA CAPITALS ·

ABACUS 0·65 × 0·58 M.

ABACUS 0·64 × 0·58 M.

IA 553

IA 1119

1962

a. Column Capitals, 32 and 44, from Stoas

DIAMETER 0.5049

IA 352 G

DIAMETER 0.4928

IA 349 D

DIAMETER 0.4871

IA 349 C

b. Profiles of Top of Column Shafts from Stoas, 25 (left), 26 (center), 27 (right)

PLATE 70

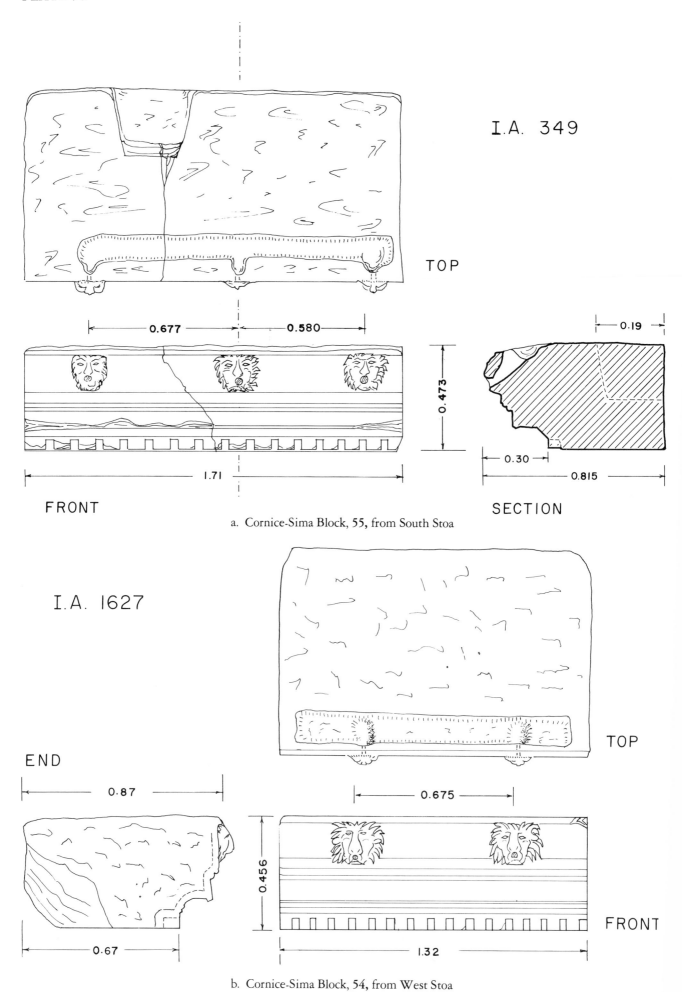

I.A. 349

0.677   0.580

TOP

0.19

0.473

0.30

0.815

1.71

FRONT

SECTION

a. Cornice-Sima Block, 55, from South Stoa

I.A. 1627

TOP

END

0.87

0.675

0.456

0.67

1.32

FRONT

b. Cornice-Sima Block, 54, from West Stoa

PLATE 71

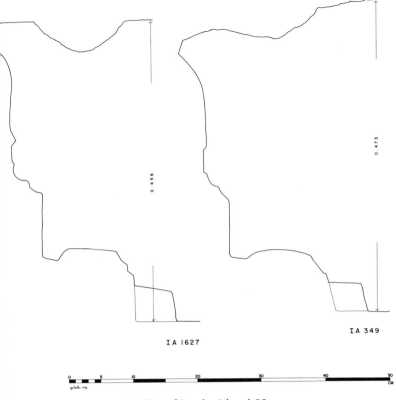

0.456

0.473

IA 1627

IA 349

0 5 10 20 30 40 50 CM

a. Profiles of Blocks 54 and 55

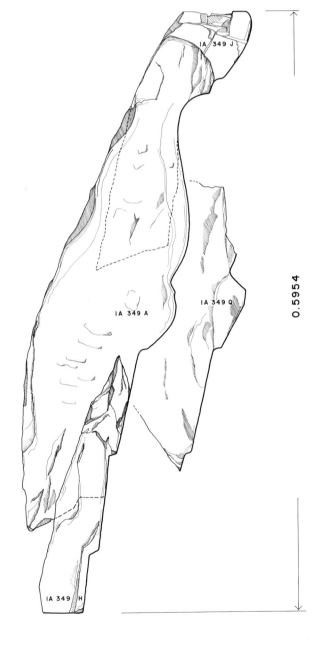

IA 349 J

IA 349 A

IA 349 Q

0.5954

IA 349 H

0 1 2 3 4 5 10 15 20 25 CM

grulich 1970 Isthmus

b. Architrave-Frieze Fragments, 45-48, from Stoas

PLATE 72

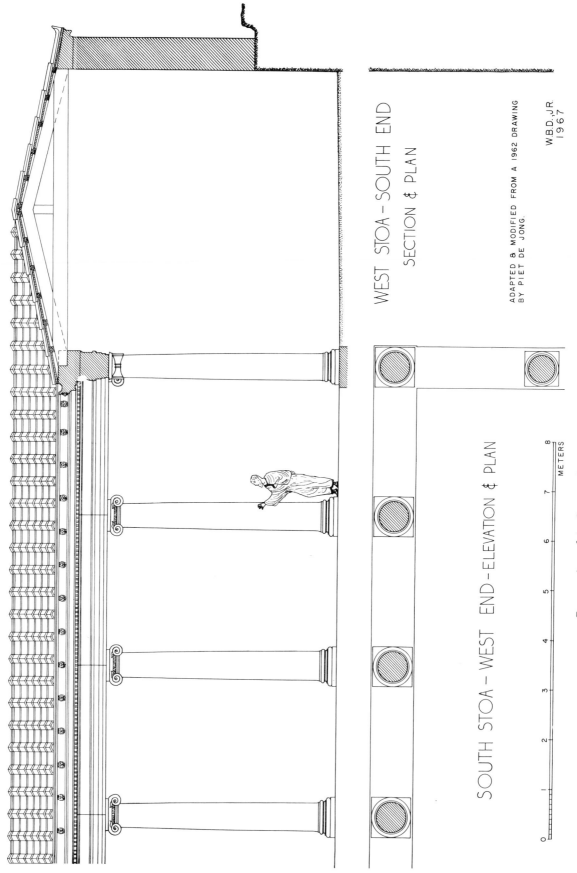

WEST STOA – SOUTH END
SECTION & PLAN

ADAPTED & MODIFIED FROM A 1962 DRAWING
BY PIET DE JONG.

W.B.D., JR.
1967

SOUTH STOA – WEST END – ELEVATION & PLAN

METERS

Restoration of the Stoas at Southwest Corner of the Colonnades

PLATE 73

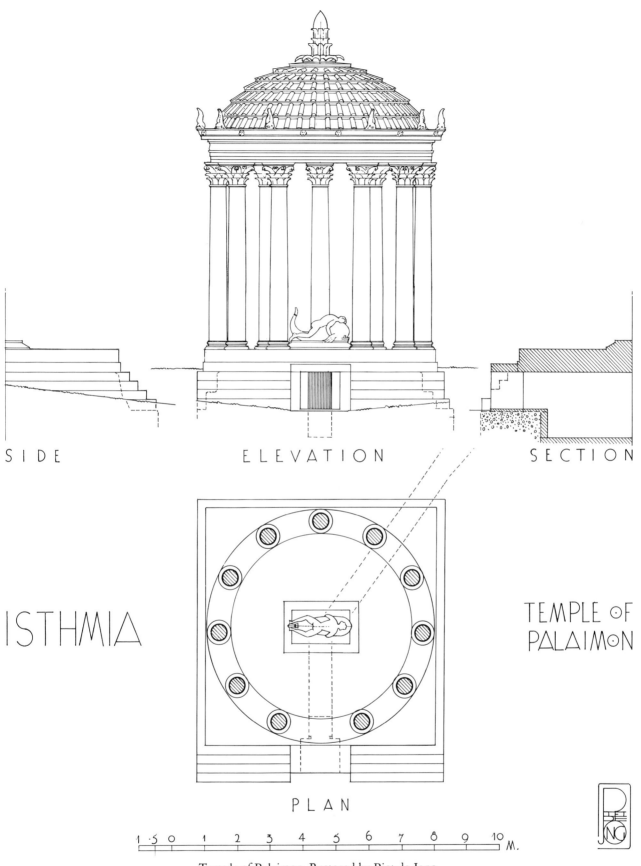

SIDE ELEVATION SECTION

ISTHMIA TEMPLE OF PALAIMON

PLAN

1·5 0 1 2 3 4 5 6 7 8 9 10 M.

Temple of Palaimon, Restored by Piet de Jong

PLATE 74

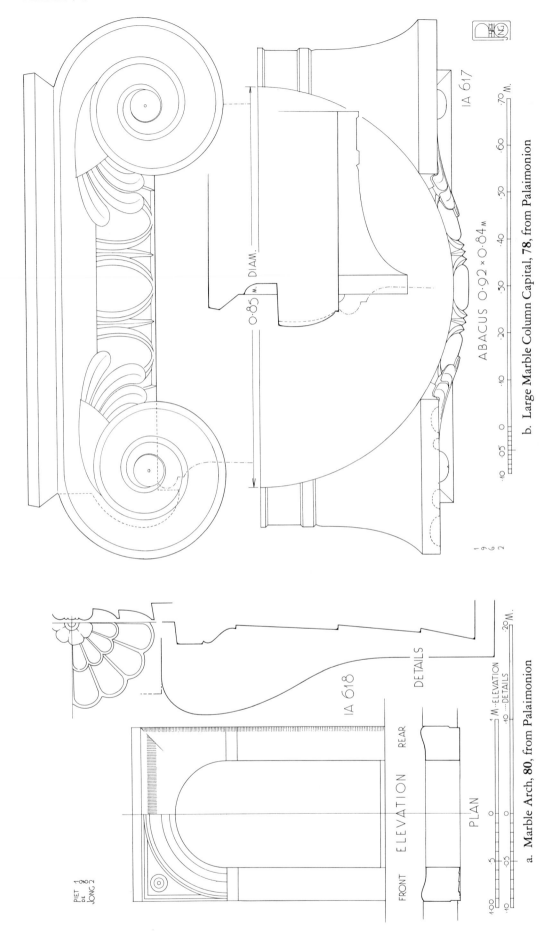

b. Large Marble Column Capital, **78**, from Palaimonion

a. Marble Arch, **80**, from Palaimonion

ABACUS 0·92 × 0·84ᴍ

IA 617

0·85 ᴍ. DIAM.

IA 618

FRONT   ELEVATION   REAR

DETAILS

PLAN

PIET DE JONG 1962

PLATE 75

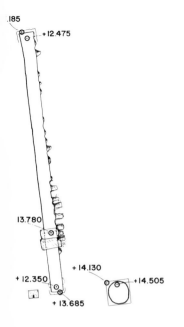

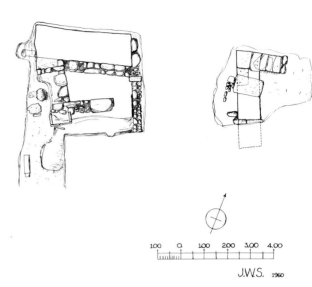

a. Plan of Sacred Glen Area

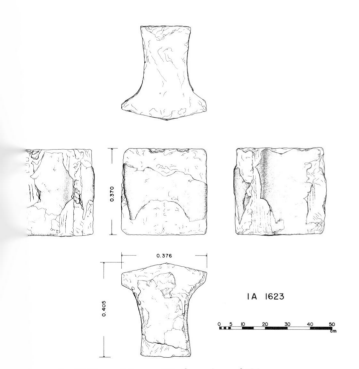

IA 1623

b. T-Shaped Stone, **81,** from Sacred Glen

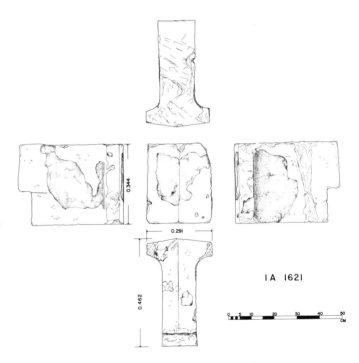

IA 1621

c. T-Shaped Stone, **83,** from Sacred Glen

PLATE 76

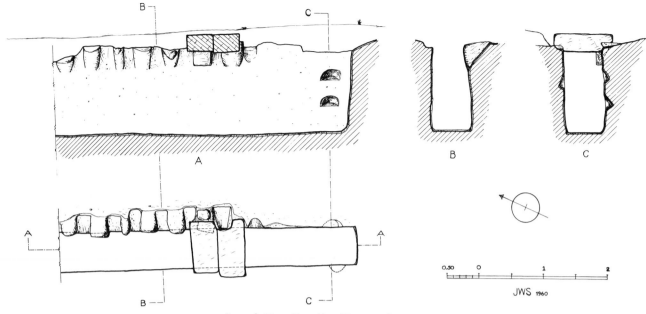

a. Sacred Glen, Details of Stuccoed Channel

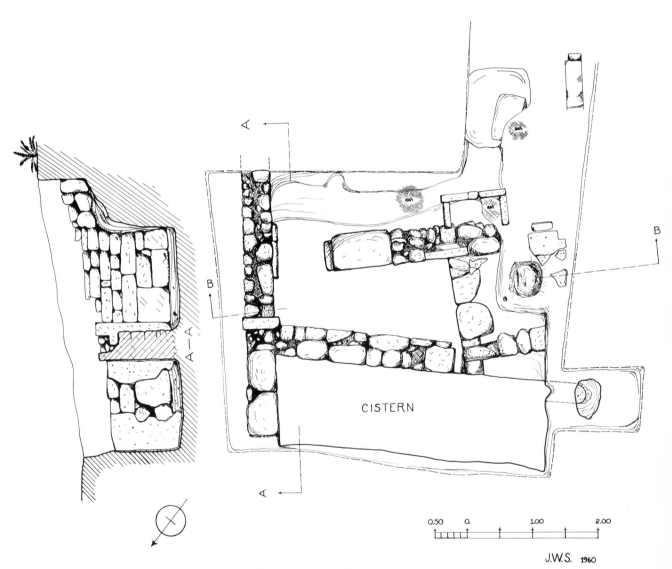

CISTERN

b. Commercial Area in Sacred Glen, Plan and Section

PLATE 77

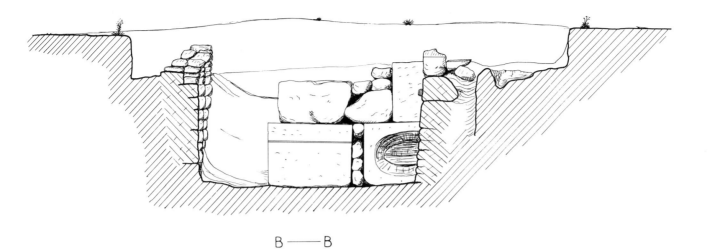

B ——— B

a. Commercial Area in Sacred Glen, Section through Larger Cistern

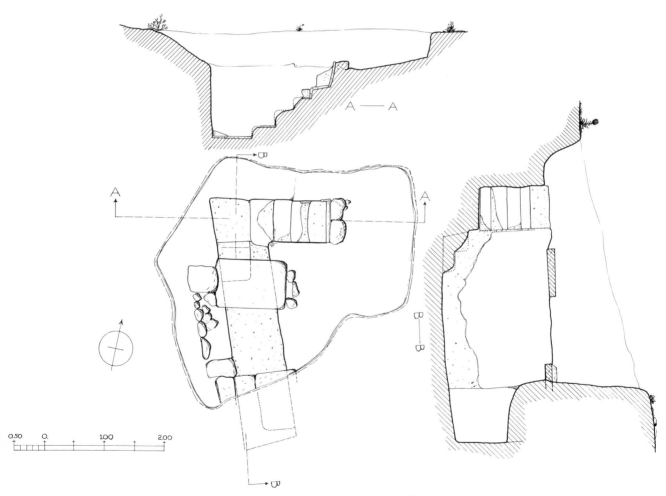

b. Smaller Cistern in Sacred Glen, Plan and Sections

PLATE 78

SECTION B-B

ASH

WEST FOUNDATION

1964

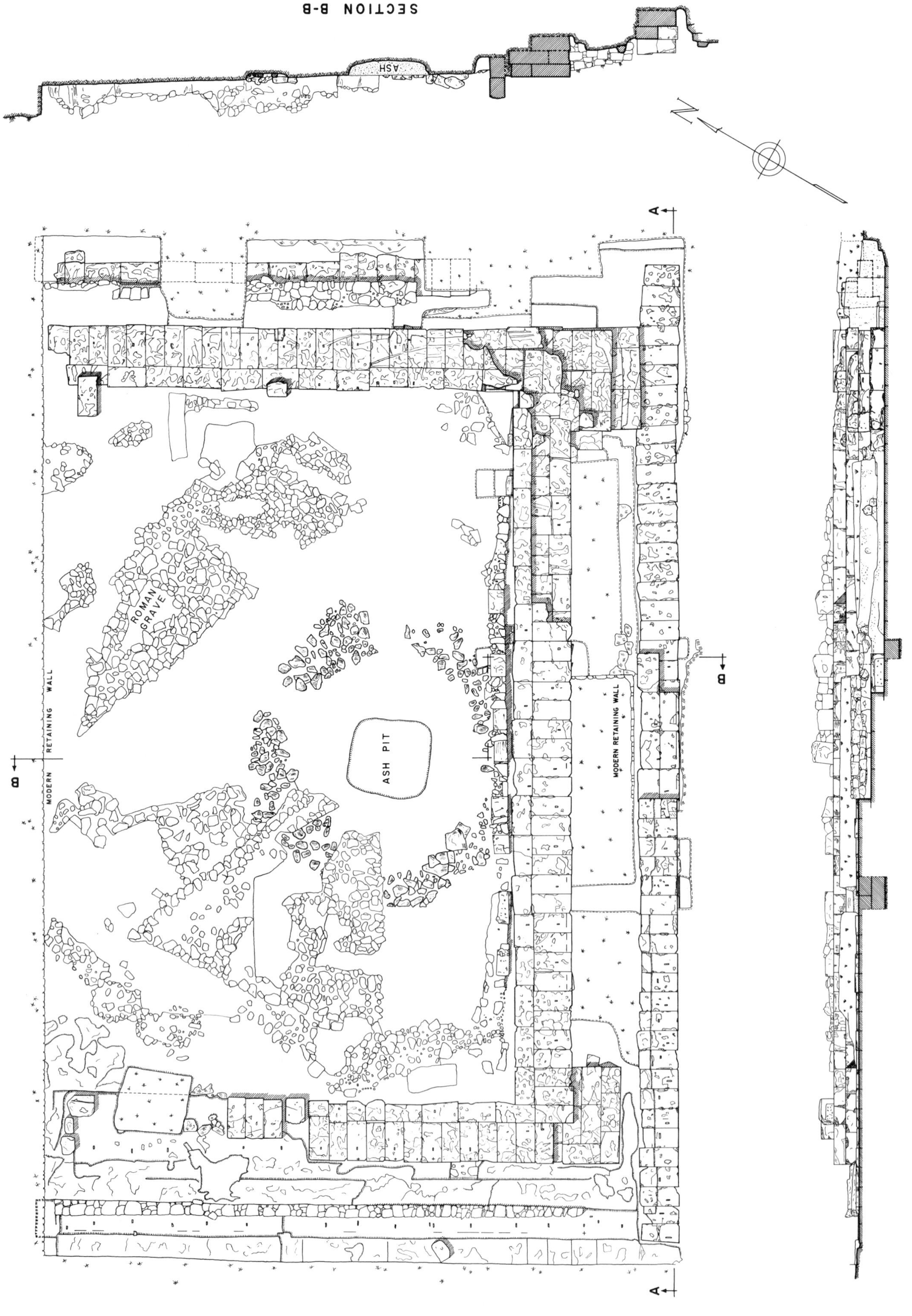

N

ROMAN GRAVE

MODERN RETAINING WALL

ASH PIT

MODERN RETAINING WALL

A

A

B

B

SECTION A-A

PLATE 79

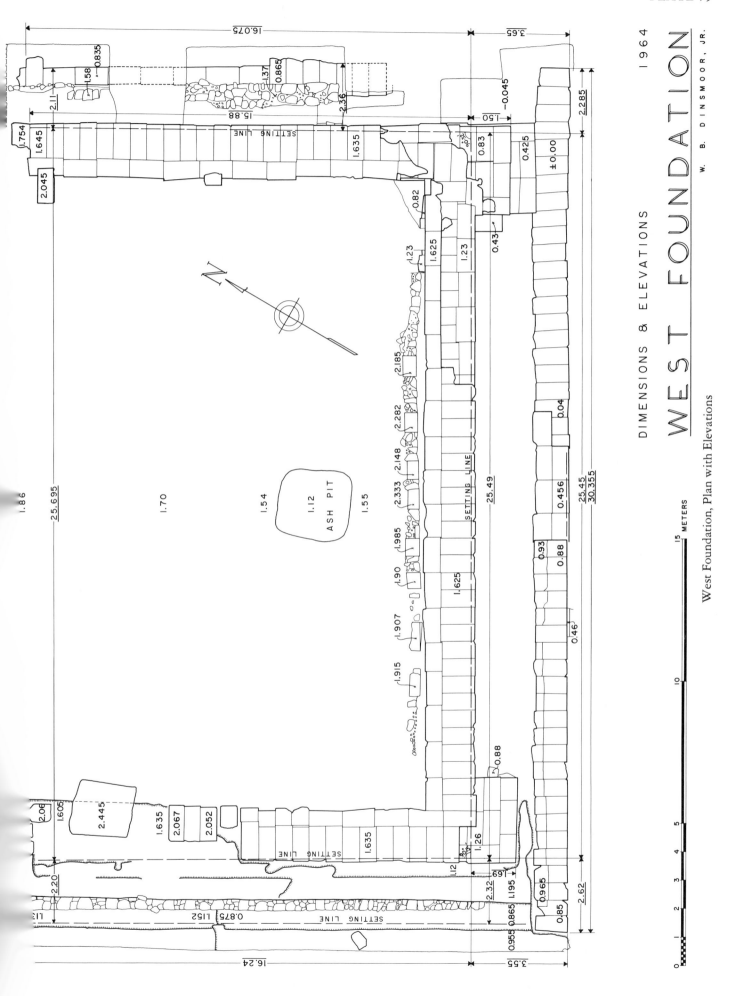

DIMENSIONS & ELEVATIONS   1 9 6 4

WEST FOUNDATION

W. B. DINSMOOR, JR.

West Foundation, Plan with Elevations

PLATE 80

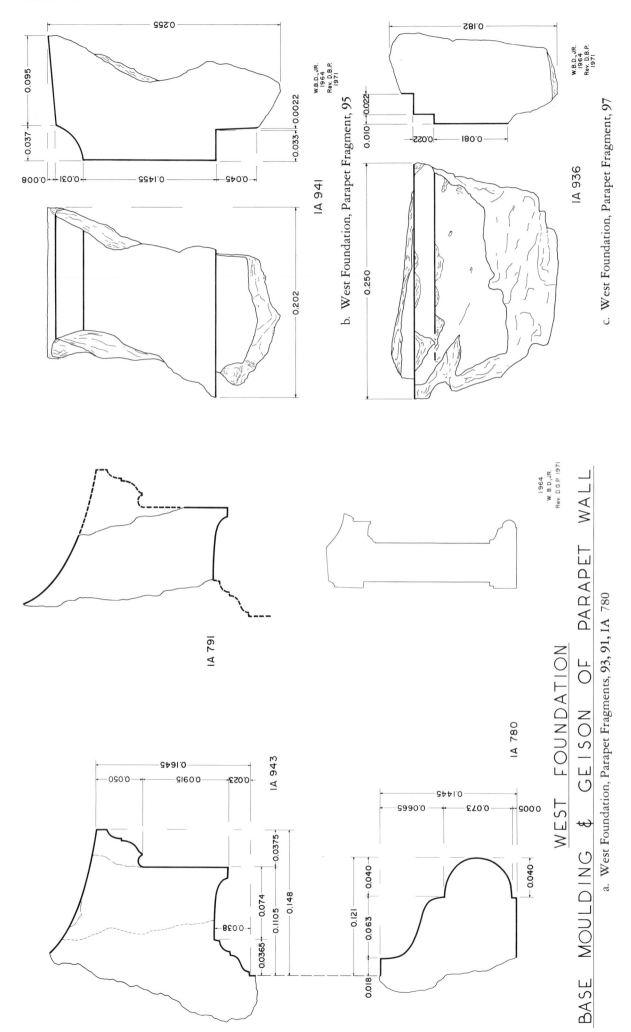

IA 941

b. West Foundation, Parapet Fragment, 95

W.B.D., JR.
1964
Rev. D.B.P.
1971

IA 936

c. West Foundation, Parapet Fragment, 97

W.B.D., JR.
1964
Rev. D.B.P.
1971

IA 791

IA 943

IA 780

a. West Foundation, Parapet Fragments, 93, 91, IA 780

1964
W. B. D., JR.
Rev. D.G.P. 1971

WEST FOUNDATION

BASE MOULDING & GEISON OF PARAPET WALL

PLATE 81

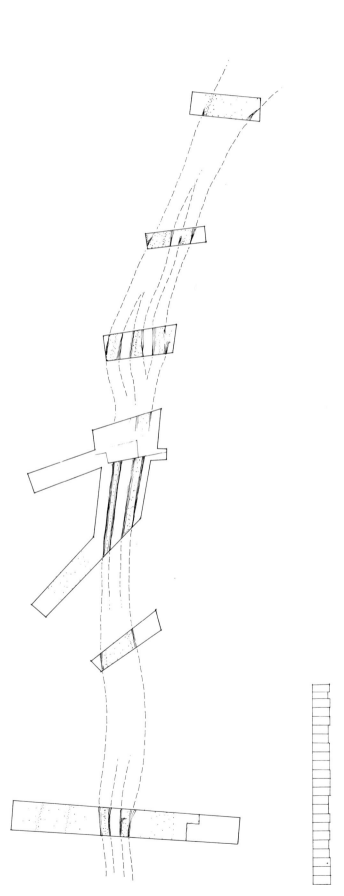

Ancient Road South of West Foundation

PLATE 82

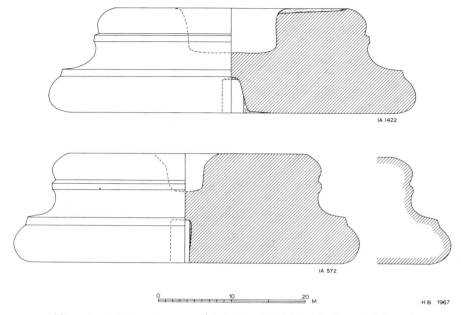

IA 1422

IA 572

H.B. 1967

a. Three Ionic Column Bases, **76, 75, 74,** of Red Marble, from Palaimonion

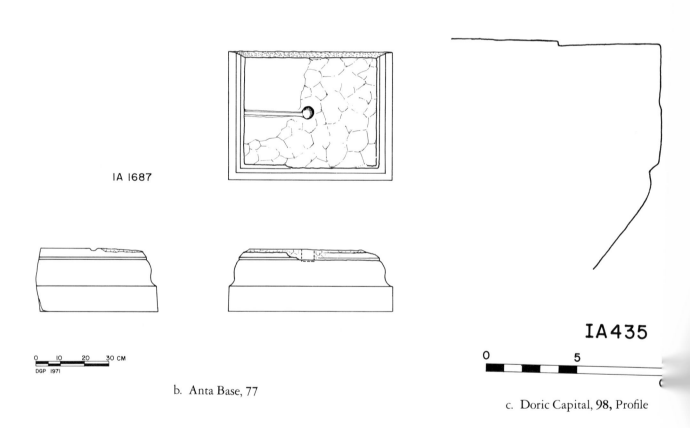

IA 1687

IA435

b. Anta Base, **77**

c. Doric Capital, **98,** Profile

PLATE 83

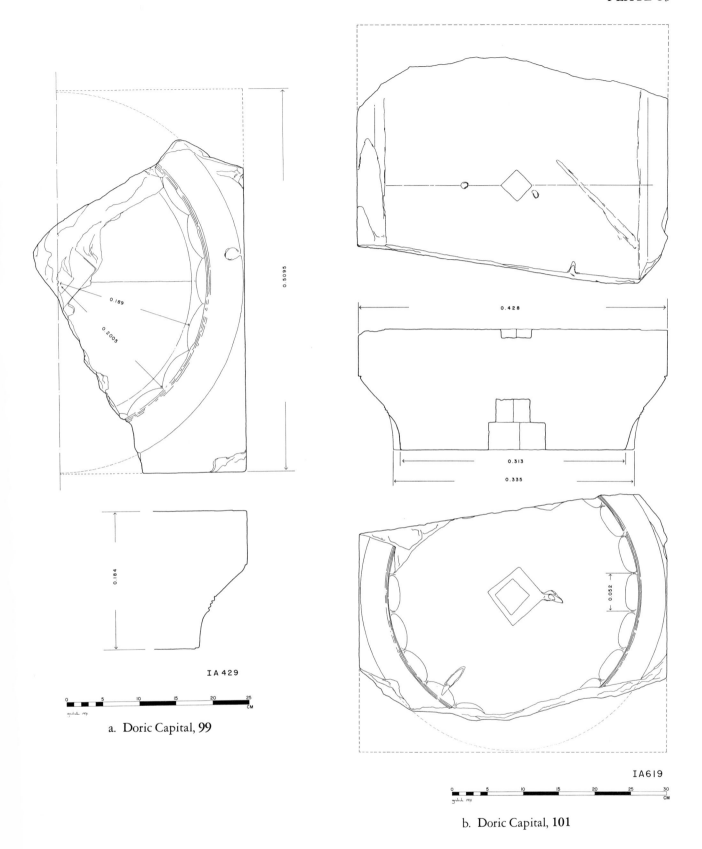

0.5095

0.189

0.2005

0.184

IA 429

0 5 10 15 20 25
CM

a. Doric Capital, **99**

0.428

0.313

0.335

0.052

IA619

0 5 10 15 20 25 30
CM

b. Doric Capital, **101**

PLATE 84

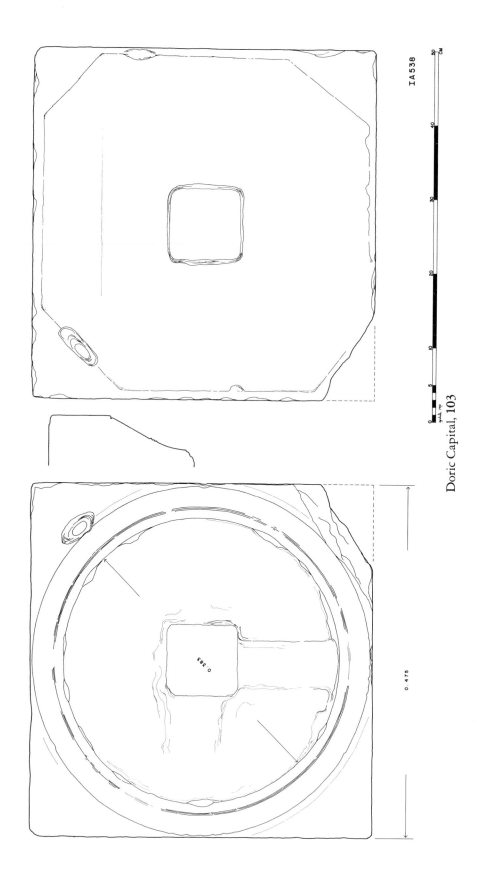

IA538

Doric Capital, 103

PLATE 85

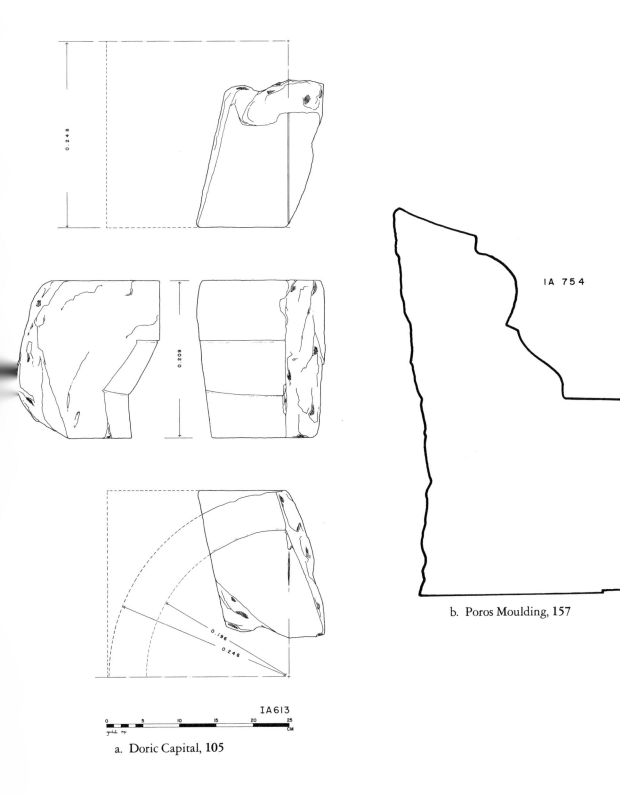

0.248

0.209

0.196

0.246

IA 754

IA613

0   5   10   15   20   25
                                                          CM

a. Doric Capital, 105

b. Poros Moulding, 157

PLATE 86

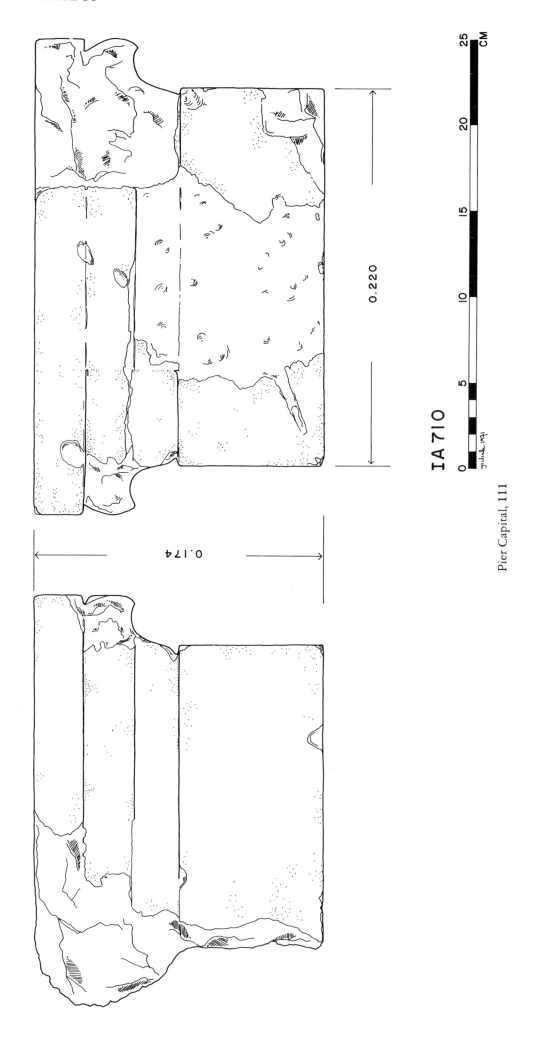

IA 710

Pier Capital, 111

PLATE 87

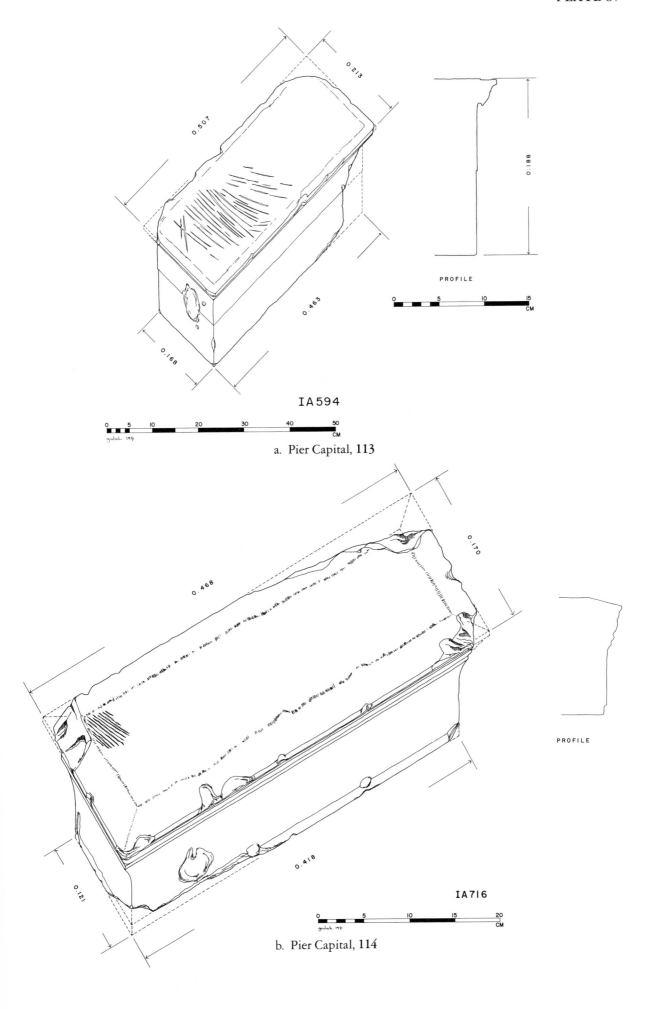

0.213

0.507

0.188

PROFILE

0.463

0.168

0   5   10   15
CM

IA594

0   5   10   20   30   40   50
CM

gulick 1971

a. Pier Capital, 113

0.170

0.468

PROFILE

0.418

0.121

IA716

0   5   10   15   20
CM

gulick 1971

b. Pier Capital, 114

PLATE 88

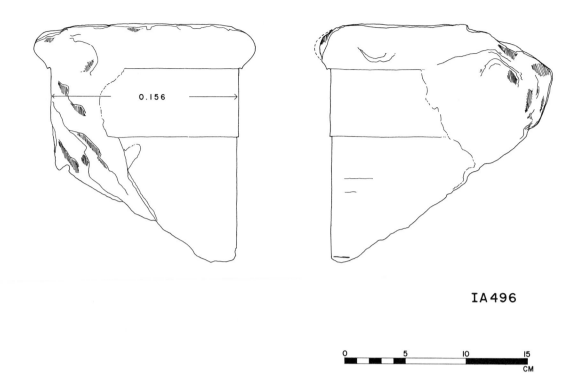

IA496

a. Pier or Anta Capital, 115

IA 569

DGP 1971

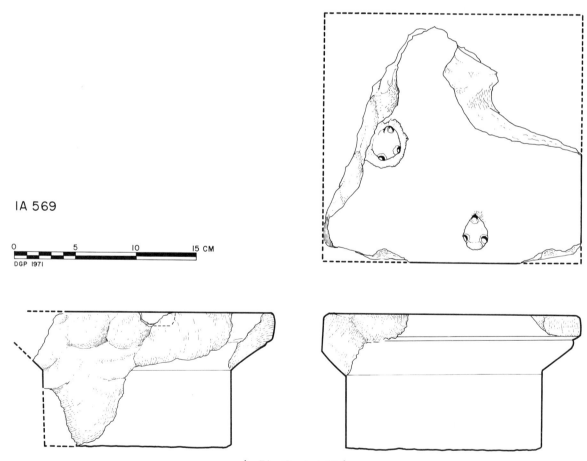

b. Pier Capital, 116

PLATE 89

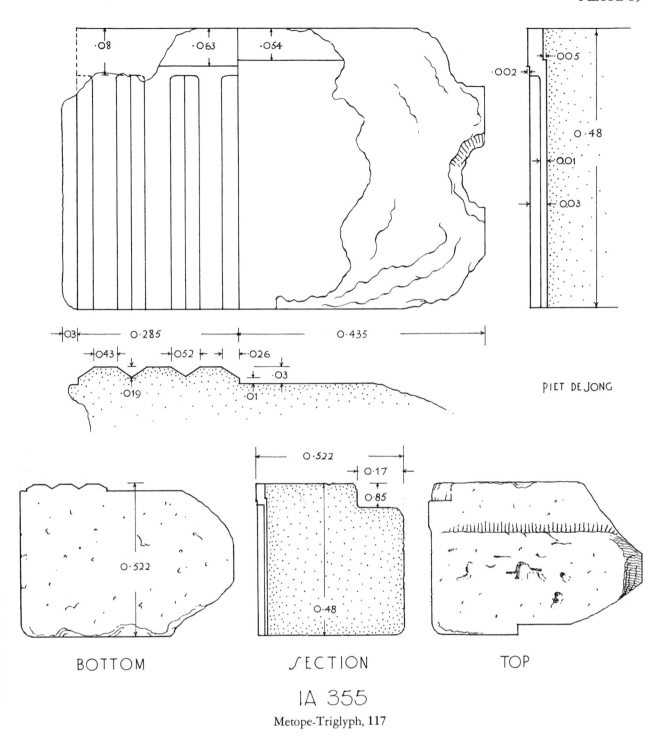

·08   ·063   ·054

·005

·002

0·48

0·01

0·03

·03   0·285   0·435

·043   ·052   ·026

·03

·019   ·01

PIET DE JONG

0·522   0·17

0·85

0·522   0·48

BOTTOM   SECTION   TOP

IA 355

Metope-Triglyph, 117

PLATE 90

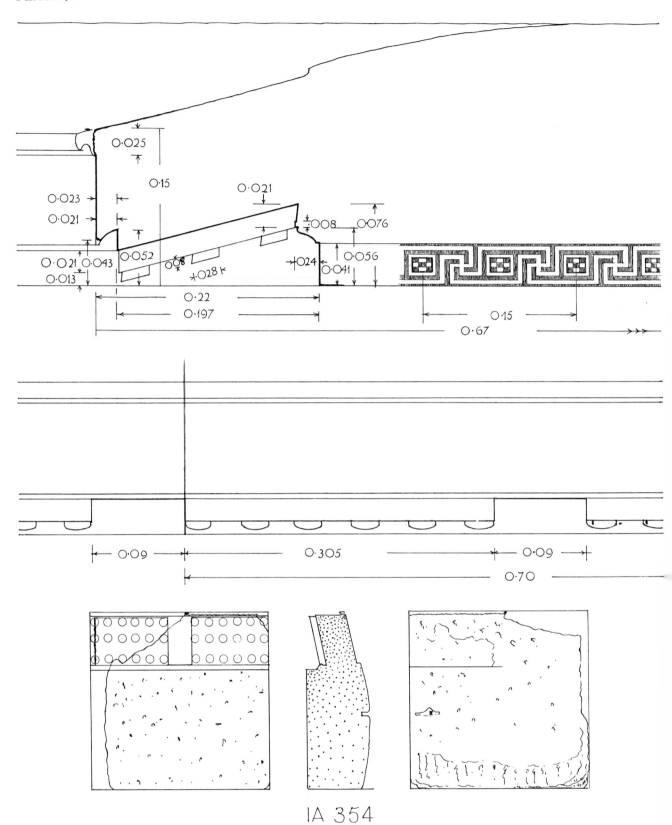

IA 354

Fragment of Doric Cornice, 118

PLATE 91

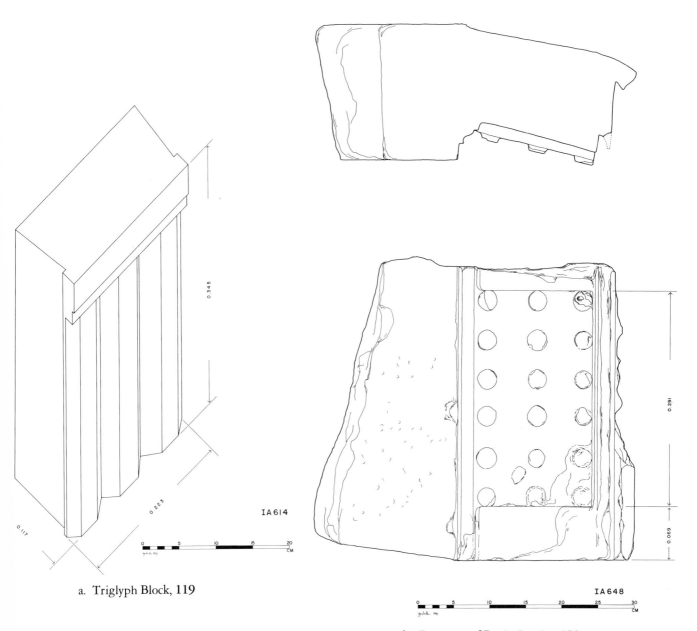

IA614

a. Triglyph Block, 119

IA648

b. Fragment of Doric Cornice, 120

PLATE 92

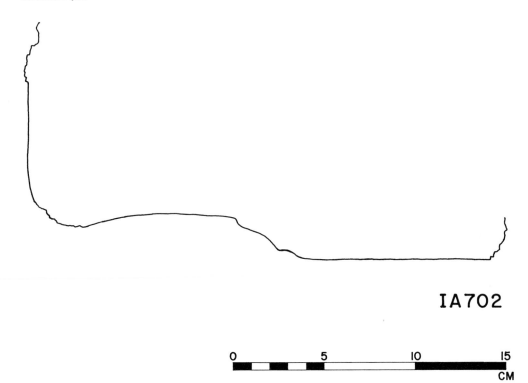

IA702

a. Piece of Raking Cornice, 124

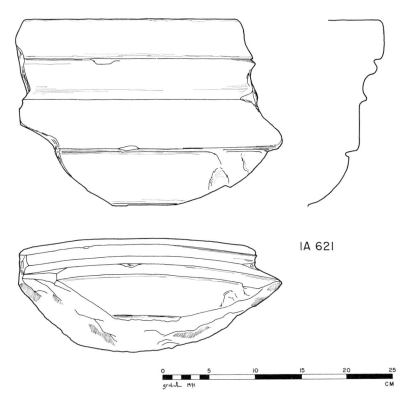

IA 621

grob 1971

b. Fragment of Circular Monument, 130

PLATE 93

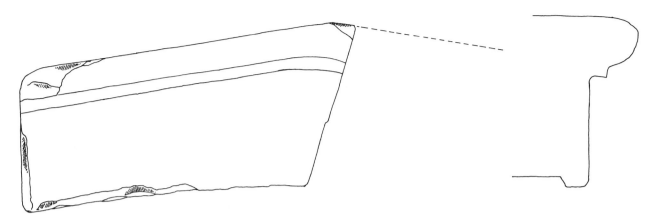

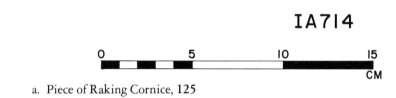

IA714

a. Piece of Raking Cornice, 125

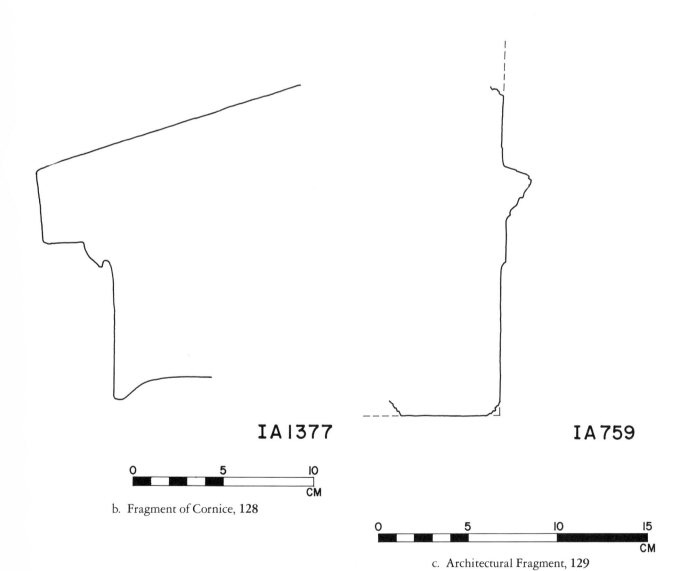

IA1377

b. Fragment of Cornice, 128

IA759

c. Architectural Fragment, 129

PLATE 94

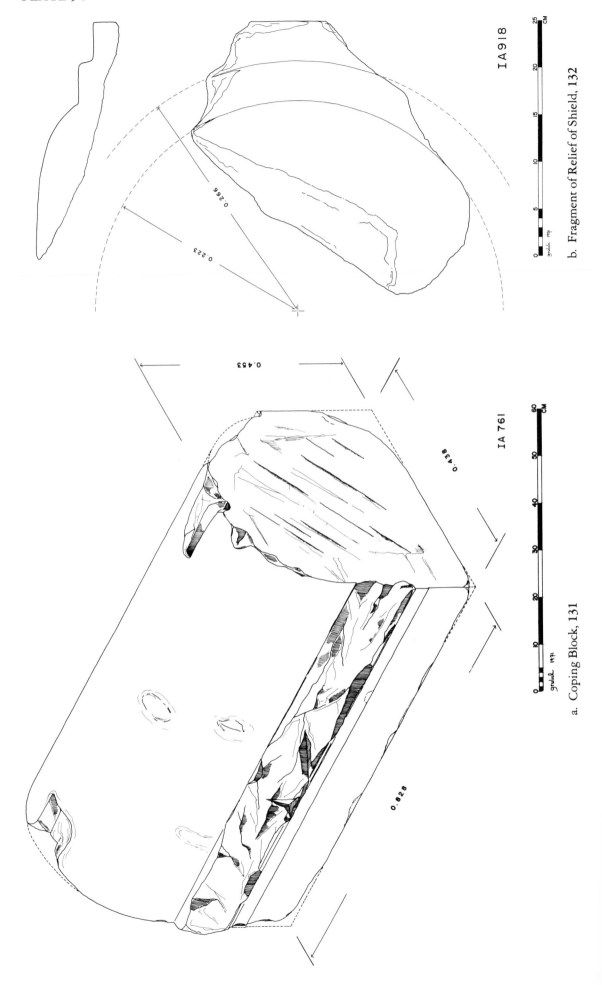

IA918

b. Fragment of Relief of Shield, 132

IA761

a. Coping Block, 131

PLATE 95

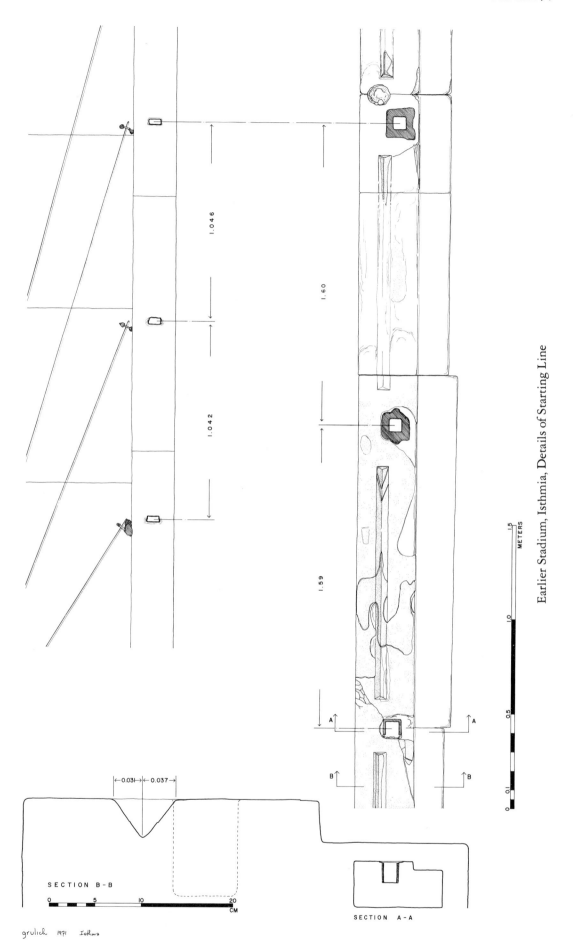

SECTION B-B

0   5   10   20
CM

SECTION A-A

Earlier Stadium, Isthmia, Details of Starting Line

0   0.1   0.5   1   1.5
METERS

grulich 1971 Isthmia

1.046

1.042

1.60

1.59

0.031   0.037

A   A

B   B

PLATE 96

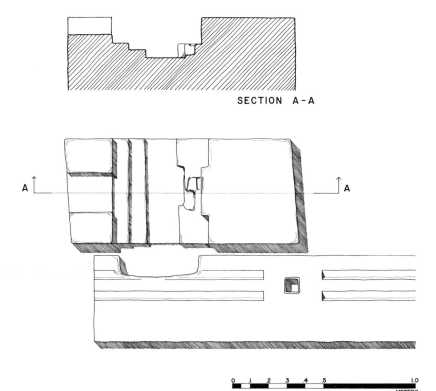

SECTION A-A

a. Later Stadium, Isthmia, Details of Starting Line

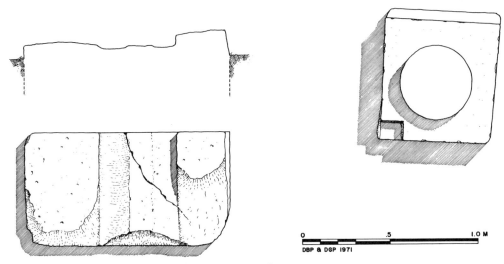

b. Open End of Stadium, Epidauros, Details of Starting Line

PLATE 97

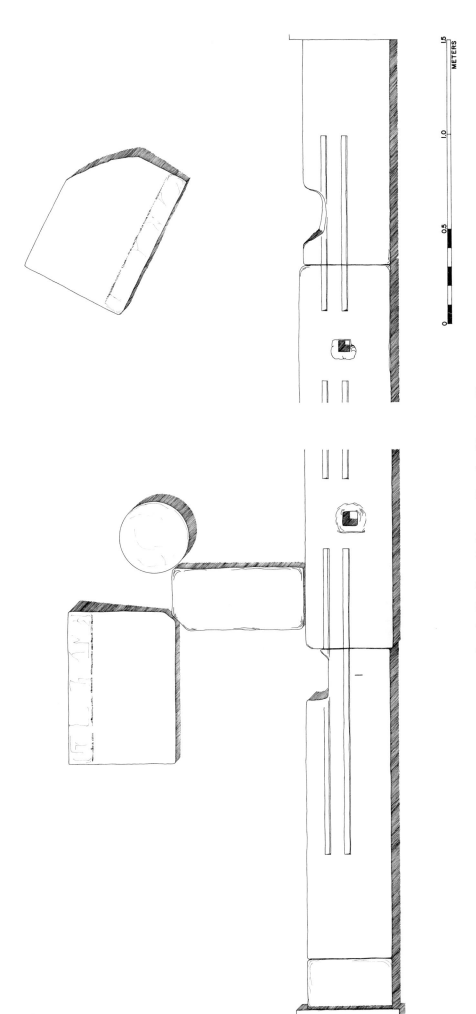

Closed End of Stadium, Epidauros, Details of Starting Line

PLATE 98

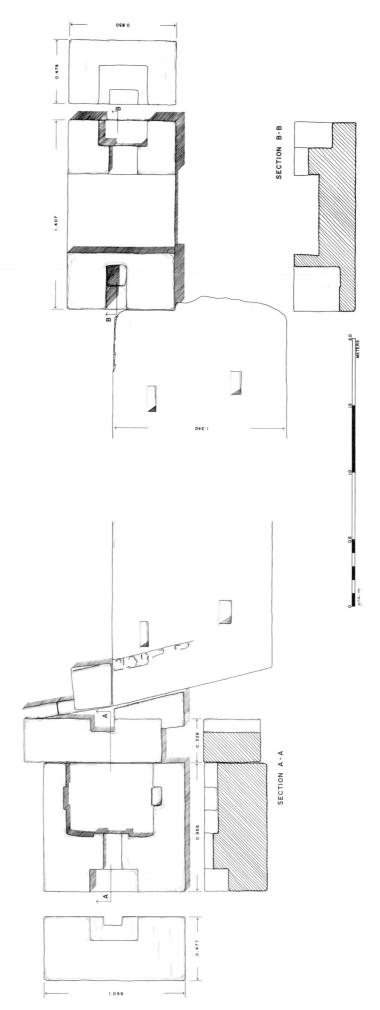

Racecourse, Corinthian Agora, Details of Starting Line

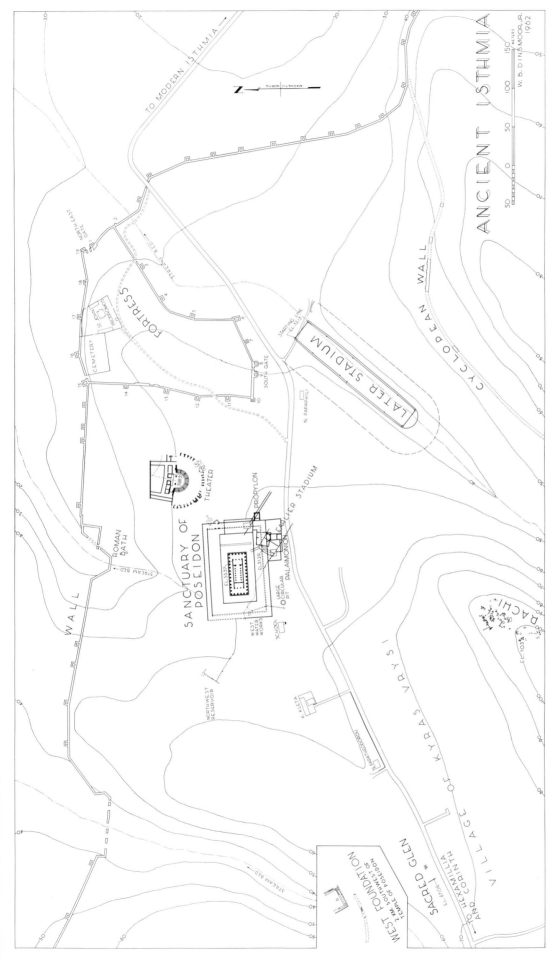

Ancient Isthmia, with Inset

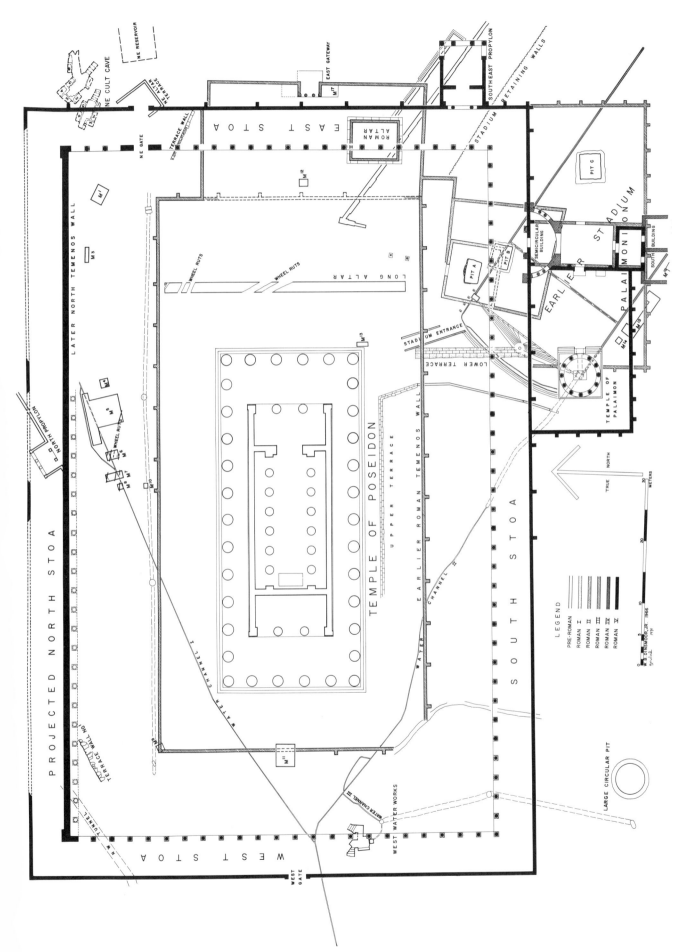

PROJECTED NORTH STOA

Later North Temenos Wall

NE CULT CAVE

NE RESERVOIR

NE GATE

TERRACE WALL

NORTH PROPYLON

TERRACE WALL NG

WEST STOA

WEST GATE

WEST WATER WORKS

WATER CHANNEL III

WATER WORKS

WATER CHANNEL I

WATER CHANNEL II

EAST STOA

EAST GATEWAY

ROMAN ALTAR

LONG ALTAR

WHEEL RUTS

WHEEL RUTS

WHEEL RUTS

TEMPLE OF POSEIDON

UPPER TERRACE

EARLIER ROMAN TEMENOS WALL

SOUTH STOA

STADIUM ENTRANCE

LOWER TERRACE

STADIUM

SOUTHEAST PROPYLON

SOUTHEAST RETAINING WALLS

PIT C

EARLIER STADIUM

PALAIMONION

SEMICIRCULAR BUILDING

PIT A

PIT B

SOUTH BUILDING

TEMPLE OF PALAIMON

LARGE CIRCULAR PIT

TRUE NORTH

LEGEND

PRE-ROMAN
ROMAN I
ROMAN II
ROMAN III
ROMAN IV
ROMAN V

METERS

W. B. DINSMOOR, JR. 1966

Period Plan of Sanctuary, with Pre-Roman Waterworks

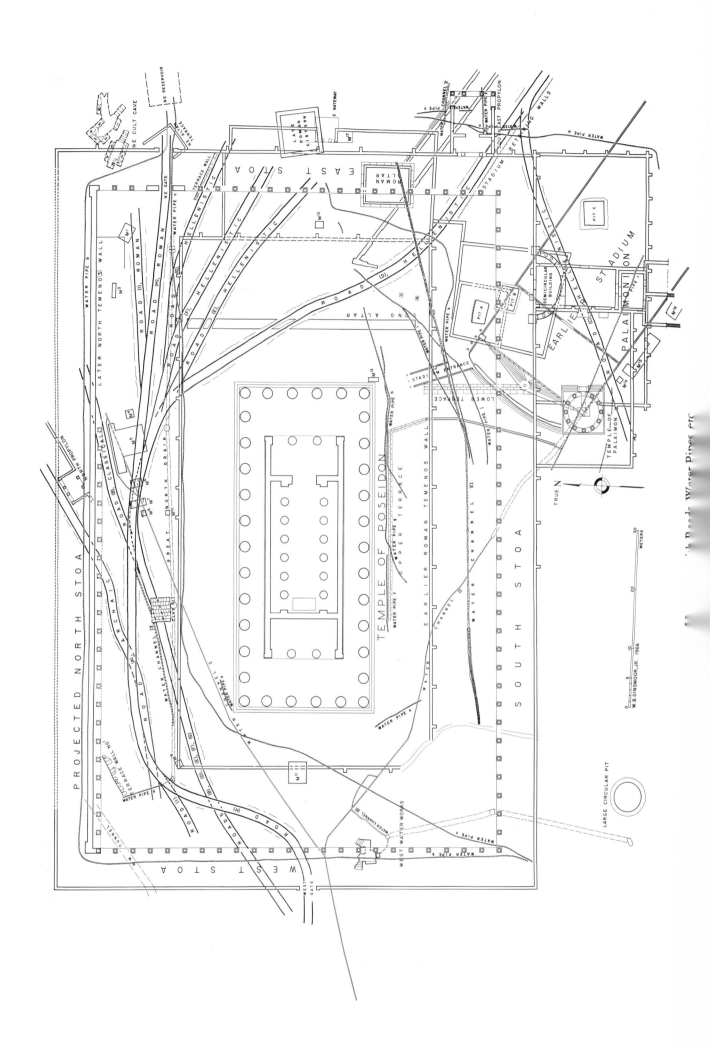

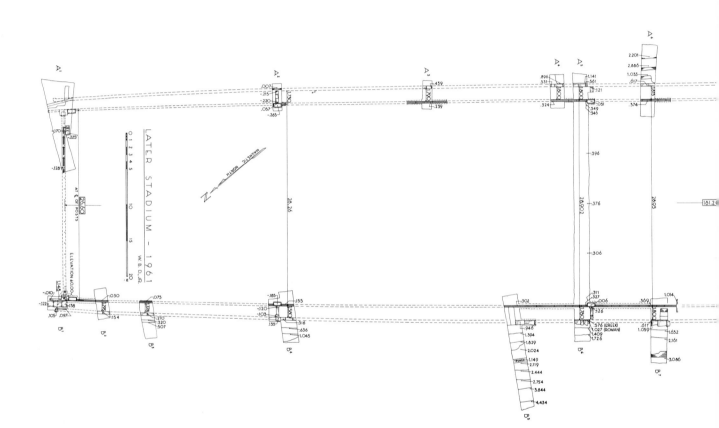

LATER STADIUM – 1961
W. B. D. Jr.

Later Stad

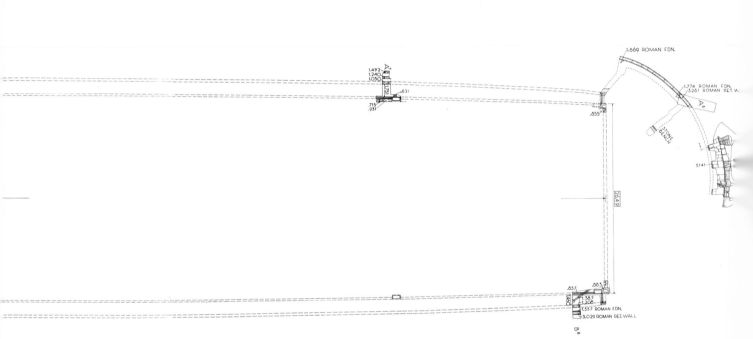

1.669 ROMAN FDN.

1.774 ROMAN FDN.
3.261 ROMAN RET. W.

STONE BENCH

3.141

1.492
1.240
1.030
1.175
.621
.715
.931

.655

26.49

.837 .663
.1.400
1.387
1.208
1.537 ROMAN FDN.
3.029 ROMAN RET WALL

ium, Overall Plan

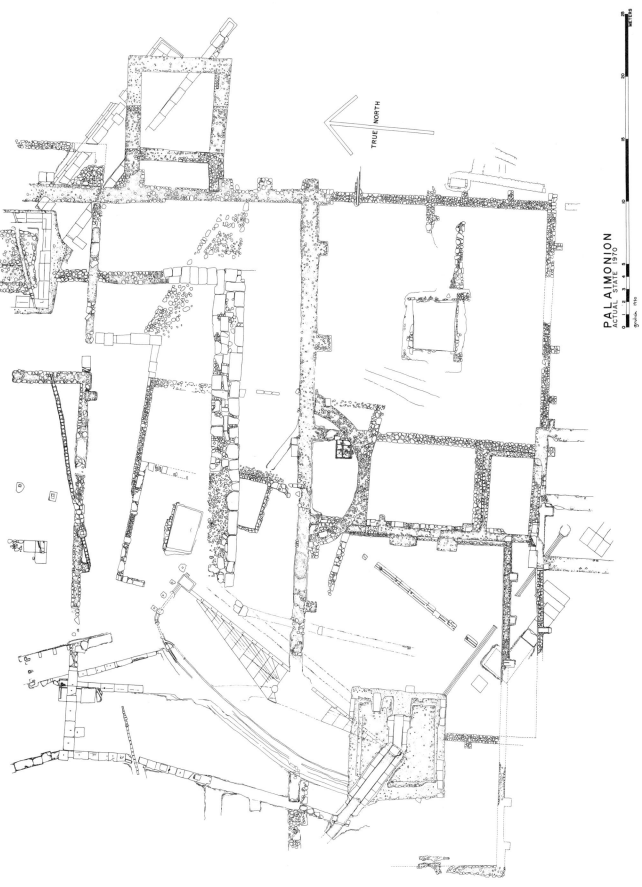

PALAIMONION
ACTUAL STATE 1970

TRUE NORTH

Palaimonion Area, Actual State Plan

PLATE VIII

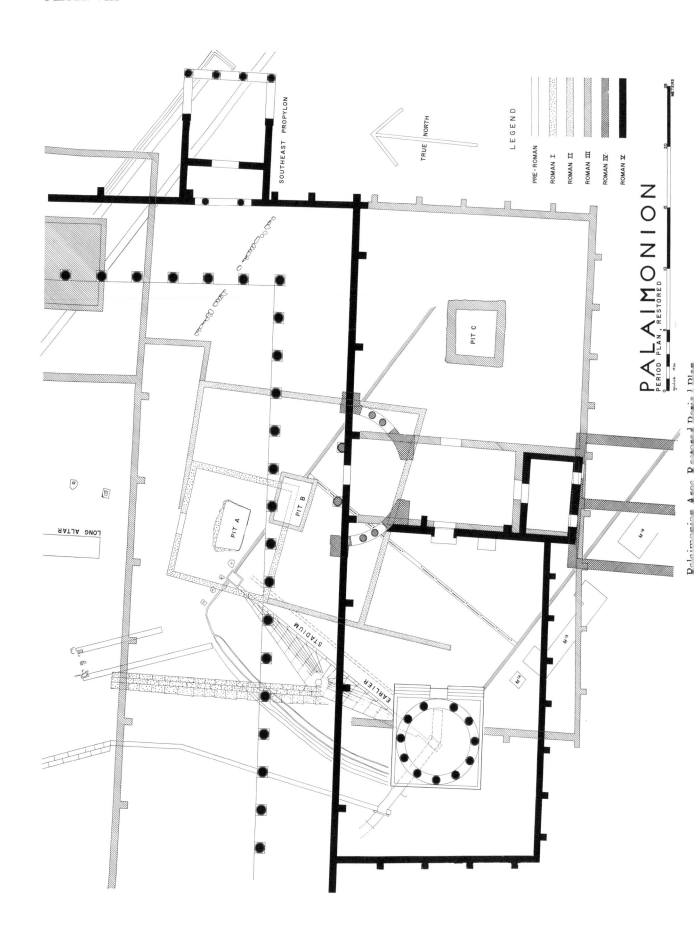

PALAIMONION
PERIOD PLAN, RESTORED

Palaimonion Area, Restored Period Plan

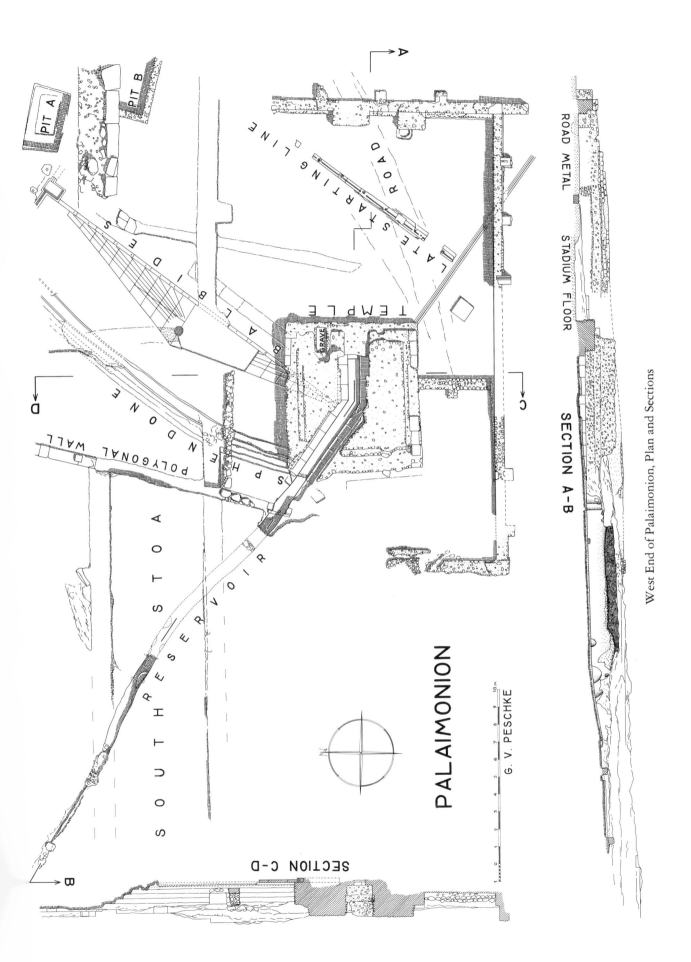

PLAN IX

PIT A

PIT B

LATE STARTING LINE

ROAD

A L B I D E S

E N D O N E

S P H

POLYGONAL WALL

SOUTH RESERVOIR

STOA

TEMPLE

GRAVE

ROAD METAL

STADIUM FLOOR

SECTION A-B

SECTION C-D

PALAIMONION

G. V. PESCHKE

0 1 2 3 4 5 6 7 8 9 10 m

West End of Palaimonion, Plan and Sections

PLAN X

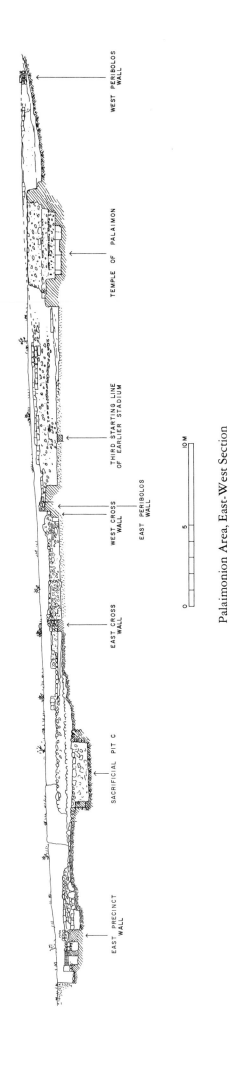

WEST PERIBOLOS
WALL

TEMPLE OF PALAIMON

THIRD STARTING LINE
OF EARLIER STADIUM

WEST CROSS
WALL

EAST PERIBOLOS
WALL

EAST CROSS
WALL

SACRIFICIAL PIT C

EAST PRECINCT
WALL

0   5   10 M

Palaimonion Area, East-West Section